The United Nations Crime Prevention and Criminal Justice Program

University of Pennsylvania Press
Procedural Aspects of International Law Series

Burns H. Weston, Series Editor (1994–   )
Robert Kogod Goldman, Editor (1977–1994)
Richard B. Lillich, Editor (1964–1977)

A complete list of the books in this series
appears at the back of this volume.

The United Nations Crime Prevention and Criminal Justice Program

Formulation of Standards and Efforts at Their Implementation

Roger S. Clark

University of Pennsylvania Press

Philadelphia

Library of Congress Cataloging-in-Publication Data
Clark, Roger Stenson.
   The United Nations Crime Prevention and Criminal Justice Program :
formulation of standards and efforts at their implementation / Roger S. Clark.
      p.   cm. — (Procedural aspects of international law series)
   Includes bibliographical references and index.
   ISBN 0-8122-3269-0
   1. Crime prevention—International cooperation.   2. Crime prevention—
Standards.   3. Criminal justice, Administration of—International
cooperation.
4. Criminal justice, Administration of—Standards.   I. Title.   II. Series.
HV7431.C555   1994
364.4'04526—dc20   94-28090
                                                                              CIP

Contents

Editor's Foreword

The *United Nations Crime Prevention and Criminal Justice Program: Formulation of Standards and Efforts at Their Implementation* is the twentieth book in the Procedural Aspects of International Law Series, and the second to be published by the University of Pennsylvania Press. Its author, Roger S. Clark, is Distinguished Professor at the State University of New Jersey Law School, Rutgers, at Camden and a noted authority in the international and criminal law fields.

This book is the first in any language to examine in depth United Nations activities since 1945 in criminal justice and to assess critically that body's evolving organizational structures and efforts at setting and implementing standards in this area. Professor Clark's interest in his subject is not merely academic. From 1987 to 1990, he was a member of the United Nations Committee on Crime Prevention and Control, a body of experts he aptly describes as the "catalyst" for the UN program, particularly in drafting standards such as model treaties, standard minimum rules and declarations of basic principles. He has also been a member of New Zealand's delegations to various US Congresses on the Prevention of Crime and Treatment of Offenders. His active involvement in helping shape the UN criminal justice program has given him a keen appreciation of the difficulties of making and implementing international criminal law and policy. These experiences uniquely qualify him to evaluate the substantive activities of the United Nations, in its criminal justice program, as well as to predict future directions it may take. This book thus makes a significant, indeed, singular contribution to knowledge about this important but largely unchronicled area of UN activity.

* * *

With the publication of this book, the editorship of this Series will pass into the capable hands of Burns H. Weston, Bessie Dutton Murray Distinguished Professor at the University of Iowa College of Law. I am particularly indebted to Professor Richard B. Lillich, PAIL president and first Series editor, for his unfaltering advice and assistance during my nearly seventeen-year tenure as Series editor. I also want to acknowledge with special thanks the important contribution made by my Dean's Fellow, Andrew M. Beato, in editing this volume.

Robert Kogod Goldman
Washington, D C

Acknowledgments

As in any enterprise of this nature, this book would not have been possible without the contributions, large and small, of a great number of people. Most of them had no idea what they were contributing to.

Rutgers University gave me a sabbatical leave in 1990 during which I collected a great deal of material and produced a first draft of several chapters. I received welcome financial support through an Andrei Sakharov Fellowship from the Jacob Blaustein Institute for the Advancement of Human Rights. I deeply appreciate the honor as well as the assistance. The former Director of the Institute, Sidney Liskofsky, was of great encouragement to me in shaping this project. The current Director, Felice Gaer, helped me to hone many of my ideas when she was Executive Director of the International League for Human Rights, and she helped mightily with the source material.

Eduardo Vetere and Kurt Neudek of the Crime Prevention and Criminal Justice Branch of the United Nations in Vienna have always been willing to share their wisdom and experience with me—to say nothing of voluminous documentation. Matti Joutsen, Director of the European Institute for Crime Prevention and Control affiliated with the United Nations, Vincent Del Buono of the International Center for Criminal Law Reform and Criminal Justice Policy in Vancouver, and Ronald Gainer, formerly Associate Deputy Attorney-General of the United States, were all kind enough to read drafts of much of the manuscript and to make suggestions that undoubtedly improved it. Matti also gave generously of his prodigious memory, his political wisdom, and his files. Several of the current and former staff of the Law Library here at Rutgers Law School in Camden went to great pains to track down elusive material for me, particularly David Batista, Lucy Cox, Anne Dalesandro, Vicki Kristian, and Marion Townend. David Batista was kind enough to prepare the bibliography. Belinda Clark, Jane Coombs and Ambassador Dame Ann Hercus, of the New Zealand Mission to the United Nations, along with David Oughton and Graheam Simpson of the New Zealand Department of Justice, educated me on many matters. They also facilitated my participation at several of the meetings discussed in the pages that follow. David Lange, as Prime Minister and

Minister of Foreign Affairs, and Sir Geoffrey Palmer, in his capacity as Minister of Justice of New Zealand, made possible my membership between 1987 and 1990 on the United Nations Committee on Crime Prevention and Control. Geoff Palmer has influenced my professional life in many other ways. William Mansfield and Ambassador David McDowell ran a brilliant election campaign on my behalf in ECOSOC which made me a member of the United Nations Committee. Yael Danieli, Past President and Senior Representative to the United Nations of the Society for Traumatic Stress Studies, taught me much about victims and about the politics of the area. Richard Lillich, of the University of Virginia School of Law, President of the Procedural Aspects of International Law Institute, and Robert Goldman, of American University's Washington College of Law, my editor, have by their insistence and sound advice ensured that the product will see the light of day. June Chaffin, my secretary, and Amanda Figland and Rani Emandi, my research assistants, along with two of Robert Goldman's Dean's Fellows at American University, Paul Barkan and Andrew Beato, provided the technical skills necessary to accuracy, consistency, and intelligibility. Seymour Clark-Reynolds found the final typos.

I am grateful to them all and to the countless others—friends and foes—who shared the journey.

And then there is Irene. Irene Melup of the Crime Prevention and Criminal Justice Branch of the United Nations persuaded me to become involved in the area of international criminal justice a decade ago. She was an enormous help in obtaining material and in criticizing my drafts. She knew where all the bodies were buried; if I failed to find any of them, it is because I failed to ask the right questions. I know that there is much in here that she can not possibly agree with, but she is the inspiration to all of us who have seriously worked the area of the United Nations and crime prevention and criminal justice.

I have endeavored to incorporate references to all relevant documentary material available to me on 1 December 1993.

Parts of Chapters 1 through 4 appeared in considerably different form in R. S. Clark, *Human Rights and the UN Committee on Crime Prevention and Control*, 506 ANNALS 68 (1989). An earlier version of Chapter 7 appeared as *The 1985 United Nations Declaration of Basic Principles of Justice for Victims of Crime and Abuse of Power* in THE LIVING LAW OF NATIONS: ESSAYS IN MEMORY OF ATLE GRAHL-MADSEN (G. Alfredsson & P. Macalister-Smith ed. 1994). An earlier version of Chapter 8 appeared as *Crime: The UN Agenda on International Cooperation in the Criminal Process*, 15 NOVA L. REV. 475 (1991).

Camden, New Jersey
December 1993

Part I
The Program in
Its Context

Chapter 1
A Brief History of the Program

A. Introduction

On December 18, 1991 the United Nations General Assembly adopted Resolution 46/152, entitled "Creation of an Effective United Nations Crime Prevention and Criminal Justice Programme."[1] That resolution resulted from recommendations made by an Intergovernmental Working Group that met in Vienna in the previous August[2] and a ministerial meeting that met in Paris in November, just a month before the General Assembly resolution was adopted.[3] These series of events focused attention on a long-existing program that has been a largely unknown part of the United Nations system, yet one I believe to be of considerable significance. In particular, the program has engaged in significant "legislative" work, reflected in the Secretariat's recently-published COMPENDIUM OF UNITED NATIONS STANDARDS AND NORMS IN CRIME PREVENTION AND CRIMINAL JUSTICE[4] and in efforts to "implement" those standards.

This book discusses the actions of the United Nations in the criminal justice area since 1945 and the organizational structure that has resulted from its substantive activities. It offers some predictions on what the future may hold, along with ideas and concrete suggestions. Particular attention is given to the efforts of the United Nations to formulate standards to which states should aspire, and even some standards to which they are legally bound.

1. G.A. Res. 46/152, U.N. GAOR, 46th Sess., Supp. No 49, at 217, U.N. Doc. A/46/49 (1992).
2. *See* U.N. Doc. A/CONF.156/2 (1991) (noting the recommendations of the Working Group).
3. *See Note by the Secretary-General, Social Development: Crime Prevention and Criminal Justice,* U.N. Doc. A/46/703 (1991).
4. U.N. Sales No. E.92.IV.1 (1992) [hereinafter THE COMPENDIUM]. The major items in THE COMPENDIUM will be discussed in Chapter 4 *infra*.

Until the recent reorganization, the organizational structure of the program consisted primarily of the work of a small Secretariat unit in Vienna entitled the Crime Prevention and Criminal Justice Branch, a set of institutes referred to collectively as the "Crime Prevention and Criminal Justice Program Network," five-yearly United Nations Congresses on the Prevention of Crime and the Treatment of Offenders, and an expert committee called the Committee on Crime Prevention and Control ("Crime Prevention Committee").[5] Between 1987 and 1990, I served as a member of the Crime Prevention Committee, a subsidiary organ of the Economic and Social Council (ECOSOC). That body oversaw the work that the Secretariat was performing, in addition to being the preparatory body for the congresses. As such, I tended to regard it as the catalyst for the system, while the congresses—a major international event by any standard—were something of a focal point or showpiece for the whole enterprise. In the last years of its life, the Crime Prevention Committee was expanding this role as a catalyst, particularly in drafting standards and in devising methods for their "implementation." More will be said about the Crime Prevention Committee in later pages. Its demise and replacement by an intergovernmental commission is the most dramatic feature of the new era ushered in by the Assembly's 1991 resolution. As an expert committee designed to play a substantial role in a highly political area, its existence was always somewhat quixotic. In place of the Crime Prevention Committee, and to some degree the congresses, is a new functional commission, which the General Assembly asked ECOSOC to create, consisting of forty government representatives designated the Commission on Crime Prevention and Criminal Justice.[6]

In the past, I have emphasized the rather obvious point that much of what the program does is of a human rights or rule of law nature.[7] At first blush, the program's area of operation is that of a sub-heading of civil and political rights, namely the protection of rights in the admin-

5. *See* M. LÓPEZ-REY, A GUIDE TO UNITED NATIONS CRIMINAL POLICY (1985); HELSINKI INSTITUTE FOR CRIME PREVENTION AND CONTROL, AFFILIATED WITH THE UNITED NATIONS (HEUNI), COURSE ON UNITED NATIONS CRIMINAL JUSTICE POLICY (1985); B.S. ALPER & J.F. BOREN, CRIME: INTERNATIONAL AGENDA (1972); UNITED NATIONS DEPARTMENT OF PUBLIC INFORMATION, THE UNITED NATIONS AND CRIME PREVENTION, U.N. DOC. DP/1143–41016 (1991) (booklet). On recent developments, *see* Note, *General Assembly Resolution on the Creation of an Effective United Nations Crime Prevention and Criminal Justice Program*, 3 CRIM. L.F. 105 (1991); K. Neudek, *United Nations Crime Prevention and Criminal Justice Programme*, 1 EUROP. J. CRIM. POL'Y & RES. 185 (1993).

6. ECOSOC responded to the General Assembly's request to create the Commission in E.S.C. Res. 1992/1, U.N. ESCOR, Supp. No. 1, at 11, U.N. Doc. E/1992/92 (1992).

7. R.S. Clark, *Human Rights and the U.N. Committee on Crime Prevention and Control*, 506 ANNALS 68 (1989).

istration of justice. Further reflection suggests that its role is wider than this. For example, some of the program's work encompasses economic, social, and cultural rights as well. The Secretariat arm in Vienna, entitled the Crime Prevention and Criminal Justice Branch, was anchored in the United Nations Centre for Social Development and Humanitarian Affairs until mid-1993, a relationship that emphasized the social affairs nature of the enterprise. Secretary-General Boutros Boutros-Ghali's reorganization decisions, which entailed moving most of that Center to New York, may de-emphasize the economic and social connection for the future.[8] Much of the documentary work output, including areas such as the prevention of juvenile delinquency and strategies for dealing with domestic violence, is decidedly in the social sphere. Indeed, some of the work[9] defies categorization in traditional human rights terms. Fundamentally, this aspect of the program involves basic efforts to free the world of crime, or at least to minimize it

---

8. The Centre was composed of two Divisions, the Division on the Advancement of Women and the Social Development Division; the Crime Prevention and Criminal Justice Branch was within Social Development. Explaining the work of the Centre, a former Director-General of the Vienna Office has commented that:

> The precise inter-relationship of what constitutes a "Society for All," based on the principle of partnership in diversity—partnership between government and a healthy "civil society" in particular—is what the United Nations Office at Vienna/ Centre for Social Development has been actively promoting for some years. Our approach is to promote integrated social policies as a general objective without which "development is meaningless" but particularly with respect to crime prevention, drugs, youth, family, women, vulnerable groups and the socially deprived.

Miss Margaret J. Anstee, speech to the Ministerial Meeting on the Creation of an Effective United Nations Crime Prevention and Criminal Justice Programme (Nov. 21–23, 1991) (on file with author). Sometimes the connections were hard to make and there was a persistent stream of thought that crime has been too closely associated at the United Nations with social and economic policy and would make more progress as a freestanding item. *See, e.g.*, M. López-Rey, *Aspects and Problems of the Role of United Nations Assistance to Developing Countries in the Field of Social Defence*, 39 REVUE INTERNATIONALE DE DROIT PÉNAL 21 (1968). The officials who composed the Division on the Status of Women and most of those in the Social Development Division (other than the Crime Prevention and Criminal Justice Branch) were transferred to New York in 1993. It does not appear that any close attention was paid to the conceptual issues surrounding where crime issues ought to fit at the time of this reorganization. Crime Prevention and Criminal Justice has been left in Vienna alongside the much larger United Nations International Drug Control Program which operates under the aegis of another ECOSOC Commission, the Commisssion on Narcotic Drugs. This connection perhaps emphasizes the "law enforcement" aspects of both programs, but the control of drugs, like crime in general, has social aspects also!

9. Such as much of the material on cooperation in criminal matters discussed in Chapter 8 *infra*.

and its harmful consequences. Such a result is sought through the means of "prevention" or "control," especially through co-operative action. There is no turn of phrase quite precise enough to catch the essence of this group of activities. With that caveat in mind, I refer to such endeavors, for want of a better term, as "law and justice" items. They emphasize such things as the exchange of information, cooperation in the criminal prosecution process, victim assistance, and methods of crime prevention.

Even the United Nations itself has tended to ignore the existence of this part of the operation.[10] I am hopeful, therefore, that the appearance of this book will help to increase the visibility of the program and contribute to informed debate about the Committee on Crime Prevention and Control and its replacement, the Commission on Crime Prevention and Criminal Justice.[11] There is a need for serious discussion about what the crime prevention and criminal justice program can do most effectively with its limited resources and what might best be left to other parts of the United Nations system that have a comparative advantage.

This chapter is largely an effort to record the essence of the United Nations crime prevention and criminal justice program and the manner in which it has developed. In part, it is a retrospective study since the restructuring of the system that came with the creation of the new ECOSOC Commission means that the unique form of law-making represented by the interplay between the expert (and somewhat independent) Committee on Crime Prevention and Control and the government-dominated congresses will become a thing of the past. But, the future will be substantially built upon the foundation of that past.

10. A striking indication of the need to raise the visibility of the program is provided by the Centre for Human Rights' Human Rights Fact Sheet, No. 1 on HUMAN RIGHTS MACHINERY (1987) which ignores the Committee. The 1988 edition of UNITED NATIONS ACTION IN THE FIELD OF HUMAN RIGHTS, U.N. Doc. ST/HR/2/Rev.3, barely notes (at 21) the existence of the Committee on Crime Prevention and Control and the Crime Prevention and Criminal Justice Branch. The existence of the Committee as a contributor to the human rights scene is noted more forcefully in the report of the independent expert, Professor Philip Alston. Philip Alston, *Effective Implementation of International Instruments on Human Rights, Including Reporting Under International Instruments on Human Rights*, at 56, U.N. Doc. A/44/668 (1989) [hereinafter Alston Report]. Theodor Meron ignores the law-making work of the Committee on Crime Prevention and Control in his excellent study, T. MERON, HUMAN RIGHTS LAW-MAKING IN THE UNITED NATIONS (1986).

11. The only significant literature focusing specifically on the Committee on Crime Prevention and Control is W. Clifford, *The Committee on Crime Prevention and Control*, 34 INT'L REV. CRIM. POL'Y 11 (1978); *Summary of the work programme of the Crime Prevention and Criminal Justice Branch of the United Nations Secretariat*, *id*. at 19; and description of the work of the Committee in UNITED NATIONS CRIME PREVENTION AND CRIMINAL JUSTICE NEWSLETTER, No. 7, at 3 (1982). *See also* Clark, *supra* note 7.

The new structure will be discussed specifically in the next two chapters that complete Part I of the book, Chapters 2 and 3. However, some speculation about how various parts of the structure might work will also appear regularly throughout succeeding chapters. Chapter 2 approaches the matter through an examination of the changes in the structure brought about in 1991 and 1992. Chapter 3 looks in more detail at the role of the numerous organs currently involved in the program—their mandates and methods of operation.

Part II, Chapters 4 and 5, addresses the adoption of United Nations norms and standards. In an effort to provide some general substantive context for the reader, Chapter 4 offers an overview of the instruments produced by this part of the United Nations system. It is organized chronologically so as to dramatize a point that must be emphasized— namely, the way in which norm production burgeoned in the past decade or so.

Chapter 5 addresses the formal and juridical nature of the instruments and examines the manner in which existing instruments were drafted. It also discusses the "legislative" role of each of the various formal organs involved in the process and of the informal network, an "invisible college" in Oscar Schachter's memorable phrase,[12] that has kept the organs in motion. Some comments will be made about what the new structure might bring to this exercise.

Part III provides a more detailed consideration of some of the major instruments adopted under the auspices of the Committee on Crime Prevention and Control and the Congresses, notably the Standard Minimum Rules for the Treatment of Prisoners (Chapter 6), the Declaration of Basic Principles of Justice for Victims of Crime and Abuse of Power (Chapter 7), and the model treaties on co-operation in the international criminal process (Chapter 8). I make no attempt at a comprehensive effort to discuss in detail all the criminal justice instruments. Rather, the items selected amount to a fair representation of the totality of the enterprise. Thus, the chapters on the Standard Minimum Rules and on the rights of victims deal largely with human rights questions, while that on international co-operation in the criminal process concerns "law and justice" issues.

The final two chapters, Part IV, examine efforts to move from the promulgation of standards and norms to their monitoring and implementation.

Needless to say, the program does not exist in a vacuum within the United Nations. The Crime Prevention and Criminal Justice Branch is located in Vienna—not the most visible location. Vienna is also where

12. O. Schachter, *The Invisible College of International Lawyers*, 72 Nw. U. L. Rev. 217 (1977).

the new commission meets. The Branch and the Commission there-fore run the risk of being marginalized within the United Nations system and there are a number of existing United Nations instruments in the crime prevention and criminal justice area that were developed with limited input from the Vienna part of the system.[13] The Branch has succeeded, however, in developing fairly good liaison in its drafting endeavors with the Centre for Human Rights in Geneva while working with the Centre on projects involving technical cooperation in the area of human rights in the administration of justice.[14] Indeed, in the first resolution adopted by ECOSOC on the recommendation of the new Commission on Crime Prevention and Criminal Justice, the Council

13. Strong criticism was voiced in the report of the third meeting of persons chairing the human rights treaty bodies about the problems caused by having the Committee on the Elimination of Discrimination against Women serviced from Vienna, as was the case before the 1993 reorganization. *See Note by the Secretary-General, Effective implementation of international instruments on human rights, including reporting obligations under international instruments on human rights,* U.N. Doc. A/45/636 at 6–7 (1990). Some of the same issues of marginalization arise in the criminal justice area. THE COMPENDIUM, *supra* note 4, con-tains the text of nine "human rights" instruments which are in whole or in part germane to the present area that were in fact produced in other parts of the system. Universal Declaration of Human Rights, G.A. Res. 217 A (III), U.N. GAOR, 3d Sess., Pt.1, Resolutions, at 71, U.N. Doc. A/810 (1948); International Covenant on Economic, Social and Cultural Rights, G.A. Res. 2200 (XXI), U.N. GAOR, 21st Sess., Supp. No. 16, at 49, U.N. Doc. A/6316 (1967); International Covenant on Civil and Political Rights, *id.* at 52; Optional Protocol to the International Covenant on Civil and Political Rights, *id.* at 59; Second Optional Protocol to the International Covenant on Civil and Political Rights, Aiming at the Abolition of the Death Penalty, G.A. Res. 44/128, U.N. GAOR, 44th Sess., Supp. No. 49, at 206, U.N. Doc. A/44/49 (1990); Convention against Torture and Other Cruel, Inhuman or Degrading Treatment or Punishment, G.A. Res. 39/46, U.N. GAOR, 39th Sess., Supp. No. 51, at 197, U.N. Doc. A/39/51 (1985); Principles of Medical Ethics Relevant to the Role of Health Personnel, Particularly Physicians, in the Protection of Prisoners and Detainees against Torture and Other Cruel, Inhuman or Degrading Treatment or Punishment, G.A. Res. 37/194, U.N. GAOR, 37th Sess., Supp. No. 51, at 210, U.N. Doc. A/37/51 (1983); Body of Principles for the Protection of All Persons under Any Form of Detention or Imprisonment, G.A. Res. 43/173, U.N. GAOR, 43rd Sess., Supp. No. 49, at 297, U.N. Doc. A/43/49 (1989); Convention on the Rights of the Child, G.A. Res. 44/25, U.N. GAOR, 44th Sess., Supp. No. 49, at 166, U.N. Doc. A/44/49 (1990). Coordination within the United Nations remains a continuing challenge. *See also infra* note 16. The problem even extends to coordination of the Specialized Agencies which occasionally foray into the criminal justice area. *See generally,* K.T. Samson, *Human Rights Co-ordination within the UN System,* in THE UNITED NATIONS AND HUMAN RIGHTS 620 (P. Alston ed. 1992).

14. *See Crime Prevention and Criminal Justice, Report of the Secretary-General,* at 6, U.N. Doc. E/1990/36 (1990). Like the Committee, though, the Branch has made little impact on the literature. A computer search of periodical literature in the past decade revealed only one article that mentioned the Branch—and that was, like most of the material on the U.N. program in general, written by an officer of the Branch, A. Viccica, *World Crime Trends,* 24 INT'L J. OFFENDER THERAPY & COMP. CRIMINOLOGY 270 (1980).

stressed the importance of this cooperation.[15] Thus it will be necessary from time to time in the discussion that follows to place the crime and criminal justice program in the broader context of the human rights system and of other parts of the organization that address many of the issues touched upon in its work.[16] Nevertheless, my main focus is on this relatively lesser-known part of the United Nations picture.

Much of the discussion in later chapters concerns material on the table between 1987–1990 when I was a member of the Committee on Crime Prevention and Control; when I was a participant at the 1990 Havana Congress on the Prevention of Crime and the Treatment of

15. The Council "Requests the Secretary-General to strengthen cooperation between the Centre for Human Rights and the Centre for Social Development and Humanitarian Affairs of the Secretariat, including in particular preparations for the World Conference on Human Rights and coordination of the various technical advisory services provided by both Centres in order to undertake joint programmes and to strengthen existing mechanisms for the protection of human rights in the administration of justice." E.S.C. Res 1992/22, pt. IV, para. 6, U.N. ESCOR, Supp. No. 1, at 22, U.N. Doc. E/1992/92 (1992). *See also id.* pt. IV, para. 5 (urging the Commission on Crime Prevention and Criminal Justice to "cooperate closely with the Commission for Social Development, the Commission on Human Rights, the Commission on Narcotic Drugs, the Commission on the Status of Women and other bodies, including the International Law Commission, and specialized agencies, including the United Nations Educational, Scientific and Cultural Organization, whose activities may have crime prevention and criminal justice aspects, in order to increase the efficiency and effectiveness of the United Nations activities in the areas of mutual concern and to ensure proper coordination and avoidance of possible duplication").

16. For example, a number of seminars organized by the Division for Human Rights under the advisory services program have discussed issues of human rights in the administration of justice. *See, e.g., 1960 Seminar on the Role of Substantive Criminal Law in the Protection of Human Rights and the Purposes and Legitimate Limits of Penal Sanctions, Tokyo, Japan,* U.N. Doc. ST/TAO/HR/7 (1960). The question of "crime" appears throughout the United Nations system. The allocation to particular organs is quite irrational. For example, the International Law Commission has grappled with the drafting of a Code of Offenses Against the Peace and Security of Mankind and the question of creating an international criminal court. The General Assembly adopted such treaties as the Convention on the Prevention and Punishment of the Crime of Genocide, G.A. Res. 260A (III), U.N. GAOR, 3d Sess., pt. 1, Resolutions 174, U.N. Doc. A/810 (1948), and the International Convention on the Suppression and Punishment of the Crime of Apartheid, G.A. Res. 3068, U.N. GAOR, 28th Sess., Supp. No. 30, at 75, U.N. Doc. A/9030 (1973), without any serious involvement of the "criminal law" branch of the system. The same is true of the treaties adopted in the "terrorism" area by the U.N. and its specialized agencies. In what might have represented a minor trend towards consulting the Committee in this area, the Eighth Congress adopted a resolution on terrorism which included language encouraging input from the Committee on Crime Prevention and Control in drafting an international penal code and considering an international criminal tribunal. *Eighth United Nations Congress on the Prevention of Crime and the Treatment of Offenders Report Prepared by the Secretariat,* Other Resolution No. 25, at 181, paras. 30–31, U.N. Doc. A/CONF.144/28 (1990).

Offenders, which I attended as part of the New Zealand delegation; and at subsequent meetings in 1991 and 1992 on the future of the whole program, which I attended in the same capacity. I have tried to locate this recent discussion in the framework of all the United Nations work in the area since the 1940s. Not *everything* has been said, done or tried before, but much of it has![17]

B. Development of the Program

The interest of the United Nations in the criminal justice area stems from the basic statement in Article 1, paragraph 3 of the Charter of the "Purpose" of the organization: "[t]o achieve international cooperation in solving international problems of an economic, social, cultural, or humanitarian character, and in promoting and encouraging respect for human rights and for fundamental freedoms for all without distinction as to race, sex, language, or religion."[18] Later, in Article 55, the Charter speaks of certain goals which are to be promoted "[w]ith a view to the creation of conditions of stability and well-being which are necessary for peaceful and friendly relations among nations." Included in these goals are "higher standards of living, full employment, and conditions of economic and social progress and development[19]. . . . [and] solutions of international economic, social, health and related problems."[20] These generalities, as they affect the criminal justice area, are given more concrete expression in several provisions of the Universal Declaration of Human Rights.[21] Thus, Article 28 of the Declaration asserts that "Everyone is entitled to a social and international order in which the rights and freedoms set forth in this Declaration can be fully realized." These rights include notably those in Article 3, the "right to life, liberty and security of person." In other words, the Declaration itself implies some obligation on states to control the extent to which the criminal classes prey on their citizenry. Moreover, several provisions of the Declaration deal with human rights in the administration of justice.[22] Article 12 provides that "No one shall be subjected to

17. *See generally* ALPER & BOREN, *supra* note 5 (sameness about the items on the international agenda).

18. U.N. CHARTER art. 1, para. 3.

19. *Id.* art. 55a.

20. *Id.* art. 55b.

21. G.A. Res. 217A (III), U.N. GAOR, 3d Sess., pt. 1, Resolutions 71, U.N. Doc. A/810 (1948).

22. *See, id.*, art. 5 (no torture, or cruel, inhuman or degrading treatment or punishment), art. 9 (no arbitrary arrest, detention or exile), art. 10 (fair trial), art. 11 (presumption of innocence, no ex post facto crimes).

arbitrary interference with his privacy, family, home or correspondence, nor to attacks on his honour and reputation. Everyone has the right to the protection of the law against such interference or attacks." And Article 17(2) insists that "No one shall be arbitrarily deprived of his property."

In short, there are two kinds of obligations on states in the area of crime and criminal justice. As the United Nations Department of Public Information has put it:

> The import of [the relevant] provisions [of the Charter and the Universal Declaration of Human Rights] cuts in two directions. They posit the right of the people of the world to enjoy domestic tranquillity and security of person and property without the encroachment of criminal activity. At the same time, they predicate efficient criminal justice systems that do not deprive citizens of their rights.[23]

As early as 1946, ECOSOC[24] established a Temporary Social Commission which, *inter alia*, was to "report to the Council on the advisability of bringing under the Council the activities in the social field hitherto carried on by the League of Nations, and such other activities as the work on the treatment of offenders now carried on by the International Penal and Penitentiary Commission."[25] The main activities of the League of Nations in the area had been to encourage work relating to the traffic in women and children and to questions of child welfare. However, the League had been expanding its field of interest in the 1930s, most notably by the endorsement of the Standard

23. THE UNITED NATIONS AND CRIME PREVENTION AND CRIMINAL JUSTICE, *supra* note 5, at 28–29.

24. ECOSOC is described in the U.N. Charter, art. 7, as one of the "principal organs" of the organization. ECOSOC assists the General Assembly in carrying out the organization's functions in the economic and social area and has independent powers, primarily of a recommendatory nature, in that area. *See* U.N. CHARTER, art. 7.

25. E.S.C. Res. 7 (I), 1 U.N. ESCOR, 1st Sess., Resolutions, at 127 (1946). The history of the U.N.'s involvement in this area is discussed in an article by the Secretariat. *The Work of the United Nations in the Field of the Prevention of Crime and the Treatment of Offenders*, 1 INT'L REV. CRIM. POL'Y 3 (1951); M. LÓPEZ-REY, A GUIDE TO UNITED NATIONS CRIMINAL POLICY 1–9 (1985); T. Sellin, *Lionel Fox and the International Penal and Penitentiary Commission*, STUDIES IN PENOLOGY DEDICATED TO THE MEMORY OF SIR LIONEL FOX, C.B., M.C. 194 (M. López-Rey & C. Germain eds. 1964); ALPER & BOREN *supra* note 5, at 77–112; J.L. Robson, *Criminology in Evolution—The Impact of International Congresses*, 3 OTAGO L. REV. 5 (1973). *See infra* notes 28, 47, 48 (discussing in greater detail the International Penal and Penitentiary Commission, I.P.P.C.). *See also* W.H. Nagel, *International Collaboration in the Field of Criminology*, LE DROIT PENAL: RECUEIL D'ETUDES EN HOMMAGE A JACOB MAARTEN VAN BEMMELEM 193 (1965) (providing a good historical overview of international efforts in the area).

Minimum Rules for the Treatment of Prisoners, drafted by the International Penal and Penitentiary Commission.[26] The Temporary Social Commission recommended continuing where the League of Nations left off and ECOSOC immediately created a permanent Social Commission.[27] That crime was regarded as a core social issue was reflected in the request by ECOSOC that the new Social Commission

consider how effective machinery can be developed for studying on a wide international basis the means for the prevention of crime and the treatment of offenders, undertake consultation with the International Penal and Penitentiary Commission, and recommend a scheme by which this whole subject can be fruitfully dealt with on a broad international basis in close association with other social problems.[28]

The United Nations quickly took over the depositary functions of the League and of the French Government concerning a series of treaties adopted since the turn of the century on traffic in women and children. These instruments were then consolidated and up-dated in the 1949 Convention for the Suppression of the Traffic in Persons and of the Exploitation of the Prostitution of Others,[29] which represents one of the earliest United Nations human rights treaties. Some work was done on the issue within the "social defense" part of the organization (the early description given to the criminal justice unit) in the following decade.[30] However, the topic was not one which was actively addressed in the Committee on Crime Prevention and Control or at

26. *See* League of Nations Docs. C.620.M.241.1930.IV; A.26.1933.IV; A.44.1933.IV; A.45.1934.IV. Annex (containing in the last document the Rules as modified by the I.P.P.C. in response to governmental comments at the League). Approval is recorded in League of Nations O.J., Spec. Supp. 123, at VI.4 (1934). The League recommended that governments take the Rules "into consideration," requested them to "consider the possibility of adapting their penitentiary system to the Standard Minimum Rules if that system is below the minimum laid down in the said rules," and requested them to submit regular reports regarding their application and on prison reforms achieved in their respective countries. The League's somewhat tentative language of approval would find its counterpart in the U.N. period. *See infra* Chapter 5, at notes 28–30. The reporting theme also continues to run through the U.N. era. *See infra* Chapter 9.

27. E.S.C. Res. 10 (II), 1 U.N. ESCOR, 2d Sess., Resolutions, at 522 (1946). The Commission is now known as the Commission on Social Development.

28. *Id.* para. 3 (b) (iii).

29. G.A. Res. 317 (IV), U.N. GAOR 4th Sess., Resolutions, at 33, U.N. Doc. A/1251 (1949); THE COMPENDIUM, *supra* note 4, at 230; K. Silfverberg, *Suppression of the Traffic in Persons and the Exploitation of the Prostitution of Others*, 2 FINNISH Y.B. INT'L L. 66 (1991).

30. The thirteenth issue of the INTERNATIONAL REVIEW OF CRIMINAL POLICY appeared in 1958 devoted to the problem of prostitution, and a 1959 Secretariat study was entitled TRAFFIC IN PERSONS AND PROSTITUTION. U.N. Doc. ST/SOA/SD/8, U.N. Sales No. 59.IV.5 (1959).

the Congresses. A recent resurgence of interest in the traffic in persons has been centered in the Slavery Working Group of the Sub-Commission on Prevention of Discrimination and Protection of Minorities, the secretariat of which (in the Centre for Human Rights) was designated as a focal point in this endeavor.[31] In any event, the focus of the United Nations in the criminal justice area would be much broader than that of the League of Nations.

In 1948, the United Nations set up a Secretariat unit (originally known as the Social Defense Section)[32] to work in the area. The same year, ECOSOC endorsed the position that

in view of the importance of the study, on an international basis, of the problem of the prevention of crime and treatment of offenders, the United Nations should assume leadership[33] in promoting this activity, having regard to inter-

31. E.S.C. Res. 1983/30, U.N. ESCOR, Supp. No. 1, at 22, U.N. Doc. E/1983/83 (1983). The Human Rights Centre in Geneva seems to have won a turf war here. *See also Report of the Working Group on Contemporaneous Forms of Slavery on its Fourteenth Session*, U.N. Doc. E/CN.4/Sub.2/1989/39 (1989); E.S.C. Decision 1990/240, U.N. ESCOR, Supp. No. 1, at 55, U.N. Doc. E/1990/90 (1990) (appointing a Special Rapporteur to consider matters relating to the sale of children, child prostitution and child pornography, including the problem of adoption for commerial purposes). E.S.C. Res. 1991/35, U.N. ESCOR, Supp. No. 1, at 31, U.N. Doc. E/1991/91 (1991), urged the Commission on the Status of Women and the Committee on Crime Prevention and Control to collaborate closely with the Centre for Human Rights on the issue.

32. The original title reflected something of a vogue in the area, although an early Chief of the Section claimed that "The term 'social defense' is somewhat misleading, cannot be considered as particularly fortunate and should not be taken to refer to any school of penal or criminological thought." M. López-Rey, *The First U.N. Congress on the Prevention of Crime and the Treatment of Offenders*, 47 J. Crim. L. Criminology & Police Sci. 526, 527 n.1 (1957). The subsequent semantics are curious: the Committee was on Crime Prevention and Control, the Secretariat deals with Crime Prevention and Criminal Justice, and the quinquennial Congresses deal with the Prevention of Crime and the Treatment of Offenders. The terminology now seems to be stabilizing on "Crime Prevention and Criminal Justice." The location of the Section on Social Defense/Crime Prevention and Criminal Justice Branch within the Secretariat seems to have been a little haphazard in the outset and the section might well have ended up as part of the Human Rights Center had it not been for the predilections and personalities involved. According to his Deputy, Kamleshwar Das, in a conversation with the author, John Humphrey, the first head of the Human Rights Division had an opportunity in 1948 to have Social Defense within his bailiwick but declined. Some of the Social Defense personnel moved from New York to Geneva in the early 1960s. The unit was reunited in New York in the mid-60s and the whole enterprise eventually found its present home in Vienna between 1979 and 1981. There is always (conflicting) speculation that the Branch might be (re-)combined with other social items in New York, with human rights in Geneva, or even more closely tied to the drug program in Vienna.

33. *See* M. López-Rey, *The Role of the United Nations Congresses on the Prevention of Crime and the Treatment of Offenders*, Fed. Probation, Sept. 1973, at 24 (questioning the commitment to leadership).

national and national organizations which have interests and competence in this field, and making the fullest use of their knowledge and experience.[34]

A representative example of the subject matter entailed in this early period is contained in the following 1951 summary of the United Nations program of research and study in the field of the prevention of crime and the treatment of offenders which appeared in the first issue of the Secretariat's fledgling INTERNATIONAL REVIEW OF CRIMINAL POL-ICY[35]:

1. Probation and related matters.
2. Juvenile delinquency in all its phases, including the study of advanced legislation on the subject.
3. Criminal statistics.
4. The formulation of standard rules for the treatment of prisoners.
5. Medico-psychological and social examination of offenders before the final disposition of the case and as a guide for treatment.
6. The detention of adults prior to sentence.
7. The indeterminate sentence and other measures designed for adapting the duration of treatment in correctional or penal institutions to the needs of the individual offender and to the protection of society.
8. Parole and after-care.
9. Open penal and correctional institutions.
10. Habitual offenders and recidivists.
11. The institutional treatment of women offenders.
12. The selection and training of correctional personnel.
13. The use of short-term imprisonment.
14. The system of payment of fines in installments.
15. Police programs and activities positively directed at the prevention of crime.
16. Forfeitures and loss of civil rights.

34. *Report of the Third Session of the Social Commission*, E.S.C. Res. 155 C (VII), U.N. ESCOR, 7th Sess., Resolutions, at 32, U.N. Doc. E/1065 (1948).

35. *See supra* note 25, at 21. The REVIEW was designed as a significant part of the program's networking endeavors. According to the Preface the REVIEW would "be primarily devoted to the methods and techniques employed in the prevention of crime and the treatment of offenders. It is therefore intended to be a journal of *applied* criminological science rather than a scientific journal in the narrower sense." *Id*. at 1. *See also* M. López-Rey, *United Nations Activities in the Prevention of Crime and the Treatment of Offenders*, AM. J. CORRECTION, May-June 1960, at 4 (discussing early United Nations work); F. Ferracuti, *The Role of Social Defense in the United Nations*, 32 REV. JUR. U. P.R. 683 (1963) (elaborating upon early United Nations work).

17. Constructive methods of treatment applied in penal and correctional institutions, and specifically designed for the re-socialization of the offenders.
18. The role of prison labour in the training of the prisoner and in the economy of the institution, as well as in its relationship to the national economy and in relation to the maintenance of the prisoner's dependants.
19. Governmental action for assistance to the dependants of the prisoners.
20. Capital and corporal punishment.
21. The collection of information with respect to the precise ways in which knowledge of, and training in, the behaviour sciences are at present being used in practice in the prevention of crime and the treatment of offenders.

Devising this shopping list was not entirely free from controversy. At the seventh session of ECOSOC, the representatives of the U.S.S.R. and Byelorussia criticized the items proposed for study as being domestic, rather than international questions. Those Members would have limited efforts to (1) questions on which relevant decisions by international organs already existed, such as measures to be taken against propaganda and the inciters of a new war and genocide; and (2) questions on which relevant international conventions existed, such as slavery, narcotic drugs and the suppression of the traffic in women and children and of obscene publications. Their efforts were soundly defeated. The British and French representatives, who had the votes, expressed the view that these matters were already being addressed and that "an international exchange of views on the prevention of crime and the treatment of offenders would be valuable."[36] In recent years, reflecting one of the many ironies of the end of the Cold War, most of the eastern European states have been keenly interested in all aspects of the program, while some of the Western states would prefer to concentrate on transnational crime.

Some differences in emphasis, some new items and a sophisticated structure for the allocation of budgetary resources are features of more recent statements of the program, but most of these original issues still found a home in the early 1990s. The section of the United Nations Proposed Program Budget for the Biennium 1992–1993[37] devoted to crime prevention and criminal justice, produced on the eve of the

36. 1947–48 U.N.Y.B. 613–14, U.N. Sales No. 1949.I.13.
37. The U.N. budget operates at two levels of specificity. A general Medium Term Plan which operates on a five-year cycle is the basic policy document of the organization. The Program Budget which is done on a biennial basis contains more working detail.

restructuring, included activities to give practical effect to the recommendations of the Eighth Congress of 1990, as endorsed by the General Assembly. This entailed "namely, minimizing crime and its harmful consequences, while simultaneously increasing the fairness and effectiveness of the criminal justice system, with due protection of human rights."[38] Three "subprogrammes" were listed: collaborative action against transnational crime, crime prevention planning and criminal justice management, and crime prevention and criminal justice standards and norms.

The first subprogram, which was to take up 40.3 percent of the regular budget and 57.2 percent of extrabudgetary resources, would aim at (a) strengthening international cooperation in preventing and combatting crime, particularly in its most dangerous transnational forms, and (b) assisting states in improving the capability of their criminal justice systems to deal with transnational crime. This latter objective would be achieved by technical cooperation activities and by formulating international instruments, model treaties, and agreements designed to promote and facilitate the collaboration of states in criminal justice matters. Attention was to be given to the means and methods for countering transnational forms of criminality, such as organized crime, terrorism, environmental offenses, crime against the cultural patrimony, and computer crimes.[39]

Subprogram 2 was to receive 26.3 percent of the regular budget and 19.6 percent of extrabudgetary resources. Activities here would aim at promoting criminal justice management and planning by (a) providing guidelines for the formulation of national policies and programs in those areas, (b) increasing awareness of governments about trends in crime and areas of concern, and (c) assisting in upgrading national criminal justice capabilities in data collection on crime and analyses for rational decision-making. Efforts were to be made to assist states in community education in crime prevention. Special attention was to be paid to the prevention of juvenile delinquency and improvement of the administration of juvenile justice. Ways and means for dealing with

---

38. *Proposed Programme Budget for the Biennium 1992–1993, pt. IV, International Cooperation for Development, Sec. 21, Social Development and Humanitarian Affairs* 39, U.N. Doc. A/46/6, Sec. 21 (1991). At the time of writing, alterations to this budget based on the restructuring, in particular to add a sub-program on operational activities, planning and overall coordination, were still working their way through the budget process. *See* Chapter 2 *infra*, at note 76, and *Proposed Programme Budget for the Biennium 1994–1995, pt. IV, International Cooperations for Development, Sec. 13, Crime Control,* U.N. Doc. A/48/6 Sec. 13 (1993). The clear understanding was that significant resources from the regular budget would now be devoted to technical cooperation and much less to activity connected with the drafting of standards and norms.

39. *Id.* at 40.

prisoners suffering from AIDS or who are infected with HIV would be explored. The United Nations Crime Prevention and Criminal Justice Information Network (UNCJIN) would be developed and maintained.[40]

Subprogram 3, on standards and norms, was to take 33.4 percent of the regular budget and 23.2 percent of extrabudgetary resources. It was aimed at "fostering progressive crime prevention and criminal justice practice, in line with United Nations standards."[41] In accordance with the recommendations of the Eighth Congress, primary emphasis was to be placed on the application of existing norms and on consolidating and rationalizing the arrangements for the effective monitoring and evaluation of the progress achieved. New guidelines would be developed in priority areas.

More recent items since the 1950s were, of course, terrorism and organized crime—the latter with strong overtones of the drug problem. Indeed, there has been increasing attention given in the program to the broad issue of transnational crime, or crime which operates across national boundaries, of which terrorism and organized crime are seen as examples.[42] The newer emphasis was an even greater insistence than in the earlier days of the program that crime must be placed in its wider social and economic setting, including questions of development.[43] The newer formulations are indicative of an expansion

40. *Id.* at 41. This network, authorized by ECOSOC in 1986, E.S.C. Res. 1986/11, U.N. ESCOR, Supp. No. 1, at 16, U.N. Doc. E/1986/86 (1986), is discussed further in Chapter 3 *infra*, at notes 143–145. A related effort, the World Criminal Justice Library Network, is also discussed in Chapter 3 *infra*, at notes 146–147.

41. *Id.* at 43.

42. *See Report of the Ad Hoc Expert Group Meeting on Strategies to Deal With Transnational Crime, Smolenice Castle, Bratislava, Czech and Slovak Federal Republic, 27–31 May 1991*, U.N. Doc. E/CN.15/1992/4/Add.1 (1992) (drawing many of the transnational threads together); *The impact of organized criminal activities upon society at large, Report of the Secretary-General*, U.N. Doc. E/CN.15/1993/3 (1993); *Control of proceeds of crime, Report of the Secretary-General*, U.N. Doc. E/CN.15/1993/4 (1993).

43. The high water mark of this expansion was probably the Sixth Congress's discussion of "Crime and the Abuse of Power: Offences and Offenders Beyond the Reach of the Law." *See Report prepared by the Secretariat, Sixth United Nations Congress on the Prevention of Crime and the Treatment of Offenders*, at 67–70, U.N. Doc. A/CONF.87/14/Rev.1 (1981). The theoretical basis seems to have been elaborated for the first time in reports submitted to the Second Congress in 1960 that "examined the relationship between socioeconomic development and crime prevention in the light of available data on demography, the environment, economics, culture, town planning, industrialization and migration." THE UNITED NATIONS AND CRIME PREVENTION, *supra* note 5, at 15. *See also Ad hoc Meeting of Experts on Social Defence Policies in relation to development planning*, 27 INT'L REV. CRIM. POL'Y 57 (1969); *Economic Commission for Africa, Report of the Seminar on Planning for Crime Prevention and Criminal Justice in the Context of Development, Addis Ababa, Ethiopia, 3–12 June 1987*, U.N. Doc. ECA/SDEHSD/UNAFRI/14 (1987).

of the organization's field of interest well beyond the "crime in the street" focus which typified the early years. However, this is not to imply that "crime in the street" is no longer of any moment!

It must be conceded that the resources devoted to the program are modest in the extreme. Despite repeated entreaties at the Committee on Crime Prevention and Control and at the congresses to devote more resources to the program, during 1992–1993 the total staff establishment was only eleven in the professional category and above, and six in the general service category.[44] The regular budget estimates (including $728,500 in "common staff costs") amount to $3,284,900 out of a total regular U.N. budget of $2,363,000,000 for the biennium (a little over an American billion a year), that is to say less than 0.15 percent of the total budget.[45] Extrabudgetary resources are estimated at an even more modest $561,100, of which $540,000 is a small part of a very generous contribution from the Italian Government which goes to support the United Nations Interregional Crime and Justice Research Institute (UNICRI) located in Rome.[46]

---

44. U.N. Doc. A/46/6, Sec. 21, *supra* note 38, table 21.13. This represented an increase over the 8 professionals and 5 general service posts budgeted for 1990–91. *Id.* From time to time, especially in a congress year, the actual numbers will be increased marginally by secondments from governments and from elsewhere in the Secretariat. Three more posts promised early in 1993 had been filled only on a temporary basis by late in 1993. Ultimate responsibility for actual staffing size lies in the complex relationship between the Secretary-General's overall responsibility for the bureaucracy and the arcane budget approval process which ultimately wends its way to the Fifth Committee of the General Assembly.

45. *Id.* table 21.12; U.N. Doc. A/46/6 (1991) (overview tables and annexes to the introduction). This is not quite the whole cost of the enterprise since conference servicing (the meeting and paper generation costs of the Committee/Commission, congresses, etc.) is buried elsewhere in the budget. According to figures provided by the Secretariat at the August 1991 Intergovernmental Working Group on the program, the paper production and interpretation costs of a meeting of the Committee or of the new Commission would amount to about $400,000. Over the five-year cycle leading up to and including a congress, another $1,900,000 in servicing costs would normally have been incurred. Of this, $700,000 is for the regional preparatory meetings, $370,000 for the interregional preparatory meetings and the remainder for the congress itself. (Secretariat explanations on the costing of draft resolutions, on the author's file.) The interregional meetings will no longer take place under the recent reorganization. *See* Chapter 3 *infra*, at note 70. The budgetary estimates for 1994–1995 suggest a 32 percent increase in the budget, which appears to be accounted for largely by increased staff costs (including the permanent addition of three more professional staff) and expenses connected with the 1995 Congress. *See Proposed Programme Budget for the Biennium 1994–1995, supra* note 38, at 3.

46. *Id.* table 21.12 (the crime program is found in Sec. 21 of the U.N. Budget). By way of comparison, the newly reorganized U.N. International Drug Control Program (Sec. 22 of the Budget) had, to deal with only one type of crime, a regular budget allocation of $13,851,900 for the 1992–93 biennium. *Proposed Programme Budget for The Biennium*

C. Machinery—The Congresses, the Committee, and the Commission

In 1950, the United Nations had accomplished the transfer to itself of the functions of the International Penal and Penitentiary Commission (IPPC).[47] During the League of Nations period, the IPPC, an informally organized intergovernmental organization, had served as a prototype of what were to become the United Nations Specialized Agencies. The most notable of the IPPC's functions since 1885 had been the holding of congresses in the correctional field.[48] These had occurred quinquennially, except during the two world wars. The later congresses would become, in turn, the most visible part of the United Nations activities in the criminal justice field. The First Congress under United Nations auspices was held in Geneva in 1955 while the Eighth took place in 1990 in Havana. The Ninth Congress is scheduled for early 1995.[49]

The Assembly's 1950 Resolution[50] called for the Secretary-General to assemble a small international Ad Hoc Advisory Committee of Experts to advise the Secretary-General and the Social Commission of ECOSOC in "devising and formulating programmes for study on an international basis and policies for international action in the field of the prevention of crime and the treatment of offenders." This Ad Hoc Committee of seven members evolved in 1965 into a ten-person Advisory Committee of Experts on the Prevention of Crime and the Treatment of Offenders.[51] In May 1971, ECOSOC made the Committee a subsidiary organ of the Council, continuing its status as a body of

---

1992–1993 (Overview tables and annexes to the introduction), at 17, U.N. Doc. A/46/6 (1991). The drug program also has staggering extrabudgetary resources for "support services" ($4,512,200), "substantive activities" ($280,000), and "operational projects" ($177,110,000), *id*. at 86,93,98. The political commitment to the drug program appears to be stronger. In allocating resources for international law enforcement, the United States also seems to place disproportionate emphasis on drug control. *See generally*, E.A. NADELMANN, COPS ACROSS BORDERS: THE INTERNATIONALIZATION OF U.S. CRIMINAL LAW ENFORCEMENT, Chapters 3–5 (1993). On UNICRI (referred to in the text), *see* Chapter 3 *infra*, at notes 117–122 (describing UNICRI and noting that this organization is also better funded than the Branch).

47. G.A. Res. 415 (V), U.N. GAOR, 5th Sess., Supp. No. 20, at 37, U.N. Doc. A/1775 (1950).

48. *See generally* N.K. TEETERS, DELIBERATIONS OF THE INTERNATIONAL PENAL AND PENITENTIARY CONGRESSES: QUESTIONS AND ANSWERS 1872–1935 (1949).

49. *See* THE UNITED NATIONS AND CRIME PREVENTION, *supra* note 5, at 12–26 (giving a synopsis of the topics of the Congresses).

50. *See supra* note 47.

51. *Organizational Arrangements for the United Nations Social Defence Programme*, E.S.C. Res. 1086 B, U.N. ESCOR, 39th Sess., Supp. No. 1, at 9, U.N. Doc. E/4117 (1965). The Advisory Committee was to report "as appropriate" to the Social Commission. *Id*. para. 3.

experts, while renaming it the Committee on Crime Prevention and Control and increasing its membership to fifteen persons elected by ECOSOC on the nomination of Governments.[52] By doing so, ECOSOC was reacting to the concerns expressed at the 1970 Kyoto Congress that the United Nations program should be strengthened.[53] In 1977, the General Assembly solidified the principle of geographical representation.[54] In 1979, the Committee was again increased to its final size of twenty-seven members with an explicit geographical distribution of seats: seven to African states, six to Asian states, three to Eastern European states, five to Latin American states, and six to Western European and other states.[55]

At the same time, ECOSOC summarized the "main functions" of the Crime Prevention Committee as follows:

52. E.S.C. Res. 1584, U.N. ESCOR, 50th Sess., Supp. No. 1, at 12, U.N. Doc. E/5044 (1971). The Committee on Crime Prevention and Control reported to what was now the Commission on Social Development. *Id.* para 6. This arrangement continued until 1983 when ECOSOC, acting on the recommendation of the Committee, decided that the Committee should report directly to ECOSOC. E.S.C. Res. 1983/25, U.N. ESCOR, Supp. No. 1, at 20, U.N. Doc. E/1983/83 (1983). The Commission on Social Development meets every other year and its consideration of the crime items had become perfunctory. Members of the Committee evidently thought that the existing reporting procedures "had resulted in considerable delays in the taking of decisions by the Council." *Commission for Social Development, Report on the Twenty-Eighth Session, 7–16 Feb. 1983*, U.N. ESCOR, Supp. No. 4, at 53, U.N. Doc. E/1983/14 (1983). The Commission on Social Development is another part of the U.N. whose existence has escaped the academic community (as well as many diplomats). I could find no significant academic discussion of its work.

53. Clifford, *supra* note 11.

54. *See* G.A. Res. 32/60, U.N. GAOR, 32d Sess., Supp. No. 45, at 135, U.N. Doc. A/32/45 (1977) (insisting on geographical representation, and providing that members would be elected to a four year term with half the membership elected every two years). Nominations for election were to be made by states. Since the Committee met only once every two years, the four-year term meant that some members were able to attend only two meetings of the Committee before their term was over. There was ongoing discussion about whether the Committee should retain its status as an expert body or whether it should simply consist of representatives of states. *See, Report of Australian Delegation, Fifth United Nations Congress on the Prevention of Crime and the Treatment of Prisoners*, at 152 (1975). Like other "expert" United Nations bodies it probably contained a mixture of independent experts and people who might well have been knowledgable but were instructed by their governments. Committee members had to run the gauntlet of nomination by states, the usual horse-trading and then election by ECOSOC. *See generally*, Lopez-Rey, *supra* note 33, at 25–26.

55. E.S.C. Res. 1979/30, U.N. ESCOR, Supp. No. 1, at 16, U.N. Doc. E/1979/79 (1979). The author, elected by ECOSOC on the nomination of New Zealand, held one of the West European and Other Group's (WEOG) seats. *See* J.L. ROBSON, SACRED COWS AND ROGUE ELEPHANTS (1987) (detailing the activities of New Zealand and the Congresses in chapters 14 and 29).

a) Preparation of the United Nations congresses on the prevention of crime and the treatment of offenders with a view to considering and facilitating the introduction of more effective methods and ways of preventing crime and improving the treatment of offenders;

b) Preparation and submission to the competent United Nations bodies and to those congresses for their approval, of programmes of international cooperation in the field of crime prevention on the basis of principles of sovereign equality of States and non-interference in internal affairs, and other proposals related to the prevention of offences;

c) Provision of assistance to the Economic and Social Council in the co-ordination of the activities of the United Nations bodies in matters concerning crime control and the treatment of offenders, and preparation and submission of findings and recommendations to the Secretary-General and the appropriate United Nations bodies;

d) Promotion of exchanges of experience gained by States in the field of crime prevention and the treatment of offenders;

e) Discussion of major issues of professional interest, as a basis for international co-operation in this field, particularly those related to the prevention and reduction of crime.[56]

Plainly, a substantial part of the mandate of the Committee, which has now passed to the new commission, was to foster the exchange of information, to provide policy advice and to facilitate networking among criminal justice professionals—with the Congresses as the major focal point[57] and the reduction of crime as the main object of the endeavor.

Yet, much more than exchange, or the "clearing-house function,"[58]

56. E.S.C. Res. 1979/19, U.N. ESCOR, Supp. No. 1, at 16, U.N. Doc. E/1979/79 (1979).

57. The Committee meetings themselves were becoming an increasingly significant opportunity for networking. The Committee's 1990 meeting was attended by observer missions of some 67 states and representatives of 47 non-governmental organizations. *Committee on Crime Prevention and Control, Report on the Eleventh Session, Vienna, 5–16 February 1990*, U.N. ESCOR, Supp. No. 10, at 255–57, U.N. Doc. E/1990/31 (1990). This trend seems likely to continue with the Commission. Indeed, with the Commision meeting annually, compared with the Committee's biennial cycle, the networking momentum may well be greater. In addition to most of its members, its first meeting in 1992 was attended by observers of 35 other states and 27 NGOs; that in 1993 was attended by 37 of its 40 members, by observers from 55 other states and 40 NGOs.

58. *See Education, Training and Public Awareness in the Field of Crime Prevention*, E.S.C. Res. 1990/24, U.N. ESCOR, Supp. No. 1, at 26, U.N. Doc. E/1990/90 (1990) (speaking of

has occurred. The program has been deeply involved in generating standards against which state performance may be judged. These two functions of the United Nations program are concisely summarized in a document prepared in the course of developing the organization's Medium Term Plan for the Period 1992–1997.[59] It reads

Mindful of the negative impact of criminality on economic, social, political and cultural processes, and on the quality of life, the international community is committed to the task of minimizing crime and its harmful consequences, while simultaneously increasing the fairness and effectiveness of the criminal justice system, with due protection of human rights. Crime prevention is now deemed essential to the well-being of all people, to national development and public safety.

These two aims, embracing both law and justice and human rights aspects, thus characterize the work of the program.

In dealing with the United Nations norms and standards, I think of the Crime Prevention Committee and the new Crime Prevention Commission in terms of "catalysing" or "generating" the material in question. I do this bearing in mind that during the life of the Crime Prevention Committee only some of the drafting was done by committee members themselves, either at meetings of the full group, at informal gatherings, or at the structured regional and inter-regional preparatory meetings for the Congresses. Much of the nitty-gritty work, of course, was done by the very able, but understaffed, Secretariat in the Crime Prevention and Criminal Justice Branch, by paid consultants, and by an army of underpaid non-governmental representatives, many of whom have given freely of their time and expertise to lobby or to participate directly in the work. Some governments made suggestions or funneled draft documents into the system. Independently funded "institutes," which are members of the United Nations Crime Prevention and Criminal Justice Program Network,[60] have contributed to

---

the "policy, standard-setting and clearing-house functions and central co-ordination role" of the organization). *See generally* UNITED NATIONS DEPARTMENT OF ECONOMIC AND SOCIAL AFFAIRS, A POLICY APPROACH TO SOCIAL DEFENCE, U.N. Doc. ST/SOA/114 (1972) (several essays on the policy generating function of the organization).

59. *Programme Questions*, at 17, U.N. Doc. E/AC.57/1990/CRP.2 (1990).

60. The institutes with the closest connection to the United Nations are the U.N. Interregional Crime and Justice Research Institute (UNICRI) in Rome, the United Nations Asia and the Far East Institute for the Prevention of Crime and the Treatment of Offenders (UNAFEI) in Tokyo, the United Nations Latin American Institute for the Prevention of Crime and the Treatment of Offenders (ILANUD) in San José, Costa Rica, the European Institute for Crime Prevention and Control affiliated with the U.N. (HEUNI) in Helsinki, Finland, and the African Regional Institute for the Prevention of Crime and the Treatment of Offenders (UNAFRI) in Kampala, Uganda. Four other

efforts to make the whole program operational by technical co-operation projects, seminars and training courses, and by sharpening the issues with research and position papers.

The Committee on Crime Prevention and Control, then, was not a lone operator. But, as the preparatory body for the congresses, possessed of a certain continuity in membership, the Crime Prevention Committee had a central role in shaping the whole agenda. This ultimately affected not only a whole body of professional discourse,[61] but also the development of a corpus of international standards in the area—much of it of the "weak" or "soft" variety of law.[62]

It remains to be seen precisely how the dynamics of the process will ultimately be affected by the new structure erected in 1991 and 1992. In particular the question arises whether the Crime Prevention Commission will have a greater or a lesser role than the Crime Prevention Committee and how the role of the congresses will be affected by the existence of an intergovernmental body which meets on an annual basis. It is to those developments that I now turn.

---

institutes co-operate closely with the U.N., the Arab Security Studies and Training Centre in Riyadh, Saudi Arabia, the Australian Institute of Criminology in Canberra, Australia, the International Centre for Criminal Law Reform and Criminal Justice Policy in Vancouver, British Columbia, Canada, and the International Institute for Higher Studies in Criminal Sciences in Siracusa, Italy. *See* Chapter 3 *infra*, at notes 112–142 (describing these bodies in greater detail).

61. There has been a subtle process of symbiosis whereby what has been on the agendas of the Committee and Congress has affected what work is done in the field and, at the same time, that which people who found their way to meetings regarded as important worked its way into the proceedings.

62. *See* Chapter 5 *infra*, at notes 62–71 (discussing the jurisprudential nature of the texts).

Chapter 2
Recent Reorganization of the Program

A. Introduction

As noted in Chapter 1, the United Nations Program has recently undergone significant reorganization. This chapter is devoted to examining those changes in three parts. The first is a chronology of the events; the second examines some of the main issues that were debated during the reorganization and the conclusions that were reached on them; the third examines the reorganizing instrument, General Assembly Resolution 46/152.[1]

B. Chronology

Efforts by members of the Committee on Crime Prevention and Control to gain more attention and resources for the program date back at least to a successful move in 1983 to have the Crime Prevention Committee report directly to ECOSOC, rather than through the Commission on Social Development.[2] Crime items had tended to be treated perfunctorily in that forum[3] and were buried amongst matters with which there was undoubtedly some affinity at a high level of generality—as they were all "social" questions—but with which it was sometimes difficult to make concrete connections.[4]

1. G.A. Res. 46/152, U.N. GAOR, 46th Sess., Supp. No. 49, at 217, U.N. Doc. A/46/49 (1992).
2. E.S.C. Res. 1983/25, U.N. ESCOR, Supp. No. 1, at 20, U.N. Doc. E/1983/83 (1983), discussed in Chapter 1 *supra* at note 52.
3. Like the Committee on Crime Prevention and Control, the Commission on Social Development met (and meets) only every other year. Further momentum was lost for the crime items by this situation.
4. Crime prevention and criminal justice was the last sub-item under an item on the Commission's agenda entitled *Programmes and Policies for Social Integration*, which con-

The Seventh Congress was persuaded to include in one of its major instruments, the Milan Plan of Action,[5] a request to the Secretary-General to review the functioning and program of work of the organization in crime prevention and criminal justice. This review would occur in consultation with the Committee on Crime Prevention and Control and would include the United Nations regional and interregional institutes. The aim of the Secretary-General's evaluation would be to establish priorities and to ensure the continuing relevance and responsiveness of the United Nations to emerging needs. In its general resolution on the Seventh Congress, the General Assembly both approved the Milan Plan and added a specific paragraph ordering the review. [6]

At its 1986 meeting, the Committee on Crime Prevention and Control had a general discussion of the matter on the basis of an initial review made by the Secretary-General.[7] The Committee recommended

---

tained: A. Youth, B. Aging, C. The welfare of children and families, D. Migrant workers, E. Social welfare, F. Disabled persons, G. Crime prevention and criminal justice. *See, e.g.*, *Commission for Social Development, Report on the Twenty-Seventh Session, 9–19 February 1981*, U.N. ESCOR, Supp. No. 6, at iii, U.N. Doc. E/1981/26 (1981). The Assistant Secretary-General for Social Development and Humanitarian Affairs explained "social integration" as follows:

> That aimed at securing for the less advantaged groups in society full access to their country's social and economic institutions on the basis of full equality. It implied the creation of conditions to ensure the contribution of less advantaged groups to the development process, notably youth, the aging, disabled persons, women and migrant workers and, in turn, their receiving a fair share of the benefits.

Id. at 23. *See also* Chapter 1 *supra* note 8.

5. *Seventh United Nations Congress on the Prevention of Crime and the Treatment of Offenders, Milan, 26 August-6 September 1985, Report prepared by the Secretariat*, at 2, para. (j), U.N.Doc. A/CONF.121/22/Rev.1 (1986). The General Assembly approved the Milan Plan. G.A. Res. 40/32, U.N. GAOR, 40th Sess., Supp. No. 53, at 204, U.N. Doc. A/40/53 (1986). The Milan Plan is also discussed in Chapter 4.

6. G.A. Res. 40/32, U.N. GAOR, 40th Sess., Supp. No. 53, at 204, U.N. Doc. A/40/53 (1986). The Plan is approved in the third paragraph while the review is authorized specifically in the thirteenth paragraph. The Secretary-General was requested to make an initial review for the Crime Prevention Committee, with a final report to be made to ECOSOC in 1987.

7. *See Report of the Secretary-General, Initial Review of the Functioning and Program of Work of the United Nations in the Field of Crime Prevention and Criminal Justice*, U.N. Doc. E/AC.57/1986/4 (1986). The Committee's discussion is in *Committee on Crime Prevention and Control, Report on the Ninth Session, Vienna, 5–14 March 1986*, U.N. ESCOR, Supp. No. 5, at 9–11, 25–31 U.N. Doc. E/1986/25 (1986). Additional thought was given to the review at an informal meeting involving some members of the Crime Prevention Committee and other experts held at the HEUNI offices in Helsinki in December 1986. Particular attention was given to strengthening the Secretariat and giving more focus to

to ECOSOC the adoption of a resolution which encouraged both the continuation of the process and the creation of a global crime prevention and criminal justice network.[8] The following year, ECOSOC adopted a much broader decision setting up a Special Commission to do an "in-depth study of the United Nations intergovernmental structure and functions in the economic and social fields."[9] There was some fear that this study might lead to the merging of the Crime Prevention Committee with other bodies, thus losing even more momentum for the Crime Program.[10] Since the Crime Prevention Committee would not meet before the Special Commission did, Simone Rozes, who chaired the Committee at its Ninth Meeting in 1986, circulated among the committee members a draft paper for the Special Commission which was revised in the light of members' comments and then submitted to the Special Commission.[11] Strong suppport was expressed at the Special Commission for the work of the Committee on Crime Prevention and Control and the Crime Program in general, although there was some criticism of the lack of resources. Fears that the Crime Prevention Committee might find itself absorbed somewhere else thus proved unfounded.

Having had its views sharpened during this exercise, however, the Crime Prevention Committee returned to the fray with some enthusiasm at its 1988 Session. It adopted a resolution[12] requesting that the chair of the Crime Prevention Committee, on the basis of informal

---

the Congresses. *See* The Helsinki Paper on the Work of the United Nations in the Field of Crime and Criminal Justice, Helsinki (Dec. 1, 1986)(on file with author).

8. The draft was adopted by ECOSOC as E.S.C. Res. 1986/11. E.S.C. Res. 1986/11; U.N. ESCOR, Supp. No. 1, at 16, U.N. Doc. E/1986/86 (1986). *See* Chapter 3 *infra* at notes 143–45 (detailing information on the network).

9. E.S.C. Decision 1987/112, U.N. ESCOR, Supp. No. 1, at 50, U.N. Doc. E/1987/87 (1987).

10. ECOSOC's action followed the appearance of the recommendations of the General Assembly's Group of High-Level Intergovernmental Experts to Review the Efficiency of the Adminstrative and Financial Functioning of the United Nations. U.N. GAOR, 41st Sess., Supp. No. 49, U.N. Doc. A/41/49 (1986). Recommendation 8 of the Group, referred to the need to "[i]dentify measures to rationalize and simplify the intergovernmental structure, avoid duplication and consider consolidating and co-ordinating overlapping activities and merging existing bodies in order to improve their work and make the structure more responsive to present needs." *Id.* at 7.

11. *See* U.N. Doc. E/AC.57/1988/CRP.5 (1988)(reproducing the paper along with comments made at the Special Commission).

12. *Committee on Crime Prevention and Control, Report on the Tenth Session, Vienna, 22–31 August 1988*, C.C.P.C. Res. 10/1, U.N. ESCOR, Supp. No. 10, at 48, U.N. Doc. E/1988/20 (1988). By the time of the Committee's Tenth Session, the Secretary-General had completed the review of the functioning and programme of work. *See Report of the Secretary-General, Review of the Functioning and Programme of Action of the United Nations in the Field of Crime Prevention and Criminal Justice*, U.N. Doc. E/1978/43 (1987).

consultations with committee members, appoint a sub-committee composed of the bureau and other designated members, with due regard to the principles of geographical distribution, working in collaboration with the directors of the regional and interregional institutes. The sub-committee would provide an overview of the problem of crime; assess the most efficient means of stimulating practical action in support of Member States; and make recommendations to the Crime Prevention Committee concerning the most effective mechanisms for the implementation of the overview.

The sub-committee met at Riyadh, Saudi Arabia, on January 18–19, 1989 under the auspices of the Arab Security Studies and Training Center. Its report, drafted by Co-Rapporteurs Ronald L. Gainer (Member of the Committee from the United States), Vasily P. Ignatov (Member of the Committee from the U.S.S.R.) and Matti Joutsen (Director of HEUNI) over the next few months, was presented to the Crime Prevention Committee at its Eleventh (and, as it turned out, last) Meeting in February 1990.[13] After considerable debate in the Crime Prevention Committee, a revised version of the document appeared as an addendum to the Report of the Committee on that session, under the provocative title "The need for the creation of an effective international crime and justice programme."[14]

The document made a fairly tightly crafted case. In an introductory section, it was argued that "The effective control of crime and protection of citizens are at the heart of governmental responsibility . . .", that "Effective international co-operation is necessary to help countries to deal with problems of national and transnational crime . . .", and that "Such a programme should stem from an unqualified commitment of the world community of States to invest the necessary human capital and ingenuity, financial resources and modern technical means in the preservation of law, justice and security."[15] The document then turned to "the problem of contemporary crime," offering some analyses of the extent, nature and costs of crime, both at the international and the national level.[16] Following this was a chapter on the need for international cooperation and assistance both in respect of national and international crime.[17] Next was a chapter on the inadequacy of present

---

13. *The Need for the Creation of an Effective International Crime and Justice Programme, Report of the Subcommittee Established by the Tenth Session of the United Nations Committee on Crime Prevention and Control, Vienna, 22–31 August 1988*, U.N. Doc. E/AC.57/1990/6 (Rev.1) (1990).

14. U.N. Doc. E/1990/31/Add.1 (1990) [hereinafter The Need].

15. *Id.* at 3.

16. *Id.* at 3–8.

17. *Id.* at 8–10.

cooperation and assistance, particularly the activities of the United Nations.[18] A final chapter spoke to the development of an effective program[19] while offering views on the functions of the program, the elements of the program, organizational structure, and the mechanism for restructuring. The bulk of the ideas contained in this document were in due course incorporated in the General Assembly's resolution setting out the parameters of the new program.[20]

As drafted by the Co-Rapporteurs and adopted by the Crime Prevention Committee, the addendum to the Committee report was accompanied by a document entitled "World-Wide Crime and the Responsibility of the International Community: A Declaration of the End of Complacency." Signed by most of the Committee members and the heads of the various institutes, the declaration was apparently framed in tones too lively for the organization and it did not achieve the ultimate imprimatur of appearing as a United Nations document.[21] It is a *cri de coeur* of the Crime Prevention Committee's frustrations:

There comes a time when patience loses virtue. There comes time when good intentions stand alone as futile. There comes a time when human tragedy is so compounded that honest men and women must seek effective remedies or lose their self-respect.

The tragedy is world-wide crime. The men and women who must speak out include the undersigned. The time is overdue.[22]

---

18. *Id.* at 10–15. The report argues

The United Nations crime and justice programme has been embarrassingly inadequate for years. Over and over, countries that have recognized their need for outside assistance in meeting problems of crime have requested urgent assistance from the United Nations. Often they have obtained only heartfelt expressions of sympathy and formal regrets. Other countries have wanted to request United Nations help in developing particular programmes to assist them in combating crime, but have faced the reality that the United Nations is not equipped, in terms of personnel, structure or budget supplied by Member States to undertake such assistance projects. The problem is not alleviated by a system of technical assistance on a bilateral basis. Over and over, the United Nations policy-making bodies have called for the needed strengthening of the Crime Prevention and Criminal Justice Branch and the upgrading of its status, but without success.

(*Id.* at 14. Footnotes omitted.)

19. *Id.* at 15–20.

20. G.A. Res. 46/152, *supra* note 1.

21. *See World-Wide Crime and the Responsibility of the International Community: A Declaration of the End of Complacency*, 1 CRIM. L.F. 571 (1990)(reproducing the text of the document).

22. *Id.*

In its Report, the Committee on Crime Prevention and Control forwarded a draft resolution on restructuring to the Congress.[23] Under this draft, the Congress, in turn, would ask the General Assembly to establish an "expert working group" which, "subject to the availability of extrabudgetary funds, would further elaborate the proposed international crime and justice programme referred to in the . . . report of the Committee, as well as the mechanisms required for implementing the proposed programme."[24] This would be followed by a "summit or ministerial meeting" to consider the proposals.[25]

There were those among the strategists of the Committee on Crime Prevention and Control who were confident that the Eighth Congress, with its wide constituency of criminal justice professionals, would be a favorable forum for a broad airing of the Committee's ideas for reform. In fact, the Eighth Congress approached the matter with some enthusiasm and adopted a modified version of the Crime Prevention Committee's draft.[26] There were two main changes. The first modification was that the expert working group became an intergovernmental one[27] (with the corollary that extrabudgetary funds were no longer necessary); the second was that the high level meeting now became "an early ministerial meeting."

Accordingly, in its Resolution 45/108,[28] the General Assembly, acting on the recommendation of the Eighth Congress, took note "with appreciation"[29] of the Committee on Crime Prevention and Control's report on "The need for the creation of an effective international crime

23. *Review of the functioning and programme of work of the United Nations in crime prevention and criminal justice, Committee on Crime Prevention and Control, Report on the Eleventh Session, Vienna, 5–16 February 1990*, Decision 11/122, U.N. ESCOR, Supp. No. 10, at 169, U.N. Doc. E/1990/31 (1990).

24. *Id.* para. 1.

25. *Id.* para. 2.

26. Draft resolution 2 recommended for adoption by the General Assembly, *Eighth United Nations Congress on the Prevention of Crime and the Treatment of Offenders, Havana, 27 August–7 September 1990, Report prepared by the Secretariat*, at 9, U.N. Doc. A/CONF.144/28/Rev.1 (1991). *See id.* at 220–21 (summarizing the discussion).

27. The strategy of the Committee had been that the expert meeting would emphasize the technical side of the exercise and then the summit would give the political input. In the event, the intergovernmental meeting held in Vienna was more political than had originally been intended and in some delegations the foreign affairs representatives dominated. From the point of view of political commitment, this may have been an advantage in some instances.

28. G.A. Res. 45/108, U.N. GAOR, 45th Sess., Supp. No. 49A, at 193, U.N. Doc. A/45/49 (1991).

29. *Id.* para. 8 (preamble). The Assembly also noted the endorsement of the report by the Eighth Congress, as well as the deliberations of the Congress thereon. *Id.*

and justice programme."[30] It decided to establish an intergovernmental working group which, on the basis of the Committee's report, would produce a report elaborating proposals for the program and suggesting how that program could most appropriately be implemented. This working group would comprise no more than thirty states, appointed by the President of the Assembly in consultation with the chairs of the regional groups.[31] In order to take the work to the next level and ensure the necessary political impact, the Assembly foresaw the calling of the "early" ministerial meeting. This meeting would consider the report of the working group "in order to decide what the future crime prevention and criminal justice programme should be."[32] It would also "consider, in this context, the possible need for a convention or other international instrument to develop the content, structure and dynamics of that programme, including mechanisms for setting priorities, securing the implementation of the programme and monitoring the results achieved."[33]

Various proposals were circulated informally in the months leading up to the August 1991 meeting of the Intergovernmental Working Group.[34] One that was to prove quite influential in shaping the final product was a discussion paper dated June 10, 1991, circulated by HEUNI.[35] The paper argued that the main problems facing the program appeared to be the diffuse nature of the program; the laxity with

30. *See supra* note 14.

31. G.A. Res. 45/108, *supra* note 8, para. 1.

32. *Id.* para. 2(a).

33. *Id.* para. 2(b).

34. One proposal, referred to as an "Informal Draft Document," dated June 25, 1991, was eventually circulated at the Working Group. It was produced by "interested and like-minded permanent missions in Vienna" operating under the chairmanship of the German delegation. U.N. Doc. A/AC.239/CRP.5 (1991). While some of these documents were eventually circulated in revised form as official documents, many others were never released officially. Within the West European and Other Group, for example, papers were produced in Paris, London, Washington, Ottawa, the Hague and Canberra—and no doubt elsewhere as well. The most eloquent and ambitious effort was a draft dated July 9, 1991, by Ronald Gainer, the United States national on the Committee on Crime Prevention and Control. It was entitled *Charter of the United Nations Crime and Justice Programme*. (While styled a "Charter," it was apparently meant to be adopted by General Assembly resolution.)

35. HEUNI, A Plan for the Restructuring of the United Nations Crime Prevention and Criminal Justice Programme, (Discussion paper for the Intergovernmental Working Group, Vienna)(Aug. 5–9, 1991)(on file with author) [hereinafter "HEUNI Paper"](also circulated at the meeting of the Working Group as U.N. Doc. A/AC.239/CRP.2 (1991)). The paper was drafted by a small ad hoc working group that met in Helsinki in May 1991. *See* HEUNI, Organization and Activities 1992, at 11 (1993). Present at the meeting, in addition to the Director of HEUNI, Matti Joutsen, were Vasily P. Ignatov (U.S.S.R.), Gioacchino Polimeni (Italy), Julian Schutte (Netherlands) and the author.

which new elements are included; the disproportion between the mandates and the available resources; and the absence of clear priorities for action. In the view of the authors of the paper, the root cause of these problems lay in the mechanism for the development of the program. Thus, the main change proposed was the establishment of a new Crime Prevention Commission of the Economic and Social Council. Such a commission would be the principal mechanism for establishing priorities and ensuring the political support of states. Establishment of priorities by an intergovernmental body, it was argued, would encourage more active and more direct participation of the policy-making elements of the Member States. The Crime Prevention Commission also would provide a forum for overseeing and evaluating implementation of standards and norms.[36]

The Intergovernmental Working Group met in Vienna, August 5–9, 1991.[37] It was attended by the thirty states which had been selected as members, by observers from thirty-nine other states, several other intergovernmental organizations and NGOs, and representatives of the institutes.[38]

The businesslike tone of the meeting was set in the Opening Statement made by Margaret Anstee, Director-General of the United Nations Office at Vienna.[39] Anstee referred to increasing international concern over crime which was generating what the Secretary-General had called "a haunting sense of insecurity."[40] A new concept of security

---

36. This paragraph is based on the unpaginated summary to the HEUNI Paper which was not included in the version circulated at the Working Group. *Id.*

37. *Report of the Meeting of the Intergovernmental Working Group on the Creation of an Effective International Crime and Justice Programme, held at Vienna from 5 to 9 August 1991,* U.N. Doc. A/CONF.156/2 (1991).

38. *Id.* at 20.

39. *See* Notes prepared for the Director-General, circulated to delegates (on file with the author), and *Report of the Intergovernmental Working Group, supra* note 37, at 18 (summarizing the tone of the meeting).

40. *Report of the Secretary-General on the Work of the Organization,* U.N. GAOR, 44th Sess., Supp. No. 1, at 11, U.N. Doc. A/44/1 (1989). This fetching phrase would appear later in the Message of the Secretary-General to the Ministerial Meeting: "Inhabitants of the world's cities live with a haunting sense of fear and insecurity." The Secretary-General continued:

In my report on the work of the Organization, addressed to the current forty-sixth session of the General Assembly, I have stressed that if the security of nations is not to be viewed in terms of external threat alone, if progress is to be measured not only by economic indicators, and if change is to be understood also from the perspective of human welfare, then the social agenda of the United Nations is in equal rank with the political, economic or environmental agendas. It is, therefore, imperative that crime in its many forms and dimensions be addressed as a critical problem requiring

was emerging in which, with the end of the cold war, the focus has shifted to internal strife, maintenance of socio-economic stability, and respect for human rights.[41] This has led to the United Nations being called to play many new roles, such as those in Namibia, El Salvador, Northern Iraq, and Cambodia,[42] where the crime prevention program was required to lend expertise in areas such as public service and justice reforms, reconciliation policy and the creation of non-miliary police forces. Another aspect of this new concept of security was related to development: the non-violent resolution of conflicts, effective judicial systems and redress of grievances, all of which have been seen increasingly as a means of assuring stability and conditions propitious to development without repression. This was particularly important for countries moving towards a market economy and greater democracy. Nevertheless, there was a gap between the demands for assistance being made by States and the response of the United Nations. The meeting was thus faced with the quandary of escalating demands versus static resources. However, as Anstee saw it, there were some broad areas of agreement including the establishment of a vigorous United Nations Crime Prevention, Justice and Security program; the creation of an intergovernmental commission; the strengthening of the Secretariat unit; and increased technical co-operation.

Three main[43] draft resolutions were put before the meeting which

---

coordinated national and international action, with close judicial and police cooperation among states.

Message of the Secretary-General to the Ministerial Meeting (on file with author).

41. This argument is an interesting play on the meaning of "security" in the phrase "international peace and security," the maintenance of which is one of the "Purposes" of the United Nations. *See* U.N. CHARTER art. 1, para. 1. *See also An Agenda for Peace: Preventive diplomacy, peacemaking and peace-keeping, Report of the Secretary-General pursuant to the statement adopted by the Summit Meeting of the Security Council on 31 January 1992*, U.N. Doc. A/47/277 (1992)(detailing new approaches to security).

42. Since the time of the Intergovernmental Working Group, the United Nations has also become involved in the former Yugoslavia, in Angola, in Somalia and in South Africa. The Secretary-General does not have a cadre of people sitting around waiting for new assignments and must redeploy to deal with new mandates—sometimes at serious cost to day-to-day operations. The Crime Branch obviously has some relevant expertise. Ultimately the Chief of the Crime Prevention and Criminal Justice Branch was assigned to Phnom Penh as director of civilian administration of the province. *See Report of the Secretary-General, Progress Report on United Nations Activities in Crime Prevention and Criminal Justice, including detailed information on current programme budget and extrabudgetary activities of the Crime Prevention and Criminal Justice Branch of the Centre for Social Development and Humanitarian Affairs*, at 13, U.N. Doc. E/CN.15/1992/2 (1992). The work in Cambodia included drafting a penal code and a code of criminal procedure as well working on anti-corruption measures.

43. Costa Rica also floated a conference room paper proposing an international convention for the area. *See infra* note 126.

provided the basis for the final result. The first (and lengthiest) was submitted by the leader of the Australian delegation to the Working Group, Herman Woltring, and tabled on the first day by Australia, on behalf also of India, Indonesia, Japan, Libyan Arab Jamahiriya and Malaysia.[44] It was drawn, in significant part, from the HEUNI paper[45] but went into more detail and reflected widespread consultations in which the Australians had engaged. The second draft resolution was tabled the following day by France—which would be the host for the planned ministerial meeting.[46] The United States also tabled a draft resolution on the second day.[47]

As had been suggested,[48] there seemed to be agreement on creating a commission. Each of the drafts would do this. Beyond that, though, some sharp differences were revealed.

Aside from disbanding the Crime Prevention Committee and creating a commission, the Australian draft would keep most of the existing program, including the congresses, intact.

The United States draft, the sparsest both in terms of its length and its approach to the program, would replace both the Committee on Crime Prevention and Control and the congresses with the new commission.[49] It would take a quite narrow view of the objects of the program which would be "devoted to providing practical assistance to States, such as data collection, information sharing, and training, to achieve the goals of preventing crime within and among States and of

---

44. U.N. Doc. A/AC.239/L.3 (1991) [hereinafter "Australian Draft"].

45. *Supra* note 35. The most interesting feature of the HEUNI paper which was not presented in the Australian draft was article 12 which provided that:

A Member State may at any time declare under this Article that it recognizes the competence of the Commission to mediate in the settlement of a dispute with another Party, having lodged the same declaration, as to the application of a Treaty or Convention in force between them on co-operation in criminal matters, or as to the compatibility with general rules of public international law of an act of criminal legislation, adjudication or law enforcement by such other Party.

Having a political body exercising such adjudicative powers apparently did not command widespread support, although the concept is not unprecedented. *See* Convention on International Civil Aviation, Dec. 7, 1944, art. 84, 59 Stat. 1516, 15 U.N.T.S. 295 (detailing the powers accorded the Council of the International Civil Aviation Organization). An expert Sub-Commission, if created, or something more akin to the human rights treaty bodies, would have been a more logical body to exercise a power like this. If used often, which is unlikely, a dispute settlement power might drain off a lot of the Commission's resources.

46. U.N. Doc. A/AC.239/L.4 (1991) [hereinafter French Draft].

47. U.N. Doc. A/AC.239/L.5 (1991) [hereinafter U.S. Draft].

48. *See supra* note 39.

49. U.S. Draft, *supra* note 47, para. 3.

improving the response to crime by developing enhanced criminal justice systems within States."[50] Implicit in this draft was that there would be no new resources devoted to the program, and even that there might be a reduction. The United States has always been somewhat ambivalent towards United Nations programs with a human rights dimension, particularly those emphasizing economic, social and cultural rights. This ambivalence seemed at the time to have carried over into the attitudes of the then-current administration in Washington towards the crime prevention and criminal justice program.

The French draft, on the other hand, would retain both the Crime Prevention Committee, as an expert body, and the congresses, as well as creating a commission. It invited the Secretary-General to double the "material and human resources at the disposal of the Branch over a period of five years."[51] The French draft also recommended the creation of a foundation with the task of mobilizing, under the auspices of the Crime Prevention and Criminal Justice Branch, international initiatives aimed at raising funds to support projects involving practical measures to implement the program at the local, national, and international level, and to facilitate the establishment of information exchange and cooperation and assistance networks at the local, national and international level.[52]

The result of the discussion was a draft for the Ministerial Meeting that came quite close to what was adopted by that meeting and ultimately by the General Assembly.[53]

The Ministerial Meeting took place in Versailles, November 21–23,

---

50. *Id.* para. 5. Essentially, identical language is repeated in G.A. Res. 46/152, but in a context which suggests that it is not the *only* thing to which the program is "devoted." G.A. Res. 46/152, *supra* note 1, para. 5.

51. French Draft, *supra* note 46 (paragraphs are not numbered in this draft).

52. This proposal, aimed at tapping funds from private sources and from governments other than the central one, was raised again by France at Versailles and again at the first meeting of the Commission. *See Note on the Foundation*, U.N. Doc. E/CN.15/1992/CRP.7 (1992). At this point, no action has been taken. An earlier version of the idea emerged from the Committee on Crime Prevention and Control at its Eleventh Session in C.C.P.C. Res. 11/1, entitled *World foundation on crime control and assistance to victims. Report of the Committee on Crime Prevention and Control on its Eleventh Session, supra* note 23, at 171. This resolution did not proceed at the Congress but the idea of a foundation was included in two Congress resolutions, para. 5 of Other Resolution 27, entitled *Protection of human rights of victims of crime and abuse of power* (international fund for victims), and para. 4(g) of Other Resolution 1, on *Prevention of urban crime, Report of the Eighth Congress, supra* note 26, at 124, 194 (international foundation for the prevention of urban crime). There is, in fact, an existing organ, now known as the Crime Prevention and Criminal Justice Fund, that could probably fill the objectives of the French proposal. *See infra* note 60.

53. *See infra* notes 136–166 (discussing the contents of G.A. Res. 46/152).

1991.[54] It was attended by 114 Member States and two non-Members. After a debate which essentially tracked that which occurred at the Working Group, the Ministerial Meeting recommended a draft for acceptance by the General Assembly with only minor drafting changes from that of the Working Group. The hoped-for high level political commitment was, at last, behind the whole enterprise.

By then, it was late in the General Assembly's session, but the Third Committee of the Assembly debated the matter briefly between December 9 and 11.[55] With only one substantial change, the draft was adopted and sent to the Plenary of the Assembly for final approval. The substantial change was an increase in the number of members proposed for the Commission from thirty-two in the Ministerial Meeting draft to forty in the final Assembly version, thereby increasing the representation of the developing countries.[56] This was the number ultimately adopted by the Economic and Social Council.

C. Major Issues

1. Resources

As noted in Chapter 1,[57] the resources devoted to the program in the past have been very modest, some 0.15 percent of the United Nations' annual operating budget, itself of modest proportions by any calculation. Many of the governments participating in the 1991 meetings were in favor of devoting more resources to the program.[58] On the other hand, a few significant contributors to the budget seemed to be proceeding on the basis that smaller was better. The upshot was inevitably some compromise in Resolution 46/152.

The final paragraph of the Annex to the resolution[59] states that the program is to be funded from the regular budget of the organization. Funds allocated for technical assistance may be supplemented by direct

54. *See Note by the Secretary-General, Report of the Ministerial Meeting on the Creation of an Effective United Nations Crime Prevention and Criminal Justice Programme, 21–23 November 1991*, U.N. Doc. A/46/703 (1991).

55. *See Social Development: Crime Prevention and Criminal Justice, Report of the Third Committee (Part II)*, U.N. Doc. A/46/704/Add. 1 (1991).

56. *See* Chapter 3 *infra* at note 8 (discussing the composition of the Commission). The increase was sufficiently controversial that, in committee, the United States voted "no" and 34 states from the West European and Other and East European groups abstained. In Plenary, the resolution was adopted without a vote.

57. *See* Chapter 1 *supra* at notes 44 and 45.

58. France, for example, would have doubled the level of resources and size of the Branch by 1995. *See supra* note 51.

59. G.A. Res. 46/152, *supra* note 1, Annex, para. 44.

voluntary contributions from Member States and interested funding agencies. Member States also are encouraged to make contributions to the United Nations Trust Fund for Social Defense, now renamed the United Nations Crime Prevention and Criminal Justice Fund.[60] They similarly are encouraged to contribute in kind for the operational activities of the program, particularly by seconding staff, organizing training courses and seminars, and providing the requisite equipment and services.

Paragraph 4 of the adopting resolution requests the Secretary-General to "give a high level of priority within the United Nations framework, and within the overall existing United Nations resources" to the program.[61] Paragraph 6 invites Member States to "give their political and financial support and to take measures that will ensure the implementation of the provisions [of the resolution] as they relate to the strengthening of the United Nations crime prevention and criminal justice programme in terms of its structure, content and priorities."[62] Paragraph 32 of the Annex to the resolution is perhaps the high-water mark of exhortations to provide resources. It recommends to the Secretary-General that, "in recognition of the high priority that should be accorded to the programme, an upgrading of the Crime Prevention and Criminal Justice Branch into a Division should be effected as soon as possible."[63] Upgrading is to be done, however, "bearing in mind the structure of the United Nations Office at Vienna,"[64] and "within the framework of the total available resources of the United Nations."[65] At the time, the Center for Social Development and Humanitarian Affairs of the Vienna Office comprised two Divisions, the Division on the

60. In E.S.C. Res. 1086 B (XXXIX), U.N. ESCOR, 39th Sess., Supp. No. 1, at 9, U.N. Doc. E/4117 (1965), ECOSOC established a special fund, the United Nations Trust Fund for Social Defense, to permit Member States and other donors to support United Nations endeavors in crime prevention and criminal justice. The General Assembly, in 1982, placed this Fund on the agenda of the annual Pledging Conference for Development Activities. In spite of some apparent early enthusiasm, *see Report of the Secretary-General*, U.N. Doc. E/CN.5/409/Add.4 (1967), the level of contributions has remained low and much of the fund represents contributions by the Italian Government which are a relatively small part of a large contribution which it makes to the Rome-based United Nations Interregional Crime and Justice Research Institute. The objects of this Trust Fund are apparently broad enough to encompass the objects of the proponents of a new foundation. *Supra* note 52.

61. G.A. Res. 46/152, *supra* note 1, para. 4. *See also id.* para. 7 (requesting "appropriate resources").

62. *Id.*

63. *Id.* Annex, para. 32.

64. *Id.*

65. *Id.* (referring back to para. 14 of the Annex to the Resolution).

Advancement of Women and the Social Development Division. The Crime Prevention and Criminal Justice Branch was part of the latter division. (The Division on the Advancement of Women and the Social Development Division, minus the Crime Branch which remains in Vienna, were moved to New York in 1993.) Both the Division on the Advancement of Women and the Social Development Division were formerly branches and had been upgraded. Upgrading the Crime Prevention and Criminal Justice Branch to a Division in its own right presumably would give it more autonomy, visibility, and leverage within the bureaucracy. A commission is normally serviced by a Division. While there are no hard and fast rules, changing the Branch to a Division should result in increasing to at least fifteen the current complement of eleven permanent professional posts. At the time of writing, the upgrading is still a matter for further negotiation. In the absence of additional earmarked resources, the Secretary-General is being urged to rob Peter to pay Paul.

2. Priorities

Until now, the primary focus of the program had been on the holding of the congresses. These meetings, as places for the exchange of ideas and networking in general, had been seen as a useful end in themselves. Especially in recent years, they also had played a dramatic part in the preparation of instruments which would provide standards for states in the crime area and would encourage international cooperation in general.[66] Voices were heard to the effect that this was not enough and that there should be both a change in priorities and more attention paid to the process followed in setting priorities. The creation of the Crime Prevention Commission was, in part, a response to these

---

66. The new Commission has described the instruments as "the most visible aspect" of United Nations work in the area. The Commission has noted that:

Other activities that the programme has carried out include the development of model agreements, surveys, research, the establishment of the United Nations Criminal Justice Information Network and the development of manuals on issues such as national criminal statistics, crime prevention measures, the prevention of corruption, and assistance to victims of crime. In addition, a broad range of activities involving, among other things, training courses, research and advisory services, are provided by the programme, including the network of institutes.

Strategic Management by the Commission on Crime Prevention and Criminal Justice of the United Nations crime prevention and criminal justice programme, Report of the Commission on Crime Prevention and Criminal Justice on its First Session, Vienna, 21–30 April 1992, C.C.P.C.J. Res. 1/1 at 38, paras. 26–27, U.N. Doc. E/1992/30 (1992).

observations. The reasoning underlying these suggestions was that with the proper (intergovernmental) procedure in place and some agreed upon general criteria, the result would be proper decisions.[67]

This thought is followed through in Paragraph 21 of Resolution 46/152, which speaks to "Programme Priorities." The paragraph suggests that in developing the program and, thereby, tackling the general goals of the exercise,[68] areas of priority shall be determined in response to the needs and concerns of Member States, giving particular consideration to the following:

(a) Empirical evidence, including research findings and other information on the nature and extent of crime and on trends in crime;[69]

(b) The social, financial and other costs of various forms of crimes and/or crime control to the individual, the local, national and international community, and to the development process;

(c) The need of developing or developed countries, which are confronting specific difficulties related to national or international circumstances, to have recourse to experts and other resources necessary for establishing and developing programmes for crime prevention and criminal justice that are appropriate at the national and international levels;

(d) The need for balance within the programme of work between programme development and practical action;

(e) The protection of human rights in the administration of justice and the prevention and control of crime;

(f) The assessment of areas in which concerted action at the interna-

---

67. *See, e.g.*, HEUNI Paper, *supra* note 35, at 3.

68. *See infra* note 158 (discussing goals).

69. The Secretariat has previously conducted a series of global surveys of crime trends, although obtaining and comparing criminal statistics is a daunting challenge. *See, e.g., Third United Nations Survey of Crime Trends, Operation of Criminal Justice Systems and Crime Prevention Strategies, covering the period 1980–1986*, U.N. Doc. A/CONF.144/6 (1990)(presented to the 8th Congress). Some 95 countries provided information—a record. As part of a strategy to develop a broader information base, UNICRI convened a Planning Meeting on the Development of a United Nations Criminal Justice Information Programme in June 1991, the Report of which was before the Intergovernmental Working Group. U.N. Doc. A/AC.239/CRP.4 (1991). In E.S.C. Res. 1992/22, pt. I, para. 3 (f), U.N. ESCOR, Supp. No. 1, at 22, U.N. Doc. E/1992/92 (1992), ECOSOC decided that the surveys should in future be carried out at two-year intervals, with preparations for the next survey (1990–1992) commencing at the end of 1993. Recent efforts have been made to supplement this data, which is based on official statistics, with victim surveys carried out in 1989 and 1992 in 37 countries. *See Criminal Victimization in the World*, U.N. Doc. E/CN.15/1993/CRP.6 (1993).

tional level and within the framework of the programme would be most effective;

(g) Avoidance of overlap with the activities of other entities of the United Nations system or of other organizations.[70]

To underscore that the program cobbled together in the past was not carved in stone, the subsequent paragraph provides that the Commission "shall not be bound by mandates conferred prior to its formation, but shall assess them on their merits by applying the above-mentioned principles."[71]

There is probably something in this Resolution for everyone; the formulation hardly takes the matter of priority-setting far into the realm of the concrete. Indeed, one might interpret the matter of priorities either as a question going to which "areas" or "topics" or "themes" of criminal justice should be given most prominence, or as referring to questions of technique—how might the selected areas best be tackled by means of specific activities. The distinction may perhaps be described as one between "thematic" and "operational" priorities.

That both of these rather different notions might even be intended is suggested by the complex priorities provisions contained in the first resolution prepared in 1992 by the Crime Prevention Commission for approval by ECOSOC. That instrument begins by determining that "the following priority themes should guide the work of the Crime Prevention Commission in the development of a detailed programme and the budget allocations for the period 1992–1996":

(a) National and transnational crime, organized crime, economic crime, including money laundering, and the role of criminal law in the protection of the environment;

(b) Crime prevention in urban areas, juvenile and violent criminality;

(c) Efficiency, fairness and improvement in the management and administration of criminal justice and related systems, with due emphasis on the strengthening of national capacities in developing countries for the regular collection, collation, analysis and utilization of data in the development and implementation of appropriate policies.[72]

---

70. G.A. Res. 46/152, *supra* note 1, Annex, para. 21.

71. *Id.* Annex, para. 22.

72. E.S.C. Res. 1992/22, *supra* note 69, pt. VI, para. 1. These priorities were reaffirmed by the Commission and ECOSOC in 1993. *See* E.S.C. Res. 1993/34, pt. I, para. 1 (1993).

So far as techniques for giving operational effect to these themes are concerned, the next paragraph of the ECOSOC resolution recommends that "in the course of the programme budget planning process, allocation should be made for special operational activities and advisory services in situations of urgent need and for programme organization, evaluation and reporting obligations."[73] The resolution goes on to determine that "in the areas" of the priority themes, "the objectives [for the operation of the Secretariat] should be":

(a) To concentrate the majority of programme resources on the provision of training, advisory services and technical cooperation in a limited number of areas of recognized need, taking into account the need for technical assistance to developing countries, in order to achieve a synergetic effect, allowing intense and effective use of materials, resources and experience from both regular budgetary resources and voluntary contributions;

(b) In the case of special operational activities and advisory services in situations of urgent need, to offer timely and practical assistance to Governments, upon request, in situations that do not permit a problem to be adopted as a regular priority by the Commission . . . ; in implementing these special operational activities and advisory services, the Secretariat should place major emphasis on serving as a broker and clearing-house, providing advisory services and training to Member States from within existing budgetary resources and through voluntary contributions; the Secretariat should submit to the Commission at its second session a narrative and statistical report on the implementation of these special operational activities and advisory services, together with a statement of expenditure and any appropriate recommendations;

(c) With regard to programme organization, evaluation and reporting obligations, to assist the Commission in reaching agreement on the general goals of the programme and the needs to be met; to ascertain the capacity available to meet those needs; to determine the objectives, specific activities and mechanisms to be used for that purpose; to remain cognizant of and advise the Commission on pertinent developments and discharge other reporting responsibilities; and to mobilize support for the programme.[74]

Here is a strongly asserted preference for putting resources into training, advisory services and technical cooperation. This preference was

73. E.S.C. Res. 1992/22, *supra* note 69, pt. VI, para. 2.

74. *Id.* pt. VI, para. 3. The provisions of E.S.C. Res. 1992/22, *supra* note 69, paras. 2, 3(b), just discussed, suggest a disposition on the part of some members to keep the Secretariat on a short leash, almost to the point of micro management. The Secretary-General has complained that ;

there sometimes seems to be a blurred perception of the exact delimitation of functions between the Secretariat, headed by the Secretary-General and the other princi-

followed up by revisions to the organization's medium term plan for 1992–1997,[75] in particular, to include in the Crime Prevention Branch's overall plan of work a sub-program on operational activities, planning and overall coordination which emphasizes practical assistance and technical cooperation.[76]

Another example of the current disposition to stress procedures for choosing priorities and some basic criteria is the Crime Prevention Commission's own Resolution 1/1 of its first session, in which it decided to apply the principles of strategic management in carrying out its mandate.[77] According to this resolution, the principles of strategic management require that the Crime Prevention Commission agree on the general goals of the programme with regard to both program development and implementation (its mission); the needs to be met; the capacity available to meet those needs; the objectives for program development; the specific activities to be carried out to promote the achievement of those objectives; the mechanisms to be used in determining the objectives and the specific activities; measures for evaluating program implementation; and measures for evaluating programme accomplishments.[78] In the present context, the most concrete reference is that to "specific activities" to give effect to whatever objectives have been decided upon. "These activities could be, for example,

---

pal organs. Article 101 of the Charter empowers the General Assembly to establish regulations for the appointment of staff. Regulations, however, should mean broad guidelines under principles set out in the Charter and not detailed or rigid directives that can only upset operational efficiency and dilute the authority of the Secretary-General. Judicious use of funds is naturally a matter of concern to all Member States, particularly the principal contributors. However, beyond the legislative responsibility of scrutinizing expenditures and ensuring as wide a geographical basis for recruiting staff as possible, the management of the Secretariat needs to be left in the hands of the chief administrative officer. . . . Over-legislation itself can cause strains that are wholly avoidable.

Report of the Secretary-General on the Work of the Organization, at 8, U.N. GAOR, 46th Sess., Supp. No. 1, U.N. Doc. A/46/1 (1991).

75. *See* G.A. Res. 45/253, U.N. GAOR, 45th Sess., Supp. No. 49A, at 352, U.N. Doc. A/45/49 (1990)(restating in paragraph 2 "that the Medium Term Plan, as adopted, is the principal policy directive of the United Nations and shall serve as the framework for the formulation of the biennial programme budgets").

76. *See Proposed Revisions to the Medium-Term Plan for the Period 1992–1997, Major Programme V, International Cooperation for Social Development, Programme 29, Crime Prevention and Criminal Justice*, U.N. Doc. A/47/6 (1992)(Prog. 29); *Proposed Programme Budget for the Biennium 1994–1995, pt. IV, Sec. 13, Crime Control*, U.N. Doc. A/48/6 Sec. 13 (1993).

77. C.C.P.C.J. Res. 1/1, *supra* note 66.

78. *Id.* Annex, para. 10.

the arrangement of a meeting, the performance of research, the preparation of a manual or the development of guidelines. Ideally, several activities should be carried out in pursuit of any one objective, and the outcomes would cross-fertilize one another."[79]

3. The Use of Experts

Two types of arguments were made for replacing the Committee on Crime Prevention and Control with a commission. One type tended to be articulated in the documents and argued that the Crime Prevention Committee had done excellent work, but the task now was to create an organ with more political clout.[80] The other (articulated by a small minority) suggested that the Committee had been either a failure, or worse, a menace that interfered too much in what sovereign states were doing. The clash between the opposing positions developed especially in the context of a debate about whether the Crime Prevention Committee might be retained in some form after the creation of a commission, perhaps as an expert sub-commission.[81] An analogy was drawn by some speakers with the role of the Commission on Human Rights, a

79. *Id*. Annex, para. 29. The resolution continues:

Thus, if the Commission determines that one objective is to enable countries to increase the effectiveness of their criminal justice system in the control of environmental pollution, the specific activities could include a research project comparing the effectiveness of different approaches in control, the organization of an expert meeting on the sentencing of persons and corporations guilty of criminal pollution, the preparation of guidelines on the prevention of international dumping of hazardous wastes, and the organization of training courses for law enforcement agencies in the investigation of cases involving pollution.

Id. Annex, para. 30.

80. *See, e.g., Report of the Intergovernmental Working Group, supra* note 37, at 22.

81. *See Report of the Intergovernmental Working Group, supra* note 37, at 23 (summarizing some aspects of this debate). A subsidiary argument suggested that there could be some savings from the dissolution that could either be re-cycled elsewhere in the program or saved. *Id.* The savings were not enormous. According to figures supplied by the Secretariat at the Intergovernmental Meeting, the U.N. was spending about $100,000 once every two years for travel and subsistence to get the members of the Crime Prevention Committee together. Members were not paid for their services. The real cost of the enterprise was about $400,000 for conference-servicing per meeting, including document cost and simultaneous translation in six languages. Under the new arrangements, the United Nations will pay the expenses only of those members of the Crime Prevention Commission who are from the least developed countries. The Crime Prevention Commission presumably costs somewhere around the $400,000 formerly spent on the Crime Prevention Committee's meeting, but it is, of course, annual. *See also* Chapter 1 *supra* note 45; Chapter 3 *infra* note 67 (describing the costs of the congresses).

governmental body, and its Sub-Commission on Prevention of Discrimination and Protection of Minorities, an expert body.[82]

In the writer's view, there must be a place in the process for a
combination of political and expert inputs. Commentators have noted
the importance of those with expertise in various parts of the United
Nations system (and even of those responsible for their education).[83]
Professor Theodor Meron, in a work that is highly critical of current
law-making modalities in the human rights area, has suggested that
there is much to be learned from the procedures both of expert bodies
like the International Law Commission and of intergovernmental entities such as the United Nations Commission on International Trade
Law (UNCITRAL).[84] A focus of UNCITRAL's work is to encourage
governments to send genuine experts to its working groups—where
the laborious work is performed. The experience of UNCITRAL and
the Council of Europe, Meron suggests, "has shown that when governments are interested enough in influencing the formulation of an
instrument of importance to them, they can and do appoint competent
experts. . . . The crucial point, therefore, is not that members be elected
in their individual capacity, but that they should be genuine experts."[85]
In proposing the creation of a new and expert United Nations Human
Rights Law Commission ("UNHRLC") to perform the major drafting
work in the human rights area, Professor Meron argues for a better
balance between the participation of experts and that of generalist
diplomats.[86] "In any event," Meron adds, "the political perspective
would be provided by constant input from governmental comments,
guidelines and instructions from the political organs, and by the
knowledge of the UNHRLC members that their drafts would be submitted for adoption by the political organs."[87]

I think that the notion of an expert requires more exploration than
that given by Professor Meron. In particular, it appears to me that

---

82. Reference might also be made to the way in which the International Labor
Organization utilizes a combination of expert and political committees in the supervision
of the organization's conventions and recommendations. *See generally*, HUMAN RIGHTS
SOURCEBOOK 402–419 (A.P. Blaustein, R.S. Clark & J.A. Sigler eds. 1987); S.A. Ivanov,
*The International Labour Organisation: Control Over Application of the Conventions and Recom-
mendations on Labour*, in CONTROL OVER COMPLIANCE WITH INTERNATIONAL LAW 153,
154–56 (W.E. Butler ed. 1991).

83. *See, e.g.*, J. Sundberg, *The Wisdom of Treaty Making: A Glance at the Machinery behind
the Production of Law-Making Treaties and A Case Study of the Hague Hijacking Conference of
1970*, 16 SCANDINAVIAN STUD. IN L. 285, 288–90 (1972).

84. T. Meron, HUMAN RIGHTS LAW-MAKING IN THE UNITED NATIONS, 280–82 (1986).

85. *Id.* at 290.

86. *Id.*

87. *Id.*

there are at least two broad categories of experts in the crime prevention and criminal justice area. One category contains the person at-
tached to a government, who follows the issue in question and who
understands the policy issues and the details while perhaps having
policy-making or policy-implementation responsibilities.[88] The other is
the non-official expert—a judge, an academic, an NGO person—who
brings both a knowledge of the issues and a different perspective to
bear. Such non-official experts are often more free to float new ideas
and be critical of government positions than officials can be.[89] This is
the kind of person who is crucial to the success of a human rights
monitoring body like the various treaty committees. Such persons are
also essential if serious efforts are to be made of the implementation of
the United Nations standards and norms in the criminal justice area.[90]
Both kinds of experts have a substantial role to play in the system.

There is a more general point about the cadre of people who work in
the international criminal justice area, sometimes in different roles at
various stages of a career. Oscar Schachter has spoken elegantly of the
"invisible college of international lawyers." Schachter states that the

professional community [of international lawyers], though dispersed throughout the world and engaged in diverse occupations, constitutes a kind of invis-

88. The authors of the draft from "interested and like minded" missions in Vienna,
apparently understood this distinction and had this kind of expert in mind when they
suggested the appointment of a Sub-Commission or Standing Working Group. *Supra*
note 34. Selected Governments among the new Commission would assign "Expert
Representatives" to serve on this body which would, notably, oversee the implementation
of standards and norms. Members of the group should have experience in the areas of
crime prevention and criminal justice, and/or should have knowledge of social or humanitarian matters, and/or should already have some experience about the functioning
of the U.N. system. *Id.* at 5. G.A. Res. 46/152, exhorts Member States to include in their
delegation to the Commission on Crime Prevention and Criminal Justice experts and
senior officials with training and practical experience in crime prevention and criminal
justice, especially those with policy responsibility in the field. G.A. Res. 46/152, *supra*
note 1, Annex, para. 24. *See* Chapter 3 *infra*, at note 10.

89. The Minister of Justice of the Netherlands, speaking on behalf of the Member
States of the European Community at the Ministerial Meeting, conceded that existing
budgetary constraints made the continuation of the Committee impossible once the
Commission had been created. He continued: "Yet we should not believe that the new
Programme can be realised without the help of individual, independent experts. The
world of legal science, of law faculties and criminological and penological institutes has
an important contribution to make to the formulation and articulation of policies on
crime prevention, criminal justice and protection of the public. Governments would be
presumptuous to ignore their influence" (Text on file with author). At the Intergovernmental Working Group, M. Gilbert Bonnemaison, representing France, insisted that
there is an ethical dimension to the concept of an expert. Even a governmental expert
owes an obligation to the truth which is a higher obligation than that owed to the expert's
government (on file with author).

90. *See* Chapter 9 *infra*.

ible college dedicated to a common intellectual enterprise. As in the case of other disciplines, its members are engaged in a continuous process of communication and collaboration. Evidence of this process is found in the journals and yearbooks of international law, in the transnational movement of professors and students, and in the numerous conferences, seminars and colloquia held in all parts of the globe. But this communication is by no means confined to the realm of scholarship. For the international bodies and conferences of an official character are largely composed of jurists who are part of the active professional community and who maintain intellectual contact with the scholarly side of the profession. The invisible college thus extends into the sphere of government, resulting in a *pénétration pacifique* of ideas from the nongovernment into official channels. It would be unrealistic, however, to think of this as a one-way penetration. Individuals who move from one role to another are unlikely to remain uninfluenced by the ideas and considerations which impinge on them in their different capacities. The mingling of the scholarly and the official affects both categories, and often creates tension as individuals move from one role to another or perceive themselves as acting in the dual capacity of objective scientist and government advocate.[91]

My experience in the criminal justice area would suggest that the phenomenon of which Schachter writes is broader than that of international lawyers. While there are many lawyers active in the area of criminal justice, there are also numerous people from other disciplines, such as criminology, penology, medicine, social work, anthropology and psychology, who are a vital part of the interdisciplinary college.

In the end, the abolition of the Committee on Crime Prevention and Control was accompanied by a carefully crafted and somewhat delphic two paragraphs including a footnote of Resolution 46/152.[92] Paragraph 27 of the Annex to the resolution, after referring to the dissolution of the Crime Prevention Committee, asserts that "There will be a basic need for involving independent experts in the area of crime prevention and control."[93] This is followed by Paragraph 28 and its footnote, which states

28. The commission shall, when necessary, use the services of a limited number of qualified and experienced experts, either as individual consultants or in working groups, in order to assist in the preparations for and follow-up work of the commission. Their advice shall be transmitted to the commission for consideration. The commission shall be encouraged to seek such advice whenever

91. O. Schachter, *The Invisible College of International Lawyers*, 72 Nw. U. L. Rev. 217, 217 (1977).

92. The rather complex arrangement, a compromise between strongly-held French and United States views, was based on a procedure developed in the work of the Commission on the Status of Women. *See* E.S.C. Res. 1987/24, *Long-term programme of work of the Commission on the Status of Women to the year 2000*, U.N. ESCOR, Supp. No. 1, at 18, U.N. Doc. E/1987/87 (1987).

93. G.A. Res. 46/152, *supra* note 1, Annex, para. 27.

such expertise is needed. One of the major tasks of the experts shall be to assist in the preparations for the congresses.[94]

** The Secretariat shall keep a list of such experts. The experts shall be selected by the commission in collaboration with the Secretariat, the United Nations institutes for the prevention of crime and the treatment of offenders and non-governmental organizations. The commission, in consultation with Member States, shall develop a mechanism for that purpose. Such experts, who may be either governmental officials or other individuals, shall be chosen on the basis of equitable distribution. They should be available to the programme in their individual independent capacity for at least three years. Expert group meetings shall take place subject to the conditions set out in paragraph 14 [i.e. "within the framework of the total available resources of the United Nations."][95]

Both kinds of experts to which I have referred—governmental and independent—seem to be contemplated, and the types of tasks which might be assigned to them could include drafting instruments, working up discussion papers for a congress, or monitoring progress on implementation of norms and standards.[96]

The first two meetings of the Commission on Crime Prevention and Criminal Justice in 1992 and 1993 were well attended by governmental experts. There was no attempt, however, to make these paragraphs operational.[97] It remains to be seen what use is made in the future of experts who are relatively free of governmental ties.

4. A Convention or Other International Instrument

The question of the possible need for a convention or other instrument, referred to in General Assembly Resolution 45/108,[98] was open

94. *Id.* para. 28.

95. *Id.* (material marked by double asterisk is in footnote in Resolution). The bracketed reference to "available resources" implies that new budgetary provisions would need to be made, or more likely, that extrabudgetary funds would have to be found. Nothing in this somewhat formal procedure, which will produce experts to assist *the Commission* in some form of committee or rapporteur format, seems intended to prevent *the Secretariat* from using individual consultants on an individual basis (as it has always done) to assist *it*, for example with a technical assistance project.

96. *See* Chapter 9 *infra*.

97. A proposal made in 1992 by France on behalf of itself, Austria, Canada, the Netherlands and the United Kingdom for a sessional working group to deal with implementation, including monitoring, of norms and standards, apparently contemplated governmental not independent expertise. The plan was ultimately withdrawn. *See Report of the Commission on Crime Prevention and Criminal Justice on its First Session, supra* note 66, at 76–77. Follow-up discussion in 1993 did not broach the subject of non-governmental experts.

98. *See supra* notes 28, 33.

to a number of interpretations and analogies. The General Assembly has wide express powers under Article 22 of the Charter[99] and inherent ones as well[100] to engage in structural innovation. ECOSOC has the power to create commissions[101] and also probably has some implied creative powers. Given the way the General Assembly in the past has exercised its powers to create such substantial entities as the office of the High Commissioner for Refugees[102] or the United Nations Environmental Program,[103] it was obvious that what was involved was not a question of *vires*. The General Assembly and ECOSOC have plenty of power to act on their own pursuant to the Charter, without the necessity of further treaty authorization. Rather, what was involved was a question of political judgment about what could best move the program along at this stage.

The Committee on Crime Prevention and Control's 1990 Report[104] contains a fairly balanced summary of the arguments for and against a convention:

An appropriate measure for eliciting international support and for developing the programme would be the adoption of an international instrument on crime prevention and criminal justice. Such an instrument could be an international convention. The past two decades have made it clear that a United Nations programme commensurate with the needs expressed by Member States will not evolve through arguments, exhortations, programme reviews and resolutions alone. Drafting a convention can well be a lengthy process and, if poorly designed, a convention may impose a degree of rigidity on the programme that negates what has been underlined above on the need for flexibility in the face of the possible differences in priorities between States, and of changing circumstances. However, a well-planned, carefully considered and meticulously drafted United Nations convention would provide an authoritative framework for the needed programme and the dynamics for its continued development.

As Matti Joutsen, the Director of HEUNI, noted in a background paper made available at the 1990 meeting of the Crime Prevention Committee, the idea of a convention on crime prevention and criminal

---

99. U.N. Charter art. 22 says that the Assembly "may establish such subsidiary organs as it deems necessary for the performance of its functions." U.N. CHARTER art. 22.

100. *See* Effect of Awards of Compensation Made by the United Nations Administrative Tribunal, 1954 I.C.J. 47 (describing the power to create an administrative tribunal).

101. U.N. CHARTER art. 68.

102. G.A. Res. 428 (V), U.N. GAOR, 5th Sess., Supp. No. 20, at 46, U.N. Doc. A/1775 (1950).

103. G.A. Res. 2997 (XXVII), U.N. GAOR, 27th Sess., Supp. No. 30, at 43, U.N. Doc. A/8730 (1973).

104. The Need, *supra* note 14, at 18–19.

justice was not new.[105] It had been debated at some length during the Fourth Congress, with reference to the implementation of the Standard Minimum Rules for the Treatment of Prisoners;[106] and during the Fifth Congress, in its discussion of the item on "Changes in forms and dimensions of criminality—transnational and national."[107] More recently, the idea of a Convention had re-emerged and been discussed at two of the Interregional Preparatory Meetings for the Eighth Congress, as well as at all the regional preparatory meetings for that Congress.[108] Joutsen pointed out, however, that "these discussions reflect two different ways of viewing the role of such a Convention," namely:

— The first would call for a convention that should *consolidate* all the existing crime prevention and criminal justice provisions of multilateral and bilateral conventions, treaties, agreements and norms. Its objective would be to strengthen international co-operation, particularly in relation to transnational crimes and to mobilize multilateral efforts while avoiding fragmentation and overlapping.

— The second would call for a convention that should provide a *framework* for international co-operation in crime and justice in general. Its main goal would be to provide the international community with a solid formulation for a more effective worldwide programme to meet the challenge of escalating crime.[109]

What a framework treaty might look like was suggested by the HEUNI document circulated at the Intergovernmental Working Group.[110]

An example of what a consolidating treaty might contain was pro-

105. M. Joutsen, Development of a United Nations Convention on Crime Prevention and Criminal Justice 1 (Jan. 23, 1990)(background paper, on file with author).

106. *Fourth United Nations Congress on the Prevention of Crime and the Treatment of Offenders, Kyoto, Japan, 17–26 August 1970, Report prepared by the Secretariat,* at 20–21, U.N. Doc. A/CONF. 43/5 (1971). *See* Chapter 5 *infra,* at notes 31–34.

107. *Fifth United Nations Congress on the Prevention of Crime and the Treatment of Offenders, Geneva, 1–12 September 1975, Report prepared by the Secretariat,* at 9–18, U.N. Doc. A/CONF.56/10 (1976).

108. *See* Topic I: *Crime Prevention and Criminal Justice in the Context of Development: Realities and Perspectives on International Cooperation,* at 6–7, U.N. Doc. A/CONF.144/IPM.1 (1988); Topic III: *Effective National and International Action Against (a) Organized Crime; (b) Terrorist Criminal Activities,*" at 8, 20, U.N. Doc. A/CONF.144/IPM.2 (1988); U.N. Doc. A/CONF.144/RPM.1 (1989) at 12 (Asia and Pacific region); U.N. Doc. A/CONF.144/RPM.2 at 18 (1989) (European region); U.N. Doc. A/CONF.144/RPM.3, at 8 (1989)(Latin American and Caribbean region); U.N. Doc. A/CONF.144/RPM.4, at 5 (1989) (Western Asia region); U.N. Doc. A/CONF.144/RPM.5 (1989) (African region).

109. Joutsen, *supra* note 105, at 2. Emphasis in the original footnote is omitted from the first quoted paragraph. *See Report of the Committee on its Eleventh Session, supra* note 23, at 245 (stating, less elegantly, the distinctions Joutsen makes).

110. *See supra* note 35, Annex 2.

vided by General Ignatov, the Soviet expert on the Committee on Crime Prevention and Control. He drafted and circulated informally early in 1991 a "United Nations Convention on Crime Control."[111] The draft applied both to international crimes (such as genocide, terrorism, and serious drug offenses) and to conventional criminal offenses with an international element. The draft also contained provisions on sentencing principles, confiscation of proceeds of crime, protection of victims, rights of the accused, extradition, mutual legal assistance, and technical assistance. While it was an ambitious attempt at a broad multilateral consolidation, the Ignatov proposal contained too much substance for the system to digest and was ultimately overtaken by events.[112]

Some of the early discussions favoring a treaty relied upon an analogy to the United Nations drug program which had been more successful in attracting resources than the crime control program.[113] While the drug program was itself in the process of being rationalized by action of the General Assembly and the Secretary-General,[114] it had some basic treaty provisions at its core, namely the 1961 Single Convention on Narcotic Drugs,[115] the 1971 Convention on Psychotropic Substances[116] and the 1988 United Nations Convention Against Illicit Traffic in Narcotic Drugs and Psychotropic Substances.[117] Parts of the machinery of the drug program were created by these treaties. The International Narcotics Control Board, for example, is constituted under the Single Convention, and the treaties can be read together as something of a policy framework. All of the activity surrounding the

111. United Nations Convention on Crime Control (1991)(on file with author).

112. *See* Chapter 8 *infra* (discussing the model treaties which appear to be the maximum load which may be borne at present by the system).

113. *See Report of the Intergovernmental Working Group, supra* note 37 at 26. *See also* Chapter 1 *supra*, at note 46 (citing figures on resource disparities). Narcotic Drugs had been staffed by a Division right from the very first days of the Secretariat. *See generally* 1946–47 U.N.Y.B. 623 (describing the Secretariat).

114. On December 21, 1990, between the time of the Crime Committee's 1990 Report and the 1991 Intergovernmental Meeting, the General Assembly adopted G.A. Res. 45/179, *Enhancement of the United Nations Structure for Drug Abuse Control,* U.N. GAOR, 45th Sess., Supp. No. 49A, at 292, U.N. Doc. A/45/49 (1991). This resolution combined the three separate bureaucracies in Vienna that had worked the drug area, the Division on Narcotic Drugs of the Secretariat, the secretariat of the International Narcotics Control Board and the extrabudgetarily funded United Nations Fund for Drug Abuse Control. The single program became known as the United Nations International Drug Control Program.

115. 520 U.N.T.S. 204 (1964). *See also* 1972 Protocol Amending the Single Convention on Narcotic Drugs, 976 U.N.T.S. 3 (1972).

116. 1019 U.N.T.S. 175 (1971).

117. U.N. Doc. E/CONF.82/15 (1988).

drafting of the 1988 Convention[118] had served to focus considerable attention on the program.

Nevertheless, the drug program is still a part of the Secretariat structure and was cobbled together largely by actions of the Assembly and the Secretary-General. Its main policy-making body, the Commission on Narcotic Drugs, was created by resolution of the Economic and Social Council.[119] Indeed, the drug area had provided in 1987 a dramatic example of a world ministerial meeting called to draw attention to the problem.[120] This ministerial meeting was at least part of the inspiration for the 1991 Versailles Ministerial Meeting. Analogies to the drug program thus pointed both in the direction of working on a convention and of seeking high level ministerial support, with the General Assembly and the Secretary-General tidying up the details.

At an early stage of the debate in the Committee, there was some suggestion that the best way to ensure that the program was taken seriously was to go even further than had the drug program by removing it from the United Nations as such and to create a new Specialized Agency which would take over the operation.[121] Such an agency, like the existing sixteen Specialized Agencies, would have its constituent basis in a multilateral treaty and would enter into a "relationship" agreement with the United Nations. Reference was sometimes made in this context to the International Penal and Penitentiary Commission's relationship with the League of Nations. Specialized agency status did not exist during the League of Nations period. The International Penal and Penitentiary Commission was, however, seen by some as a kind of prototype for what became the specialized agencies under the United Nations Charter.[122]

This idea of a new specialized agency probably received its clearest

118. *Id.* In Matti Joutsen's terms, the 1988 treaty itself is something of a hybrid between a consolidation instrument and a framework instrument. *Supra* note 109.

119. 1946–47 U.N.Y.B. 532.

120. *See Report of the International Conference on Drug Abuse and Illicit Trafficking Vienna, 17–26 June 1987,* U.N. Doc. A/CONF.133/12 (1987), in particular its Comprehensive Multidisciplinary Outline of Future Activities in Drug Abuse Control. *Id.* at 3.

121. *See* The Need, *supra* note 14, at 18. "The logical administrative placement of such a programme would be either in a new United Nations agency established and maintained with separate funding, or in a new, major unit of the Secretariat." Some variants of the "agency" argument considered the Office of the High Commissioner for Refugees (UNHCR) or the United Nations Children's Fund (UNICEF) which had been structured by resolution rather than treaty as available examples. In Joutsen's typology, a treaty creating a separate agency would be the ultimate in framework treaties. *Supra* note 109.

122. The I.P.P.C. did not have a treaty basis, but was essentially an intergovernmental organization.

exposition in the report of a meeting held at the Max Planck Institute in Freiburg in May of 1991.[123] The author understands that the idea was given some careful governmental attention in the weeks following that meeting. It did not, however, garner significant support at the Intergovernmental Working Group three months later. Creating a new specialized agency presumably would have entailed a large commitment of resources that states were not prepared to make, at least for the moment.[124] The suggestion of such an agency, not having been pursued at the Intergovernmental Working Group, was not raised seriously at the Ministerial Meeting. The idea of a specialized agency probably makes sense only if it entails combining the resources of the Crime Prevention and Criminal Justice Branch, the International Drug Control Program and the interregional and regional institutes. Since I suspect that the idea may be appealing to some in the longer term, I have included in Appendix 2, under the heading "Alternative Visions," the relevant provisions of the Freiburg report.[125]

Yet another variant on the treaty theme was introduced by Costa Rica at the Intergovernmental Working Group in the form of an "International Convention on Cooperation in Crime Prevention and Criminal Justice."[126] Under this draft, the states parties thereto would undertake to develop further the content, structure and practical application of the United Nations program and to strengthen international cooperation in those areas, bearing in mind the fundamental principles of their respective legal systems.[127] In order to support the program, states would adopt such legislation as would be required and

---

123. THE SOCIETY FOR THE REFORM OF CRIMINAL LAW AND THE MAX PLANCK INSTITUTE FOR FOREIGN AND INTERNATIONAL CRIMINAL LAW, FINAL REPORT OF THE INTERNATIONAL WORKSHOP ON PRINCIPLES AND PROCEDURES FOR A NEW TRANSNATIONAL CRIMINAL LAW (1991) (reproduced in relevant part in the Appendix hereto). *See also* on the possibility of a new agency, Chief Adedokun A. Adeyemi, Crime Prevention and Criminal Justice in the Context of Development: Realities and Perspectives on International Co-operation (paper distributed to members of Committee on Crime Prevention and Control under cover of letter dated January 29, 1990, on file with author).

124. As of December 31, 1989, one of the largest employers among the Specialized Agencies, the Food and Agriculture Organization, had 6331 employees, while the smallest, the Universal Postal Union, had 169. *See United Nations System, Personnel Statistics*, at 10 (Table 1A), U.N. Doc. ACC/1990/PER./R.6 (1990). The Universal Postal Union, in short, had about ten times as many people as the Crime Branch.

125. *See supra* note 123.

126. U.N. Doc. A/AC.239/CRP.6 (1991). *See Report of the Intergovernmental Working Group, supra* note 37, at 25–26. An edited version of the draft was put before the Ministerial Meeting. *See* U.N. Doc. A/CONF.156/CRP.1 (1991).

127. *Id.* art. I.

would "assist in the drafting, consolidation, revision and application of . . . international instruments containing regulations and standards relating to crime prevention and criminal justice."[128] Such instruments might be annexed to the Convention in the form of Protocols with the agreement of the states parties.[129] Viewed through the prism of the Joutsen typology,[130] the basic Costa Rican treaty itself was a framework document, while the protocols would be consolidating ones. A Committee for Cooperation in Crime Prevention and Criminal Justice would be created along the lines of the human rights treaty supervisory committees.[131] The Cooperation Committee would examine reports submitted by states that became parties to the Protocols.[132]

This idea was never fully considered in the Working Group or at the Ministerial Meeting, although Costa Rica produced a draft resolution for the latter meeting which would have had a working group of the new Crime Prevention Commission and the Ninth Congress in 1995 contributing to a drafting process. That process would result in a convention being approved by the 50th Session of the General Assembly that year.[133]

In the end, the Ministerial Meeting adopted the resolution rather than the treaty approach to the defining instrument, but included in its report the following:

Although some delegations were in favour of the development of an international convention in order to continue the work of the United Nations in codification of international criminal law, others felt that such a project was premature. In fact such work would consume time and resources, something impracticable under the present constraints. After having considered the proposals made by the delegation of Costa Rica, the Meeting decided that: (a) the Commission on Crime Prevention and Criminal Justice to be established shall be competent to examine the desirability of a Convention or of another instrument; (b) the Commission shall examine that possibility and shall take appropriate action.[134]

A judgment that proceeding by resolution was the most practical way to advance had carried the day, at least for the moment.[135] There was

---

128. *Id.* art. III, para. 1.

129. *Id.* art. III, para. 2.

130. *See supra* note 109.

131. *See supra* note 126, art. IV. The model was apparently such committees as the Committee on Human Rights, the Committee on the Elimination of Racial Discrimination, and the Committee Against Torture.

132. *Id.* art. V.

133. *Letter dated 8 November 1991 from the First Alternate Representative of Costa Rica to the United Nations addressed to the Secretary-General*, U.N. Doc. A/CONF.156/4 (1991).

134. *Report of the Ministerial Meeting, supra* note 54, at 38.

135. At its first meeting the Commission on Crime Prevention and Criminal Justice

considerable fear that a convention, whatever form it might take, would take a long time to draft and even then might not garner enough ratifications to be of much use. I doubt that we have heard the final word on this idea and have, accordingly, reproduced the Costa Rican draft in Appendix 2 as an "Alternative Vision."

D. The Culmination—General Assembly Resolution 46/152

General Assembly resolution 46/152[136] was adopted on December 18, 1991 without a vote. It consists of a two-page adopting resolution and a lengthy Annex, as adopted in Versailles, entitled "Statement of Principles and Programme of Action of the United Nations Crime Prevention and Criminal Justice Programme."

The adopting portion of the resolution begins with preambular material recalling the history of the item and recognizing the urgent need to improve international cooperation.[137] The operative part of the resolution then approves the statement of principles and program of action[138], and supports a clearer definition of the program's mandate.[139] The Secretary-General[140] and Member States[141] are requested to give their support, as are all entities of the United Nations system, including the regional commissions, the congresses, the specialized agencies, and relevant intergovernmental and non-governmental organizations.[142] Developed countries are exhorted to review their aid programs in order to ensure that there is a full and proper contribution in the field of criminal justice within the overall context of development priorities.[143] The General Assembly asks the ECOSOC to create a new commission and to cancel the meeting of the Committee on Crime

---

adopted Decision 1/102 in which it "decided to consult the Governments of States Members of the United Nations on the matter [of a convention] and, for that purpose, to forward to them all relevant material and information with a view to having available at its second session sufficient background data to enable it to conduct a well-informed discussion." *Report of the Commission on Crime Prevention and Criminal Justice on its First Session, supra* note 66, at 50. Of the 15 responses received by the end of January 1993, only three were positive. *See Progress made in the implementation of Economic and Social Council Resolution 1992/22, Report of the Secretary-General*, at 16, U.N. Doc. E/1993/10 (1993). There was in fact no debate at the 1993 session of the Commission.

136. *See supra* note 1. The text of the resolution is reproduced in the Appendix.
137. *Id.* preamble.
138. *Id.* para. 2.
139. *Id.* para. 3.
140. *Id.* paras. 4 and 7. *See also supra* notes 63–65.
141. *Id.* para. 6.
142. *Id.* para. 8.
143. *Id.* para. 9.

Prevention and Control scheduled for February 1992.[144] Funds currently allocated to the program, as well as any savings realized by restructuring, are to be retained for the program, without prejudice to additional funds that may be made available by the Secretary-General.[145] Finally, the Secretary-General is requested to report on developments to the General Assembly.[146]

The Statement of Principles section of the Annex begins with an ideological underpinning, namely a recognition that the world is experiencing very important changes resulting in a political climate conducive to democracy, international cooperation, more widespread enjoyment of basic human rights, and the realization of the aspirations of nations to economic development and social welfare. Notwithstanding these developments, the world is still beset by violence and other forms of serious crime. These phenomena constitute a threat to the rule of law.[147] In this context, according to the resolution, a humane and efficient criminal justice system can be an instrument of equity and constructive social change and social justice, protecting basic values and peoples' inalienable rights.[148]

The view is also espoused that the lowering of the world crime rate is related to, among other factors, the improvement of the social conditions of the population. Both developed and developing countries are experiencing difficult situations in this respect. Nevertheless, the specific problems encountered by the developing countries justify priority being given to addressing the situation confronting those countries.[149]

Another noteworthy paragraph deals with mutual assistance and other forms of cooperation.[150] It recognizes that many criminal offenses have international dimensions. Thus, while respecting state sovereignty, there is an urgent need to address problems arising in collecting evidence, extraditing offenders and promoting mutual legal assistance when, for example, such offenses are committed across frontiers or when frontiers are used to escape detection or prosecution. Despite differences in legal systems, the resolution argues, experience

144. *Id.* paras. 10 and 11. As has been noted in Chapter 1, ECOSOC created the Commission on 6 February 1992, pursuant to E.S.C. Res. 1992/1, U.N. ESCOR, Supp. No. 1, at 11, U.N. Doc. E/1992/92 (1992), and the first meeting of the Commission took place soon thereafter at the end of April 1992.

145. *Id.* para. 13.

146. *Id.* para. 14.

147. *Id.* Annex, para. 1

148. *Id.* Annex, para. 2.

149. *Id.* Annex, para. 3.

150. *See generally* Chapter 8 *infra.*

has shown that mutual assistance and cooperation can be effective counter-measures, and can help to prevent conflicts of jurisdiction.[151]

Echoing the comment about security made at the opening of the Intergovernmental Working Group[152] and the strong feeling of many of those involved in the process that the protection of human rights is a fundamental dimension in the whole area, the Statement of Principles also recognizes that democracy and a better quality of life can flourish only in a context of peace and security for all. "Crime prevention and criminal justice, with due regard to the observance of human rights, is thus a direct contribution to the maintenance of peace and security."[153]

All of this leads to the not-surprising conclusions that there must be intensified international cooperation in crime prevention and criminal justice,[154] that Governments should define more clearly the role and function of the United Nations program[155] and that the review of the program should aim at strengthening its effectiveness, improving its efficiency, and establishing an adequate Secretariat support structure.[156]

Part II of the Annex to the resolution sets forth a Program of Action. It begins by "defining" the United Nations crime prevention and criminal justice program as to

bring together the work of the commission on crime prevention and criminal justice, the interregional and regional institutes for the prevention of crime and the treatment of offenders, the network of government-appointed national correspondents in the field of crime prevention and criminal justice, the Global Crime and Criminal Justice Information Network and the United Nations congresses on the prevention of crime and the treatment of offenders in providing assistance to Member States in their efforts to reduce the incidence and costs of crime and in developing the proper functioning of the criminal justice system.[157]

The resolution continues with a statement of the "Goals" of the Program, which, in general, are to assist both the international com-

---

151. *Id.* Annex, para. 6. Efforts to prevent conflicts of jurisdiction have not gone very far. *See* Chapter 8 *infra*, at notes 92–97.

152. *See supra* note 41.

153. *Id.* Annex, para. 7.

154. *Id.* Annex, para. 11.

155. *Id.* Annex, para. 12.

156. *Id.* Annex, para. 13.

157. *Id.* Annex, para. 14. This paragraph concludes that: "The establishment of this programme will be effected in accordance with the procedures defined below and within the framework of the total available resources of the United Nations." *See* discussion *supra* notes 63–65.

munity and individual countries in meeting pressing needs in the area.[158] The program is thus expected to contribute to the prevention of crime within and among States; the control of crime both nationally and internationally; the strengthening of regional and international cooperation in crime prevention, criminal justice and the combatting of transnational crime; the integration and consolidation of the efforts of Member States in preventing and combating transnational crime; the development of more efficient and effective administration of justice, with due respect for the rights of those affected by crime and all those involved in the criminal justice system; and the promotion of the highest standards of fairness, humanity, justice and professional conduct.[159]

A section of the resolution on the "Scope" of the Program suggests the kinds of cooperation that may be appropriate: research and studies, regular international surveys, exchange and dissemination of information, and training. Cooperation also encompasses

technical assistance, including advisory services, particularly in respect of the planning, implementation and evaluation of crime prevention and criminal justice programmes, training and the use of modern communication and information techniques; such assistance may be implemented by means of, for example, fellowships, study tours, consultancies, secondments, courses, seminars and demonstration and pilot projects.[160]

The reference to implementation in the "Scope" section is particularly significant. The Program "may also include, as appropriate, while respecting the sovereignty of States, a review of the effectiveness and application of and, where necessary, further development and promotion of international instruments on crime prevention and criminal justice."[161] This is followed by a section on Priorities[162] which has already been discussed at length.[163]

A section entitled "Structure and Management"[164] addresses in detail the Crime Prevention Commission, the congresses and the organizational structure of the Secretariat. These items will be dealt with in Chapter 3. So, too, will the contents of the penultimate section of the resolution, on program support.[165] That section deals with the role of

158. *Id.* Annex, para. 15.
159. *Id.* Annex, para. 16.
160. *Id.* Annex, para. 17.
161. *Id.* Annex, para. 20. *See* Chapter 9 *infra* (discussing implementation).
162. *Id.* Annex, paras. 21–22.
163. *See supra* notes 66–79.
164. *See supra* note 1, Annex, paras. 23–34.
165. *Id.* Annex, paras. 35–43.

the institutes and their coordination, the network of government-appointed national correspondents, the global information network, and intergovernmental and non-governmental organizations. The final provision of the resolution,[166] on funding, has already been discussed in the context of resources.[167]

The next chapter discusses the organs that exist after the restructuring and examines their mandates and methods of operating.

---

166. *Id.* Annex, para. 44.
167. *See supra* text accompanying note 59.

Chapter 3
The Organs Involved in the Crime Prevention and Criminal Justice Process, Their Mandates and Methods of Operation

A. Introduction

In this chapter, I examine the main organs involved in the Crime Prevention and Criminal Justice process including the Commission on Crime Prevention and Criminal Justice, the Secretariat, the Economic and Social Council (ECOSOC), the preparatory meetings for the Congresses, the Congresses, the Third Committee of the General Assembly, the Institutes, the Criminal Justice Information Network (UNCJIN), the World Criminal Justice Library Network, the network of government-appointed correspondents, and the International Scientific and Professional Advisory Council (ISPAC). In focusing individually on these organs, I shall attempt to elucidate both the formal structure and the informal sub-structure[1] and to give particular attention to the "legislative" process—the way in which the normative instruments have been developed.

B. The Commission on Crime Prevention and Criminal Justice

As suggested in the discussion in Chapter 2 of the restructuring of the U.N. program,[2] the Commission is apparently intended to be the most active part of the new system, a role occupied in the past by the congresses. Proponents of the restructuring particularly emphasized the Crime Prevention Commission's function, as a collection of govern-

1. *See also* the discussion of the "invisible college" in Chapter 2 *supra*, at note 91.
2. *See* Chapter 2 *supra*.

mental representatives, in galvanizing the support of governments for the endeavor.

Article 68 of the U.N. Charter empowers ECOSOC to "set up commissions in economic and social fields and for the promotion of human rights, and such other commissions as may be required for the performance of its functions."[3] Such organs are known collectively as "functional commissions" (there appear to be, by definition, no non-functional ones!) and operate under Rules of Procedure adopted by the Council.[4] ECOSOC created the Commission on Crime Prevention and Criminal Justice in February 1992,[5] acting on the request of the General Assembly in its restructuring resolution.[6] The Crime Prevention and Criminal Justice Commission's terms of reference are those set out in paragraphs 23–26 of the Statement of Principles and Programme of Action annexed to the Assembly's 1991 Resolution.[7]

The Crime Prevention Commission consists of forty Member States of the United Nations, elected on the basis of equitable geographical distribution. Members serve for a term of three years, except that the terms of one-half of the first elected members, whose names were chosen by lot, expire after two years.[8] I have discussed in an earlier

3. U.N. CHARTER art. 68.

4. *Rules of Procedure of the Functional Commissions of the Economic and Social Council*, U.N. Doc. E/5975/Rev.1 (1983).

5. E.S.C. Res. 1992/1, U.N. ESCOR, Supp. No. 1, at 11, U.N. Doc.E/1992/92 (1992).

6. G.A. Res. 46/152, U.N. GAOR, 46th Sess., Supp. No. 49, at 217, Annex, para. 11(b), U.N. Doc. A/46/49 (1992).

7. *Id.* Annex, paras. 23–26. R. 34 of the Rules of Procedure of the Functional Commissions of the Economic and Social Council, provides that no summary records of a commission shall be provided unless specifically authorized by ECOSOC. *Supra* note 4, at 9. Like the Committee on Crime Prevention and Control before it, the Commission on Crime Prevention and Criminal Justice has not been authorized to keep summary records. Thus the only widely available account of its deliberations is in the narrative summary contained in its reports. The United Nations Vienna Office issues press releases on the meetings of the Commission under the symbol UNIS/CP/—, but these are neither official records nor widely circulated.

8. *Id.*, Annex, para. 24. The size and geographical distribution may be reviewed two years after the first session of the commission. *Id.* The initial members of the Commission, elected in Feb. 1992, with the year at the end of which their term expires noted in parentheses, are, for the twelve African States: Burkina Faso (1993), Gabon (1993), Ghana (1994), Guinea-Bissau (1993), Libya (1993), Madagascar (1994), Malawi (1993), Nigeria (1994), Sierra Leone (1994), Tunisia (1993), Uganda (1993), Zaire (1993); for the nine Asian States: China (1994), Indonesia (1994), Iran (1994), Japan (1993), Malaysia (1993), Philippines (1994), Republic of Korea (1994), Saudi Arabia (1993), Sri Lanka (1993); for the four Eastern European States: Bulgaria (1994), Hungary (1993), Poland (1994), Russian Federation (1993); for the eight Latin American and Caribbean States: Bolivia (1994), Costa Rica (1993), Cuba (1993), Dominican Republic (1993), Nicaragua (1994), Paraguay (1994), Peru (1994), Uruguay (1994); and for the seven Western

chapter the question of the involvement of experts, both governmental and nongovernmental, in the process.[9] Member States are exhorted in Resolution 46/152 to make every effort to ensure that their delegations include experts and senior officials with special training and practical experience in crime prevention and criminal justice, especially with policy responsibility in the field.[10] The Commission has power, not yet exercised at the time of this writing, to create ad hoc working groups and to appoint special rapporteurs as it deems necessary.[11] Annual sessions of the Commission are held in Vienna and extend no longer than ten working days.[12] The Rules for commissions of ECOSOC contemplate that, in addition to its members, meetings of the Commission will be attended by other ("observer") states,[13] specialized agencies of the U.N. family,[14] other intergovernmental organizations,[15] and non-governmental organizations in consultative status.[16] Other parts

European and Other States: Australia (1994), Austria (1993), Finland (1993), France (1994), Germany (1993), Italy (1994), United States of America (1994).

9. *See* Chapter 2 *supra*, at notes 80–97.

10. G.A. Res. 46/152, *supra* note 6, Annex, para. 24. Empirically testing how well this exhortation was obeyed at the Commission's initial meetings in 1992 and 1993 was not possible, but the author's impression was that a reasonably high proportion of states (both members and observers) had tried to send people with some expertise and even policy responsibilities.

11. *Id.* Annex, para. 23.

12. *Id.* Annex, para. 25. The initial meeting in 1992 occupied eight working days; that in 1993 occupied nine. The meeting has been fitted into the U.N. calendar for the latter part of April each year.

13. *Rules of Procedure of Functional Commissions of the Economic and Social Council, supra* note 4, R. 69. Some 35 observer states were present (on short notice) in 1992 and 55 in 1993.

14. *Id.* R. 71.

15. *Id.* R. 74. Typical examples include the Council of Europe and INTERPOL.

16. *Id.* R. 75, and R. 76. Article 71 of the U.N. Charter, empowers ECOSOC to "make suitable arrangements for consultation with non-governmental organizations which are concerned with matters within its competence." Some 27 NGOs were represented at the first meeting of the Commission and 40 at the second. Many of the NGOs have people who are stationed in Vienna; others come in from Geneva or from further afield for meetings like this. In November 1980, a Vienna NGO Alliance on Crime Prevention and Criminal Justice was formed to coordinate efforts. It complemented the existing New York Alliance devoted to the same task which dates from the late 1960s. Subsequently, NGO Committees on Narcotic Drugs were formed in Vienna and New York. *See* R. Linke, *The Cooperation between Non-Governmental Organizations and the United Nations in the Field of Crime Policy, in* Helsinki Institute for Crime Prevention and Control affiliated with the United Nations, Course on United Nations Criminal Justice Policy 90 (1985) [hereinafter "HEUNI Course"]; Letter from Joseph M. Callan, Executive Secretary, Alliance of NGOs on Crime Prevention and Criminal Justice to Roger S. Clark (Oct. 12, 1992).

of the U.N. Secretariat, notably the Centre for Human Rights and the Drug Program, are also represented.

The functions of the Crime Prevention Commission are described as follows:

(a) To provide policy guidance to the United Nations in the field of crime prevention and criminal justice;

(b) To develop, monitor and review the implementation of the programme on the basis of a system of medium-term planning in accordance with the priority principles provided in paragraph 21 above;[17]

(c) To facilitate and help to co-ordinate the activities of the interregional and regional institutes;

(d) To mobilize the support of Member States for the United Nations crime and criminal justice programme;

(e) To prepare the congresses and to consider suggestions regarding possible subjects for the programme of work as submitted by the congresses.[18]

At its first meeting in 1992, largely an occasion to note the changing of the guard from the Crime Prevention Committee, the Crime Prevention Commission included strong language addresssing its place in the scheme of things in a lengthy draft resolution which it prepared for adoption by ECOSOC.[19] The resolution[20] recognizes the Crime Prevention Commission "as the principal policy-making body of the United Nations in the field of crime prevention and criminal justice and requests it to coordinate, as appropriate, relevant activities in this field." The resolution also requests that the Commission closely cooperate with the Commission for Social Development; the Commission on Human Rights; the Commission on Narcotic Drugs; the Commission on the Status of Women and other bodies, including the International Law Commission; and specialized agencies, including the United Nations Educational, Scientific and Cultural Organization, whose activities

---

17. *See* Chapter 2 *supra*, at note 70 (discussing Annex, para. 21).

18. G.A. Res. 46/152, *supra* note 6, Annex, para. 26.

19. *See Implementation of General Assembly Resolution 46/152: Operational activities and coordination in the field of crime prevention and criminal justice, Report of the Commission on Crime Prevention and Criminal Justice on its First Session, Vienna, 21 to 30 April 1992*, U.N. ESCOR, Supp. No. 10, at 4 (Draft Resolution I), U.N. Doc. E/1992/30 (1992). The resolution was adopted as E.S.C. Res. 1992/22, U.N. ESCOR, Supp. No. 1, at 22, U.N. Doc. E/1992/92 (1992).

20. E.S.C. Res. 1992/22, *id.* pt. IV, para. 4.

may have crime prevention and criminal justice aspects. The objective of such close cooperation is to increase the efficiency and effectiveness of U.N. activities in areas of mutual concern and to ensure proper coordination and avoidance of duplication.[21]

Beyond the generalities of the Crime Prevention Commission's roles as principal policy-making body and coordinator extraordinaire rest areas of more substance. Thus the 1992 ECOSOC resolution indicates two main areas in which future activity will occur by deciding, in a section provocatively entitled "Follow-Up," on two standing items to be included in subsequent agendas, beginning with the Crime Prevention Commission's second session. One item for future consideration concerns "technical assistance which would deal with the most practical course of action to be followed to render the programme fully operational and enable it to respond to the specific needs of Governments, including financial needs, if possible."[22] The other is an "item on existing United Nations standards and norms in the field of crime prevention and criminal justice, which serve as recommendations to Member States, including [and in the light of] their use and application."[23]

C. The Secretariat

An outstanding feature of the modern international organization is a permanent secretariat whose members' primary loyalty is to the organization rather than to their state of origin.[24] The U.N. Charter is somewhat terse in setting up the Secretariat as one of the "principal organs"[25] of the U.N. The Secretariat is said to "comprise a Secretary-

21. *Id.* pt. IV, para. 5.
22. *Id.* pt. VII, para. 2.
23. *Id.* pt. VII, para. 3. The bracketed words, the subject of hard bargaining at the Commission, were apparently dropped by the editors. They turned up in the Secretary-General's report made pursuant to the paragraph. *See Existing United Nations standards and norms, which serve as recommendations to Member States, in the field of crime prevention and criminal justice in the light of and including their use and application, Report of the Secretary-General,* U.N. Doc. E/CN.15/1993/6 (1993).
24. *See, e.g.,* U.N. CHARTER art. 100:

1. In the performance of their duties the Secretary-General and the staff shall not seek or receive instructions from any government or from any authority external to the Organization. They shall refrain from any action which might reflect on their position as international officials responsible only to the organization.
2. Each Member of the United Nations undertakes to respect the exclusively international character of the responsibilities of the Secretary-General and the staff and not to seek to influence them in the discharge of their responsibilities.

25. U.N. CHARTER art. 7.

General and such staff as the Organization may require."[26] The Secretary-General is described as "the chief administrative officer of the Organization."[27] The staff are to be appointed by the Secretary-General under regulations established by the General Assembly.[28] Appropriate staffs are to be "permanently assigned to the Economic and Social Council, the Trusteeship Council, and as required, to other organs of the United Nations."[29]

As chief executive, the Secretary-General is in a position somewhat analogous to a chief executive in a national government. He has considerable leeway in deploying resources but is ultimately subject to the power of the purse, exercised in this instance by the General Assembly.[30] Under the arrangements existing at the time of this writing, which are reflected in the program budget for the biennium 1992–1993,[31] the crime prevention and criminal justice program is staffed by a modest complement of eleven professional and six general service officers who constitute the Crime Prevention and Criminal Justice Branch.[32] Three additional posts promised early in 1993 were filled,

---

26. U.N. CHARTER art. 97.

27. *Id.*

28. *Id.* art. 101, para. 1.

29. *Id.* art. 101, para. 2

30. Article 17 of the U.N. Charter provides that "The General Assembly shall consider and approve the budget of the Organization." U.N. CHARTER art. 17, para. 1. Article 101 provides that the staff shall be appointed by the Secretary-General "under regulations established by the General Assembly." *See* Chapter 2 *supra*, at note 74 (discussing the tension between the Secretary General and the General Assembly).

31. *Proposed Programme Budget for the Biennium 1992–1993, pt. IV, International Cooperation for Development, Section 21, Social Development and Humanitarian Affairs* 39, U.N. Doc. A/46/6 (sec. 21) (1991). Chapter 1 *supra*, at notes 44–46.

32. Some countries and NGOs have also contributed in kind:

A number of countries have supported the programme through the secondment of Junior Professional Officers (Germany, Italy and Japan). Other Governments have cooperated with the Secretariat through ad hoc assignments of their nationals (Netherlands and the former Union of Soviet Socialist Republics) and other forms of assistance on specific projects. Similar support has also been provided by nongovernmental organizations. For example, the Friends World Committee for Consultation financed a one-year internship of a junior expert to work on questions related to life imprisonment, and the American Association for the Advancement of Science donated $12,000 for the printing of the *Manual on Effective Prevention and Investigation of Extralegal, Arbitrary and Summary Executions*.

Report of the Secretary-General, Progress report on United Nations Activities in Crime Prevention and Criminal Justice, including detailed information on current programme budget and extrabudgetary activities of the Crime Prevention and Criminal Justice Branch of the Centre for Social Development and Humanitarian Affairs, at 19, U.N. Doc. E.CN.15/1992/2 (1992) [hereinafter *Progress Report on United Nations Activities*]. Extrabudgetary grant money is also sometimes received from governments for specific projects.

but only on a temporary basis, later that year. As has been noted,[33] the Crime Prevention Branch was, for several years, a part of the Centre for Social Development and Humanitarian Affairs, located in Vienna. That Centre has now been dismantled and most of its personnel transferred to New York. The Crime Prevention and Criminal Justice Branch remains in Vienna, at least for the time being, and the Commission meets there. The Crime Prevention Branch is, of course, responsible for the paper flow, an enterprise that always partakes of the mysterious. In the course of the restructuring exercise an attempt was made to spell out what this means, in the following language:

The Secretariat shall be the permanent body responsible for facilitating the implementation of the programme, the priorities of which shall be established by the commission, and for assisting the commission in conducting evaluations of the progress made and analyses of the difficulties encountered. For that purpose, the Secretariat shall:

(a) Mobilize existing resources, including institutes, intergovernmental organizations, non-governmental organizations and other competent authorities for the implementation of the programme;

(b) Coordinate research, training and the collection of data on crime and justice, and provide technical assistance and practical information for Member States, particularly through the global information network on crime and criminal justice;

(c) Assist the commission in the organization of its work and in the preparation, in accordance with the directions of the commission, of the congresses and any other events relating to the programme;

(d) Ensure that the potential donors of criminal justice assistance are put in touch with countries needing the help in question;

(e) Make the case for assistance in the field of criminal justice to the appropriate funding agencies.[34]

The General Assembly also recommended to the Secretary-General that, in recognition of the high priority that should be accorded to the program, an upgrading of the Crime Prevention and Criminal Justice Branch into a Division[35] should be effected as soon as possible.[36] Upgrading was to be done, however, "within the framework of the total available resources of the United Nations"[37] and "bearing in mind the

33. *See* Chapter 1 *supra*, at note 8.
34. G.A. Res. 46/152, *supra* note 6, Annex, para. 31.
35. *See* Chapter 2 *supra*, at notes 63–64. The upgrading was still being sought at the April 1993 meeting of the Commission on Crime Prevention and Criminal Justice.
36. G.A. Res. 46/152, *supra* note 6, Annex, para. 32.
37. *Id.* para. 14.

structure of the United Nations Office at Vienna."[38] Upgrading was, in short, to be attained by stealing resources from some other part of the system. It has not yet occurred.

Given the heightened emphasis on technical assistance in the reorganized program,[39] it is likely that increased attention will be given to the Crime Prevention and Criminal Justice Branch's capacity to engage in such activity or to facilitate others in so engaging. Assistance to Governments has essentially taken the form either of fellowships or the provision of experts.[40] Fellowships permit professionals to study the practice in other countries as a way of appreciating solutions to their own problems.[41] Some assistance projects involved the provision of experts for as long as one or two years.[42] In 1970, the position of Interregional Adviser was created within the Branch to provide more flexible services on a short term basis.[43] A careful review of what can be provided is at present underway.[44]

D. The Economic and Social Council (ECOSOC)

Like the Secretariat, ECOSOC is established under the United Nations Charter as one of the "principal organs" of the United Nations.[45] It consists of fifty-four members of the United Nations elected by the General Assembly.[46] Eighteen members are elected each year for a term of three years. A retiring member is eligible for immediate re-election. The pattern of geographical distribution of seats consists of fourteen African, eleven Asian, ten Latin American and Caribbean, thirteen Western European and Other, and six Eastern European.[47]

38. *Id.* para. 32.

39. *See* Chapter 2 *supra*, at notes 73–76.

40. United Nations, The United Nations and Crime Prevention 48, U.N. Doc. DPI/1143–41016 (1991).

41. *Id.*

42. *Id.* at 48.

43. *Id. See generally, Interregional Advisory Services in the Field of Crime Prevention and the Treatment of Offenders*, 8 Crime Prevention and Crim. Just. Newsletter 6 (1983).

44. *See The need to identify the most practical course of action to fully operationalize the United Nations crime prevention and criminal justice programme, including financial possibilities, Report of the Secretary-General*, U.N. Doc. E/CN.15/1993/5 (1993); *Operational activities completed by or proposed to the United Nations Crime Prevention and Criminal Justice Branch since the First Session of the Commission Crime Prevention and Criminal Justice in April 1992*, U.N. Doc. E/CN.15/1993/CRP.9 (1993). *See also* Chapter 10 *infra*.

45. U.N. Charter art. 7. On ECOSOC in general, *see* D. O'Donovan, *The Economic and Social Council*, in The United Nations and Human Rights: A Critical Appraisal 107 (P. Alston ed. 1992) (good discussion by an experienced Irish representative).

46. U.N. Charter art. 61.

47. G.A. Res. 2847 (XXVI), U.N. GAOR, 26th Sess., Supp. No. 29, at 67, U.N. Doc. A/8429 (1972).

In the Charter, the main functions and powers of ECOSOC are described thus:

1. The Economic and Social Council may make or initiate studies and reports with respect to international economic, social, cultural, educational, health, and related matters and may make recommendations with respect to any such matters to the General Assembly, to the Members of the United Nations, and to the specialized agencies concerned.
2. It may make recommendations for the purpose of promoting respect for, and observance of, human rights and fundamental freedoms for all.
3. It may prepare draft conventions for submission to the General Assembly, with respect to matters falling within its competence.
4. It may call, in accordance with the rules prescribed by the United Nations, international conferences on matters falling within its competence.[48]

Consequently, ECOSOC's legislative work in the criminal justice area falls squarely within paragraphs 1 and 2 of this mandate. The congresses are convened by ECOSOC under its general conference power in paragraph 4 and in accordance with General Assembly Resolution 415 (V) of 1950 which dealt with the plan relating to the transfer of the functions of the International Penal and Penitentiary Commission to the United Nations.[49]

---

48. U.N. CHARTER art. 62. Many commentators have argued that ECOSOC has become moribund. A recent high-level meeting suggested that:

> Those participants who saw a chance for ECOSOC to become more effective agreed that it must become the final decision-making body in economic and social areas, just as the Security Council has become the final arbiter of security matters. The current practice of merely debating items and then passing them on to the Assembly for decision should be abandoned.

STANLEY FOUNDATION, REPORT OF THE TWENTY-SECOND UNITED NATIONS ISSUES CONFERENCE, THE UNITED NATIONS: STRUCTURE AND LEADERSHIP FOR A NEW ERA 19 (1991). In the criminal justice area ECOSOC occasionally functions as the "final arbiter" in the sense that it adopts the definitive resolution on the subject on the recommendation of the Commission on Crime Prevention and Criminal Justice, or its predecessor, the Committee on Crime Prevention and Control. Not everyone is eager for ECOSOC to exercise too much of its own discretion. *See infra* note 59.

49. U.N. GAOR, 5th Sess., Supp. No. 20, at 37, U.N. Doc. A/1775 (1950). *See also infra* note 76. The Secretary-General was asked to take the necessary steps to convene the Eighth Congress and the provisional agenda was approved in E.S.C. Res. 1987/49, U.N. ESCOR, Supp. No. 1, at 33, U.N. Doc. E/1987/87 (1987). The venue was selected in

ECOSOC meets briefly each year in New York in January/February for an organizational session. Formerly, a first regular session for the year was held in New York for some three weeks in May,[50] and a second regular session in Geneva for the same length of time in July. Beginning in 1992, there has been only one substantive session of four to five weeks which takes place in alternate years in New York and Geneva between May and July.[51] Three Committees of the whole are created by the ECOSOC Rules—the First (Economic) Committee, the Second (Social) Committee and the Third (Programme and Co-ordination) Committee.[52]

Crime prevention and criminal justice does not have a high profile in ECOSOC's deliberations. It does not appear as a separate item on the agenda. Instead, this topic is included as a sub-item in a general "Social Development" item which is allocated to the Second (Social) Committee[53] and dealt with at the substantive session. In practical terms, this means crime prevention and criminal justice is bracketed for discussion with matters such as a report of the Secretary-General on the status and role of cooperatives in the light of new economic and social trends, the Secretary-General's report on the world social situation, the possibility of convening a world summit for social development and the Decade of Disabled Persons.[54] A speech by an individual delegate and the debate at any particular meeting may range randomly over one or all of these as well as crime.

In due course, a plenary meeting of ECOSOC formally adopts what has been decided in committee, normally without debate.[55] About three working days are allocated to the Second (Social) Committee's

---

E.S.C. Decision 1989/134, U.N. ESCOR, Supp. No. 1, at 81, U.N. Doc. E/1989/89 (1989).

50. The crime item was then dealt with annually in the first regular session in New York.

51. G.A. Res. 45/264, *Restructuring and Revitalization of the United Nations in the Economic, Social and Related fields*, para. 5, U.N. GAOR, 45th Sess., Supp. No. 49 A, at 2, U.N. Doc. A/45/49/Add.1 (1991).

52. *See generally* the *Rules of Procedure of the Economic and Social Council*, U.N. Doc. E/5715/Rev.1 (1983) (setting out the council's mode of operation).

53. *See, e.g., Report of the Economic and Social Council for the year 1989*, U.N. GAOR, 44th Sess., Supp. No. 3, at vii, U.N. Doc. A/44/3/Rev.1 (1989) [hereinafter *1989 ECOSOC Report*]. The other items allocated to the Social Committee were entitled Human rights questions, Women, and Narcotic Drugs.

54. These were the sub-items on the 1992 Agenda.

55. Rule 53 of the ECOSOC Rules of Procedure, provides: "Discussion of a report of a sessional committee of the whole in a plenary meeting of the Council shall take place if at least one third of the members present and voting at the plenary meeting consider such discussion to be necessary. A motion to this effect shall not be discussed but shall be put to the vote immediately." *Supra* note 52.

work on the whole item. In short, the Crime Prevention Commission's Report hardly receives detailed attention.

Since 1982[56] there have been no summary records of the sessional committees and the account of deliberations in the ECOSOC Report is sparse at best. Occasionally, states that have not been able to strike a compromise in the Social Committee will make an appropriate statement in plenary so as to be recorded there,[57] but it is unusual for anyone to bother to do so in the criminal justice area.

However, it would be incorrect to regard ECOSOC as merely a rubberstamp for the Committee on Crime Prevention and Control and now the Commission on Crime Prevention and Criminal Justice, although ECOSOC does seem to operate on the basis that there is a strong presumption that the reporting body knew what it was doing and that all appropriate compromises had been reached there.[58] Speaking also on behalf of Canada and New Zealand, the representative of Australia articulated the principle as the following:

At the inaugural session [of the Commission on Crime Prevention and Criminal Justice], a lot of goodwill was exhibited in order to reach shared objectives and priorities and to accommodate the interests of all parties. After significant discussions, consensus was eventually achieved. Mr. Chairman, it would now seem appropriate for ECOSOC to adopt the results, which comprise a delicate balance and a clear consensus of the Commission. Indeed, it would be in the interests of the future development and work of the new commission, particularly in its early days, to adopt these tightly-crafted resolutions before us

56. E.S.C Decision 1982/105, U.N. ESCOR, Supp. No. 1, at 35, U.N. Doc. E/1982/82 (1982).

57. To the extent that states accept that at least some of the resolutions adopted by ECOSOC or the General Assembly contribute to international customary law, or otherwise create expectations, dissenters may wish to reserve their position. Those who merely express their reservations in Committee will not have those views recorded. Hence, anyone who feels strongly enough—and thinks the point through—will want to go on the record in plenary so as to appear in the summary records which are kept there. Rule 62 of the *Rules of Procedure of the Economic and Social Council*, provides: "Representatives may make brief statements consisting solely of explanation of their votes [known to insiders as "EOVs"], before the voting has commenced or after the voting has been completed. The representative of a member sponsoring a proposal or motion shall not speak in explanation of the vote thereon, except if it has been amended." *Supra* note 52. A member may also wish to record its opposition to a decision that has no "legislative" overtones but is nonetheless contrary to its policy positions. *See* note 62 *infra* (citing an example).

58. Given that the Committee was not an intergovernmental body, one might perhaps surmise that its drafts would be given less deference than those of the Commission on Human Rights, but I have been able to find no empirical support for any difference in the way in which ECOSOC treated its work compared with the way it treated the work of obviously governmental subordinate bodies.

and carry forward the spirit of cooperation and goodwill that was achieved by all parties [at] the Commission.[59]

On rare occasions where sufficient members of ECOSOC care enough, a draft resolution from the Crime Prevention Committee or the Crime Prevention Commission may be revised[60] or held over to the session the following year while something is worked out.[61] In the latter years of the Crime Prevention Committee, the most contested item seems to have been a matter on which the Crime Prevention Committee itself had made no formal recommendation, that of the invitation by Cuba to hold the Eighth Congress in Havana. The United States lobbied hard in ECOSOC for Vienna as the site and introduced a resolution to this effect. Ultimately, Havana won out against the sole negative vote of the United States.[62]

Occasionally, members of the Crime Prevention Committee would find their way to the meetings of ECOSOC, either as members of their national delegations, or simply to engage in informal lobbying. One might have expected that there would be some formal procedure whereby the Chair of the Crime Prevention Committee, or some other delegate thereof, might make a presentation of the Report or answer

59. Statement by Dr. Martin Sharp, Australian Delegation, ECOSOC, Substantive Session (July 23, 1992) (on file with author).

60. *See, e.g., Report of the Economic and Social Council for the year 1986*, U.N. GAOR, 41st Sess., Supp. No. 3, at 105–107, U.N. Doc. A/40/3/Rev.1 (1985) (noting the amendments by the U.S, demanding a higher priority to work on transnational crime, and the U.K., emphasizing budgetary constraints. These are issues of particular importance to the two countries).

61. *See, e.g., Report of the Economic and Social Council for the year 1987*, U.N. GAOR, 42d Sess., Supp. No. 3, at 116–17, U.N. Doc. A/42/3/Rev. 1 (1987) (noting the fate of the Committee's two 1986 resolutions on preparations for the Eighth Congress and a review of the functioning and program of work of the United Nations in crime prevention and criminal justice which were held over for a year and then adopted in amended form).

62. *1989 ECOSOC Report, supra* note 53, at 116–18. (There were no abstentions.) The United States, which had complained previously about the Cuban human rights record, its relationship with the drug cartel, and about its quick execution of alleged Cuban drug dealers, recorded a more neutral explanation of vote:

[The U.S. representative] said that the decision to hold the Congress away from the United Nations office at Vienna was regrettable. Her delegation was concerned that the resources available to the Crime Prevention and Criminal Justice Branch of the Centre for Social Development and Humanitarian Affairs had decreased, even as its commitments had increased. Moreover, holding the Congress in Vienna would have made it possible for all members to attend.

U.N. Doc. E/1989/SR.15, at 19 (1989).

questions, but this was not the case.[63] Similarly, there is no formal procedure for representation of the Crime Prevention Commission at the ECOSOC meeting at which its report is being adopted, although the Secretariat will normally make a brief introduction[64] (which some members of ECOSOC may even contrive to find brilliant or masterful).

Occasionally, for the crime questions, a national delegation will be joined in ECOSOC by personnel from the nation's capital representing Justice, Interior, the Attorney-General's Department, the Home Office, or the like. However, the cast of characters present is usually from the permanent missions in New York or Geneva, as the case may be.[65] This cast typically includes the same foreign affairs personnel who cover human rights issues and attend the Third Committee of the General Assembly later in the year. Some decisions on speeches, votes, and co-sponsorships will be taken entirely in New York. Others will be filtered through the capital—including departments other than foreign affairs. It all depends on the particular issue and on how much discretion the delegation in question is afforded at United Nations headquarters. Many of the delegates in fact work on the criminal justice issue throughout a New York posting lasting for several years and gain considerable expertise on it. Some of them even attend meetings of the Commission in Vienna as part of their country's delegation, although they are more likely to work New York/Geneva—the standard human rights axis—than New York/Vienna.[66]

---

63. *See Rules of Procedure of the Economic and Social Council, supra* note 52 at chapter XII. Entitled "Participation by Non-Members of the Council," this chapter deals with the participation of states that are not members of the Council (or even of the U.N.); National Liberation Movements; the President of the Trusteeship Council; representatives of the Specialized Agencies; and other intergovernmental organizations. Surely, in such a context, it ought to refer to representatives of the Council's subsidiary organs.

64. Rule 37 of the *Rules of Procedure of the Functional Commissions of the Economic and Social Council*, provides:

> The commission shall submit to the Council a report, which shall normally not exceed thirty-two pages, on the work of each session containing a concise summary of recommendations and a statement of issues requiring action by the Council. It shall as far as practicable frame its recommendations and resolutions in the form of drafts for approval by the Council.

Supra note 4. The thirty-two page limit appears to have fallen into desuetude. The Commission is not authorized to keep summary records. *Supra* note 7.

65. Some New York-based personnel will find their way to Geneva and, less often, vice versa.

66. Although a number of them followed the women's human rights issues when those issues were staffed out of Vienna.

E. The Interregional and Regional Preparatory Meetings

Congresses have in the past been preceded by a series of smaller scale[67] meetings devoted to a preliminary exploration of the topics selected for discussion at the larger gathering. This included, to the extent available, an examination of the documentation and draft instruments for the congress.[68] For example, in preparation for the 1990 Havana Congress, five Interregional Preparatory Meetings took place in Vienna during 1988,[69] one devoted to each of the five congress "topics." The primary players in each of these meetings were the members of a group of ten experts assembled by the Secretary-General, a different group for each meeting. The experts on each occasion were a mix of government officials, academics, and members of the judiciary. Each group included one or two members of the Committee on Crime Prevention and Control, that was also represented "officially" by one other member who was an additional participant with the ten. A number of governments sent observers. The crime prevention and criminal justice institutes associated with the United Nations, intergovernmental organizations and several non-governmental organizations were also represented. Each of these meetings engaged in serious work at drafting details of the instruments which the Committee on Crime Prevention and Control would ultimately forward to the congress. These interregional meetings

67. Despite the smaller scale of these meetings, they have tended to be costly. According to figures supplied by the Secretariat to the 1991 Intergovernmental Working Group, the Interregional Meetings cost the organization $220,000 for travel costs and $150,000 for conference servicing (documents and interpretation). The Regional Preparatory Meetings cost $200,000 in travel and $500,000 in conference servicing. The total cost for a congress over the five-year period was said to be $1,100,000 for conference servicing and $800,000 for "other requirements" including travel, staff support and the public information programme. This latter figure apparently included the regional and inter-regional costs. No doubt this does not fully account for the salary costs involved. *See* Chapter 2 *supra* at note 81 (noting the costs of meetings of the Committee on Crime Prevention and Control and the new Commission).

68. *See e.g., Discussion Guide for the Interregional and Regional Preparatory Meetings for the Eighth United Nations Congress on the Prevention of Crime and the Treatment of Offenders*, U.N. Doc. A/CONF.144/PM.1 (1988) (example of the discussion guide produced in the past under the auspices of the Committee). The Guide summarized the issues arising under each of the five congress topics and posed some questions for discussion. *See also Draft Discussion Guide, Ninth United Nations Congress on the Prevention of Crime and the Treatment of Offenders*, U.N. Doc. E/CN.15/1993/L.1 (1993); *Research and demonstration workshops proposed for the Ninth United Nations Congress on the Prevention of Crime and the Treatment of Offenders*, U.N. Doc. E/CN.15/1993/CRP.2 (1993).

69. *See* U.N. Docs. A/CONF.144/IPM/1–4 and A/CONF.144/IPM/5 and Corr.l. (1988) (detailing the records of these meetings).

will not be staged in the lead up to the next congress and their functions will essentially be taken over by the Commission on Crime Prevention and Criminal Justice.[70]

Further, five regional meetings took place at various sites in 1989.[71] Participation in these meetings was primarily by governmental representatives and the invitation to participate was based on membership of the five United Nations Economic Commissions—for Asia and the Pacific, Europe, Latin America and the Caribbean, Western Asia, and Africa. Discussion at these regional meetings covered all five of the congress topics. Various suggestions and re-drafts were floated at them. These were taken into account by the Committee on Crime Prevention and Control when it met early in 1990 to fine-tune the material which it was forwarding to the congress.[72] These meetings seem to have been well regarded during the reorganization process, especially by delegates from developing countries. Something the same may be expected in the preparations for 1995.[73]

70. *See* G.A. Res. 46/152, *supra* note 6, Annex, para. 30(c) (detailing preparations for the congresses only in terms of regional meetings and the potential involvement of the interregional and regional institutes therein, apparently assuming that the interregional meetings will fall by the wayside). Discontinuing these meetings is another way of emphasizing the more overtly governmental nature of the new dispensation. At the first meeting of the Commission, the Chief of the Crime Prevention and Criminal Justice Branch commented that:

> In lieu of interregional preparatory meetings . . . the Commission had been given the task of defining and considering in depth the substantive items for the provisional agenda of the Ninth Congress.

Report of the Commission on Crime Prevention and Criminal Justice on its First Session, *supra* note 19, at 78. *See also infra* note 73.

71. *See* U.N. Docs. A/CONF.144/RPM.1, A/CONF.RPM.1 Corr.1, A/CONF.144/RPM.2, A/CONF.144/RPM.2 Corr.1, A/CONF.144/RPM.3, A/CONF.144/RPM.3 Corr.1, A/CONF.144/RPM.3 Corr.2, A/CONF.144/RPM.4, A/CONF.144/RPM.4 Corr.1, A/CONF.144/5, A/CONF.144/5 Corr.1, A/CONF.144/5 Corr.2 (1989) (summarizing the events occurring at these meetings).

72. Some governments in fact raised points again in Havana that they had made in the regional meetings but which had not carried the day.

73. G.A. Res. 46/152, *supra* note 6, Annex, para. 30, subpara. (c). This states that:

> Quinquennial regional meetings should be held under the guidance of the commission on matters related to the agenda of the commission or the congresses, or on any other matters, except when a region does not consider it necessary to hold such a meeting. The interregional and regional institutes should be fully involved, as appropriate, in the organization of these meetings. The commission shall give due consideration to the need to finance such meetings, in particular in developing regions, through the regular budget of the United Nations.

Id. The region most likely to consider it not necessary is the European, where there is a

F. The Congresses

1. The Congresses in the U.N. Scheme

The congresses[74] are convened by ECOSOC every five years pursuant to its powers under Article 62 of the Charter[75] and General Assembly Resolution 415 (V) of 1950.[76] Resolution 415 (V), in the plan relating to the transfer of the functions of the International Penal and Penitentiary Commission which is annexed to it, records laconically that "The United Nations shall convene every five years an international congress similar to those previously organized by the IPPC. Resolutions adopted at such international congresses shall be communicated to the Secretary-General and, if necessary, to the policy-making bodies."

General Assembly Resolution 46/152 crystallized the common law on the congresses in the following terms:

29. The United Nations congresses on the prevention of crime and the treatment of offenders, as a consultative body of the programme, shall provide a forum for:

(a) The exchange of views between States, intergovernmental organizations, non-governmental organizations and individual experts representing various professions and disciplines;

---

considerable amount of other activity. Regional meetings in preparation for the 1995 Congress were planned for all regions to take place early in 1994. *See Progress made in the preparations for the Ninth United Nations Congress on the Prevention of Crime and the Treatment of Offenders, Report of the Secretary-General*, at 2–3, U.N. Doc. E/CN.15/1993/7 (1993).

74. *See* J. Robson, *Criminology in Evolution—The Impact of International Congresses*, 3 OTAGO L. REV. 5 (1973); M. Lopez-Rey, *The Role of the United Nations Congresses on the Prevention of Crime and the Treatment of Offenders*, FED. PROBATION, Sept. 1973, at 24; M. Lopez-Rey, *The First U.N. Congress on the Prevention of Crime and the Treatment of Offenders*, 47 J. CRIM. L. CRIMINOLOGY. & POLICE. SCI. 526 (1957); J.E. Hall Williams, *Two International Congresses*, 1 BRIT. J. CRIMINOLOGY 254 (1961); T.P. Morris, *Second United Nations Congress on Prevention of Crime and the Treatment of Offenders*, 1 BRIT. J. CRIMINOLOGY 261 (1961); W.H. Nagel, *United Nations Congress on Prevention of Crime and Treatment of Offenders, London, August, 1960*, 1 EXCERPTA CRIMINOLOGICA 161 (1961); T. Mathiesen, *The U.N. Congress as a Culture* (delivered at the 18th Annual Conference of the European Group for the Study of Deviance and Social Control, in cooperation with the Coornhert-League for Penal Reform, Amsterdam) (Sept. 1990) (on file with author). Professor Mathiesen's paper is a delightful send-up of his experience as a member of the Norwegian delegation to the 1985 Congress in Milan. It should be required reading for anyone who takes the enterprise too seriously. Professor Mathiesen discusses five "cultural norms" of the congresses: "Always show that what you are doing at the conference is of the greatest importance," "Show that you know and are known by many others," "Always show the greatest possible respect for everyone else at the conference," "Do everything you can to reach agreement on the issues raised," "Make sure that what is decided never conflicts with the rules of your own country."

75. *See supra* note 48.

76. *See supra* note 49.

(b) The exchange of experiences in research, law and policy development;

(c) The identification of emerging trends and issues in crime prevention and criminal justice;

(d) The provision of advice and comments to the commission on crime prevention and criminal justice on selected matters submitted to it by the commission;

(e) The submission of suggestions, for the consideration of the commission regarding possible subjects for the programme of work.[77]

The resolution goes on to provide for certain "arrangements" that should be implemented "in order to enhance the effectiveness of the programme and to achieve optimal results."[78] The congresses should be held every five years, for a period between five and ten working-days. The Crime Prevention Commission must select precisely defined topics for the congresses, in order to ensure a focused and productive discussion. Finally, action-oriented workshops on topics selected by the Commission, as part of a congress program, and ancillary (NGO) meetings associated with the congresses, should be encouraged.[79]

2. The Eighth Congress as an Example

In the discussion that follows, I shall use the Eighth Congress in Havana as exemplary of the way in which congresses have been proceeding.[80] The discussion will include some suggestions for the more efficient conduct of business by the congresses and I return to the theme of improving the modus operandi of the congresses in Chapter 5.[81]

Invitations to attend the Havana Congress were issued by the United Nations Secretary-General to the following, now "traditional," list: representatives of states; observers from organizations and from national liberation movements that have received a standing invitation from the General Assembly to participate in the sessions and work of all international conferences convened under its auspices; representa-

77. G.A. Res. 46/152, *supra* note 6, Annex, para. 29.

78. *Id.* Annex, para. 30.

79. *Id.* Workshops are being planned for 1995 on extradition and international cooperation; mass media and crime prevention; urban policy and crime prevention; prevention of violent crime; environmental protection at the national and international levels; and international cooperation and assistance in the management of the criminal justice system.

80. *See also* R.S. Clark, *The Eighth United Nations Congress on the Prevention of Crime and the Treatment of Offenders*, 1 CRIM. L. F. 513 (1990); Note, *Eighth UN Crime Congress*, 16 COMMONWEALTH L. BULL. 1381 (1990) (discussing the Havana Congress).

81. Chapter 5 *infra*, at notes 2–23.

tives designated by organs of the United Nations; representatives of the specialized agencies of the United Nations and the International Atomic Energy Agency, as observers; observers designated by interested governmental organizations; observers designated by interested non-governmental organizations in consultative status with the Economic and Social Council; individual experts invited to participate as observers in their individual capacity; expert consultants invited by the Secretariat; officials of the Secretariat; and other persons invited by the United Nations.[82] So far as states are concerned, the invitation suggested that "Delegations may include experts in the field of crime prevention and criminal justice and those concerned with policies and programs affecting the prevention and control of crime and delinquency."[83] Individual experts were said to include "members of the teaching staff of universities, of criminological or social research institutes and of national non-governmental organizations concerned with crime prevention and the treatment of offenders, staff of correctional establishments and institutions for juvenile delinquents, members of courts and bar associations, social workers, youth workers, specialists in education, specialists in behavioral sciences and police officials."[84] The gathering, then, potentially and in practice, includes a very wide mix of officials, scholars, and other practitioners of the criminal justice area. The range of views represented at the gatherings is thus much larger than is the case with ordinary governmental meetings within the United Nations. Because of the technical nature of much of the discussion, the meetings are perhaps less politicized than is the case of many international gatherings. Nevertheless, since the 1970s, the congresses have ultimately become substantially intergovernmental meetings with everybody else there more or less on sufferance, and only governments may vote on the adoption of resolutions.

The 1990 Congress was attended by representatives of one hundred twenty-seven governments,[85] and delegations from Palestine, the African National Congress, various United Nations offices and organs, two

---

82. *See Eighth United Nations Congress on the Prevention of Crime and the Treatment of Offenders, Information for Participants* 4–5, U.N. Doc. A/CONF.144/INF.1 (1990). *See also Memorandum to the Assistant Director, Crime Prevention and Criminal Justice Section, Fifth United Nations Congress on the Prevention of Crime and the Treatment of Offenders—Question of Issuing Invitation to States not Members of the United Nations and to Individual Participants from such States,* 1975 U.N. Jurid. Y.B. 174.

83. *Information for Participants supra* note 82, at 4.

84. *Id.* at 5.

85. Amongst these one hundred twenty-seven participants were four non-Member States of the United Nations, namely the two Koreas, Switzerland and the Holy See. The two Koreas have since become Members.

specialized agencies, six other intergovernmental organizations, and fifty nongovernmental organizations, along with about four hundred individuals who participated in a personal capacity. Several smaller countries could manage only one person in their delegation—either from the capital, the country's diplomatic mission in Havana or somewhere relatively nearby. Such delegations were hard-pressed to follow what were often three simultaneous formal meetings[86] and some informal ones as well[87] and were obviously forced to be selective.[88]

ECOSOC produces Provisional Rules of Procedure for the congresses[89] which are adopted (with any necessary modifications) by the Congress at its first meeting. At the first ceremonial and plenary meeting, the Havana Congress, in accordance with tradition, elected the head of the Cuban delegation as President of the Congress. The plen-

86. *See infra* note 91.

87. *See infra* pp. 78–79.

88. The New Zealand delegation, of which I was part, had four members and we were able to cover the formal field quite well, but had some difficulty attending the ancillary meetings. *See infra* at note 93 (describing the ancillary meetings).

89. *See Eighth United Nations Congress on the Prevention of Crime and the Treatment of Offenders, Rules of Procedure*, U.N. Doc. A/CONF.144/2 (1990). After each Congress, the Committee on Crime Prevention and Control used to be charged with making appropriate recommendations for amendments it deems necessary in the light of experience. *Id.* R. 61. There was some awkwardness at the Sixth Congress when some delegations insisted upon changing, in a particular case and by a simple majority, the requirement of a two-thirds majority for the adoption of substantive resolutions. *See* U.N. Doc. E/AC.57/43 (1980), and *Sixth Congress United Nations Congress on the Prevention of Crime and the Treatment of Offenders, Caracas, Venezuela, 25 August–5 September 1980, Report prepared by the Secretariat*, at 79, U.N. Doc. A/CONF.87/14/Rev.1 (1981). The Secretariat's suggestions for avoiding that problem in the future were not followed. U.N. Doc. E/AC.57/43, The Rules adopted for Milan in E.S.C Decision 1985/134, U.N. ESCOR, Supp. No. 1, at 43, U.N. Doc. E/1985/85 (1985), were not sorely tested as all decisions at Milan were made by consensus. When the Committee took up the Rules after Milan, draft standards for U.N. conferences in general were before the General Assembly U.N. Docs. A/40/611 Add. 1 (1985); G.A. Decision 40/421, U.N. GAOR, 40th Sess., Supp. No. 53, at 346, U.N. Doc. A/40/53 (1986). Hence the Committee deferred the item. *See Committee on Crime Prevention and Control, Report on the Ninth Session, Vienna, 5–14 March 1986*, at 21, U.N. Doc. E/1986/25 (1986). Nothing relevant came of the exercise in the General Assembly. Thus, ECOSOC ultimately approved for Havana the same rules of procedure adopted by the Seventh Congress "on the understanding that the Eighth Congress should make every effort to reach a consensus on all substantive matters." E.S.C. Res. 1989/69, para. 14, U.N. ESCOR, Supp. No. 1, at 58, U.N. Doc. E/1989/89 (1989). Rules prepared for the 1995 Congress by the Commission on Crime Prevention and Criminal Justice are essentially the same as for 1990 with one dramatic difference. Rule 28 provides that draft resolutions must be submitted to the Secretary-General of the Congress four months prior to the Congress. *See Draft Rules of Procedure for the United Nations Congresses on the Prevention of Crime and the Treatment of Offenders*, Annex to E.S.C. Res. 1993/32 (1993).

ary then adopted the Provisional Rules of Procedure by consensus, whereupon the President of the Congress made the following statement:

Without prejudice to the rules of procedure adopted by the Congress, my understanding is that this Congress should make every effort to attain consensus in all substantive matters.[90]

Under the rules the 1990 Congress was to conduct its business in a plenary group and in two committees of the whole, Committee I and Committee II. Should a vote be necessary on a substantive matter in the plenary, a two-thirds vote of the representatives present and voting would be required.[91] "Present and voting" was defined as meaning casting an affirmative or negative vote, so that abstentions would not be counted for this purpose. The plenary elected a Chair of each of the Committees, and the Committees themselves elected a Vice-Chair and a Rapporteur. A Rapporteur-General and a First Vice-President of the congress were also chosen, as were twenty-three states (as opposed to individuals) as Vice-Presidents. Together with the President, these officers constituted the General Committee—a kind of steering committee, responsible for the smooth flow of the business of the congress. Several of these officers participated vigorously in the inevitable "informal consultations" which are necessary to keep such an international gathering afloat.

The overall theme for the 1990 Congress was "International Cooperation in Crime Prevention and Criminal Justice for the Twenty-First Century." Within this general theme were five topics:

- Crime prevention and criminal justice in the context of development: realities and perspectives of international co-operation (Topic I);
- Criminal justice policies in relation to problems of imprisonment, other penal sanctions and alternative measures (Topic II);
- Effective national and international action against:
  (a) Organized crime,
  (b) Terrorist criminal activities (Topic III);
- Prevention of delinquency, juvenile justice and the protection of the young: policy approaches and directions (Topic IV); and

90. *Eighth United Nations Congress on the Prevention of Crime and the Treatment of Offenders, Havana, 27 August–7 September 1990, Report prepared by the Secretariat,* at 215, U.N. Doc. A/CONF.144/28/Rev.1 (1991).

91. *Rules of Procedure, supra* note 89, R.33.

- United nations norms and guidelines in crime prevention and criminal justice: implementation and priorities for future standard-setting (Topic V).

Topic I, which included such matters as crime trends, prevention of urban crime, international co-operation and mutual assistance, organized crime, and drug trafficking, was considered directly in plenary. Topic II, which included computerization of criminal justice, alternatives to imprisonment, principles for the treatment of prisoners, and prisoners with HIV/AIDS, together with Topic IV, which included the prevention of juvenile delinquency and domestic violence, were dealt with in Committee I. Topic III opened up such questions as model treaties on extradition and mutual assistance and action against terroristic criminal activities. Both Topic III and Topic V, which invited a discussion of new instruments (such as those on the use of force and firearms by police, the role of lawyers and of prosecutors), capital punishment, and procedures for evaluating the extent to which states implement United Nations norms and guidelines, would be considered in Committee II.

In addition to attending the plenary and committee sessions, delegates to a congress need to keep track of meetings of their regional grouping which take place throughout the congress to share information and discuss strategy. For example, the West European and Other Group, which was perhaps the most active regional grouping in Havana, met the day before the congress began and again on each working day before that day's congress meetings began. (It was preceded, even earlier in the morning, by a European Community meeting.)

As will be discussed further in Chapter 5, the Eighth Congress adopted a total of forty-five resolutions, twenty-one on the recommendation of the Committee on Crime Prevention and Control and twenty-four introduced by governments in Havana.[92] This undoubtedly placed some stress on the system and it is unlikely that such a marathon effort will occur in subsequent meetings.

3. The Ancillary Meetings

As has been noted, the congresses are attended by a large number of NGO representatives and by unaffiliated individual experts. Numerous ancillary meetings organized by the NGOs are a striking feature of the occasion. In fact, many of the most interesting sessions in terms of the basic networking function of the congresses—the sharing of

92. Chapter 5 *infra*, at notes 2–9.

ideas—are the ancillary ones. Yet, it is difficult for government delegates to attend ancillary meetings which are often scheduled at the same time as the formal meetings. The feedback between the two spheres is haphazard at best. NGO representatives do not speak in the official meetings as frequently as one might expect or even as frequently as the congress rules seem to contemplate—although many of them lobby vigorously behind the scenes and have had some more direct input earlier in the whole process.

Given the importance of the networking aspect of the congresses, how to get the twain to meet more ought to receive further thought before the 1995 congress. At the first meeting of the Commission, I made the suggestion that, for at least two days of the congress, the formal part of the meetings should be suspended so that delegates might attend the NGO meetings without the fear of missing something.[93] The suggestion went nowhere.

4. Giving More Focus to the Congresses

The congresses have always been something of a three-ring circus (four rings, if the ancillary meetings are counted) and the relevant provisions of Resolution 46/152[94] both assume that the congresses will continue and that some efforts will be made to rationalize the proceedings. Criticism of the modus operandi of the gatherings is hardly new. Speaking of the Second Congress, held in London in 1960, Professor Hall Williams commented:

The overall impression of the Congress was one of confusion of aims and dispersion of energies which could have been used to better effect. One cannot attend one of these vast international jamborees without wondering who is benefiting from the experience, and what contribution is being made in the debates (and outside) towards a deeper knowledge and understanding of the subject. Admirable as were the preliminary papers, excellent as were the rapporteurs, distinguished as were many of the participants, one felt a sense of dissatisfaction at the level of debate and the impossibility of getting anywhere

93. Statement of the Observer of New Zealand to the Commission on Crime Prevention and Criminal Justice (April 24, 1992) (on file with author). *See Report of the Commission on Crime Prevention and Criminal Justice on its First Session, supra* note 19, at 80. The suggestion in the text that Governments might learn something from NGOs was hardly greeted with vast enthusiasm. Some governments are, however, evidently supportive of the meetings: the Alliance of NGOs on Crime Prevention and Criminal Justice, which coordinates the ancillary meetings, reports that funding is received from two different governments for the simultaneous translation of the meetings. Letter from Joseph M. Callan, Executive Secretary, Alliance of NGOs on Crime Prevention and Criminal Justice, to Roger S. Clark (Oct. 12, 1992).

94. *See supra* notes 77 & 78.

through listening to them. Surely it is not beyond the wit of man to devise a scheme for an international convention where some really intelligent discussion could be assured to those who attend and by those who take part. Much of the time in London was occupied in dreary accounts by government delegates of the situation in their respective countries, and what was being achieved. Much of the rest of the time went in banal remarks and puerile arguments unworthy of such a distinguished gathering.[95]

His suggestions about what might be done to improve the situation still have a timely ring:

(1) delegates should be screened in some way for their credentials, so as to achieve a uniformly high standard of representation; (2) small group discussions by experts on particular subjects should be an important part of the proceedings; (3) governments should be encouraged to submit their progress reports in advance and they should be circulated in the papers rather than orally delivered; (4) there should be more lectures, by carefully chosen persons, followed by free discussion; (5) broad general topics should not be selected for general discussion, and broad general discussions should be discouraged: there must be some specific focus of attention.[96]

At least some of these concerns were on the minds of the Crime Prevention Commission in its 1992 resolution on preparations for the 1995 congress, which it forwarded to ECOSOC.[97] After making some provisional choices in topics,[98] the resolution requested the Crime Prevention Commission to finalize the matter at its 1993 session, taking into account that the Ninth Congress should deal with a limited number of precisely defined substantive topics that reflect urgent needs of the world community; the final selection should be made in accordance with the priorities set by the Crime Prevention Commission; and there should be action-oriented research and demonstration workshops and ancillary meetings.[99]

---

95. Hall Williams, *supra* note 74, at 260–61. U.N. congresses are not the only international meetings accused of being circuses or jamborees. Similar criticism of the congresses of the International Political Science Association has also been found. J. Barents, *Vanity Fair? International congresses reconsidered*, 53 AM. POL. SCI. REV. 1090 (1959).

96. Hall Williams, *supra* note 74, at 261.

97. E.S.C. Res. 1992/24, U.N. ESCOR, Supp. No. 1, at 32, U.N. Doc. E/1992/92 (1992).

98. *Id.* para. 1. For the final topics, *see infra* note 99.

99. *Id.* para. 2. The final topics chosen for 1995 are

(a) International cooperation and practical technical assistance for strengthening the rule of law: promoting the United Nations crime prevention and criminal justice programme;

(b) Action against national and transnational economic and organized crime, and the

G. The General Assembly

The General Assembly holds its regularly scheduled annual meeting in New York between the third Tuesday in September and mid-December.[100] It functions through the instrumentality of a plenary and six committees of the whole.[101] One of these committees is the Third Committee which deals with Social, Humanitarian and Cultural matters. To it are assigned, *inter alia*, human rights issues and crime prevention and criminal justice issues. Crime Prevention and Criminal Justice appears each year as a separate item or sub-item on the agenda,[102] although aspects of the matter inevitably arise under the various human rights items also.[103]

---

role of criminal law in the protection of the environment: national experiences and international cooperation;

(c) Criminal justice systems: management and improvement of police and other law-enforcement agencies, prosecution, courts, corrections; and the role of lawyers;

(d) Crime prevention strategies, in particular as related to crimes in urban areas and juvenile and violent criminality, including the question of victims: assessment and new perspectives.

E.S.C. Res. 1993/32, entitled *Preparations for the Ninth United Nations Congress on the Prevention of Crime and the Treatment of Offenders*.

100. *Rules of Procedure of the General Assembly*, R. 1, U.N. Doc. A/50/Rev.15 (1985). Sometimes, it is necessary to resume the session at a low key level in the New Year with whoever is around in order to conclude business.

101. *Id.* R. 98. Through 1992 there were seven committees. For some useful background on the Assembly, *see* J. Quinn, *The General Assembly into the 1990s*, in THE UNITED NATIONS AND HUMAN RIGHTS: A CRITICAL APPRAISAL, *supra* note 45, at 55 (thoughtful comments by experienced Australian representative). Quinn, *id.* at 60–61, has some thoughts on the relationship between the "social" and "human rights" issues in the work of the Assembly.

102. *See, e.g., Annotated Preliminary List of Items to be Included in the Provisional Agenda of the Forty-Fifth Regular Session of the General Assembly*, Agenda Item 103, at 298–300, U.N. Doc. A/45/100 (1990) (referring to congresses since 1955 and action taken by the Assembly in the past five sessions). The 1990 Agenda, however, did not specifically refer to the *Report of the Eighth Congress, supra* note 90, that was in fact the main subject of the discussion. In a resolution adopted by the Assembly that year, entitled *Rationalization of the Work of the Third Committee*, the Assembly determined that in the future there would be a general "Social development" item, with two sub-items to be discussed separately: (a) Questions relating to the world social situation and to youth, aging, disabled persons and the family; and (b) Crime prevention and criminal justice. G.A. Res. 45/175, *Rationalization of the Work of the Third Committee*, U.N. GAOR, 45th Sess., Supp. No. 49A, at 287, U.N. Doc. A/45/49 (1991). Under the crime prevention and criminal justice rubric, the Third Committee would discuss crime prevention and criminal justice in 1991, 1993, etc.; international co-operation in combating organized crime in 1992, 1994, etc.; and the congresses every five years beginning in 1995.

103. *See, e.g.*, Chapter 5 *infra*, at notes 47–49, 52 (detailing the resolutions adopted in 1985 and 1990 under the human rights in the administration of justice item).

The diplomats who work the Third Committee are, by and large, the same people who operate at ECOSOC, either because their states are members of the Council or because they attend the Council as observers. They are usually expert in human rights matters. Especially at the General Assembly session immediately following a congress, Third Committee diplomats numbers may be augmented for the crime prevention item by extras from central casting in the capital. These will typically be personnel from justice, police or interior departments who were associated with the congress in some way, including in the past a handful of members of the Committee on Crime Prevention and Control. As in the case of ECOSOC meetings,[104] some of the delegations to the Third Committee have freedom of action in New York while others must clear their position through the capital. A cadre of delegates whose countries have a special interest in the topic has formed in New York. These delegates, in conjunction with the Secretariat, tend to anchor the many consultations that are necessary for a satisfactory draft to emerge in the Third Committee, to provide co-sponsorships and to ensure the necessary votes. Representatives of the country which has been the host for a congress will normally play a prominent role in steering through approval of any instruments adopted at that congress.

The Third Committee is authorized to keep summary records of its meetings.[105] Thus, to the extent that discussion takes place on the record, it can be researched. Occasionally, governments will repeat statements in plenary in explanation of a vote that they consider important. There a verbatim record is kept.[106]

In the case of the earlier United Nations congresses, a report went to ECOSOC from the Secretary-General and the General Assembly did not formally concern itself with the results.[107] Thus, as will be noted, it was initially ECOSOC that, in 1957, passed on the work-product of the First United Nations Congress of 1955—the Standard Minimum Rules for the Treatment of Prisoners (Rules).[108] It was not until 1971 that the General Assembly first added its imprimatur to those Rules.[109] In recent years, however, the congress report has been considered at the

104. *See supra* p. 70.

105. *See Control and Limitation of Documentation, Note by the Secretary-General*, at 23, U.N. Doc. A/INF.46/1 (1991).

106. *Id.* at 21.

107. *See* G.A. Res. 415 (V), *supra* note 49 (allowing for some flexibility by stating that the resolutions of the congresses "shall be communicated to the Secretary-General and, if necessary, to the policy-making bodies").

108. *See* Chapter 5 *infra*, at note 28.

109. *Id.* at note 35.

session of the General Assembly which begins shortly after the end of the congress, without first being passed upon by ECOSOC. (The congresses have been fitted into the United Nations calendar in such a way as to take place in late August to early September.) This pattern seems about to change: the Ninth Congress is currently scheduled for January or February 1995; it seems likely that its recommendations will go to the Commission on Crime Prevention and Criminal Justice in April, to ECOSOC in July and then, if relevant, to the General Assembly at the end of the year.

The Report of the Commission on Crime Prevention and Criminal Justice is not formally placed before the Third Committee for action. However, aspects of the Council's work may be referred to in the course of debate and the relevant portions of the Report of ECOSOC are before the Assembly's Third Committee.

At least in the past, members of the Third Committee tended to consider resolutions from the congresses with some care but then conclude that only the most minor changes were possible. Two arguments predominated. One was that the congress and the Committee on Crime Prevention and Control were experts. They had passed on the documents and were presumed to have known what they were doing. The second argument was that, in retrospect, no one in New York was able to be sure that they could reconstruct those political compromises which were necessary in the prior forums—the Committee and the congress—especially since explanations in the preparatory work are seldom revealing. In such a situation, it is best to let sleeping dogs lie, lest, to mix a metaphor, the whole package should unravel.[110] The upshot is that, subject to occasional, quite minor tinkering and possible dispute about the strength of the approving verbs,[111] the work of the recent congresses has quickly received some sort of General Assembly seal of approval. It seems reasonable to assume that, with the new governmental structure of the Crime Prevention Commission as the main preparatory body, this deference will be at least as striking.

---

110. *See* L.L. Lamborn, *The United Nations Declaration on Victims: Incorporating "Abuse of Power"*, 19 RUTGERS L.J. 59, 80 (1987) (discussing reluctance even to clean up drafting anomalies in the 1985 Victims Declaration); *Crime Prevention and Criminal Justice, Report of the Third Committee*, at 4–7, U.N. Doc. A/45/756 (1990) (noting the minimal changes made by the Third Committee to the Havana instruments in 1990. In the case of the 1990 Congress, the main advocate of some changes was the U.S. which had, however, offended some by not attending the meeting in Cuba and had some difficulty in getting anyone to focus on the merits of its positions. The United States was able to garner only minimal support).

111. *See* Chapter 5 *infra*, at notes 59–61.

H. The Institutes

What are often referred to as "United Nations Institutes,"[112] or the "Crime Prevention and Criminal Justice Program Network,"[113] is a heterogeneous collection of bodies, each with a relationship arrangement with the Secretariat, not all of which use the word "Institute" in their names. Included in these bodies are:

(a) the Rome-based United Nations Interregional Crime and Justice Research Institute (UNICRI), a United Nations entity that operates on an inter-regional basis;

(b) four affiliated regional institutes: the United Nations Asia and Far East Institute for the Prevention of Crime and the Treatment of Offenders (UNAFEI), at Fuchu, Japan (covering Asia and the Pacific); the United Nations Latin American Institute for the Prevention of Crime and the Treatment of Offenders (ILANUD), at San José, Costa Rica (covering Latin America and the Caribbean); the European Institute for Crime Prevention and Control, affiliated with the United Nations (HEUNI), at Helsinki, Finland (covering Europe); and the United Nations African Regional Institute for the Prevention of Crime and the Treatment of Offenders (UNAFRI), at Kampala, Uganda (covering Africa);

(c) three associate entities that also cooperate closely with the United Nations: the Arab Security Studies and Training Centre (ASSTC), at Riyadh, Saudi Arabia (a regional center covering the Arab world); the Australian Institute of Criminology (AIC), at Woden, Australia (a sub-regional institute, covering the Pacific), and the International Centre for Criminal Law Reform and Criminal Justice Policy, at Vancouver, Canada (an international centre).[114]

---

112. *See* THE UNITED NATIONS AND CRIME PREVENTION, *supra* note 40, at 36 (explaining the derivation of this term).

113. *See Progress report of the Secretary-General, Activities of the United Nations Interregional Crime and Justice Research Institute and the regional institutes for crime prevention and criminal justice*, U.N. Doc. E/CN.15/1992/3 (1992) (referring to the term used in this report) [hereinafter *Progress report on the institutes*]. The *Progress report* is reprinted in 3 CRIM. L. F. 481 (1992).

114. *Id.* at 3–4. E.S.C. Res. 1992/22, pt. IV, para. 3(h) foreshadows the affiliation of more entities. It encourages the Secretary-General to develop "criteria and procedures for the creation and affiliation of new United Nations institutes or centres that would join those referred to in paragraph 35 of General Assembly resolution 46/152 for consideration by the Commission at its second session, and the favourable review of requests by groups of States to establish United Nations subregional institutes." A fourth associate entity, the International Institute of Higher Studies in Criminal Sciences, is formally joining the network after a long informal relationship. This Institute, founded in 1972 at Siracusa, Italy, is devoted to studies, research and the advancement of criminal sciences,

As well as cooperating with the Crime Prevention and Criminal Justice Branch, the institutes also cooperate with the United Nations regional economic and social commissions, other regional organizations, the governments of countries in their regions, other entities, and experts.

General Assembly Resolution 46/152 contemplates that increased use should be made of the institutes for program support. It exhorts the organization and the Member States to support their activities, giving particular attention to the needs of institutes located in developing countries. "Given the important role of such institutes," the resolution provides, rather clumsily, "their contributions to policy development and implementation, and their resource requirements, should be fully integrated into the overall programme, especially those of the African Regional Institute for the Prevention of Crime and the Treatment of Offenders."[115] The resolution also suggests that the Commission may request that the institutes, subject to the availability of resources, implement selected elements of the program. The Commission may also suggest areas for inter-institute activities.[116]

UNICRI has been described,[117] with perhaps a little hyperbole, as the "centerpiece" of the network. When it was originally established as the United Nations Social Defense Research Institute (UNSDRI) in 1968, it was conceived as the research arm of the crime program. Its work, however, expanded naturally from research to training and field activities, especially to assist developing countries. Hence, in 1989 a new Statute was adopted transforming it into its present guise.[118] According to the Statute[119]:

The objective of the Institute shall be to contribute, through research, training, field activities and the collection, exchange and dissemination of information, to the formulation and implementation of improved policies in the field of crime prevention and control, due regard being paid to the integration of such policies within broader policies for socio-economic change and development, and to the protection of human rights.

---

with particular emphasis on the development of human rights. *See Activities of the United Nations Interregional Crime and Justice Research Institute and other institutes, Progress report of the Secretary-General*, U.N. Doc. E/CN.15/1993/8 (1993). Negotiations have been entered into with a proposed International Center for the Prevention of Crime at Montreal.

115. G.A. Res. 46/152, *supra* note 6, Annex, para. 35.

116. *Id.* Annex, para. 37.

117. *The United Nations and Crime Prevention, supra* note 40, at 42.

118. *Statute of the United Nations Interregional Crime and Justice Research Institute*, E.S.C. Res. 1989/56, U.N. ESCOR, Supp. No. 1, at 41, U.N. Doc. No. (1990).

119. *Id.* art. 1.

UNICRI regularly reports an impressive amount of activity under these general rubrics. A recent report lists numerous research projects and scientific meetings; training courses in Tunisia, Malta, Rome, Naples, and Verona; technical co-operation efforts in Italy, Argentina, Uruguay, and Egypt (and a gala fund raising effort for a project supporting juvenile justice reform in Myanmar); and publication, library, and documentation services.[120] Apart from the Arab Security Studies and Training Center,[121] UNICRI is the best-heeled part of the enterprise—better staffed and funded than the Crime Prevention Branch itself. In 1992, UNICRI's core staff consisted of twenty-four members, shortly to be augmented by the arrival of three additional researchers. About fifty international consultants participate in the implementation of the work program on a regular basis. The projected budget for 1992 was $4,850,409.[122]

The United Nations regional institutes have an active program of research, training courses, technical assistance, seminars, and publications. The establishment of these institutes was originally suggested during regional meetings held in 1953 and 1954 in preparation for the First Congress. The Secretariat has explained the background to them in the following manner:

> It was never intended that United Nations recommendations on criminal justice policies would be adopted wholesale and uniformly by all Member States. There are just too many differences in national histories, cultures, economic structures and governmental institutions for this to be feasible or desirable, at least within the foreseeable future. Yet, if all Member States are left entirely to their own devices in the implementation of policies, the impact of carefully considered and formulated standards and the world-wide improvement of the functioning of criminal justice would be eroded. . . . Regional centers of activity, which can take into account the cultures and traditions of groupings of nations integrally linked by geography and contiguous histories, serve as effective halfway houses between the dual exigencies of national sovereignty and international standardization. They exist closer to the ground, so to speak, than the central bodies of the United Nations and are more convenient when requests for guidance and assistance are submitted by Member States.[123]

---

120. *Report on the Activities of the United Nations Interregional Crime and Justice Research Institute for the Period 1 November 1989 to 31 March 1992*, U.N. Doc. E/CN.15/1992/CRP.6 (1992).

121. *See infra* note 137.

122. *See supra* note 120, at 2 (including salaries for the budget figure). The Secretary-General's *Progress report on the institutes*, states that UNICRI's "operational budget for 1992 is $2.8 million (excluding salaries)." *Supra* note 113. At the same time, the Crime Branch's 1992 budget of about $1.6 million, most of it for salaries, supported eleven professional and six general service posts. *See* Chapter 1 *supra*, at notes 44–46.

123. THE UNITED NATIONS AND CRIME PREVENTION, *supra* note 40, at 36.

First of the regional institutes to be operative was UNAFEI, established under a 1961 agreement between the U.N. and the Government of Japan.[124] A 1959 agreement with the Government of Brazil for a Latin American institute[125] never became operative and ILANUD, the next institute to emerge, eventually came into being in Costa Rica in 1975.[126] HEUNI was established by a 1981 agreement with the Government of Finland.[127] The most recent institute, UNAFRI, was established in Uganda in 1987 under the auspices of the Economic Commission for Africa.[128] For the most part, UNAFEI, ILANUD, and HEUNI are supported by the host government, although ILANUD in particular relies on some grant funds from agencies such as the United Nations Development Fund (UNDP).[129] UNAFRI, the weakest of the institutes in terms of resources, is at present funded largely by UNDP, with a contribution of premises and facilities by the host government and assessed contributions (the overwhelming majority of them unpaid) from the parties to its Statute.[130] Of the regional institutes, UNAFEI has the largest complement of staff, with nine "faculty" and twenty administrative, clerical, and technical staff, all seconded by the Japanese Government. Four or five visiting experts from abroad are also invited to each training program.[131] The staffs of the other United Nations institutes are quite modest. HEUNI, for example, has five full-time people, a director, one senior researcher, two program officers

124. *Asia and Far East Institute for the Prevention of Crime and the Treatment of Offenders*, 20 INT'L REV. CRIM. POL'Y 76 (1962); Agreement between the United Nations and the Government of Japan for the Establishment of the Asia and Far East Institute for the Prevention of Crime and the Treatment of Offenders, *signed on* March 15, 1961, 397 U.N.T.S. 200 (1961).

125. *Id.* at 76, n.1.

126. *Establishment of the United Nations Latin American Institute for the Prevention of Crime and the Treatment of Offenders*, 33 INT'L REV. CRIM. POL'Y 65 (1977); Agreement between the United Nations and the Government of Costa Rica for the Establishment of the Latin American Institute for the Prevention of Crime and the Treatment of Offenders, *signed on* July 11, 1975, 973 U.N.T.S. 175 (1975).

127. Agreement between the Government of Finland and the United Nations for the Establishment of the Helsinki Institute for Crime Prevention and Control, Affiliated with the United Nations, *signed* Dec. 23, 1981, *amended and extended*, April 14, 1987 (on file with author).

128. *See A Brief on the African Institute for the Prevention of Crime and the Treatment of Offenders (UNAFRI): Establishment, Objectives, Progress and Work Implementation to Date*, U.N. Doc. E/CN.15/1992/CRP.8 (1992). Of the 50-odd potential members, some 26 had acceded to its Statute by 1992. *Id.* at 2.

129. *Progress Report on the Institutes, supra* note 113, at 6–14. HEUNI gets regular financial support from the Governments of Denmark, Norway, Sweden, and Finland, and, in addition, several governments have funded specific projects. *Id.* at 14.

130. *Id.* at 15.

131. *Id.* at 8.

and an office secretary.[132] UNAFRI has four officers and two support people.[133]

The Arab Security Studies and Training Center (ASSTC) was established at Riyadh in 1978 by a decision of the Second Meeting of Arab Ministers of the Interior.[134] It is both an intergovernmental organization and a specialized regional center servicing the Arab world. The ASSTC operates under the aegis of the Council of Ministers of the League of Arab States. According to the United Nations Secretariat, the ASSTC "assists Arab States in the context of the Islamic legal system, and participates in international efforts to prevent crime and victimization, maintain security and peace, promote sustained development in the context of socio-economic and cultural conditions and foster justice."[135] One special aspect of its work is program network coordination, and it has acted as host to a series of annual joint program coordination meetings among the Crime Prevention Network since 1985.[136] A second special aspect is that its training programs include advanced academic components leading to Master's degrees and other diplomas, offered through the ASSTC Graduate School of Criminal Justice at the Higher Institute of Studies. ASSTC funding comes from the Arab States. Its 1992 budget, which supported a staff of around two hundred, amounted to $11,000,000, twenty-five percent of which was allocated to staffing and seventy-five percent of which was distributed among the various programs.[137]

The Australian Institute of Criminology (AIC) was established in 1971 to provide a range of policy-related research and allied services to all Australian governments, state and federal, to criminal justice agencies, and to other client groups.[138] As a result of a memorandum of understanding which was signed between the United Nations and AIC in 1989, the Institute cooperates closely with the United Nations program. AIC does extensive research, holds conferences and seminars, has an extensive publication program, and is moving into the area of

132. *Id.* at 14.

133. *Id.* at 15.

134. Much of the information in this and the following paragraphs is derived from the *Progress Report on the Institutes, supra* note 113, at 16–18.

135. *Id.* at 16.

136. *See Report of the Seventh Joint Programme Co-ordination Meeting of the United Nations Crime Prevention and Criminal Justice Programme Network, Dharan, Kingdom of Saudi Arabi, 7–8 January 1992,* U.N. Doc. E/CN.15/1992/CRP.5 (1992). ECOSOC expressed its appreciation of this coordinating effort in E.S.C. Res. 1992/22, pt. IV, para. 1, U.N. ESCOR, Supp No. 1, at 22, U.N. Doc. E/1992/92 (1992).

137. *Progress Report on the Institutes, supra* note 113, at 18.

138. Information on the AIC has largely been derived from the *Progress Report on the Institutes, supra* note 113, at 18–20.

training and technical cooperation. AIC is funded principally by the Australian Government, supplemented by returns from contract research, conferences, and publications, and its annual budget of about three million Australian dollars supports a staff of about forty-five.

A recent addition to the group is the International Centre for Criminal Law Reform and Criminal Justice Policy (the Centre)[139] in Vancouver, British Columbia, Canada. In July 1991, following action in ECOSOC,[140] the Government of Canada entered into a memorandum of understanding with the United Nations concerning the role of the Centre.[141] The program of the Centre focuses on research and other activities related to the development and reform of criminal law. The Centre was founded by the Society for the Reform of Criminal Law, Simon Fraser University and the University of British Columbia. As an Institute, it is unique in that its resources are expected to come from a variety of public and private sources including its founders and other contributors. The Centre has obtained funding and other resources from the Canadian federal Departments of External Affairs and International Trade, Justice, and Solicitor-General, the British Columbia Law Foundation, and the Vancouver Foundation, one of the largest civic foundations in North America.

How far all these resources can be harnessed in support of the U.N. program is an open question. As the Secretariat subtly stated:

A coordination mechanism has been established and maintained by means of the annual joint programme coordination meetings, generously hosted by ASSTC. The meetings have proved a valuable contribution to the coordination effort but have not led to a consolidated alignment of programme activities within the framework of the programme budget and medium-term plan, partly because of the competing priorities of the institutes, as determined by the voluntary contributions received.[142]

I. The United Nations Criminal Justice Information Network (UNCJIN)

In 1986, ECOSOC invited the Secretariat to "establish in cooperation with the United Nations Institutes and other entities concerned, a

139. Information on the Centre has been obtained mainly from the *Progress Report on the Institutes*. *Id.* at 20–21.

140. E.S.C. Res. 1991/15, U.N. ESCOR, Supp. No. 1, at 18, U.N. Doc. E/1991/91 (1991).

141. Memorandum of Understanding Between the Government of Canada and the United Nations Concerning the International Centre for Criminal Law Reform and Criminal Justice Policy in Vancouver, Canada, signed on July 11, 1991, *annexed to* U.N. Doc. UNIS/CP/177 (1991).

142. *Progress Report on the Institutes, supra* note 113, at 22.

global crime prevention and criminal justice information network . . . including a mechanism for the centralization of inputs from non-governmental organizations and scientific institutions."[143] The result is a worldwide computer network linked through a major non-profit organization called Telecommunications Cooperative Network (TCN). This network, known popularly as UNCJIN, aims to facilitate information exchange among policy-makers, planners, practitioners, scholars, and other experts, as well as United Nations national correspondents and research institutions; provide gateways permitting the transfer of knowledge, including research results; link criminal justice documentation centers and libraries around the world; and support the establishment of computerized national and local criminal justice systems.[144] The operation was coordinated in its early life by Professor Graeme Newman at the School of Justice, State University of New York at Albany, but moves were afoot in 1993 to move its operation to the Crime Prevention and Criminal Justice Branch itself.

The following is a list of services provided to members:

Electronic Mail—members may send messages and files to other users
Public Bulletin Boards—used for open forums and group exchanges on selected topics
International Calendar of Events and Meetings—includes updates on legislative reforms and court decisions
International Crime Statistics Database
Software Library—includes sources of software for criminal justice automated systems
Listing of Training Workshops and Seminars
Selected Bibliographies and Rare Data Sets
Gateways—links to other commercial data bases and services[145]

J. The World Criminal Justice Library Network

The World Criminal Justice Library Network (Library Network),[146] coordinated by the School of Criminal Justice at Rutgers University in Newark, New Jersey, was established at a conference convened by Rutgers in April 1991 in cooperation with the Crime Prevention and

143. E.S.C. Res. 1986/11, para. 5(a), U.N. ESCOR, Supp No. 1, at 16, U.N. Doc. E/1986/86 (1986).
144. AUSTRALIAN INSTITUTE OF CRIMINOLOGY, UNITED NATIONS CRIMINAL JUSTICE INFORMATION NETWORK 1 (1990).
145. *Id.* at 2.
146. *See Progress Report on United Nations Activities, supra* note 32, at 16–17.

Criminal Justice Branch.[147] Working closely with UNCJIN, the Library Network aims at making scientific and academic literature accessible to criminal justice professionals throughout the world. Among its projects, the Library Network is in the process of creating a list of criminal justice periodicals and developing plans for the sharing of bibliographical material internationally.

K. The Network of Government-Appointed National Correspondents

The General Assembly's 1950 resolution ratifying the transfer to the United Nations of the functions of the International Penal and Penitentiary Commission (IPPC)[148] contained a provision that all Members of the United Nations, and all existing members of the IPPC which are not Members of the United Nations, and any other States designated by the Economic and Social Council, shall be invited by the Council to appoint one or more representatives of expert qualifications or experience, professional or scientific, in the field of the prevention of crime and the treatment of offenders. These representatives would act as "individual correspondents."[149] Over the years, the network has grown to over 300 correspondents in 135 countries.[150]

The material received through the correspondent network is of decidedly uneven quality and it is hard to say that, as a network, the group has made a very obvious contribution to the work of the organization. It does, however, represent a reasonably informed constituency which is committed to the enterprise and can at least facilitate paper flow, in particular by contributing to the dissemination of U.N. material in the states from which the members come. Many of the group have contributed in other capacities, by becoming members of the Committee on Crime Prevention and Control or representing their countries at various meetings.

The discussion surrounding a resolution of the Eighth Congress[151]

---

147. Report of the Preparatory Conference for a World Criminal Justice Library Network (1991) (on file with author).

148. *See supra* note 49.

149. *Id.* Annex II, para. (a).

150. *Progress Report on United Nations Activities, supra* note 32, at 15.

151. *See Consolidation of the role of national correspondents, Eighth United Nations Congress on the Prevention of Crime and the Treatment of Offenders, Havana, 27 August-7 September 1990, Report prepared by the Secretariat,* at 133, U.N. Doc. A/CONF.144/28/Rev.1 (1991) (Other Resolution 5). *See also Note by the Secretary-General, United Nations Network of Government-Appointed National Correspondents in the Field of Crime Prevention and Control,* U.N. Doc. E/AC.57/1990/4 (1990).

on the consolidation of the role of the correspondents focused more attention on the group, and the Second General Meeting of National Correspondents was held during the congress.[152] In particular, the resolution tried to systematize the way data is transferred to the U.N. and to make sure that the correspondents pay particular attention to the need to update the U.N. Criminal Justice Information Network regularly. As a follow-up to these developments at the Eighth Congress, HEUNI organized the First European Seminar for National Correspondents at Helsinki in 1990. That meeting, which was attended by national correspondents from over 20 countries, adopted a set of draft guidelines on the role and functions of national correspondents, in an effort to maximize their contribution to and support of the U.N. program. These comments have been forwarded to correspondents from other regions for their critique.[153]

There is some hope for breathing life into this part of the enterprise.

L. The International Scientific and Professional Advisory Council (ISPAC)

Inclusion of the NGO and professional communities along with governmental representation has always been a feature of the crime prevention and criminal justice area. Earlier we have seen some of the tensions in the way this relationship has played out in respect of the Committee on Crime Prevention and Control and the Congresses.[154] In both New York and Vienna, an energetic Alliance of Non-Governmental Organizations on Crime Prevention and Criminal Justice (known as "The Alliance") works to coordinate efforts.[155] The Interna-

152. The first meeting had been held at the Milan Congress. In E.S.C. Res. 1989/58, ECOSOC, for the first time, provided guidelines for the appointment of correspondents. E.S.C. Res. 1989/58, U.N. ESCOR, Supp. No. 1, at 44, U.N. Doc. E/1989/89 (1989).

153. *Progress Report on United Nations Activities, supra* note 32, at 15.

154. *See supra* pp. 42–46, 78–79. Historically, the involvement of non-governmental personnel goes back at least to the early nineteenth century congresses. *See* Chapter 1 *supra* at note 48. *See also* M. López-Rey, *The Co-Operation of Non-Governmental Organizations with the United Nations in the Field of the Prevention of Crime and the Treatment of Offenders,* Associations Internationales, No. 1, 21 (1957) (describing NGOs and the program in general); Chapter 5 *infra,* note 16 (concerning NGOs and the Committee on Crime Prevention and Control).

155. Letter from Joseph M. Callan, *supra* note 16. Callan notes that:

We [members of the Alliance] were the initiating organization in developing the thrust for implementing the international prison transfer treaties that are extant today. Also, we have published a booklet on children in prison with their mothers after having surveyed systems throughout the world. In addition, we have done work on

tional Scientific and Professional Advisory Council of the United Nations for Crime Prevention and Criminal Justice (ISPAC) is an effort to further systematize some aspects of the relationship between the United Nations and those outside government. ISPAC's main object is to serve as a focal point for input into the United Nations program from nongovernmental and academic organizations active in crime prevention and criminal justice. Its work is carried out through a set of functional and resource committees. ISPAC meets annually in Milan or at a location agreed upon with the Crime Prevention Branch (its 1992 and 1993 meetings were in Courmayeur, Italy) and its work is coordinated by the Centro Nazionale di Prevenzione e Difesa Sociale, a highly regarded non-governmental organization in consultative status with the Economic and Social Council.[156] The Centro was the local organizer of the 1985 Milan Congress and is the seat of the International Coordinating Committee of four major organizations active in the crime field.[157] While the creation of such a body was foreshadowed in the Guiding Principles for Crime Prevention and Criminal Justice in the Context of Development and a New International Economic Order adopted at the Seventh Congress[158], it was not until 1991 that a generous grant from the Italian Government made possible the first meeting of the Council.[159]

The Council has a number of Resource Comittees on subjects such as

---

alternatives to incarceration and treatment of foreign prisoners. At present, we have a Working Party on Prison Health Care and one on crime prevention.

Id.

156. Relations between the Centro and the U.N. are governed by a Memorandum of Understanding Between the Centro Nazionale di Prevenzione e Difesa Sociale and the Centre for Social Development and Humanitarian Affairs of the United Nations Office that was signed at Vienna, on December 20, 1990. *See Report, International Scientific and Professional Advisory Council of the United Nations Crime Prevention and Criminal Justice Programme, First Session, Milan, Italy, 21–23 September 1991 (ISPAC 1991 Report)* (reproducing the contents of the memorandum) [hereinafter *ISPAC 1991 Report*].

157. These four major organizations are the International Association of Penal Law, International Penal and Penitentiary Foundation, International Society for Criminology, International Society of Social Defence. *See* H. Rostad, *The History of International Collaboration in Crime Prevention and Treatment of Offenders—with Special Emphasis on the Activities of the International Penal and Penitentiary Foundation*, in HEUNI Course, *supra* note 16, at 79.

158. *See Guiding Principles for Crime Prevention and Criminal Justice in the Context of Development and a New International Economic Order, Seventh United Nations Congress on the Prevention of Crime and the Treatment of Offenders, Milan, 26 August-6 September 1985, Report Prepared by the Secretariat*, Decision B of the Congress, at 5, para. 46, U.N. Doc. A/CONF.121/22/Rev.1 (1986).

159. *See generally, ISPAC 1991 Report, supra* note 156.

Victim Protection and Conflict Resolution, Crime and Justice Policy, Rights of the Child, Prisoners' Rights, Human Rights in Criminal Justice, Women in Criminal Justice and Transnational Crime. It actively facilitates expert meetings on various topics and is in the process of developing programs and activities in the following areas:

(a) Research and policy development;
(b) Implementation of United Nations norms and guidelines;
(c) Documentation and information exchange;
(d) Training; and
(e) Pilot and demonstration proposals, as well as other activities requested by the Commission or the Branch.

All of these are expected to have an operational component in terms of technical assistance and collaborative action programs.[160]

While there would undoubtedly have been a role for such a body to play when the Committee on Crime Prevention and Control composed of experts was the main catalyst in the crime prevention and criminal justice program, ISPAC may well be able to command an even more significant constituency given the intergovernmental nature of the new Crime Prevention Commission.

160. Doc. ISPAC/1 of Sept. 21, 1991, at 2, *annexed to ISPAC 1991 Report, supra* note 156.

Part II
Formulation of Norms and Standards

Chapter 4
Standard-Setting Instruments—A
Chronological Overview

A. Introduction

The absolute number of standard-setting instruments emanating from the early United Nations committees and congresses was quite small. There seems to have been a tacit understanding that the meetings would devote themselves primarily to the exchange of views and information, rather than to normative drafting. By 1985 and 1990, however, a vast amount of normative material was emerging from the congresses.[1] At the same time, more material was coming through the Committee on Crime Prevention and Control for approval by the Economic and Social Council. There is, in short, a striking contrast between the early and more recent periods so far as sheer quantity of material is concerned.

Johan Kaufmann, in his perceptive analysis of "conference diplomacy," has suggested a typology (obviously overlapping) of kinds of intergovernmental conferences which he calls "deliberative," "legislative," and "informational." A deliberative conference concentrates on general discussions and exchanges points of view on certain topics. A legislative conference endeavors to make recommendations to governments, or makes decisions which are binding upon them. An informational conference has as its main purpose the international exchange of information on specific questions.[2] In the case of earlier congresses, the understanding was that the event was mostly of a deliberative and informational nature. In the decade between 1980 and 1990, this understanding broke down and there was a veritable flood of instru-

1. *See* UNITED NATIONS DEPARTMENT OF PUBLIC INFORMATION, THE UNITED NATIONS AND CRIME PREVENTION, at 12–27, U.N. Doc. DP/1143–41016 (1991) (summarizing the subjects discussed at each of the congresses).

2. J. KAUFMANN, CONFERENCE DIPLOMACY: AN INTRODUCTORY ANALYSIS 6–7 (2d rev. ed. 1988).

ments, making the congresses more of a legislative, policy-formulating occasion.[3] Undoubtedly these were mostly worthwhile exercises, but the question was raised whether there has not, in fact, been simply too much material to absorb.[4] In part, the new arrangements for the program are designed to slow down the creation of new normative material.

Some comments on the most significant instruments follow.

B. The Instruments

1. The Standard Minimum Rules for the Treatment of Prisoners

The best known of the United Nations instruments in the area, and for two decades the only one, is the Standard Minimum Rules for the Treatment of Prisoners (Rules).[5] Major credit for the formulation of this document does not, in fact, belong to the United Nations, although the Ad Hoc Committee of Experts and the 1955 Congress both had a hand in final drafting. Standard Minimum Rules were first developed in 1926 by the International Penitentiary Commission (as it was then known—later the International Penal and Penitentiary Commission or IPPC) and were revised in 1933. The League of Nations "took note" of

---

3. The Secretariat produced in time for the Eighth Congress a draft of a COMPENDIUM OF UNITED NATIONS STANDARDS AND NORMS IN CRIME PREVENTION AND CRIMINAL JUSTICE, which contained most of the material adopted up to 1989. U.N. Doc. A/CONF.144/INF.2 (1990). The COMPENDIUM was revised to take account of the 1990 output and then published in English only in 1992. U.N. Doc. ST/CSDHA/16, U.N. Sales. No. E.92.IV.1 (1992). (Efforts are afoot to have other language editions.) The appearance of this collection marked the first time that many people, including some close to the area, realized the scope of the material. Of course, some judgment was required as to which material emerging from the system is entirely ephemeral and best forgotten, and which should be collected for posterity, but the Secretariat and those members of the Committee on Crime Prevention and Control who advised it seem to have done a good job. Occasionally, the Compendium included some items the author would regard as inconsequential and failed to include others that perhaps belong. *See*, *e.g.*, *infra* note 168.

4. *See* Chapter 10 *infra*, at notes 108–110.

5. E.S.C. Res. 663 (XXIV) C, U.N. ESCOR, Supp. No. 1, at 11, U.N. Doc. E/3048 (1957). E.S.C. Resolution 663 was amended in 1977 to extend coverage to those arrested or imprisoned without charge ("detained"). The provisions of E.S.C. Res. 663 were "endorsed" by the General Assembly in G.A. Res. 2858 (XXVI) and again in G.A. Res. 3144 (XXVIII). G.A. Res. 2858 (XXVI), U.N. GAOR, 26th Sess., Supp. No. 29, at 94, U.N. Doc. A/8429 (1972); G.A. Res. 3144 (XXVIII), U.N. GAOR, 28th Sess., Supp. No. 30, at 85 (1974). The content of the Standard Minimum Rules will be discussed in Chapter 6. *See* Chapter 6 *infra*, at notes 10–104.

the Rules in 1934.[6] The Ad Hoc Committee recommended further up-dating in 1949 and the IPPC put forward a new draft in one of its last official acts before its dissolution in 1951. The 1955 Congress adopted a revision of this work and ECOSOC duly approved in 1957.[7]

The Rules deal with a whole range of institutional issues, such as maintaining a register of prisoners, separation of categories, accommodation, personal hygiene, clothing and bedding, food, exercise and sport, medical services, discipline and punishment, instruments of restraint, information to and complaints by prisoners, contact with the outside world, religion, retention of prisoners' property, notification of death, illness, transfer and the like, removal of prisoners, institutional personnel, and rules applicable to special categories of prisoners. According to the "Preliminary Observations" of the Rules, they

are not intended to describe in detail a model system of penal institutions. They seek only, on the basis of the general consensus of contemporary thought and the essential elements of the most adequate systems of today, to set out what is generally accepted as being good principle and practice in the treatment of prisoners and the management of institutions.[8]

Nonetheless, the spirit or letter of the Rules is often invoked in complaints of human rights violations made by non-governmental organizations, such as the International League for Human Rights, Amnesty International and the International Commission of Jurists—usually in the company of the Universal Declaration of Human Rights and the Covenant on Civil and Political Rights. There are indeed those who argue that the Rules have entered the corpus of general customary human rights law or that they are binding *qua* treaty law as an authoritative interpretation of the human rights provisions of the U.N. Charter.[9]

The influence of these Rules is pervasive in the United Nations crime prevention and criminal justice system. The way in which the organization "legislated" them will be discussed in Chapter 5. I shall

6. *See* Chapter 1 *supra* note 26; P. Cornil, *International Standards for the Treatment of Prisoners*, 26 INT'L REV. CRIM. POL'Y 3 (1968) (describing the early history of the Rules).

7. E.S.C. Res. 663 (XXIV) C, *supra* note 5.

8. Standard Minimum Rules for the Treatment of Prisoners, *supra* note 5, R. 1.

9. *See, e.g.,* R.B. LILLICH, INTERNATIONAL HUMAN RIGHTS: PROBLEMS OF LAW POLICY AND PRACTICE 233–307 (2d ed. 1991); HUMAN RIGHTS SOURCEBOOK 115 (A.P. Blaustein, R.S. Clark & J.A. Sigler eds., 1987); *United Nations Norms and Guidelines in Crime Prevention and Criminal Justice: Implementation and Priorities for Further Standard-Setting, Working Paper prepared by the Secretariat*, U.N. Doc. A/CONF.144/18, at 7 (1990). *See also* Chapter 6 *infra*, at notes 140–145 (discussing the application of the Rules in domestic law).

offer some more detailed analysis of the content of the Rules and an assessment of their impact in Chapter 6. It will be necessary to return to them again in the general discussion of efforts at implementation in Chapter 9.

2. The Torture Declaration

The next document to be significantly shaped in the criminal justice part of the United Nations system was the 1975 Declaration on the Protection of All Persons from Being Subjected to Torture and Other Cruel, Inhuman or Degrading Treatment or Punishment.[10] The problem of torture had been before the United Nations General Assembly since 1973, largely in the context of Amnesty International's Campaign for the Abolition of Torture, which had been launched at the end of 1972, and the events surrounding the overthrow of the Allende government in Chile in September of 1973. In November 1974, the General Assembly requested the Fifth Congress, which was to take place the following year, to examine "rules for the protection of all persons subjected to any form of detention or imprisonment against torture and other cruel, inhuman or degrading treatment or punishment."[11] The Assembly's resolution also requested the Fifth Congress "to give urgent attention to the question of the development of an international code of ethics for police and related law enforcement agencies." Further, the resolution invited the World Health Organization to draft "an outline of the principles of medical ethics which may be relevant to the protection of persons subjected to any form of detention or imprisonment against torture and other cruel, inhuman or degrading treatment or punishment."

Evidently, some tactical decisions had been made that running the torture and police items through the congress part of the system, rather than the regular human rights organs, might be an expeditious way of dealing with them. Amnesty International's former Legal Adviser, Nigel Rodley, has suggested some explanations for this.[12] Rodley

10. G.A. Res. 3452 (XXX), U.N. GAOR, 30th Sess., Supp. No. 34, at 91, U.N. Doc. A/10034 (1976). *See* J. BURGERS & H. DANELIUS, THE UNITED NATIONS CONVENTION AGAINST TORTURE (1988) (describing the drafting of the Declaration and the later Convention); J. Burgers, *An Arduous Delivery: The United Nations Convention Against Torture (1984)*, *in* EFFECTIVE NEGOTIATION: CASE STUDIES IN CONFERENCE DIPLOMACY 45 (J. Kaufmann ed. 1989).

11. G.A. Res. 3218 (XXIX), U.N. GAOR, 29th Sess., Supp. No. 31, at 82, U.N. Doc. A/9631 (1975).

12. N.S. RODLEY, THE TREATMENT OF PRISONERS UNDER INTERNATIONAL LAW 26–27 (1987). Rodley's book, which devotes much of its text to analyzing the Committee on Crime Prevention and Control's work, perhaps unwittingly demonstrates how seriously

notes first that the Fifth Congress already had on its agenda two related items, one on the implementation of the Standard Minimum Rules and one on "the emerging roles of the police and other law enforcement agencies, with special reference to changing expectations and minimum standards of performance."[13] These items had an obvious relationship with official torture—and one should never underestimate the value of latching on to an existing agenda item! Second, Rodley notes that the problem of torture is a problem of criminal activity, albeit criminality typically committed by those charged with crime prevention.[14] As the most significant argument, Rodley next notes that

the participants in the Congress are drawn largely from the ranks of national administrations of justice (judges, prosecutors, senior police officers, and so on) rather than from foreign offices, as is the case with most UN meetings. It might be expected that representatives with this background might want to confirm that torture was the antithesis of their calling.[15]

---

the major human rights organization which he represented with great skill for many years, Amnesty International, viewed the Committee. Not everyone is as enthusiastic as Rodley about the human rights emphasis of the work of the Committee and the congresses. The late William Clifford, a former Assistant Director-in-charge of the Crime Prevention and Criminal Justice Section, complained that: "As evidenced by the discussions of the Congress and the Committee, by 1975 the emphasis had shifted from the concern with crime control to a wider and less controversial preoccupation with human rights and with standards—embodied in a Congressional resolution against torture, a move to establish the rights of prisoners more effectively, and an interest in developing standards of performance for law enforcement." W. Clifford, *The Committee on Crime Prevention and Control*, 34 INT'L REV. CRIM. POL'Y 11, 15–16 (1978). There is something a little bizarre about the argument that human rights are less controversial than crime control! The emphasis on human rights was itself under some attack during the restructuring debate in 1991 and 1992.

13. *See Fifth United Nations Congress on the Prevention of Crime and the Treatment of Offenders, Geneva, 1–12 September 1975, Report prepared by the Secretariat*, at 25 and 32, U.N. Doc. A/CONF.56/10 (1976).

14. RODLEY, *supra* note 12, at 26. At its Third Session, the Committee on Crime Prevention and Control described torture as a "major [crime] of transnational concern." *Report of the Committee on Crime Prevention and Control on its Third Session*, paras. 27 and 39, U.N. Doc. E/CN.5/516 (1974).

15. RODLEY, *supra* note 12 at 27. Professor Alfred Heijder has stated:

When an individual is part of a professional group, he will be aware of what his colleagues do in the same situation. Since not only general recognition but a prolonged specialized training is a precondition for an occupation being recognized as a profession, he will have undergone during that training a process of anticipatory socialization. He is taught not only the skills of the job but also is oriented to the professional values and norms. The generative traits of a profession call for a measure of professional autonomy against the pressures of the general political system, public opinion and sometimes even one's own value orientation. Codes of professional conduct can be seen as a formalization of the more or less diffuse colleague opinion in

This aspect of professionalism on the part of those involved with the U.N.'s criminal law bodies is, I believe, enormously important to successful development of criminal justice standards.[16] Rodley then argues that since the congress meets only once every five years, deferral of the issue, the traditional tactic of those wishing to obstruct an initiative, was less likely to be successful. (I doubt this—a five year delay is not unheard of in the U.N.) Finally, he notes that in 1955 the First Congress had successfully completed and adopted the Standard Minimum Rules. Thus, there would be some political momentum for a dramatic landmark twenty years on.

In the event, largely because of efforts by Sweden and the Netherlands, an informal sessional working group was set up at the Fifth Congress in early September 1975 to address the General Assembly's requests. For the most part, the group's work concentrated on torture and no text emerged on a code of police ethics[17] or on any amendments to the Standard Minimum Rules. The text of a Declaration against torture was adopted by the Fifth Congress and, with minor changes, speedily and unanimously approved by the General Assembly on December 9, 1975.[18]

The Declaration condemns torture and other cruel, inhuman or degrading treatment or punishment as an offense to human dignity, a denial of the purposes of the Charter of the United Nations and a

---

the professional field. Sometimes the existence of a full-fledged code is even mentioned as one of the main traits of a profession. A code of professional conduct will help the individual to cope with the problems arising from the different demands of a situation. Its influence may even reach beyond that.

A. Heijder, *Codes of Professional Ethics Against Torture, in* AMNESTY INTERNATIONAL, CODES OF PROFESSIONAL ETHICS 3, 6 (2d ed. 1984). In a report to the Human Rights Committee, the New Zealand Government noted that this Amnesty document (and sometimes Amnesty personnel) formed part of a police training module on ethical issues. *See* MINISTRY OF EXTERNAL RELATIONS AND TRADE, HUMAN RIGHTS IN NEW ZEALAND: THE PRESENTATION OF NEW ZEALAND'S SECOND PERIODIC REPORT TO THE HUMAN RIGHTS COMMITTEE, 25 (Information Bulletin No. 30) (1990).

16. The same considerations apply to efforts to draft standards for doctors, lawyers, prosecutors, judges, and psychiatrists, as witness international professional attitudes towards Soviet mental health practitioners believed to be involved in the incarceration of dissidents. *See* R. Bonnie, *Coercive Psychiatry and Human Rights: An Assessment of Recent Changes in the Soviet Union*, 1 CRIM. L. F. 319 (1990).

17. *See* RODLEY, *supra* note 12, at 279–81 (discussing the texts considered but not adopted at the Congress).

18. G.A. Res. 3452 (XXX), *supra* note 10 (adopting the Declaration on the Protection of All Persons from Being Subjected to Torture and Other Cruel, Inhuman, or Degrading Treatment or Punishment). *See* U.N. GAOR, 30th Sess., 3d Comm., 2167th mtg., at 321, U.N. Doc. A/C.3/SR.2167 (1975) (describing the minor amendments made in the Third Committee, before the resolution was approved "by acclamation").

violation of the human rights and fundamental freedoms proclaimed in the Universal Declaration of Human Rights. States are required to take steps to prevent such practices, and to provide for complaint procedures, impartial investigations, and criminal proceedings against the guilty as well as redress and compensation for victims.

The strategy of using the congressional route for drafting purposes worked. The instrument was adopted with vast despatch by United Nations standards. Its text would later prove fundamental to the drafting of the Convention Against Torture and Other Cruel, Inhuman or Degrading Treatment or Punishment adopted by the General Assembly in 1984[19] and provide the basis for the work of the Special Rapporteur on Torture.[20]

3. The Code of Conduct for Law Enforcement Officials

The Code of Conduct for Law Enforcement Officials and the Principles of Medical Ethics which had been contemplated at the same time as the Torture Declaration eventually emerged from the General Assembly in 1979 and 1982 respectively.[21] The Committee on Crime Prevention and Control provided the forum for the development of a generally acceptable text of the Code of Conduct for Law Enforcement officials at its Fourth Session in June 1976.[22] The draft then found its way through the Commission for Social Development and ECOSOC to the General Assembly.[23]

19. G.A. Res. 39/46, U.N. GAOR, 39th Sess., Supp. No. 51, at 197, U.N. Doc. A/39/51 (1985). *See also supra* note 10.

20. *See* C.H.R. Res. 1985/33, U.N. ESCOR, Supp. No. 2, at 71, E/1985/22 (1985) (containing the original provisions for appointment). C.H.R. Res. 1990/34, U.N. ESCOR, Supp. No. 2, at 92, U.N. Doc. E/1990/22 (1990) (extending the mandate).

21. G.A. Res. 34/169, U.N. GAOR, 34th Sess., Supp. No. 46, at 185, U.N. Doc. A/34/46 (1980) (adopting Code of Conduct for Law Enforcement Officials); G.A. Res. 37/194, U.N. GAOR, 37th Sess., Supp. No. 51, at 210, U.N. Doc. A/37/51 (1983) (adopting the Principles of Medical Ethics). *See* L.F. Molina, *Comments on the "Universality" of the Code of Conduct for Law Enforcement Officials,* 1990 THIRD WORLD LEGAL STUD. 59 (suggesting that the Code of Conduct, and presumably others of the U.N.'s instruments, is Euro-centric and may not be ideologically transferable to local socioeconomic practices).

22. *Committee on Crime Prevention and Control, Report on the Fourth Session,* ch. 1A, Annex V, U.N. Doc. E/CN.5/536 (1976). RODLEY, *supra* note 12, at 280–81.

23. *Supra,* note 21. The *Principles of Medical Ethics relevant to the Role of Health Personnel, Particularly Physicians, in the Protection of Prisoners and Detainees against Torture and Other Cruel, Inhuman or Degrading Treatment or Punishment,* G.A. Res. 37/194, U.N. GAOR, 37th Sess., Supp. No. 51, at 210, U.N. Doc. A/37/51 (1983), were developed, as the Assembly envisaged in 1974, under the aegis of the World Health Organization rather than that of the Committee on Crime Prevention and Control. *See* RODLEY, *supra* note 12, at 291– 301. *See also,* K.T. Samson, *Human Rights Co-ordination within the UN System,* in THE

The main thrust of the Code is that officials are to respect the law and basic human rights. Given the realities of who exercises power in some jurisdictions, the Commentary to the Code notes that "In countries where police powers are exercised by military authorities, whether uniformed or not, or by state security forces, the definition of law enforcement officials shall be regarded as including officers of such forces." Force may be used only when strictly necessary and to the extent required for the performance of an official's duty. The use of firearms is considered as an extreme measure. No law enforcement official may inflict, instigate, or tolerate any act of torture or other cruel, inhuman, or degrading treatment or punishment. Nor may any law enforcement official invoke superior orders or exceptional circumstances such as a state of war or threat of war, a threat to national security, internal political instability, or any other public emergency as a justification of torture or other cruel, inhuman, or degrading treatment or punishment.

4. The Caracas Declaration

The Sixth United Nations Congress of 1980 did not produce any dramatic human rights instruments akin to the Standard Minimum Rules or the Torture Declaration for adoption by the General Assembly. However, it did produce the Caracas Declaration which was duly endorsed by the Assembly[24] and included as an annex to the Assembly's resolution receiving the Report on the Sixth Congress. Additionally, the Congress, acting in a more formal way than previous Congresses, adopted a number of resolutions that may only be located in the Report of the Sixth Congress.[25]

United Nations and Human Rights: A Critical Appraisal 620, 641 (P. Alston ed. 1992) (regarding this as an unusual but commendable model of cooperation between the U.N. and one of its Specialized Agencies).

24. G. A. Res. 35/171, U.N. GAOR, 35th Sess., Supp. No. 48, at 193, U.N. Doc. A/35/48 (1981) [hereinafter Caracas Declaration].

25. *Report Prepared by the Secretariat, Sixth United Nations Congress on the Prevention of Crime and the Treatment of Offenders, Caracas, Venezuela, 25 August–5 September 1980*, at 5–23, U.N. Doc. A/CONF.87/14/Rev.1 (1981). The resolutions deal with such topics as developing minimum standards for juvenile justice, extra-legal executions ("a particularly abhorrent crime the eradication of which is a high international priority"), torture and inhuman treatment (encouraging, for example, the development of a Convention Against Torture which the Assembly in fact completed in 1984), prevention of abuse of power, specific needs of women prisoners, development of measures for the social resettlement of the imprisoned, transfer of offenders, and exhorting follow-up to previous standard-setting resolutions. None of these resolutions is sufficiently definitive as a U.N. statement of the item to require further comment here.

The Caracas Declaration was largely a crime and development oriented document which nevertheless had a distinct emphasis on economic, social, and cultural rights. The Caracas Declaration's first paragraph, for example, declares:

the success of criminal justice systems and strategies for crime prevention, especially in the light of the growth of new and sophisticated forms of crime and the difficulties encountered in the administration of criminal justice, depends above all on the progress achieved throughout the world in improving social conditions and enhancing the quality of life; it is thus essential to review traditional crime prevention strategies based exclusively on legal criteria.[26]

The second paragraph insists that "crime prevention and criminal justice should be considered in the context of economic development, political systems, social and cultural values and social change, as well as in the context of the new international economic order."[27]

5. The Capital Punishment Safeguards

The abolition of capital punishment has been a controversial item at the United Nations,[28] as elsewhere. Although the General Assembly went on record in 1971 in support of the proposition that "the main objective to be pursued is that of progressively restricting the number of offences for which capital punishment may be imposed with a view to the desirability of abolishing this punishment in all countries,"[29] the objective has proved difficult to achieve. A desultory discussion of the subject at the Sixth Congress in 1980, in which both abolition of the

26. Caracas Declaration, para. 1
27. Caracas Declaration, para. 2.
28. The 1989 Second Optional Protocol to the International Covenant on Civil and Political Rights, aiming at the abolition of the death penalty, was adopted by a vote of 59 to 26 with 48 abstentions—a very sparse vote for the adoption of a human rights treaty. G.A. Res. 44/128, U.N. GAOR, 44th Sess., Supp. No. 49, at 206, U.N. Doc. A/44/49 (1989). At the 1990 Congress, a group of states, anchored by Italy, introduced a resolution which would have invited states retaining the death penalty to "consider the possibility of establishing, within the framework of their national legislations, a moratorium on its application, at least on a three-year basis, or creating other conditions under which capital punishment is not imposed or executed, so as to permit a study of the effects of abolition on a provisional basis." The resolution failed to garner the two-thirds majority required under congress rules. *See Eighth United Nations Congress on the Prevention of Crime and the Treatment of Offenders, Havana, 27 August–7 September 1990, Report Prepared by the Secretariat*, at 266–70, U.N. Doc. A/CONF.144/28/Rev.1 (1991).
29. G.A. Res. 2857 (XXVI), U.N. GAOR, 26th Sess., Supp. No. 29, para. 3, U.N. Doc. A/8429 (1972). Support was hardly overwhelming then either, since the vote was 59 for, 1 against (Saudi Arabia), 54 abstaining, and 18 absent. *See also* W.A. SCHABAS, THE ABOLITION OF THE DEATH PENALTY IN INTERNATIONAL LAW (1993).

penalty and safeguards in its imposition were stressed, failed to produce a resolution which would command a consensus.[30] However, in 1981 the General Assembly referred an area to the Committee on Crime Prevention and Control on which it had been possible to obtain some degree of consensus—the need for safeguards in the imposition of the penalty. This resulted in the formulation of a set of Safeguards Guaranteeing Protection of the Rights of Those Facing the Death Penalty (Safeguards), which were adopted by ECOSOC in 1984.[31] These Safeguards, and subsequent ECOSOC action in 1989 adding to them, will be discussed together here. In a later section,[32] mention will be made of a related 1989 resolution on the prevention and investigation of extra-legal, arbitrary, and summary executions.

The Council's resolution on Safeguards makes the point emphatically that the standards are being accepted "on the understanding that they shall not be invoked to delay or to prevent the abolition of capital punishment."[33] The Safeguards are both substantive and procedural. They provide that, in countries which have not abolished the death penalty, capital punishment may be imposed only for the most serious crimes, it being understood that their scope should not go beyond intentional crimes with lethal or other extremely grave consequences.[34] Capital punishment may be imposed only for a crime for which the death penalty was prescribed by law at the time of its commission. If, subsequent to the commission of the crime, provision is made by law for the imposition of a lighter penalty, the offender shall benefit thereby.[35] Persons below eighteen years of age at the time of the commission of the crime shall not be sentenced to death, nor shall the sentence be carried out on pregnant women, new mothers, or those who have become insane.[36] The Safeguards also impose a standard of proof requirement.

30. *Report prepared by the Secretariat, Sixth United Nations Congress on the Prevention of Crime and the Treatment of Offenders, Caracas, Venezuela, 25 August–5 September 1980*, at 50–52, U.N. Doc. A/CONF.14/Rev.1 (1981).

31. E.S.C. Res. 1984/50, U.N. ESCOR, Supp. No. 1, at 33, U.N. Doc. E/1984/84 (1984). The resolution was later endorsed by the General Assembly. G.A. Res. 39/118, U.N. GAOR, 39th Sess., Supp. No. 51, at 211, U.N. Doc. A/39/51 (1985) [hereinafter "Safeguards"].

32. *Infra* notes 95–111.

33. *See supra* note 31, para. 3 (adopting the Resolution).

34. Safeguards, *supra* note 31, para. 1. This and other provisions of the Safeguards resolution both incorporate and give more detail to the generalities of art. 6 of the International Covenant on Civil and Political Rights. G.A. Res. 2200 (XXI), U.N. GAOR, 21st Sess., Supp. No. 16, at 52, U.N. Doc. A/6316 (1967) [hereinafter International Covenant on Civil and Political Rights].

35. *Id.* para. 2.

36. *Id.* para. 3. Article 6, para. 5 of the International Covenant on Civil and Political

Capital punishment may be imposed "only when the guilt of the person charged is based upon clear and convincing evidence leaving no room for an alternative explanation of the facts."[37] A fair trial is guaranteed "including the right of anyone suspected or charged with a crime for which capital punishment may be imposed to adequate legal assistance at all stages of the proceedings."[38] Anyone sentenced to death is entitled to a right of appeal to a court of higher jurisdiction, and steps should be taken to ensure that such appeals become mandatory.[39] Anyone sentenced to death shall have the right to seek pardon or commutation of sentence.[40] The punishment may not be carried out pending any appeal or other recourse procedure or other proceeding relating to pardon or commutation.[41] Where capital punishment occurs, it shall be carried out so as to inflict the minimum possible suffering.[42]

In 1989, ECOSOC returned to the subject in a resolution drafted in the Committee on Crime Prevention and Control entitled "Implementation of the safeguards guaranteeing protection of those facing the

---

Rights, states that "Sentence of death shall not be imposed for crimes committed by persons below eighteen years of age and shall not be carried out on pregnant women." *International Covenant on Civil and Political Rights, supra* note 34. While the U.S. was one of the many states joining the consensus on the Safeguards resolution and the 1989 resolution on implementing the Safeguards, the U.S. Supreme Court has held that it is constitutionally permissible to execute offenders who were sixteen or seventeen at the time of the killing. *See* Stanford v. Kentucky, 492 U.S. 361 (1989). In ratifying the Covenant in 1992, the U.S. entered a reservation to art. 6, to the effect that the United States "reserves the right, subject to its Constitutional constraints, to impose capital punishment on any person (other than a pregnant woman) duly convicted under existing or future laws permitting the imposition of capital punishment, including such punishment for crime committed by persons below eighteen years of age." *Multilateral Treaties deposited with the Secretary-General, Status as at 31 December 1992*, at 132, U.N. Doc. ST/LEG/SER.E/11 (1993). Amnesty International reports that as of May 1, 1991, 31 persons were on death row with death sentences received for crimes committed when they were under the age of 18; since 1976 four executions of young people have taken place (in South Carolina, Louisiana and Texas (2)). The United States is one of only seven countries known to have carried out such executions in the last decade, the others being Barbados (which has since raised the age to 18), Iran, Iraq, Nigeria, Pakistan and Bangladesh (the latter one execution only). AMNESTY INTERNATIONAL, UNITED STATES OF AMERICA: THE DEATH PENALTY AND JUVENILE OFFENDERS (unpaginated summary) (1991). *See* W.A. Schabas, *International Norms Concerning Capital Punishment of the Insane*, 4 CRIM. L.F. 95 (1993) (discussing capital punishment of the insane and the mentally retarded). *See also infra* note 47.

37. *Id.* para. 4.
38. *Id.* para. 5.
39. *Id.* para. 6.
40. *Id.* para. 7.
41. *Id.* para. 8.
42. *Id.* para. 9.

death penalty."[43] That resolution contained two "procedural" principles and two "substantive" ones. On the procedural front, the first statement was a reiteration of the need for competent counsel. It was recommended that states afford special protection to persons facing charges for which the death penalty is provided, by allowing time and facilities for the preparation of their defense, including adequate assistance of counsel at every stage of the proceedings, above and beyond that afforded in non-capital cases.[44] Second, states were recommended to provide for mandatory appeals or review, with provisions for clemency or pardon in all cases of capital offenses.[45] As far as substance was concerned, states were urged to establish a maximum age beyond which a person may not be sentenced to death or executed (a position already reached in some countries),[46] and to eliminate the death penalty for persons suffering from mental retardation or extremely limited mental competence, whether at the stage of sentence or execution.[47]

6. Output of the 1985 Milan Congress

(a) In General

The Seventh Congress, held in Milan in 1985, adopted numerous substantive resolutions.[48] Three of these, the United Nations Standard

43. E.S.C. Res. 1989/64, U.N. ESCOR, Supp. No. 1, at 51, U.N. Doc. E/1989/89 (1989) [hereinafter Implementation of Safeguards]. The author was one of the sponsors of this resolution in the Committee on Crime Prevention and Control.

44. *Id.* R. 1(a). *See* F.N. Tulsky, *What Price Justice? Poor Defendants Pay the Cost as Courts Save on Murder Trials,* PHILADELPHIA INQUIRER, Sept. 3, 1992, at 1 (indicating that even in the developed world, this promise is not always kept).

45. *Id.* R. 1(b).

46. *Id.* R. 1(c).

47. *Id.* R. 1(d). The U.S. Supreme Court has held the execution of the insane to be unconstitutionally cruel and unusual punishment, but has upheld the execution of the retarded. *See* Ford v. Wainwright, 477 U.S. 399 (1986) (proscribing the execution of the insane); Penry v. Lynaugh, 492 U.S. 302 (1989) (Penry had an I.Q. of 50 to 65 and a mental age of six and a half.) *See also* Schabas, *supra* note 36; R. G. Salguero, Note, *Medical Ethics and Competency to be Executed,* 96 YALE L.J. 167 (1986); R. Bonnie, *Dilemmas in Administering the Death Penalty: Conscientious Abstention, Professional Ethics, and the Needs of the Legal System,* 14 L. & HUM. BEHAV. 67 (1990) (describing the difficult ethical problems faced by professionals involved with executions). The U.N. material does not enter directly into this ethical debate, except perhaps for Principle 3 of the Principles of Medical Ethics, which provides that "It is a contravention of medical ethics for health personnel, particularly physicians, to be involved in any professional relationship with prisoners or detainees the purpose of which is not solely to evaluate, protect or improve their physical and mental health." *Supra* note 21.

48. *See Seventh United Nations Congress on the Prevention of Crime and the Treatment of*

Minimum Rules for the Administration of Juvenile Justice (the "Beijing Rules"),[49] the Declaration of Basic Principles of Justice for Victims of Crime and Abuse of Power[50] and a resolution on Domestic Violence,[51] were specifically adopted with only minor cosmetic changes by the General Assembly and their texts appear in the Assembly's Resolutions for the fall of 1985.[52] Each of these resolutions is primarily a human rights document. Another Resolution of the Seventh Congress, the Milan Plan of Action, which contains a substantial quantity of human rights language, was approved by name[53] and the Guiding Principles for Crime Prevention and Criminal Justice in the Context of Development were recommended by name.[54] The Assembly also "endorse[d]" as a group "the other resolutions unanimously adopted by the Seventh Congress."[55] Two of these "other resolutions", the Model Agreement on the Transfer of Foreign Prisoners and the Basic Princi-

---

Offenders, Milan, 26 August-6 September 1985, Report prepared by the Secretariat, at 2–98, U.N. Doc. A/CONF.121/22/Rev.1 (1986).

49. G.A. Res. 40/33, U.N. GAOR, 40th Sess., Supp. No. 53, at 206, U.N. Doc. A/40/53 (1986) [hereinafter Beijing Rules].

50. G.A. Res. 40/34, U.N. GAOR, 40th Sess., Supp. No. 53, at 213, U.N. Doc. A/40/53 (1986) [hereinafter Declaration on Victims].

51. G.A. Res. 40/36, U.N. GAOR, 40th Sess., Supp. No. 53, at 215, U.N. Doc. A/40/53 (1986) [hereinafter Resolution on Domestic Violence].

52. *See also* Res. 40/35, U.N. GAOR, 40th Sess., Supp. No. 53, at 215, U.N. Doc. A/40/53 (1986) (draft text forwarded from Congress and adopted by the Assembly which requested the development of standards for the prevention of juvenile delinquency). These guidelines were adopted by the Eighth Congress. *See infra* notes 169–176.

53. G.A. Res. 40/32, U.N. GAOR, 40th Sess., Supp. No. 53, para. 3, at 204, U.N. Doc. A/40/53 (1986). The full enacting language is "[the General Assembly] *approves* the Milan Plan of Action, [referring to the congress report] adopted by consensus by the Seventh Congress, as a useful and effective means of strengthening international cooperation in the field of crime prevention and criminal justice." *Cf.* Caracas Declaration *supra* note 24 (the Declaration was annexed to the Assembly's adopting resolution). The Milan Plan of Action and the other Seventh Congress resolutions which are discussed *infra*, at notes 80–94, are thus not as accessible since their text appears only in the Report of the Congress and not in the more widely distributed Resolutions of the General Assembly. *See also* Chapter 5 *infra*, at notes 36–61 (discussing the Assembly's modes of approval).

54. In paragraph 4 of G.A. Res. 40/32, the Assembly "*[r]ecommends* the Guiding Principles for Crime Prevention and Criminal Justice in the Context of Development and a New International Economic Order [ref. to Congress Report] for national, regional and international action, as appropriate, taking into account the political, economic, social and cultural circumstances and traditions of each country on the basis of the sovereign equality of States and of non-interference in their internal affairs." G.A. Res. 40/32, *supra* note 53, para. 4.

55. *Id.* para. 5.

ples on the Independence of the Judiciary, were of particular interest.[56]

(b) The Standard Minimum Rules for the Administration of Juvenile Justice (Beijing Rules)

The Beijing Rules[57] aim both at protecting the basic civil liberties of alleged juvenile offenders in the criminal justice system and providing for the framework for states to "develop conditions that will ensure for the juvenile a meaningful life in the community, that, during that period in life when she or he is most susceptible to deviant behaviour, will foster a process of personal development and education that is as free from crime and delinquency as possible."[58] The rules insist that the juvenile justice system should emphasize the well-being of the juvenile and ensure that any reaction to juvenile offenders shall always be in proportion to the circumstances of both the offender and the offense.[59] Juveniles must be guaranteed at all stages basic procedural safeguards such as the presumption of innocence, the right to be notified of the charges, the right to remain silent, the right to counsel, the right to the presence of a parent or guardian, the right to confront and cross-examine witnesses, and the right to appeal to a higher authority.[60] Nonetheless, the juvenile's right to privacy is to be respected at all stages in order to avoid harm being caused to her or him by undue publicity or by the process of labeling.[61] Deprivation of liberty as a sanction shall occur only after careful consideration and "shall be limited to the possible minimum."[62] Indeed, it shall not occur unless the juvenile is "adjudicated of a serious act involving violence against another person or of persistence in committing other serious offences and unless there is no other appropriate response."[63] Capital and corporal punishment are prohibited.[64]

---

56. Other Congressional resolutions, such as those dealing with fair treatment of women by the criminal justice system, with professional standards for prosecutors and other criminal justice personnel, and on extra-legal, arbitrary, and summary executions represent continued interest in such items, but were largely derivative of other work in the U.N. system. The two noted in the text above and discussed *infra*, at notes 85–94, represent a more original contribution.

57. *See supra* note 49.

58. *Id.* R. 1.2.

59. *Id.* R. 5.1.

60. *Id.* R. 7.1

61. *Id.* R. 8.1

62. *Id.* R. 17.1(b).

63. *Id.* R. 17.1(c).

64. *Id.* R. 17.2 and R. 17.3.

Non-institutional treatment is thus to be the norm. Such treatment is to be accompanied by efforts to provide the necessary assistance such as lodging, education or vocational training, employment, or any other assistance in order to facilitate the rehabilitative process.[65] Similar care is, of course, to be provided to those in institutions.[66]

(c) Basic Principles of Justice for Victims

The Declaration of Basic Principles of Justice for Victims of Crime and Abuse of Power (Victims Declaration)[67] will be discussed in detail in Chapter 7. The Declaration contains two parts, one concerning Victims of Crime and another addressing Victims of Abuse of Power. There is some overlap between the categories.

In the "Crime" section, "victims" is defined to mean "persons who, individually or collectively, have suffered harm including physical or mental injury, emotional suffering, economic loss or substantial impairment of their fundamental rights, through acts or omissions that are in violation of criminal laws operative within Member States, including those laws proscribing criminal abuse of power."[68] This definition is broad enough to encompass those who are the victims of such human rights abuses as torture, disappearances, and depredations of the environment that are proscribed under national law. Victims of crime are entitled to a package of rights, including access to justice and fair treatment,[69] restitution from the offender,[70] compensation from the state where full restitution cannot be obtained from the offender,[71] and the necessary health, psychological, and related social services.[72]

In the "Abuse of Power" section "victims" is defined to mean "persons who, individually or collectively, have suffered harm, including physical or mental injury, emotional suffering, economic loss or substantial impairment of their fundamental rights, through acts that do

65. *Id.* R. 24.1.

66. *Id.* R. 26.2. *See generally* J. Finckenauer & T. McArdle, *Institutional Treatment Possibilities for Young Offenders*, 39 & 40 INT'L REV. CRIM. POL'Y 119 (1990).

67. *See supra* note 50. *See also* Chapter 7 *infra*.

68. *Id.* para. 1.

69. *Id.* para. 4–7.

70. *Id.* para. 8–11. Paragraph 11 of the Declaration adds that: "Where public officials or other agents acting in an official or quasi-official capacity have violated national criminal laws, the victims should receive restitution from the state whose officials or agents were responsible for the harm inflicted. In cases where the Government under whose authority the victimizing act or omission occurred is no longer in existence, the State or Government successor in title shall provide restitution to the victims."

71. *Id.* para. 12–13.

72. *Id.* para. 14–17.

not yet constitute violations of national criminal laws but of internationally recognized norms relating to human rights."[73] In this instance, states are exhorted to consider incorporating into the national law norms proscribing such abuses and providing remedies to victims.[74] States are encouraged to develop more multilateral treaty law in the area[75] and to review their domestic legislation periodically.[76] This more precatory part of the Victims Declaration aims at the gradual incorporation of most situations covered in it within the regime set up in the first, or common crime, part.

(d) Domestic Violence

The Domestic Violence Resolution[77] invited states to adopt a variety of specific initiatives to deal with violence in the family setting—against spouses, children, and the elderly. Among the principles listed are treating the victim in a sensitive fashion; providing proper training for officials who must deal with individual situations; providing temporary solutions such as shelters and other services for the victims; and initiating preventive measures such as providing support and counseling to families, in order to improve their ability to create a non-violent environment, emphasizing principles of education, equality of rights and equality of responsibilities between women and men, their partnership, and the peaceful resolution of conflicts.

This was a significant initiative of the Seventh Congress in putting a hitherto taboo subject firmly on the international agenda. In the wake of the Domestic Violence Resolution have been several substantial developments in both the Committee on the Elimination of Discrimination Against Women[78] and the Commission on the Status of Women.[79]

73. *Id.* para. 18.
74. *Id.* para. 19.
75. *Id.* para. 20.
76. *Id.* para. 21.
77. *See supra* note 51.
78. *See* General Recommendation No. 19, *Violence against women, Report of the Committee on the Elimination of Discrimination Against Women on its eleventh session*, U.N. GAOR, 47th Sess., Supp. No. 38, at 5, U.N. Doc. A/47/38 (1992). *See also* UNITED NATIONS OFFICE AT VIENNA, CENTRE FOR SOCIAL DEVELOPMENT AND HUMANITARIAN AFFAIRS, VIOLENCE AGAINST WOMEN IN THE FAMILY, U.N. Sales No. E.89.IV.5 (1989).
79. The Commission on the Status of Women has been involved in the drafting of a Declaration on Domestic Violence. *See Report of the Commission on the Status of Women at its Thirty-Sixth Session, Vienna, 11–20 March 1992*, at 48, U.N. ESCOR, Supp. No. 4, U.N. Doc. E/1992/24 (1992). The Declaration was due to be adopted by the General Assembly at the very end of its 1993 Session. *See also* INTERNATIONAL LEAGUE FOR HUMAN RIGHTS,

(e) The Milan Plan of Action

The "Milan Plan of Action"[80] (Milan Plan) was intended to build on the Caracas Declaration. It lays out both the underlying assumptions of United Nations action and some recommendations about "essential elements" of the strategy which each state should adopt.

The assumptions start with the proposition that crime is a major problem of national, and in some cases, international dimensions which requires a significant amount of multilateral cooperation through the United Nations. Certain forms of crime can hamper the political, economic, social and cultural development of peoples and threaten human rights and peace, stability, and security. [81] The Milan Plan goes on to assert that development "is not criminogenic *per se*, especially where its fruits are equitably distributed among all the peoples, thus contributing to the improvement of overall social conditions; however, unbalanced or inadequately planned development contributes to an increase in criminality."[82] In such a context the Milan Plan asserts that "The multisectoral and interdisciplinary nature of crime prevention, including their linkages to peace, demands the co-ordinated attention of various agencies and disciplines."[83]

So far as the elements of a strategy are concerned, the Milan Plan refers to strengthening cooperation, prevention, and research, further exploring the connections between crime and criminality and human rights, combating terrorism, launching a major effort to control and eventually eradicate the destructive phenomena of illicit drug traffic and abuse and of organized crime, and to improve the capacity of the U.N. to expand technical cooperation in the area to developing countries particularly in training, planning, exchange of information and experiences, and reappraisal of legal systems in relation to changing socioeconomic conditions.[84] The Milan Plan thus emphasizes economic, social, and cultural issues.

COMBATTING VIOLENCE AGAINST WOMEN (1993); D. Thomas & M. Beasley, *Domestic Violence as a Human Rights Issue*, 15 HUM. RTS. Q. 36 (1993).

80. *See supra* note 53.

81. *Id.* para. 1.

82. *Id.* para. 2.

83. *Id.* para. 3.

84. *Id.* para. 5. More detail is spelled out on all of these matters in the Guiding Principles for Crime Prevention and Criminal Justice in the Context of Development and a New International Economic Order, also adopted by the Congress. *Report of the Seventh Congress on the Prevention of Crime and the Treatment of Offenders, supra* note 48, at 5. Paragraph 5 of the Milan Plan also foreshadowed the re-examination of the U.N. Program which has been discussed in Chapter 2.

(f) The Model Agreement on the Transfer of Foreign Prisoners

The Model Agreement on the Transfer of Foreign Prisoners (Model Transfer Agreement) and its accompanying Recommendations on the Treatment of Foreign Prisoners[85] will be discussed in more detail in Chapter 8.[86] These instruments recognize the difficulties of foreigners detained in prison abroad owing to differences in language, culture, customs, and religion. Both the Model Transfer Agreement and the Recommendations proceed, accordingly, on the basis that the aim of social resettlement of prisoners could best be achieved by giving foreign prisoners the opportunity to serve their sentence within their country of nationality or residence. States are therefore encouraged to enter into bilateral transfer agreements based on the model provided.

(g) Basic Principles on the Independence of the Judiciary

The final instrument of the Seventh Congress of note is the Basic Principles on the Independence of the Judiciary.[87] This document spells out the fundamental contents of the broad principle of the independence of the judiciary and the obligation on all governmental and other institutions to respect it. States are obligated to provide adequate resources to enable the judiciary to properly perform its functions.[88] Judges are to be free to form and join associations of judges or other organizations to represent their interests, to promote their professional training, and to protect their judicial independence.[89] Rules are laid down concerning qualifications, selection and training,[90] conditions of service and tenure,[91] professional secrecy and

85. *Report of the Seventh United Nations Congress on the Prevention of Crime and the Treatment of Offenders, supra* note 48, at 53.

86. *See* Chapter 8 *infra*, at notes 40–63.

87. *Supra* note 48, at 58. These Principles have been widely disseminated both by a leading non-governmental human rights organization, the International Commission of Jurists, which had been actively engaged in the drafting, and by inclusion in the most recent edition of the U.N.'s HUMAN RIGHTS: A COMPILATION OF INTERNATIONAL INSTRUMENTS (1988). *See* CENTRE FOR THE INDEPENDENCE OF JUDGES AND LAWYERS, CIJL BULLETIN, SPECIAL ISSUE No 25–26, THE INDEPENDENCE OF JUDGES AND LAWYERS: A COMPILATION OF INTERNATIONAL STANDARDS (Apr.-Oct. 1990) (detailing the International Commission of Jurists' efforts at dissemination). The introduction to the Bulletin by Reed Brody, 3–13, catches some of the interplay in this area between the Human Rights and Criminal Justice parts of the U.N. system. *See also* Chapter 5 *infra* note 53.

88. *Id.* para. 7.

89. *Id.* para. 9.

90. *Id.* para. 10.

91. *Id.* para. 11–14.

immunity,[92] on discipline, suspension, and removal.[93] These standards are of significant importance to organizations endeavoring to ensure the independence of the judiciary.[94]

7. The Principles on the Effective Prevention and Investigation of Extra-Legal, Arbitrary, and Summary Executions

The subject of extra-legal executions, and the closely associated concept of disappearances, have been on the United Nations agenda in various forums throughout the United Nations since the late 1970s.[95] At the Milan Congress, "Other resolution 11"[96] reaffirmed the strong condemnation of those present of extra-legal, arbitrary, and summary executions and looked forward to some follow-up by the Crime Prevention Committee. At its 1986 meeting, the Crime Prevention Committee sought an instruction from ECOSOC to proceed with the elaboration of principles on the effective prevention and investigation of such practices.[97] This was done by ECOSOC later in 1986.[98] There seems to have been some hesitation about whether the principles would be sent on for approval by ECOSOC or by the Eighth Congress. A Secretariat draft was considered and modified by the Interregional Preparatory Meeting for the Havana Congress, which took place in Vienna during June 27 to July 1, 1988.[99] However, as they emerged from that preparatory meeting, the principles were in the form of an ECOSOC resolution. After further modification during informal consultations at the Crime Prevention Committee,[100] they were forwarded to ECOSOC which adopted them in 1989.[101]

92. *Id.* para. 15–16.

93. *Id.* para. 17–20.

94. Note, for example, the reliance on the Principles by the International Commission of Jurists in its 1988 Report, W. BUTLER, ET AL., PALAU: A CHALLENGE TO THE RULE OF LAW IN MICRONESIA; REPORT OF A MISSION ON BEHALF OF THE INTERNATIONAL COMMISSION OF JURISTS (New York, ICJ, 1988).

95. *See generally* RODLEY, *supra* note 12; M. Berman & R. Clark, *State Terrorism: Disappearances*, 13 RUTGERS L.J. 531 (1982).

96. *Report of the Seventh United Nations Congress on the Prevention of Crime and the Treatment of Offenders, supra* note 48, at 77.

97. *Committee on Crime Prevention and Control, Report on the Ninth Session, Vienna, 5–14 March 1986*, U.N. ESCOR, Supp. No. 5, at 5, U.N. Doc. E/1986/25 (1986).

98. E.S.C. Res. 1986/10, U.N. ESCOR, Supp. No. 1, at 14, U.N. Doc. E/1986/86 (1986).

99. *See Report of the Interregional Meeting*, at 25, U.N. Doc. A/CONF.144/IPM.5 (1988).

100. *Committee on Crime Prevention and Control, Report on the Tenth Session, Vienna, 22–31 August 1988*, at 71, 1988 U.N. ESCOR, Supp. No. 10, U.N. Doc. E/1988/20 (1988). The meeting also had before it, in English only, a draft entitled the "Minnesota Protocol,"

The principles go into considerable detail and only the briefest of summaries is possible here. They are in three sections which refer respectively to prevention,[102] investigation,[103] and legal proceedings.[104] As far as prevention is concerned, governments are required to prohibit by law all extra-legal, arbitrary, and summary executions and ensure that they are punishable by appropriate penalties which take into account the seriousness of the offenses involved. Exceptional circumstances, including a state of war or threat of war, internal political instability, or any other public emergency, may not be invoked as a justification for such executions.[105] Governments must ensure strict control, including a clear chain of command over all officials responsible for apprehension, arrest, detention, custody, and imprisonment, as well as those officials authorized by law to use force and firearms.[106] Governments are required to prohibit orders from superior officers or public authorities authorizing or inciting other persons to carry out such executions. All persons shall have the right and the duty to defy such orders. Training of officials is to emphasize these provisions.[107]

As far as investigation is concerned, there shall be a thorough, prompt, and impartial investigation of all suspected cases of such executions. The investigation shall include an adequate autopsy, collection, and analysis of all physical and documentary evidence, and statements from witnesses.[108]

Finally, there is the matter of legal proceedings. Governments are to ensure that perpetrators are brought to justice, on a prosecute-or-extradite basis.[109] Under no circumstances, including a state of war, siege, or other public emergency, shall blanket immunity from prosecution be granted to any person allegedly involved in extra-legal, arbitrary, or summary executions.[110] The families and dependents of

---

containing a model autopsy protocol which was favorably viewed by some of the members. U.N. Doc. E/AC.57/1988/NGO.4 (1988). The Protocol eventually appeared in MANUAL ON THE EFFECTIVE PREVENTION AND INVESTIGATION OF EXTRA-LEGAL, ARBITRARY, AND SUMMARY EXECUTIONS, U.N. Sales No. E.91.IV.I (1991).

101. E.S.C. Res. 1989/65, U.N. ESCOR, Supp. No. 1, at 52, U.N. Doc. E/1989/89 (1989). *See* S. Rosen, *Draft Principles on the Effective Prevention and Investigation of Extra-Legal, Arbitrary and Summary Executions*, 5 NEWSLETTER AMNESTY INT'L LEGAL SUPPORT NETWORK 6 (1988) (describing the Principles in general).

102. *Id.* para. 1–8.
103. *Id.* para. 9–17.
104. *Id.* para. 18–20.
105. *Id.* para. 1.
106. *Id.* para. 2.
107. *Id.* para. 3.
108. *Id.* para. 9.
109. *Id.* para. 18.
110. *Id.* para. 19.

victims shall be entitled to fair and adequate compensation within a reasonable period of time.[111]

8. The 1990 Havana Congress

(a) Standard-Setters Among the 45 Congress Resolutions

In poundage terms, the outpouring of resolutions in 1990,[112] including standard-setting measures, represented approximately as many total pages as were produced at all previous congresses combined. This volume led to heightened pleas for restraint and was a factor in the recent discussions on rearranging the program, which have been analyzed in Chapter 2. Not all the forty-five resolutions adopted at the Eighth Congress can be described as standard-setting,[113] but a substantial number can. The standard-setting instruments fit three main categories: human rights in the administration of justice; model treaties on cooperation; and statements on crime prevention. Because of the volume, it is not possible to discuss each of the instruments here in the detail that has been devoted to some of the earlier instruments, but some comments will be made on the most significant resolutions in each of the three categories.

(b) Human Rights in the Administration of Justice

The normative instruments adopted by the Eighth Congress that fit the broad category of human rights in the administration of justice include the United Nations Standard Minimum Rules for Non-Custodial Measures (the Tokyo Rules),[114] the Basic Principles for the Treatment of Prisoners,[115] the United Nations Rules for the Protection of

---

111. *Id.* para. 20.

112. See *Eighth United Nations Congress on the Prevention of Crime and the Treatment of Offenders, Havana, Cuba, 27 August–7 September 1990, Report prepared by the Secretariat*, U.N. Doc. A/CONF.144/28 (1990).

113. A number of resolutions, for example, called for the establishment of data bases; others called for close collaboration with other parts of the United Nations system; others looked for the creation of working groups in various areas. Work on the first two categories is continuing; the creation of working groups is somewhat on hold pending decisions of the new Commission on Crime Prevention and Criminal Justice.

114. G.A. Res. 45/110, U.N. GAOR, 45th Sess., Supp. No. 49A, at 195, U.N. Doc. A/45/49 (1991). *See also International and Interregional Co-operation in Prison Management and Community-Based Sanctions and Other Matters, Report of the Eighth Congress, supra* note 112, at 167 (also addressing non-custodial sanctions).

115. G.A. Res. 45/111, U.N. GAOR, 45th Sess., Supp. No 49A, at 199, U.N. Doc. A/45/49 (1991).

Juveniles Deprived of their Liberty,[116] the Basic Principles on the Use of Force and Firearms by Law Enforcement Officials,[117] the Basic Principles on the Role of Lawyers,[118] and the Guidelines on the Role of Prosecutors.[119]

(i) *Standard Minimum Rules for Non-Custodial Measures (Tokyo Rules).* The Standard Minimum Rules for Non-Custodial Measures are designed to promote the use of non-custodial measures, as well as minimum safeguards for persons subject to alternatives to imprisonment.[120] Their essential rationale is that alternatives to imprisonment "can be an effective means of treating offenders within the community to the best advantage of both the offenders and society."[121] In order to provide greater flexibility consistent with the nature and gravity of the offense, with the personality of the offender, and with the protection of society and to avoid unnecessary use of imprisonment, states are encouraged to develop a wide range of options, from pre-trial to post-sentencing dispositions.[122] The development of new non-custodial measures is to be encouraged and closely monitored and their use systematically evaluated.[123]

(ii) *Basic Principles for the Treatment of Prisoners.* The Basic Principles[124] try to articulate the underlying basis of the Standard Minimum Rules for the Treatment of Prisoners, on the (probably naive) theory that such an articulation will facilitate the full implementation of those Rules.[125] All prisoners are to be treated with the respect due their

116. G.A. Res. 45/113, *id.* at 204.

117. *Report of the Eighth Congress, supra* note 112, at 110.

118. *Id.* at 117.

119. *Id.* at 188.

120. *Id.* R. 1.1. Non-custodial measures include such options as verbal sanctions (admonition, reprimand, and warning), conditional discharge, status penalties, fines, confiscation, suspended or deferred sentence, probation and judicial supervision, community service orders, referral to an attendance center, and house arrest. *Id.* R. 8.2. *See* INTERNATIONAL PENAL AND PENITENTIARY FOUNDATION, STANDARD MINIMUM RULES FOR THE IMPLEMENTATION OF NON-CUSTODIAL SANCTIONS AND MEASURES INVOLVING RESTRICTIONS OF LIBERTY (1989).

121. *Id.* para. 7 (preamble). The advantage to society includes not only rehabilitation of offenders but also the relief provided to prison overcrowding. *See also* W. Young, *Community Care as a Penal Sanction,* 1 CRIM. L.F. 297 (1990) (correcting overly-romantic thinking about community involvement).

122. *Id.* R. 2.3.

123. *Id.* R. 2.4.

124. *See supra* note 115.

125. *Id.* para. 5 (preamble). Some further references will be made to the Basic Principles throughout Chapter 6, *infra.*

inherent dignity and value as human beings.[126] There is to be no discrimination on the grounds of race, color, sex, language, religion, political or other opinion, national or social origin, property, birth, or other status.[127] Efforts addressed to the abolition of solitary confinement as a punishment, or to the restriction of its use, should be both undertaken and encouraged.[128] Conditions are to be created enabling prisoners to engage in meaningful remunerated employment which will facilitate their reintegration into the country's labor market and permit them to contribute to their own financial support and to that of their families.[129] Prisoners are to have access to the health services available in the country without discrimination on the grounds of their legal situation.[130] Finally, favorable conditions are to be created for the reintegration of the ex-prisoners into society.[131]

(iii) Rules for the Protection of Juveniles Deprived of Their Liberty. The Rules for the Protection of Juveniles Deprived of Their Liberty[132] (Juvenile Rules) essentially track the structure of the Standard Minimum Rules for the Treatment of Prisoners, but are designed specifically for juvenile offenders. The Juvenile Rules affirm the principle that the placement of a juvenile in an institution should always be a disposition of last resort and be carried out for the minimum necessary period.[133] They call for the separation of juveniles from adults in detention as a general matter,[134] and the classification of juveniles according to their sex, age, personality, and offense type, with a view to ensuring their protection from harmful influences. The Juvenile Rules also set forth special provisions covering various aspects of institutional life, such as physical environment and accommodation, education, recreation, religion, medical care, contacts with the outside world, inspection, complaints, and return to the community.

(iv) Basic Principles on the Use of Force and Firearms by Law Enforcement Officials. The Basic Principles on the Use of Force and Firearms by Law

126. *Id.* para. 1.
127. *Id.* para. 2.
128. *Id.* para. 7.
129. *Id.* para. 8.
130. *Id.* para. 9.
131. *Id.* para. 9.
132. *See supra* note 116.
133. *Id.*, adopting resolution, para. 1, & R. 1.
134. *Id.* R. 29. "Under controlled conditions, juveniles may be brought together with carefully selected adults as a part of a special programme that has been shown to be beneficial for the juveniles concerned." *Id. See* Chapter 6 *infra* notes 24 and 133 (discussing this controversial issue).

Enforcement officials[135] generally encourage the use of the minimum amount of force in law enforcement. The Basic Principles obligate governments and law enforcement agencies to adopt and implement rules and regulations on the use of force and firearms. In developing such rules and regulations, governments are exhorted to keep the ethical issues associated with the matter constantly under review.[136] Among the detailed provisions are the following on the use of firearms:

9. Law enforcement officials shall not use firearms against persons except in self-defence or defence of others against the imminent threat of death or serious injury, to prevent the perpetration of a particularly serious crime involving grave threat to life, to arrest a person presenting such a danger and resisting their authority, or to achieve his or her escape, and only when less extreme means are insufficient to achieve these objectives. In any event, intentional lethal use of firearms may only be made when strictly unavoidable in order to protect life.

10. In the circumstances provided for under Principle 9, law enforcement officials shall identify themselves as such and give a clear warning of their intent to use firearms, with sufficient time for the warning to be observed, unless to do so would unduly place the law enforcement officials at risk or would create a risk of death or serious harm to other persons, or would clearly be inappropriate or pointless in the circumstances of the incident.[137]

(v) *Basic Principles on the Role of Lawyers.* The Basic Principles on the Role of Lawyers[138] start from the premise that "adequate protection of human rights and fundamental freedoms to which all persons are entitled, be they economic, social and cultural, or civil and political, requires that all persons have adequate access to legal services provided by an independent legal profession."[139] Thus, all persons are entitled to call upon the assistance of a lawyer of their choice to protect and establish their rights, and to defend them in all stages of criminal proceedings.[140] Governments are required to ensure the provision of

135. *See supra* note 117.
136. *Id.* para. 1.
137. *Id.* paras. 9 & 10.
138. *See supra* note 118.
139. *Id.* 9 (preamble). *See also id.* para. 10 (preamble) (asserting that "professional associations of lawyers have a vital role to play in upholding professional standards and ethics, protecting their members from persecution and improper restrictions and infringements, providing legal services to all in need of them, and co-operating with governmental and other institutions in furthering the ends of justice and public interest").
140. *Id.* para. 1. *See id.* para. 2 (relating to "effective and equal access" without discrimination).

sufficient funding and other resources for legal services to the poor and, as necessary, to other disadvantaged persons.[141] Professional associations of lawyers are required to promote programs to inform the public about their rights and duties under the law and the important role of lawyers in protecting their fundamental freedoms.[142] Special safeguards are mandated in criminal justice matters.[143] There is a section insisting upon proper qualifications and training;[144] the duties and responsibilities of lawyers are outlined;[145] governments must ensure the freedom of lawyers to function;[146] like other citizens, lawyers are entitled to freedom of expression and association;[147] they may form and participate in professional associations;[148] and, finally, codes of professional conduct are to be established along with disciplinary committees to enforce those codes.[149]

(vi) Guidelines on the Role of Prosecutors. The Guidelines on the Role of Prosecutors[150] view the role of prosecutors as crucial in furthering the principles of equality before the law, the presumption of innocence, and the right to a fair and public hearing by an independent and impartial tribunal.[151] Accordingly, those selected as prosecutors must be individuals of integrity and ability, with appropriate qualifications and training.[152] To this end, the Guidelines address qualifications and training;[153] status and conditions of service;[154] freedom of expression and association;[155] the role of prosecutors in criminal proceedings;[156]

141. *Id.* para. 3.

142. *Id.* para. 4.

143. *Id.* paras. 5–8. Persons arrested or detained are to be imformed immediately of their right to be assisted by a lawyer of their choice; if they do not have the necessary means to pay, they are entitled to competent assigned counsel; access must be prompt; there must be facilities to be visited by and communicate with the lawyer.

144. *Id.* paras. 9–11.

145. *Id.* paras. 12–15.

146. *Id.* paras. 16–22.

147. *Id.* para. 23.

148. *Id.* paras. 24–25.

149. *Id.* paras. 26–29. Paragraph 28 provides that disciplinary proceedings against lawyers "shall be brought before an impartial disciplinary committee established by the legal profession, before an independent statutory authority, or before a court, and shall be subject to an independent judicial review."

150. *See supra* note 119.

151. *Id.* preamble.

152. *Id.* para. 1.

153. *Id.* paras. 1–2.

154. *Id.* paras. 3–7.

155. *Id.* paras. 8–9.

156. *Id.* paras. 10–16. For example, prosecutors must "[p]rotect the public interest, act with objectivity, take proper account of the position of the suspect and the victim, and

the need for rules and regulations to guide the exercise of the discretionary functions of prosecutors;[157] alternatives to prosecution;[158] relations with other government agencies or institutions;[159] disciplinary proceedings;[160] and an obligation on the part of prosecutors to observe the guidelines and to report violations to their superiors.[161]

(c) Model Treaties on Cooperation in the Criminal Process

The instruments in this category will be discussed in detail in Chapter 8. Suffice it here to note that there were five model treaties on this subject: the Model Treaty on Extradition,[162] the Model Treaty on Mutual Assistance in Criminal Matters,[163] the Model Treaty on the Transfer of Proceedings in Criminal Matters,[164] the Model Treaty on the Supervision of Offenders Conditionally Sentenced or Conditionally Released,[165] and the Model Treaty for the Prevention of Crimes that Infringe on the Cultural Heritage of Peoples in the Form of Cultural Property.[166]

(d) Instruments on Crime Prevention

Two instruments adopted by the Congress fit the crime prevention category: the United Nations Guidelines for the Prevention of Juvenile Delinquency (the Riyadh Guidelines),[167] and a resolution on Prevention of Urban Crime.[168]

(i) The (Riyadh) Guidelines for the Prevention of Juvenile Delinquency.

The Riyadh Guidelines[169] stress the need for and importance of pro-

---

pay attention to all relevant circumstances, irrespective of whether they are to the advantage or disadvantage of the suspect." *Id.* para. 13(b).

157. *Id.* para. 17.

158. *Id.* paras. 18–19.

159. *Id.* para. 20.

160. *Id.* paras. 21–22.

161. *Id.* paras. 23–24.

162. G.A. Res. 45/116, U.N. GAOR, 45th Sess., Supp. No. 49A, at 211, U.N. Doc. A/45/49 (1991).

163. G.A. Res. 45/117, *id.* at 215.

164. G.A. Res. 45/118, *id.* at 219.

165. G.A. Res. 45/119, *id.* at 221.

166. *Report of the Eighth Congress, supra* note 112, at 103.

167. G.A. Res. 45/112, U.N. GAOR, 45th Sess., Supp. No. 49A, at 200, U.N. Doc. A/45/49 (1991).

168. *Report of the Eighth Congress, supra* note 112, at 124. Surprisingly, this resolution is not included in the Compendium. *See supra* note 3 (describing the Compendium).

169. *See supra* note 167.

gressive delinquency prevention policies.[170] The measures to be taken should avoid criminalizing and penalizing the child for behavior which does not cause serious damage to the development of the child or harm to others. They should involve, among other strategies, the provision of opportunities, especially educational, to meet the varying needs of young persons, and to serve as a supportive framework for their development, particularly those who are demonstrably endangered or at social risk and are in need of special care and protection. The measures should also involve an awareness that "in the predominant opinion of experts," labeling a young person as "deviant," "delinquent," or "predelinquent" often contributes to the development of a consistent pattern of undesirable behavior by young persons.[171]

The Guidelines include a plea for the institution of plans for general prevention,[172] a lengthy discussion of socialization processes (the family, education, the community, and the mass media),[173] an exhortation to states to provide funds and resources for social policy,[174] and encouragement to re-examine legislation and juvenile justice administration.[175] The Riyadh Guidelines conclude with a strong call for multidisciplinary and interdisciplinary efforts at research, policy development, and coordination.[176]

A decent society will probably do for its people most of the things suggested in the Riyadh Guidelines, simply because they are the right thing to do. The fact that these steps should have some impact on reducing levels of delinquency is another good reason for doing them.

(ii) Prevention of Urban Crime. The resolution on Prevention of Urban Crime,[177] not surprisingly, returns to a number of the same themes as the Guidelines on the Prevention of Juvenile Delinquency. This preambular paragraph captures the basic flavor of the whole:

Prevention is the concern of all citizens, the community and all institutions in society, and that in particular:

---

170. The material in this paragraph has been taken primarily from General Assembly Resolution 45/112, para. 5, but is typical of the philosophy which pervades a lengthy document. *Id.* para. 5. The first five paragraphs are devoted to "fundamental principles."

171. *Id.* para. 5(f).

172. *Id.* para. 9.

173. *Id.* paras. 10–44.

174. *Id.* paras. 45–51.

175. *Id.* paras. 52–59.

176. *Id.* paras. 60–66.

177. *See supra* note 168.

(a) It is the task of Governments and other sectors of society to facilitate the development of local and national prevention programs;

(b) Prevention must bring together those with responsibility for planning and development, for the family, health, employment and training, housing, social services, leisure activities, schools, the police and the justice system in order to deal with the conditions that generate crime;

(c) Elected officials at all levels must employ the authority of their office and exercise their responsibilities in combating urban crime;

(d) Voluntary crime prevention initiatives should be supported;

(e) The community must be brought into this effort to encourage greater tolerance, greater social justice, equitable access to all programs and services and greater respect for the rights of all.[178]

The substantive recommendations include statements about the family, childhood, youth, justice, violence, urban housing and community development, alcohol, drugs and other substance abuse prevention, the police, victims, prevention of recidivism, and communicating knowledge about prevention to the citizenry. The resolution also encouraged support for the Second International Conference on Safety, Drugs and the Prevention of Urban Crime, which was held in Paris, November 18–20, 1991,[179] immediately before the Ministerial Meeting on the United Nations Program.

C. Conclusion

This concludes the overview of the standard-setting work-product of the congresses and the Committee on Crime Prevention and Control. It is a remarkable collection and the reader is encouraged to read the instruments themselves in the Secretariat's Compendium.[180]

One effect of the recent reorganization efforts will be to modify somewhat the way in which future instruments are prepared. In the first place, the Crime Prevention Commission rather than the congress will be where the main center of gravity lies and there will be fewer instruments sprung by governments on others at the last moment. Secondly, there is likely to be a consolidation phase during the next few years rather than continued frenzied drafting. Voices were even heard at the Intergovernmental Meeting in Vienna in 1991 and at the first meeting of the Commission on Crime Prevention and Criminal Justice suggesting that the existing instruments should in some way be re-

178. *Id.* para. 10 (preamble).
179. The "first" meeting, the European, American and North American Conference on Urban Safety and Crime Prevention, was held in Montreal, Canada in October 1989.
180. *See supra* note 3.

examined.[181] Re-examination of substance is unlikely to occur on a large scale and one can reasonably expect that the instruments already adopted will remain as the solid normative core of the organization's work in the criminal justice area. Some will certainly command more priority in their implementation than others.[182] There will no doubt be some additions through the work of the new commission, although the general disposition seems to be to pause at this point in order to digest and apply in an effective manner what has already been done.

181. *Report on the meeting of the Intergovernmental Working Group on the Creation of an Effective International Crime and Justice Programme, held at Vienna from 5 to 9 August 1991*, at 22, U.N. Doc. A/CONF. 156/2 (1991); *Report of the Commission on Crime Prevention and Criminal Justice on its First Session, Vienna, 21 to 30 April 1992*, at 71, U.N. Doc. E/1992/30 (1992).

182. *See* Chapter 9 *infra*, at notes 76–89, and Chapter 10 *infra*, at notes 4–6.

Chapter 5
The Approval Process and the Juridical Nature of the Instruments

A. Introduction

Increasing attention has been given in recent years to the multitude of non-legal, marginally legal, weak legal, or soft legal normative instruments developed under the auspices of international organizations.[1] In the manner of the approval process that has created them, in form, and in juridical status the criminal justice instruments represent striking examples of this genre.

In this chapter, then, I explore the soft nature of the instruments. I first address the way in which, until now, the material has been developed in the period leading up to and including the congresses. Second, I discuss the somewhat complicated way in which the Economic and Social Council and the General Assembly have gone about expressing their approval. (It may be that the recent restructuring will lead to more straightforward approval. It will certainly have some impact on the way the process works.) Next, I turn to a discussion of the juridical nature of the instruments. Are some or all of them "international law"? If not, how might these instruments best be characterized?

B. The Drafting Process

1. The 45 Resolutions Adopted at the Eighth Congress

The Eighth Congress in Havana was indicative of the way in which the drafting process had developed prior to the recent reorganization. The

---

1. *See e.g.*, T. BUERGENTHAL, LAW-MAKING IN THE INTERNATIONAL CIVIL AVIATION ORGANIZATION (1969) (noting expecially Part II); F. MORGENSTERN, LEGAL PROBLEMS OF INTERNATIONAL ORGANIZATIONS 119–134 (1986); D. M. LEIVE, INTERNATIONAL REGULATORY REGIMES: CASE STUDIES IN HEALTH, METEOROLOGY AND FOOD (1976) (paying

Committee on Crime Prevention and Control had forwarded a total of twenty-two draft resolutions to Havana through ECOSOC.[2] One of these[3] was not proceeded with in the form presented, although there were echoes of it in a resolution drafted at the Eighth Congress[4] and in the final version of another draft that had emerged from the Crime Prevention Committee's 1990 meeting.[5] Two others[6] were adopted with fairly substantial changes. Another was replaced by a somewhat different version.[7] The other eighteen were duly adopted with only minor fine-tuning.

As a package, the Crime Prevention Committee's instruments were the most weighty of the resolutions adopted by the congress. However, their number was exceeded by the twenty-four new resolutions that for many delegates made their first appearance at the Eighth Congress itself but were nevertheless adopted as well.[8] Dealing with these last-

---

special attention to volume II, chapter 24); R.R. Baxter, *Law in "Her Infinite Variety"* 29 INT'L & COMP. L.Q. 549 (1980). *See also infra* note 69.

2. *See Committee on Crime Prevention and Control, Report on the Eleventh Session, Vienna, 5–16 February 1990*, U.N. ESCOR, Supp. No. 10, at 21–170, U.N. Doc. E/1990/31 (1990) (containing the draft resolutions).

3. Committee Resolution 11/1, *World Foundation on Crime Control and Assistance to Victims, Committee on Crime Prevention and Control, Report on the Eleventh Session, supra* note 2, at 171.

4. Congress Other Resolution 27, *Protection of the human rights of victims of crime and abuse of power*, para. 5 (international fund for victims). *Eighth United Nations Congress on the Prevention of Crime and the Treatment of Offenders, Havana, 27 August-7 September 1990, Report prepared by the Secretariat*, at 194, U.N. Doc. A/CONF.144/28/Rev.1 (1991) [hereinafter *Report of the Eighth Congress*].

5. Other Resolution 1, *Prevention of urban crime*, para. 4(g) (international foundation for the prevention of urban crime). *Report of the Eighth Congress, supra* note 4, at 124.

6. Other Resolution 25, *Terrorist criminal activities, Report of the Eighth Congress, supra* note 4, at 181; Other Instrument 1, *The Model Treaty for the Prevention of Crimes that Infringe on the Cultural Heritage of Peoples in the Form of Movable Property, id.* at 103. After the Committee's approval in February 1990, the cultural heritage draft had been revised by an expert group in June 1990. *See* Chapter 8 *infra* note 145.

7. The Committee's Decision 11/105, was replaced in Committee 1 by a different version sponsored by the Netherlands and the United Kingdom. *See* Committee Decision 11/105, *Management of Criminal Justice and Development of Sentencing Policies, Committee on Crime Prevention and Control, Report on the Eleventh Session, supra* note 2, at 38 (the old resolution); U.N. Doc. A/CONF.144/C.1/L.6 (1990) (the new resolution). This new version, apparently an effort to simplify dealing with a number of drafting changes that the British and Dutch had agreed upon, repeated most of the Committee draft with improving alterations which included deleting a section on management and computers, a matter which was more fully dealt with in another conference resolution. *Report of the Eighth Congress, supra* note 4, at 241. The new version was then adopted by the Congress as "Other resolution" 19.

8. In addition to the 24 "new" resolutions which were adopted by the congress, four others were introduced. The plenary decided (apparently by consensus) to take no action

minute additions presented some difficulties, especially for small delegations a long way from home with less than perfect communications.
Because I was a member of the Crime Prevention Committee, my
sources had alerted me to a handful of these. The diplomatic process—
requests for support—had surfaced a few more. But the vast majority
of these twenty-four were new to my delegation and I suspect even
more so to many others. A number of delegations were scrambling, in
particular, to try to get instructions from home on the capital punishment resolution that ultimately failed.[9] I strongly suspect that some
states felt quite confident in rolling their particular interests late in the
game secure in the knowledge that others were playing the same way
and could be relied upon not to be obstructive so long as *their* pet ox was
not gored.

2. Encouraging States to Tip Their Hands in Advance

In the end, I do not believe that we found ourselves acquiescing in
Havana in anything that was an embarrassment.[10] But it was, in my
view, a far from satisfactory process. Somehow states have to be per-

---

on one resolution, introduced by Saudi Arabia, on "the need to amend the Vienna
Convention on Diplomatic Relations, with regard to the diplomatic agent and the
diplomatic bag in the light of recent crimes committed under the shelter of diplomatic
immunities, in particular, drug smuggling." *Report of the Eighth Congress, supra* note 4, at
233–34. One, on crime prevention and education, was withdrawn on the understanding
that it would be re-introduced in the General Assembly, where it was adopted as G.A.
Res. 45/122, U.N. GAOR, 45th Sess., Supp. No. 49A, at 225, U.N. Doc. A/45/49 (1991).
Chile introduced a draft which referred to the proposition that "treaty norms are all
binding in nature and take precedence over customary norms in regard to imprisonment." Chile went on to recommend that the Committee on Crime Prevention and
Control formulate "a preliminary draft universal covenant on imprisonment that would
codify, compile and establish new norms covering, as far as possible, the entire corpus of
contemporary law relating to imprisonment." The draft apparently garnered little support and was withdrawn. *Report of the Eighth Congress, supra* note 28, at 272. Finally, Italy
and other states introduced a resolution on the death penalty which ultimately failed. *See*
Chapter 4 *supra*, at note 4. The "new" resolutions were allocated between the plenary
and the two committees of the Congress according to subject-matter.

   9. *See* Chapter 4 *supra*, at note 28.

   10. One resolution which had been forwarded by the Committee came close to this
point. The resolution on *International co-operation for crime prevention and criminal justice in
the context of development*, adopted by the Congress and ultimately by the General Assembly as G.A. Res. 45/107, requested the Secretary-General to prepare at least two documents that were in fact before the Congress and which received a laudatory reception in
other resolutions. G.A. Res. 45/107, U.N. GAOR, 45th Sess., Supp. No.49A, at 190, U.N.
Doc. A/45/49 (1991). These documents had not been produced at the time the Committee passed on the draft earlier in the year, but were available for the Congress. Presumably someone forgot to make the necessary corrections as time passed.

suaded to tip their hands in advance of the congress and some fairly rigid time limit to that effect should be imposed. It is not beyond the wit of diplomats to devise limiting techniques to reign in the drafting excesses of sovereign states. For example, in the International Labor Organization, no resolution relating to a matter not included in the agenda may be moved at the annual conference unless it has been deposited with the Director-General at least fifteen days before the opening of the conference. A Resolutions Committee votes on which five of such resolutions the conference will take up and in which order. Those not included in the five will not be reached unless there is extra time available.[11] Such an approach would be useful for the congresses.

Speaking on behalf of New Zealand, I suggested at the first session of the Commission on Crime Prevention and Criminal Justice that the Rules for the next congress should include a provision that no resolutions could be considered at the congress which have not either been forwarded by the Commission, or drafts of which have been sent to states at least a month before the opening of the congress.[12] Something along these lines has in fact been incorporated into the Rules for 1995. The Draft Rules for the 1995 Congress, approved by the Commisssion on Crime Prevention and Criminal Justice and the Economic and Social Council in 1993, provide that that draft resolutions for the congress must be submitted to the Secretary-General of the congress four months prior to the congress, and distributed to all Member States not later than two months prior to the congress.[13] It remains to be seen how this will play out in practice.

3. Insufficient Involvement of States?

At least one government has offered criticism of the way in which congressional resolutions were prepared in the past, even in the case of those that were generated under the auspices of the Crime Prevention Committee. Speaking in the Third Committee of the General Assembly on the material produced at the Havana Congress, a representative of the United States said:

> But it is important to understand that until the Congress was held, governments were minimally involved in the preparation of the many resolutions

---

11. STANDING ORDERS OF THE INTERNATIONAL LABOR CONFERENCE, art. 17. *See also* J. KAUFMANN, CONFERENCE DIPLOMACY: AN INTRODUCTORY ANALYSIS 13 (2d rev. ed. 1988).

12. Statement by the Observer of New Zealand to the Commission on Crime Prevention and Criminal Justice (Apr. 24, 1992) (on file with the author).

13. Draft Rules of Procedure for United Nations Congresses on the Prevention of Crime and the Treatment of Offenders, R. 28, Annex to E.S.C. Res/1993/32.

which the Congress produced. There was no formal opportunity for governments to submit written comments, let alone participate in actual drafting, and the Crime Committee itself was only able to devote very limited time to drafting. Even for those governments represented [the U.S. did not go to Cuba], there was inadequate time to give in-depth consideration to each of the 45 resolutions and decisions adopted, and certainly insufficient time for serious drafting changes in any of the instruments.[14]

In so far as draft resolutions surface for the first time at congress, the comment is entirely accurate. Last minute drafts are prepared by governments, but by only one or by a small group of them. Other governments arrive on the scene largely in the dark. As I have suggested,[15] I do not believe that this is satisfactory.

The situation is more complicated in relation to the drafts that were prepared under Crime Prevention Committee auspices. In this case, much of the preliminary work was done by "experts"—which includes members of the Secretariat, seconded help from various generous governments, staff of the United Nations institutes, members of the Committee, academics and other consultants, and NGOs.[16] After preliminary work by such people, the material would then go to a relatively informal meeting of some sort[17] and then on to the more formal inter-regional and regional meetings.[18]

---

14. Statement by the Hon. Edward Marks, U.S. Mission to the U.N., Third Committee (Oct. 31, 1990). The same argument was reiterated by U.S. representatives at the 1991 Vienna Intergovernmental Meeting and at the first meeting of the Commission in 1992 (author's notes). *See Report on the Meeting of the Intergovernmental Working Group on the Creation of an Effective International Crime and Justice Programme, held at Vienna from 5 to 9 August 1991*, at 22–23, U.N. Doc. A/CONF. 156/2 (1991).

15. *See supra* pp. 127–29.

16. As in any legislative process, reading the formal documentation seldom reveals who drafted which document. By convention, work done by, say, members of the Secretariat or by NGOs will emerge under the name of a Government or, in the days of the Committee on Crime Prevention and Control, of a member of that body. Often even the named sponsors of a resolution will have little idea who did the detailed drafting. *See* L.L. Lamborn, *The United Nations Declaration on Victims: Incorporating "Abuse of Power"*, 19 RUTGERS L.J. 59 (1987); R. Brody, *Introduction, The Independence of Judges and Lawyers: A Compilation of International Standards* 25–26 C.I.J.L. BULL. 3 (1990) (going behind the public record to describe the drafting process for a 1985 and a 1990 instrument).

17. Such informal meetings included the Seminar on Transfer of Prisoners, held in Vienna in February 1983 under the auspices of the NGO Alliance on Crime Prevention and Criminal Justice to consider a Draft Model Agreement on the Transfer of Prisoners, the meeting held at the Arab Security Studies and Training Center in Riyadh, from February 28, to March 1, 1988 to develop draft Standards for the Prevention of Juvenile Delinquency, in preparation for the Eighth Congress, and the International Expert Meeting on United Nations and Law Enforcement, which met at Baden, near Vienna, between November 16 and 19, 1987 and produced the so-called "Baden Report" (*Report of the International Expert Meeting on United Nations and Law Enforcement, Baden near Vienna,*

Drafts would rapidly come within the public domain and be passed to governments at various stages either through participants or through the missions in Vienna. Governments (including some whose nationals, some of them officials, are participating as experts) would have observers at the inter-regional meetings devoted to particular topics. They would make statements or have informal input on those occasions. Buttonholing experts and apprising them of their concerns, either orally or with the aid of an informal text, has always been common behavior for governments—as it is for NGOs. Governments may make more suggestions at the regional meetings where they are eligible to attend either as participants or observers[19] and at meetings of the Committee on Crime Prevention and Control.[20] Alternatively, governments may call on or address memoranda to the Secretariat official most involved in drafting the particular instrument, expecting that person to ensure that their comments are taken into account. Of course, it is governments that ultimately voted on the instruments at the congresses and at the General Assembly. Only government representatives may vote at the congresses. In short, there was always ample opportunity for governmental participation in the drafting process of

---

16 to 19 November 1987). See R. Linke, *The Cooperation between Non-Governmental Organizations and the United Nations in the field of crime policy, in* HELSINKI INSTITUTE FOR CRIME PREVENTION AND CONTROL AFFILIATED WITH THE UNITED NATIONS, COURSE ON UNITED NATIONS CRIMINAL JUSTICE POLICY 90, 92 (1985) (discussing the 1983 meeting). The contribution of the 1988 meeting is acknowledged in paragraph 2 of the resolution adopting the United Nations Guidelines for the Prevention of Juvenile Delinquency, The Riyadh Guidelines. G.A. Res. 45/112, U.N. GAOR, 45th Sess., Supp. No.49A, at 200, U.N. Doc. A/45/49 (1991).

18. *See* Chapter 3 *supra*, at notes 67–73.

19. The United States, for example, was represented at two regional preparatory meetings for the Eighth Congress, the Asian and Pacific one, U.N. Doc. A/CONF.144/RPM.1, at 35 (1989) and the European one, U.N. Doc. A/CONF.144/RPM.2, at 35 (1989). The delegation to the European meeting was composed of the officials most involved with U.S. participation in the U.N. program, one of whom was also a member of the Committee on Crime Prevention and Control. Ronald Gainer, then Deputy Associate Attorney-General at the U.S. Department of Justice, and a Committee member, was one of the experts invited by the Secretary-General to the Interregional meeting on Topic I. U.N. Doc. A/CONF.144/IPM.1 at 26 (1988). The U.S. was represented by an observer at the Interregional meeting on Topic III. U.N. Doc. A/CONF.144/IPM.2, at 23 (1988). The United States does not appear to have been otherwise represented at the preparatory meetings. Australia, Canada and Cuba (the Eighth Congress host) were among those who attended more widely.

20. Presumably all governments have to make some hard decisions about how many resources to devote to such activities as monitoring and participating in such meetings. Among the most visible governments at the various meetings in recent years have been Australia, Austria, Canada, Cuba, Egypt, France, Germany, Italy, the Netherlands, the United Kingdom, the former USSR, and the former Yugoslavia.

those instruments produced under the aegis of the Committee on Crime Prevention and Control.

In other parts of the United Nations system, however, it is common for states to be asked formally for their comments on draft proposals and for any comments received to be circulated as a United Nations document. For example, another expert body, the International Law Commission, obtains state comments on its work as is required by its constituent document.[21] (The downside risk of this is that everything will take an inordinate time. The International Law Commission has a reputation in some quarters for worrying an item to death in an interminable fashion.) The Sub-Commission on Prevention of Discrimination and Protection of Minorities operates in a like fashion, although there appears to be nothing specific in the applicable rules of procedure which so requires. In the past, this formal procedure has not occurred in respect of congressional documents prior to the congress. Formal (and informal)[22] conference documents recommending amendments are of course circulated by governments at the congresses themselves. There appears to be no technical reason why formal comments from states should not have been sought by the Crime Prevention Committee prior to its finalization of the drafts, or even in the period immediately before the congress. It is to be expected that, in view of the criticisms made, there will be some effort made to have any drafting efforts in which the Commission may engage circulated to the wider membership of the U.N.[23]

21. As part of its "plan of work," art. 19 of the Statute of the International Law Commission requires the Commission, through the Secretary-General, to "address to Governments a detailed request to furnish the texts of laws, decrees, judicial decisions, treaties, diplomatic correspondence and other documents relevant to the topic being studied and which the Commission deems necessary." Article 21 reads:

1. When the Commission considers a draft to be satisfactory, it shall request the Secretary-General to issue it as a Commission document. The Secretariat shall give all necessary publicity to the document including such explanations and supporting material as the Commission may consider appropriate. The publication shall include any information supplied to the Commission by Governments in accordance with article 19. The Commission shall decide whether the opinions of any scientific institution or individual experts consulted by the Commission shall be included in the publication.
2. The Commission shall request Governments to submit comments on this document within a reasonable time.

Article 22 goes on to require the Commission to prepare a final draft and explanatory report "[t]aking such comments into consideration."

22. For example, members of a regional group may circulate an informal document among themselves and show it to other interested parties before going with an agreed text.

23. A possible indication of a disposition to move in this direction is Decision 1/102 of

C. Form and Mode of "Enactment" by ECOSOC and the General Assembly

1. Form

None of the instruments produced by the Crime Prevention and Criminal Justice Program have appeared in the form of multilateral treaties akin to major instruments in the human rights and drug areas.[24] Symbolic, perhaps, of the mindset that accompanies this fact is that when it was desired to complete the drafting of a convention based on the Torture Declaration which had emerged from the 1975 Congress,[25] the action moved into the mainstream human rights part of the United Nations system, the Commission on Human Rights and the Third Committee of the General Assembly. All the instruments relevant to the present study are, then, in the form of a resolution from the General Assembly, the Economic and Social Council, or the relevant congress. All those in resolution form of the congress were subsequently approved in some fashion by ECOSOC or the General Assembly. Approval normally occured without their text appearing amongst the annual publication of resolutions of the Assembly. All the instruments were ultimately adopted by consensus, differences of opinion had been ironed out, and none were finally put to a vote.

Generally, these instruments are presented in the nature of a normative statement of guidelines or standards.[26] A few are in the form of

---

the Commission on Crime Prevention and Criminal Justice in which the Commission decided to consult with governments about the proposal for a convention on cooperation on crime prevention and criminal justice made by Costa Rica "with a view to having available at its second session sufficient background data to enable it to conduct a well-informed discussion." *Report of the Commission on Crime Prevention and Criminal Justice on its First Session, Vienna, 21 to 30 April 1992*, at 50, U.N. Doc. E/1992/30 (1992). Few responses were received, certainly not enough for a well-informed discussion. *Progress made in the implementation of Economic and Social Council resolution 1922/22, Report of the Secretary-General*, at 16–17, U.N. Doc. E/1993/10 (1993).

24. I do not mean to suggest that the treaty form would be a definitive indicator of the hard or soft juridical nature of the instruments. I agree with those such as Baxter, who insist that even the treaty form may include soft, or hortatory, obligations. Baxter, *supra* note 1, at 550–54. As I shall suggest later in the text, many—perhaps most—of the criminal justice standards and norms are of the soft law variety. But this is not so much a question of form as of the attitude expressed by states in the internal language of the instruments, in speeches when adopting the instruments, and in subsequent dealings. *See also* Chapter 2 *supra*, at notes 98–135 (discussing whether there *should* be a treaty or treaties).

25. G.A. Res. 3452 (XXX), U.N. GAOR, 30th Sess., Supp. No. 34, at 91, U.N. Doc. A/10034 (1976). Chapter 4 *supra*, at notes 10–20 and accompanying text (discussing the Torture Declaration).

26. *See* Chapters 4, 6 & 7 *supra* (giving examples of such instruments).

resolutions annexing model draft treaties which states are urged to use as a basis for bilateral (or possibly regional or sub-regional) negotiations.[27]

2. Approval of the Standard Minimum Rules

Two years after their formulation at the First United Nations Congress in 1955, the Standard Minimum Rules for the Treatment of Prisoners were approved by ECOSOC.[28] The ECOSOC resolution read:

The Economic and Social Council

1. *Approves* the *Standard Minimum Rules for the Treatment of Prisoners* adopted by the First United Nations Congress. . . .[29]

2. *Draws the attention* of Governments to those *Rules* and *recommends:*

(a) That favourable consideration be given to their adoption and application in the administration of penal and correctional institutions;

(b) That the Secretary-General be informed every five years of the progress made with regard to their application;

(c) That Governments arrange for the widest possible publicity to be given to the *Rules*, not only among governmental services concerned but also among non-governmental organizations interested in social defence;

3. *Authorizes* the Secretary-General to make arrangements for the publication, as appropriate, of the information received in pursuance of sub-paragraph 2 (b) above and to ask for supplementary information if necessary.[30]

The verb "approves" was unequivocal enough, but the terms "recommends" and "give favourable consideration to" in the second paragraph softened any implication that the Council was speaking the language of legal obligation. In subsequent years, discussion took place in various forums about whether the stature of the Rules should be enhanced by obtaining General Assembly approval or placing them in treaty form. Thus the Consultative Group on the United Nations program that met in 1968 wondered "whether it might not be expedient to divide the Standard Minimum Rules into two parts, the first containing human rights safeguards embodied in a convention, and

27. *See* Chapter 8 *infra* (discussing the instruments of this nature).

28. E.S.C. Res. 663 C (XXIV), U.N. ESCOR, 24th Sess., Supp. No. 1, at 11, U.N. Doc. E/3048 (1957).

29. Here the text included a footnote reference to the relevant page of the Report of the Congress.

30. *See* Chapter 9 *infra*, at notes 6–42 (discussing the Secretary-General's information gathering on the Standard Minimum Rules). The Secretariat apparently balked at seeking supplementary information and paragraph 3 was never put into effect.

the second principles which would lay down guidelines for the rehabilitation of prisoners."[31] The idea did not catch on. As the Report of
the 1970 Kyoto Congress notes, some participants suggested the conclusion of a convention which would meet "the need for making the
guarantees, which were no more than mere recommendations, more
legally binding."[32] The majority, however, while not rejecting the idea
in principle, felt that the time was premature.[33] The report goes on to
assert that:

Nevertheless, the Congress was virtually unanimous in hoping that the moral
authority, and hence the relatively mandatory nature, of the Standard Minimum Rules could be reinforced by a resolution of the General Assembly of the
United Nations. Such a resolution, originating in the highest policy-making
body of the United Nations, would be justified by the consideration that the
Standard Minimum Rules were the concrete application of human rights in the
sphere of social defence, which was currently being approached from an ever
more scientific, humanitarian and social point of view. The General Assembly
resolution, which was earnestly desired by the Fourth Congress, should embody the new spirit that imbued the prevention of crime and the efforts being
made for the treatment of offenders.[34]

The General Assembly deigned to act the following year, although its
adopting language could be seen as reflecting less than total enthusiasm. In the relevant paragraph of its resolution that year on "Human
rights in the administration of justice" the Assembly, using somewhat

31. *Report of the United Nations Consultative Group on the Prevention of Crime and the
Treatment of Offenders, Geneva, 6–16 August 1968*, at 28, U.N. Doc. ST/SOA/91 (1969). *See
also* Chapter 6 *infra*, at note 7.

32. *Fourth United Nations Congress on the Prevention of Crime and the Treatment of Offenders,
Kyoto, Japan, 17–26 August 1970, Report prepared by the Secretariat*, at 20, U.N. Doc.
A/CONF.43/5 (1971) [hereinafter *Fourth Congress Report*].

33. *Id.* at 20–21. The idea of a convention is still current; the time is apparently still
not right. At the Havana Congress, Chile introduced a draft resolution which would
request the Committee on Crime Prevention and Control "to formulate as soon as
possible a preliminary draft universal covenant on imprisonment that would codify,
compile and establish new norms covering, as far as possible, the entire corpus of
contemporary law relating to imprisonment." The draft was withdrawn. *Report of the
Eighth Congress, supra* note 4, para. 333. During the 1991 restructuring process Costa Rica
proposed a framework convention for the program which would have protocols containing "regulations and standards." The idea was passed on to the new Commission on
Crime Prevention and Criminal Justice. *See supra* note 23, and Chapter 2 *supra*, at note
126. In the human rights area it is quite common for a resolution, especially a Declaration, to be followed some time later by a more detailed convention, in accordance with
the precedent set by the drafting of the Universal Declaration of Human Rights in 1948,
followed, eighteen years later, by the two Covenants, one on Economic, Social and
Cultural Rights, the other on Civil and Political Rights, which were eventually adopted
by the General Assembly in 1966.

34. *Fourth Congress Report, supra* note 32, at 21.

different language from the "approval" contained in the ECOSOC language,

Invites the attention of Member States to the Standard Minimum Rules for the Treatment of Prisoners and recommends that they shall be effectively implemented in the administration of penal and correctional institutions and that favourable consideration shall be given to their incorporation in national legislation.[35]

The word "approval" is conspicuous by its absence, and the words "invites," "recommends" and "favourable consideration" are hardly the blunt language of obligation.

3. Adoption in Individual General Assembly Resolutions

As noted in our historical survey,[36] some of the later instruments, such as the Torture Declaration,[37] and three instruments from the Milan Congress[38] were drafted in such a manner as to appear as individual resolutions of the General Assembly. The same is true of several instruments from the Havana Congress.[39] The Caracas Declaration of 1980

35. G.A. Res. 2858 (XXVI), U.N. GAOR, 26th Sess., Supp. No. 29, at 94, para. 2, U.N. Doc. A/8429 (1972). Paragraph 3 of the resolution "takes note with satisfaction" of the establishment of a Working Group on the Rules, to advise on methods of strengthening the implementation of the Rules and of improving the reporting procedures thereon. *See* G.A. Res. 3144 (XXVIII), U.N. GAOR, 28th Sess., Supp. No. 30, at 85, U.N. Doc. A/9030 (1974) (recommending that "Member States should make all possible efforts to implement [the Rules] in the administration of penal and correctional institutions and take the Rules into account in the framing of national legislation").

36. *See* Chapter 4 *supra*, at notes 18, 49–51.

37. *Declaration on the Protection of All Persons from Being Subjected to Torture and Other Cruel, Inhuman or Degrading Treatment or Punishment*, G.A. Res. 3452 (XXX), U.N. GAOR, 30th Sess., Supp. No. 34, at 91, U.N. Doc. A/10034 (1976).

38. *The Standard Minimum Rules for the Administration of Juvenile Justice (The Beijing Rules)*, G.A. Res. 40/33, U.N. GAOR, 40th Sess., Supp. No. 53, at 206, U.N. Doc. A/40/53 (1986); *the Declaration of Basic Principles of Justice for Victims of Crime and Abuse of Power*, G.A. Res. 40/34, *id.* at 213; *Domestic Violence*, G.A. Res. 40/36, *id.* at 215.

39. *The Standard Minimum Rules for Non-Custodial Measures (the Tokyo Rules)*, G.A. Res. 45/110, U.N. GAOR, 45th Sess., Supp. No. 49A, at 195, U.N. Doc. A/45/49 (1991); *the Basic Principles for the Treatment of Prisoners*, G.A. Res. 45/111, *id.* at 199; *the Guidelines for the Prevention of Juvenile Delinquency (the Riyadh Guidelines)*, G.A. Res. 45/112, *id.* at 200; *the Rules for the Protection of Juveniles Deprived of Their Liberty*, G.A. Res. 45/113, *id.* at 204; *Domestic Violence*, G.A. Res. 45/114, *id.* at 209; *Instrumental Use of Children in Criminal Activities*, G.A. Res. 45/115, *id.* at 211; *the Model Treaty on Extradition*, G.A. Res. 45/116, *id.*; *the Model Treaty on Mutual Assistance in Criminal Matters*, G.A. Res. 45/117, *id.* at 215; *the Model Treaty on the Transfer of Proceedings in Criminal Matters*, G.A. Res. 45/118, *id.* at 219; *the Model Treaty on the Transfer of Supervision of Offenders Conditionally Sentenced or Conditionally Released*, G.A. Res. 45/119, *id.* at 221.

was not so drafted, but it is in fact annexed to the resolution in which the Assembly "endorsed" it.[40]

4. Miscellaneous Omnibus References by the General Assembly

Another set of 1985 and 1990 General Assembly resolutions intro-duced a bewildering medley of ways of dealing with approval of those resolutions which did not become individual Assembly resolutions. Thus General Assembly Resolution 40/32 of November 29, 1985 en-titled "Seventh United Nations Congress on the Prevention of Crime and the Treatment of Offenders,"[41] has five paragraphs expressing approval of one sort or another for various aspects of the work of the Congress. The adopting verbs run the whole gamut of the United Nations language of praise. In one,[42] the General Assembly *"Takes note"* of the report of the Secretary-General on the conclusions of the Sev-enth Congress. In a second,[43] the Assembly *"Approves"* the Milan Plan of Action adopted by the congress, "as a useful and effective means of strengthening international co-operation in the field of crime preven-tion and criminal justice." A footnote refers the reader to the appropri-ate page of the Report of the Seventh Congress where the text of the Milan Plan may be found. A third paragraph[44] *"Recommends"* the Guid-ing Principles for Crime Prevention and Criminal Justice in the Con-text of Development and a New International Economic Order "for national, regional and international action, as appropriate, taking into account the political, economic, social and cultural circumstances and traditions of each country on the basis of the principles of sovereign equality of States and of non-interference in their internal affairs."

40. G.A. Res. 35/171, U.N. GAOR, 35th Sess., Supp. No. 48, at 193–95, U.N. Doc. A/35/48 (1981). The Assembly "endorses" the Declaration in para. 2, while in para. 8 it *"Invites* Governments to make continuous efforts to implement the principles contained in the Caracas declaration and other relevant resolutions and recommendations, as adopted by the Sixth United Nations Congress . . . in accordance with the economic, social, cultural and political circumstances of each country." What exactly are the "rele-vant" resolutions and recommendations is not clear. The Congress's Report lists 19 "Other resolutions and decisions" adopted in addition to the Declaration of Caracas. U.N. Doc. A/CONF. 87/14/Rev. 1, at iii (1981). None of them has the detail or finite quality of the congressional instruments with which this study is concerned. Most are general exhortations to keep up various items of the United Nations program or sugges-tions for matters to be worked on in anticipation of the next congress. They thus fail to qualify as normative instruments.

41. G.A. Res. 40/32, U.N. GAOR, 40th Sess., Supp. No. 53, at 204, U.N. Doc. A/40/53 (1986).

42. *Id.* para. 2.

43. *Id.* para. 3.

44. *Id.* para. 4.

Again there is a footnote referring the reader to the appropriate page of the report of the congress. Then comes a tersely worded omnibus paragraph[45] in which the Assembly *"Endorses* the other resolutions adopted unanimously by the Seventh Congress." This time there is no footnote crediting the report. "Endorses" appears to be a weaker form of acceptance than "approves." Finally, there is a longer paragraph[46] in which the Assembly:

Invites Governments to be guided by the Milan Plan of Action in the formulation of appropriate legislation and policy directives and to make continuous efforts to implement the principles contained in the Caracas Declaration and other relevant resolutions and recommendations adopted by the Sixth Congress, in accordance with the economic, social, cultural and political circumstances of each country.

A fortnight later the Assembly returned to some of the themes of the congress in its resolution under the item "Human Rights in the administration of justice."[47] Some of the instruments already approved were approved again. This time the Assembly *"Welcomes* the Basic Principles on the Independence of the Judiciary adopted unanimously [by the Congress] and invites Governments to respect them and to take them into account within the framework of their national legislation and practice."[48] It also *"Takes note with appreciation* of the Model Agreement on the Transfer of Foreign Prisoners and recommendations on the treatment of foreign prisoners, also adopted unanimously by the Seventh Congress, and invites Member States to take the Model Agreement into account in establishing treaty relations with other Member States or in revising existing treaty relations." [49]

General Assembly approval in 1990 was not quite as complex an affair. Apart from those instruments which became individual Assembly resolutions,[50] the Assembly "welcomed"[51] the Havana instruments

45. *Id.* para. 5.
46. *Id.* para. 6.
47. G.A. Res. 40/146, U.N. GAOR, 40th Sess., Supp. No. 53, at 254, U.N. Doc. A/40/53 (1986).
48. *Id.* para. 2.
49. *Id.* para. 4. Both paragraphs have appropriate references to where the texts may be found in the Eighth Congress Report. The resolution contains several other paragraphs referring to the work both of the Committee on Crime Prevention and Control and that of the Sub-Commission on Prevention of Discrimination and Protection of Minorities.
50. *See supra* note 39.
51. *See* G.A. Res. 45/121, U.N. GAOR, 45th Sess., Supp. No. 49A, at 223, para. 3, U.N. Doc. A/45/49 (1991) which "[w]*elcomes* the instruments and resolutions adopted by the

as a group in its resolution on the Eighth Congress. Again, as in 1985, in a later resolution on human rights in the administration of justice, the Assembly singled out for specific reference some of the Havana instruments which received a second welcome—this time by name. The Assembly invited governments to "respect them and take them into account within the framework of national legislation and practice."[52]

The most obvious practical effect of all of this is that the instruments adopted individually appear in the annual collection of General Assembly resolutions. The others have to be tracked into the report of the Eighth Congress—a far less accessible document—or to some secondary source.[53]

Is there some subtle juridical distinction involved, over and above this practical point? Is there some significance in the fact that some of the less accessible ones have been approved by name, instead of, or in addition to, being approved en masse? While the author's impression is that whether or not an instrument appears as an individual General Assembly resolution turns largely on the skill of its individual drafters and the cunning of its supporters, there is arguably some sort of hierarchy in the strength of General Assembly approval involved here. Those adopted individually must theoretically have more weight. That the drafters and supporters sometimes knew what they were doing is perhaps borne out by the experience of the Model Treaty for the

---

Eighth Congress, [note, A/CONF.144/28, ch.I] and invites Governments to be guided by them in the formulation of appropriate legislation and policy directives and to make efforts to implement the principles contained therein and in the relevant instruments and resolutions approved by the previous congresses and other relevant resolutions, in accordance with the economic, social, legal, cultural and political circumstances of each country." The resolutions adopted in Havana had been classified into three categories in the Report: Draft instruments and resolutions recommended for adoption by the General Assembly; Other instruments adopted by the Congress; and Other resolutions adopted by the Congress. *Supra* note 4, at 2–3. *See infra* notes 60–61 (discussing the deliberate use of "welcomed" here).

52. G.A. Res. 45/166, U.N. GAOR, 45th Sess., Supp. No. 49A, para. 4, U.N. Doc. A/45/49 (1991). The instruments were the Basic Principles on the Role of Lawyers, the Basic Principles on the Use of Force and Firearms by Law Enforcement Officials, the Guidelines on the Role of Prosecutors, the Basic Principles for the Treatment of Prisoners, the Standard Minimum Rules for Non-Custodial Measures, and the Rules for the Protection of Juveniles Deprived of Their Liberty.

53. *See* Chapter 4 *supra*, at note 87 (giving the example of the Basic Principles on the Independence of the Judiciary). Amnesty International included the Basic Principles on the Use of Force and Firearms by Law Enforcement Officials and the Basic Principles on the Role of Lawyers as appendices to its (annual) International Report in 1991. *See* AMNESTY INTERNATIONAL, AMNESTY INTERNATIONAL REPORT 1991 (1991).

Prevention of Crimes that Infringe on the Cultural Heritage of Peoples in the Form of Movable Property.[54] This document encountered less than total enthusiasm at the Committee on Crime Prevention and Control and at the Havana Congress and, therefore, found itself excluded from the individual instrument category (where the other draft treaties done at the congress were located) and lumped in the "other instruments" category to be grudgingly "welcomed" en masse. On the other hand, caprice sometimes seems the order of the day. One might have thought that the Basic Principles on the Use of Force and Firearms By Law Enforcement Officials,[55] or the Basic Principles on the Role of Lawyers,[56] both of which were part of the "welcomed" group in 1990, were (or ought to have been) just as important as the resolutions on computerization of criminal justice[57] or instrumental use of children in criminal activities[58] which appeared as individual resolutions. Yet I do not believe that any deliberate decision was ever made regarding the categorization of the instruments on use of force and on lawyers during the drafting process, up to and including the Eighth Congress, although someone in the Third Committee thought highly enough of them to welcome them twice at the General Assembly!

Moreover, the "enacting" or "approving" verbs in the omnibus resolutions may look innocuous, but they have in fact been chosen with care. Innocuousness comes in deliberate shadings in United Nations usage. "Welcoming,"[59] rather than "endorsing"[60] the 1990 resolutions (as the 1985 ones had been blessed with being endorsed) was a compro-

---

54. *See* Chapter 8 *infra*, at notes 143–155 (discussing this issue).

55. *Report of the Eighth United Nations Congress on the Prevention of Crime and the Treatment of Offenders, Havana, Cuba, 27 Aug.–7 Sept. 1990, supra* note 4, at 110.

56. *Id.* at 117.

57. G.A. Res. 45/109, U.N. GAOR, 45th Sess., Supp. No. 49A, at 194, U.N. Doc. A/45/49 (1991). This resolution had been passed on by the Committee on Crime Prevention and Control which had drafted it in the form of a congress resolution rather than a General Assembly one. *See* Decision 11/103, *Committee on Crime Prevention and Control, Report on the Eleventh Session, Vienna, 5–16 February 1990,* at 26, U.N. ESCOR, Supp. No. 10, U.N. Doc. E/1990/31 (1990). For reasons that escaped me, the resolution was "upgraded" in Committee at Havana. U.N. Doc. A/CONF.144/C.1/L.3 (1990).

58. G.A. Res. 45/115, U.N. GAOR, 45th Sess., Supp. No. 49A, at 211, U.N. Doc. A/45/49 (1991). This proposal had not even had the advantage of study by the Crime Prevention Committee. It was introduced at the congress by Italy on behalf of a broad group of sponsors. *See Report of the Eighth Congress, supra* note 4, at 247; U.N. Doc. A/CONF.144/C.1/L.5 (1990). *See also* Chapter 3 *supra*, at notes 89–92 (detailing the procedures of the congress).

59. *See supra* note 51.

60. The original draft of the resolution, sponsored by Cuba and Italy, "*Endorses* the resolutions adopted by the Eighth Congress and invites Governments to be guided by them. . . ." U.N. Doc. A/C.3/45/L.29, para. 3 (1990).

mise reached in the General Assembly with the United States, which had sought a softer formula still.[61] Does this really result in "less" approval, or is this just too subtle?

There appears, then, to be some shading in degrees of acceptance by the General Assembly, but it is not always deliberate.

D. The Juridical Nature of the Instruments

If one were to try to answer the question whether the resolutions go so far as either to reflect or to create customary international law, it would no doubt be necessary to look carefully at each individual instrument. For customary law to develop there must be both some relevant state practice and some *opinio juris*, a notion that what is done is done from a sense of legal obligation. The reporters of the Restatement Third of the Foreign Relations Law of the United States remind us that:

The practice of states that builds customary law takes many forms and includes what states do in or through international organizations. . . . The United Nations General Assembly in particular has adopted resolutions, declarations, and other statements of principles that in some circumstances contribute to the process of making customary law, insofar as statements and votes of governments are kinds of state practice . . . and may be expressions of *opinio juris*. . . . The contributions of such resolutions and of the statements and votes supporting them to the lawmaking process will differ widely, depending on factors such as the subject of the resolution, whether it purports to reflect legal principles, how large a majority it commands and how numerous and important are the dissenting states, whether it is widely supported (including in particular the states principally affected) and whether it is later confirmed by other practice. "Declarations of principles" may have greater significance than ordinary resolutions.[62]

Applying such criteria to the criminal justice instruments, one immediately notes that the 1975 instrument on torture,[63] for example, is cast in the form of a General Assembly Declaration, arguably the strongest form of General Assembly resolution so far as law-making goes. On the other hand, the titles and adopting language of many of the others are

61. The U.S., in an informal, unnumbered text circulated in the Third Committee (on file with the author) would have revised the adopting paragraph to read: "Invites Governments to give serious consideration to the resolutions adopted by the Eighth Congress" instead of the words "Endorses the resolutions . . . and invites Governments to be guided by them" as in the Cuba/Italy draft *supra* note 60. *See supra* note 14 (detailing the U.S. argument for adopting this position, which is based primarily on the contention that the states had only been minimally involved in the drafting).

62. RESTATEMENT (THIRD) OF THE FOREIGN RELATIONS LAW OF THE UNITED STATES § 102, Reporters' Note 2 (1987).

63. *See supra* note 37.

peppered with words like "guidelines," "standards," and "principles" which suggest something much softer. Even the Declaration on Victims[64] has language in its title immediately after the word "Declaration" which undercuts that word's effect—it is a "Declaration of *Basic Principles* of Justice for Victims of Crime and Abuse of Power" (emphasis added). Those documents that contain words such as "Rules" or "Code of Conduct" in their titles all contain in the body of the text precatory language indicating that "rules" or "code" is not used in any hard, black-letter law sense.[65]

Categorizing the legal nature of a specific provision of any particular instrument is in fact notoriously difficult. Some parts of some instruments, especially when reflective of what other significant instruments say (so that one is talking of a cumulative effect), must represent international law—either as an authoritative interpretation of the human rights provisions of the Charter, as customary law, or as evidence of "general principles of law recognized by civilized nations."[66] Such must be the case for the basic thrust of the torture instrument[67] or the prohibition of corporal punishment, punishment by placing in a dark cell, or cruel, inhuman, or degrading punishment contained in the Standard Minimum Rules for the Treatment of Prisoners.[68] And other material must surely be working its way into the general body of

64. *See* Chapter 7 *infra.*

65. *See* Chapter 6 *infra* (discussing the Standard Minimum Rules for the Treatment of Prisoners).

66. I have in mind, of course, the "sources" of law contained in article 38 of the Statute of the International Court of Justice. *See generally* HUMAN RIGHTS SOURCEBOOK 4–6 (A.P. Blaustein, R.S. Clark & J.A. Sigler eds. 1987); R. B. LILLICH, INTERNATIONAL HUMAN RIGHTS: PROBLEMS OF LAW, POLICY AND PRACTICE 126–162 (2d ed. 1991). *See also United Nations Norms and Guidelines in Crime Prevention and Criminal Justice: Implementation and Priorities for Further Standard-Setting, Working paper prepared by the Secretariat,* U.N. Doc. A/CONF. 144/18, at 7 (1990) (citing these authorities). B. SLOAN, UNITED NATIONS GENERAL ASSEMBLY RESOLUTIONS IN OUR CHANGING WORLD 54–91 (1991); C. M. Cerna, *The Normative Status of the Universal Declaration of Human Rights—The View from the United States, in* PROCEEDINGS AND COMMITTEE REPORTS OF THE AMERICAN BRANCH OF THE INTERNATIONAL LAW ASSOCIATION 1991–1992, at 48 (1992) (providing a good survey of the relevant literature).

67. Torture Declaration, *supra* note 37. *See* Filártiga v. Peña-Irala, 630 F.2d 876 (2d Cir. 1980) (using the Declaration and other material in support of the proposition that state-sponsored torture contravenes customary law).

68. Standard Minimum Rules for the Treatment of Prisoners, R. 31, *adopted by* E.S.C. Res. 663 C (XXIV) (1957), *supra* note 28, *amended by* E.S.C. Res. 2076 (LXII), U.N. ESCOR, 62d Sess., Supp. No. 1, at 35, U.N. Doc. E/5988 (1977). *See* Universal Declaration of Human Rights, G.A. Res. 217A (III), U.N. GAOR, 3d Sess., pt. 1, at 71, art. 5, U.N. Doc. A/810 (1948) (proscribing torture and cruel, inhuman or degrading treatment or punishment).

customary law. The rest, though, belongs in the categories of moral, political, or aspirational material, or of "weak law," or "soft law."[69]

Typical of the approach taken by states to the general body of the United Nations instruments is this comment from the New Zealand Department of Justice, made in the course of the Department's submission to a 1988 Ministerial Committee of Enquiry into the prison system:

The New Zealand attitude to international norms, guidelines and standards in the field of criminal justice and the treatment of offenders is that, whilst they are instruments for the maintenance of an effective and humane administration of criminal justice, many are in the nature of guide-posts as to acceptable minimum standards. Actual conditions in New Zealand are often in advance of such provisions. Where they are not, affirmative action will be considered to remedy the situation or, in a few cases, whilst agreeing with the fundamental principle, we have chosen to focus attention on some other method of resolving the situation. In some cases we have preferred other international guidelines, such as the Council of Europe rules. . . .

Amendments to the Penal Institutions Act 1954, Penal Institutions Regulations 1961, and the Criminal Justice Act 1985 are made from time to time and the United Nations Rules are borne in mind when proposals are framed. Indeed the Rules were taken into account when the regulations were drafted and the spirit of the rules is embodied in the legislation. However, there are a number of other factors which influence the final enactment of legislation in this country.[70]

The soft nature of such standards and norms does not mean that most states, as members of the United Nations club, do not feel some

69. *See* I. Seidl-Hohenveldern, *International Economic "Soft Law"*, 1979 II Recueil des Cours 165; A.J.P. Tammes, *Soft Law*, in T.M.C. ASSER INSTITUUT, ESSAYS ON INTERNATIONAL AND COMPARATIVE LAW IN HONOUR OF JUDGE ERADES 187 (1983); Panel, *A Hard Look at Soft Law*, 82 PROC. AM. SOC'Y INT'L L. 371 (1988); C.M. Chinkin, *The Challenge of Soft Law: Development and Change in International Law*, 38 INT'L & COMP. L.Q. 850 (1989); K.C. Wellens & G.M. Borchardt, *Soft Law in European Community Law*, 14 EUROP. L. REV. 267 (1989); G. Palmer, *New Ways to Make International Environmental Law*, 86 AM. J. INT'L L. 259, 269–70 (1992). *See also* O. Schachter, *The Twilight Existence of Nonbinding International Agreements*, 71 AM. J. INT'L L. 296 (1977); A. Aust, *The Theory and Practice of Informal International Instruments*, 35 INT'L & COMP. L.Q. 787 (1986). Professor Riphagen has argued that a simple scale or continuum running from non-law through soft law and normal law on to peremptory norms, fails to catch the full richness of modern state practice. In some cases, he suggests, the apparent scale may approach a circle with soft law running over into *jus cogens*. W. Riphagen, *From Soft Law to Jus Cogens and Back*, 17 VICTORIA U. WELL. L. REV. 81 (1987).

70. PRISONS IN CHANGE: THE SUBMISSION OF THE DEPARTMENT OF JUSTICE TO THE MINISTERIAL COMMITTEE OF INQUIRY INTO THE PRISONS SYSTEM 84 (1988) (appendix). *See* Chapter 10 *infra*, at note 22 (discussing the Ministerial Committee's views); Chapter 6 *infra*, note 147 (noting the Council of Europe Rules).

obligation to make an effort to comply—or to rationalize reasons for not complying.[71] Nor does it mean that the organization is powerless to try to encourage the implementation of the instruments, especially by means of monitoring devices.[72] Indeed, while Chapters 9 and 10 focus directly on the implementation issue, the reader should see all of this book as an effort to reflect the United Nations at work trying to promote the implementation of its material—at the very least by stimulating its dissemination and invocation, in the abstract if not in concrete cases. The soft law nature of some of the material does mean, however, that the struggle to venture into the realm of the concrete is an uphill one. Inevitably, we find ourselves in an area characterized both by soft law and by "soft procedures".[73]

71. While it was making a point about a norm now clearly regarded as one of *law*, the United States Government's Memorandum as Amicus Curiae in Filártiga v. Peña-Irala, *supra* note 67, is applicable to experience that the writer has had with soft law standards also:

> In exchanges between United States embassies and all foreign states with which the United States maintains relations, it has been the Department of State's general experience that no government has asserted a right to torture its own nationals. Where reports of such torture elicit some credence, a state usually responds by denial or, less frequently, by asserting that the conduct was unauthorized or constituted rough treatment short of torture.

Filártiga v. Peña-Irala, No. 79-6090, at 16 n.34 (1979).

72. *See generally* Chapters 9 & 10 *infra. See also* M. Bothe, *Legal and Non-Legal Norms— A Meaningful Distinction in International Relations?* 11 Neth. Y.B. Int'l L. 65, 78 (1980) (discussing human rights and self determination resolutions); *but see* Chapter 9 *infra*, note 46 (noting that the particular human rights procedures discussed by Bothe were being abandoned as he was writing).

73. The term "soft procedures" seems to have been coined by Professor Seidl-Hohenveldern. *Supra* note 69, at 225.

Part III
Some Representative
Standards

Chapter 6
The Standard Minimum Rules for the Treatment of Prisoners

A. Introduction

I discuss elsewhere the events surrounding the adoption of the Standard Minimum Rules for the Treatment of Prisoners (Rules)[1] and efforts at their "implementation."[2] The first part of this chapter is devoted more to the substance and philosophy of the Rules. The second part concerns what the United Nations surveys on the Rules' implementation have demonstrated. It is important to note at the outset that, in spite of periodic exhortations to the academic community to take a serious interest in the Rules,[3] and some enthusiasm expressed by human rights activists,[4] the significant academic literature on this subject is very sparse.[5] Most authorities who might have

1. *See* Chapter 4 *supra*, at notes 5–7; Chapter 5 *supra*, at notes 28–35.
2. *See* Chapter 9 *infra*, at notes 6–42. Note in this respect the *Reports of the Secretary-General on the Implementation of the Rules*. U.N. Doc. A/CONF.43/3, Annex (1970); U.N. Doc. A/CONF.56/6, Annex I (1975); U.N. Doc. A/CONF.87/11, A/CONF.87/11 Add. (1980); U.N. Doc. A/CONF.121/15, A/CONF.121/15 Add. 1 (1985); U.N. Doc. A/CONF.144/11 (1990) [hereinafter referred to by year].
3. *See, e.g., Report of the Secretary-General on the Meeting of the Working Group of Experts on the Standard Minimum Rules for the Treatment of Prisoners, held at United Nations Headquarters, from 25 to 29 Sept. 1972,* at 4, U.N. Doc. E/AC.57/8 (1973).
4. R.B. Lillich, *How Can the UN Create Human Rights Norms Other Than by the Treaty and Resolution Routes? (Model Laws Such as the UN Standard Minimum Rules for the Treatment of Prisoners), in* R.B. Lillich, International Human Rights: Problems of Law, Policy, and Practice 233 (2d ed. 1991); N.S. Rodley, The Treatment of Prisoners Under International Law (1987); J. Toman, *Quasi-Legal Standards and Guidelines for Protecting Human Rights, in* Guide to International Human Rights Practice 200 (H. Hannum ed., 2d ed. 1992); Human Rights Watch, The Global Report on Prisons (1993).
5. *Supra* note 4. *See* Note, *Standard Minimum Rules for the Treatment of Prisoners,* 2 N.Y.U. J. Int'l L. & Pol. 314 (1969); W. Clifford, *The Standard Minimum Rules for the Treatment of Prisoners,* 66 Proc. Am. Soc. Int'l L. 232 (1972); D.J. Besharov & G.O.W. Mueller, *The Demands of the Inmates of Attica State Prison and the United Nations Standard Minimum Rules*

been expected to include a substantial discussion of the Rules in their works have not done so.[6]

The Rules deal with the "treatment" of prisoners. "Treatment" is a word that, in the present context, is chosen for its ambiguity. Describing the Rules as pertaining to treatment captures nicely the duality of their concern—both with human rights and with endeavoring to "cure" the offender from re-offending. Periodically the question has been raised whether the Rules "should be divided into two categories: the first comprising rules pertaining to fundamental human rights, which might be embodied in a convention; and the second including rules laying down guiding principles for the treatment of offenders in accordance with an integrated and progressive social defence policy."[7] The idea has some appeal at the theoretical level, but unscrambling the two areas is problematical in practice and it seems likely not to occur.

As far as treatment in the sense of "curing" or "correcting" behavior is concerned, the Rules represent a striking affirmation of the fundamental goal of rehabilitation. As a study by the Secretariat puts it:

"Treatment" may refer to the way in which prisoners are treated in the sense of being handled or managed; or, borrowed from medicine, it may be used as a synonym for their re-education or rehabilitation. In the latter sense, it has become symbolic of the contemporary approach to social defence, which em-

---

for the Treatment of Prisoners: A Comparison, 21 BUFF. L. REV. 839 (1972); D.L. Skoler, *World Implementation of the United Nations Standard Minimum Rules for the Treatment of Prisoners*, 10 J. INT'L L. & ECON. 453 (1975); E. Vetere, *Las Reglas Minimas de las Naciones Unidas Para el Tratamiento de los Reclusos: Su Adopcion Y Application en Relacion a la Proteccion de los Derechos Humanos, in* CRIME AND SOCIAL POLICY: PAPERS IN HONOUR OF MANUEL LÓPEZ-REY Y ARROJO (P. David ed., 1985). Issue No. 26 of the INTERNATIONAL REVIEW OF CRIMINAL POLICY (1968) is devoted largely to the subject. *See also* P. Cornil, *International Standards for the Treatment of Offenders, id.* at 3; J. Carlos Garcia Basalo, *Obstacles to the Implementation of the Standard Minimum Rules in Latin America, id.* at 17; P. Cornil, *John Howard, European Social Reformer, in* CHANGING CONCEPTS OF CRIME AND ITS TREATMENT 171, 177–83 (H.J. Klare ed. 1966) (comparing Howard's views with those of the Rules).

6. *See* J.J. GOBERT & N.P. COHEN, RIGHTS OF PRISONERS 530 (1981) (carrying a Table of References to the Rules). None of the references is to material where the U.N. Rules are more than supportive of a point being made with other authority. Recent supplements to the work do not contain any new references to the Rules. *See also* S. RUBIN, THE LAW OF CRIMINAL CORRECTION 322–24 (1963) (containing two pages of general discussion of the Rules that confuses ECOSOC with UNESCO). Among the sources that, surprisingly, do *not* discuss the Rules at all are 3 CRIME AND JUSTICE: THE CRIMINAL IN CONFINEMENT (L. Radzinowicz & M.E. Wolfgang ed., 1971); S. KRANTZ, CASES AND MATERIALS ON THE LAW OF CORRECTIONS AND PRISONERS' RIGHTS (3d ed. 1986); and R.G. SINGER & W.P. STATSKY, RIGHTS OF THE IMPRISONED: CASES, MATERIALS AND DIRECTIONS (1974). *See generally infra* note 144.

7. *Report of the United Nations Consultative Group on the Prevention of Crime and the Treatment of Offenders, Geneva, 6–16 Aug. 1968*, at 28, U.N. Doc. ST/SOA/91 (1969). *See* Chapter 5 *supra*, at notes 31–34.

phasizes prevention and therefore regards treatment as "secondary preven-tion", that is, prevention of the aggravation of law-breaking when society has failed to prevent its occurrence.[8]

B. Content of the Rules

The 95 Rules are organized into three Parts: Rules 1 through 5, Preliminary Observations; Rules 6 through 55 ("Part I"), Rules of General Application; and Rules 56 through 95 ("Part II"), Rules Appli-cable to Special Categories. The comments that follow track the organi-zation of the Rules themselves.

In 1990 the General Assembly adopted a short eleven-paragraph statement of Basic Principles for the Treatment of Prisoners[9] on the recommendation of the Eighth Congress which had in turn received it from the Committee on Crime Prevention and Control. The resolution adopting the statement refers to the "concern of previous congresses regarding the obstacles of various kinds that prevent the full imple-mentation of the Rules" and expresses the belief that "the full imple-mentation of the Rules would be facilitated by the articulation of the basic principles underlying them." Among the general principles artic-ulated which seem to be well within the spirit of the 1955 formulations are propositions such as "All prisoners shall be treated with the respect due to their inherent dignity and value as human beings" and "All prisoners have the right to take part in cultural activities and education aimed at the full development of the human personality" and "The [basic] principles shall be applied impartially." But there are some

8. *Implementation of the Standard Minimum Rules for the Treatment of Prisoners*, 26 INT'L REV. CRIM. POL'Y 69, 69 (1968). *See infra* notes 71–85 (discussing Rules 57–81).

9. *Basic Principles for the Treatment of Prisoners*, G.A. Res. 45/111, U.N. GAOR, 45th Sess., Supp. No. 49A, at 199, U.N. Doc. A/45/49 (1990). The Assembly also adopted, in 1988, the *Body of Principles for the Protection of All Persons under Any Form of Detention or Imprisonment*, G.A. Res. 43/173, U.N. GAOR, 43rd Sess., Supp. No. 49, at 297, U.N. Doc. A/43/49 (1989). Final work on these Principles took place under the auspices of the Sixth (Legal) Committee of the Assembly, rather than that of the Third Committee which normally deals with human rights and criminal justice matters. There was minimal input from the Vienna part of the U.N. system. The Principles, in part, reformulate some of the material contained in the Standard Minimum Rules for the Treatment of Prisoners. Their main focus, however, was the protection of the physical integrity of those in custody. As in any effort at revisiting that which was previously agreed upon, there was the possibility that the exercise would result in some watering down of the Standard Minimum Rules. No serious mischief appears to have been done in fact. *See generally*, T. Treves, *The UN Body of Principles for the Protection of Detained or Imprisoned Persons*, 84 AM. J. INT'L L. 578, 582–83 (1990). On the drafting process of these Principles, which began late in 1975, *see* N.S. RODLEY, THE TREATMENT OF PRISONERS UNDER INTERNATIONAL LAW 256–259 (1987).

formulations in the principles which, at the very least, represent a different emphasis and perhaps even indicate a change of direction. Such nuances will be noted at the appropriate points in the discussion.

1. Preliminary Observations (Rules 1–6)

The Preliminary Observations start with the proposition that the Rules are not intended to describe in detail a model system of penal institutions. They seek only, on the basis of the general consensus of contemporary thought and the essential elements of the most adequate systems of today, to set out what is generally accepted as sound principle and practice in the treatment of prisoners and the management of institutions.[10] A corollary of this is that "in view of the great variety of legal, social, economic and geographical conditions of the world, it is evident that not all of the rules are capable of application in all places and at all times."[11] This qualification is at the same time an invitation to raise the standards even higher[12] and a delightfully vague escape hatch, of great comfort to those who would prefer to lower the floor to avoid many of the standards laid down in the Rules. When interpreting the statement as an escape hatch, it is easy to overlook the logical deduction from general statement—simply because not all Rules must be applied in all places at all times, it does not follow that it is unnecessary to apply any Rules any time or any place. On the contrary, some must be binding and even non-derogable, if you will. Ultimately, the question becomes which parts of the Rules represent black-letter human rights *law* that must be applied with no excuses, and which are more on the level of *principle* or even aspiration so as to be applied in spirit rather than in detail.[13]

10. Rule 1 of the *Standard Minimum Rules for the Treatment of Prisoners*, E.S.C. Res. 663 (XXIV) C, U.N. ESCOR, 24th Sess., Supp. No. 1, at 11, U.N. Doc. E/3048 (1957), *amended by* E.S.C. Res. 2076 (LXII), U.N. ESCOR, 62d Sess., Supp. No. 1, at 35, U.N. Doc. E/5988 (1977) [hereinafter S.M.R.].

11. S.M.R., R. 2.

12. *See, e.g., 1985 Report of the Secretary-General, supra* note 2, at 5:

> A number of countries mentioned that their prison regulations followed the norms set up by the Council of Europe [in Council Resolution (73)5 of 19 January 1973]. This by no means was to be interpreted as a departure from the United Nations Standard Minimum Rules, but as an effort to go beyond them. Several Governments in other regions also reported that their legislation went beyond the minimum standards set up in the Rules.

13. *See* S.M.R., R. 3: (stating that "[t]hey are not intended to preclude experiment and practices, provided these are in harmony with the principles and seek to further the purposes which derive from the text of the rules as a whole").

The Preliminary Observations conclude by noting that the Rules do not seek to regulate the management of institutions for young persons such as Borstals or correctional schools, but that the Rules of General Application would be equally applicable to such institutions.[14] As a general proposition, the Observations add, young persons should not be sentenced to imprisonment.[15] These brief references to standards for juveniles have, of course, been amply supplemented more recently. The relevant instruments are the 1985 United Nations Standard Minimum Rules for the Administration of Juvenile Justice ("Beijing Rules")[16] and the 1990 United Nations Rules for the Protection of Juveniles Deprived of Their Liberty.[17]

2. Rules of General Application (Rules 6–55)

Non-discrimination is the "basic principle" contained in the first of the Rules of General Application. There shall be no discrimination on grounds of race, color, sex, language, religion, political or other opinion, national or social origin, property, birth, or other status.[18] "On the

14. *Id.* R. 5(1).

15. *Id.* R. 5(2). Agreement at the international level on what constitutes a "young person" or a "juvenile" has been elusive. In this instance the matter was finessed by asserting, that "The category of young prisoners should include at least all young persons who come within the jurisdiction of juvenile courts." *Id. See The Convention on the Rights of the Child*, G.A. Res. 44/25, U.N. GAOR, 44th Sess., Supp. No. 49, at 166, U.N. Doc. A/44/49 (1989) (asserting in para. 1 that "For the purposes of the present Convention, a child means every human being below the age of eighteen years unless, under the law applicable to the child, majority is attained earlier"). Article 38, para. 4, provides, however that: "[s]tates parties shall refrain from recruiting any person who has not attained the age of fifteen years into their armed forces. In recruiting among those persons who have attained the age of fifteen years but who have not attained the age of eighteen years, States Parties shall endeavor to give priority to those who are oldest." *But see* the International Covenant on Civil and Political Rights, G.A. Res. 2200 (XXI), U.N. GAOR, 21st Sess., Supp. No. 16, at 52, art. 6, para. 5, U.N. Doc. A/6316 (1966) (capital punishment not to be imposed for crimes committed by persons below eighteen years of age); and *United Nations Rules for the Protection of Juveniles Deprived of Their Liberty*, G.A. Res. 45/113, U.N. GAOR, 45th Sess., Supp. No 49A, para. 11(a), U.N. Doc. A/45/49 (1990) (a "juvenile is every person under the age of 18.")

16. G.A. Res. 40/33, U.N. GAOR, 40th Sess., Supp. No. 53, at 206, U.N. Doc. A/40/53 (1985) (discussed in Chapter 4 *supra*, at notes 57–66).

17. G.A. Res. 45/113, U.N. GAOR, 45th Sess., Supp. No. 49A, at 204, U.N. Doc. A/45/49 (1991) (discussed in Chapter 4 *supra*, at notes 132–134).

18. S.M.R., R. 6(1). The list of proscribed grounds of distinction, now fairly much boiler plate in nature, tracks that in article 2 of the Universal Declaration of Human Rights. G.A. Res. 217A (II), U.N. GAOR, Resolutions 71, 3rd Sess., pt. 1, U.N. Doc. A/810 (1948). (Some more recent formulations add disability to the list.) This non-discrimination point is echoed in para. 2 of the 1990 Statement of Basic Principles. *Supra* note 9.

other hand," the Rule continues, "it is necessary to respect the religious beliefs and moral precepts of the group to which a prisoner belongs."[19]

The next of the general Rules deals with the keeping of records, the "Register." Each place where people are imprisoned must keep what is referred to as "a bound registration book with numbered pages." This book contains the following for each prisoner: information concerning his or her identity, the reasons for commitment and the authority therefor, and the day and hour of admission and release. No prisoner shall be admitted without a valid commitment order, the details of which are entered into the register.[20]

Different categories of prisoners must be separated.[21] They are to be kept in separate institutions or parts of institutions taking account of their age, criminal record, the legal reason for their detention, and their treatment needs. Men and women shall so far as possible be detained in separate institutions. In an institution that receives both men and women the whole of the premises allocated to women must be entirely separate. Prisoners awaiting trial must be kept separate from convicted prisoners.[22] Persons imprisoned for debt and other civil prisoners shall be kept separate from those imprisoned for

19. S.M.R., R. 6(2). *See* R. 41, *infra* note 56.

20. S.M.R., R. 7. This Rule has probably to be read in the light of technological developments since the invention of the bound register. As a New Zealand report notes, "The reason for the Rule is obviously to ensure that inmates do not 'disappear' and that their whereabouts can always be traced, but the present state of the art in computer technology is such that a computer register would enhance the manual system while maintaining the necessary security." MINISTERIAL COMMITTEE OF INQUIRY INTO THE PRISONS SYSTEM, PRISON REVIEW, TE ARA HOU: THE NEW WAY 191 (1989). A related perspective was noted in the *1985 Report of the Secretary-General on the Rules*:

> An increased use of computerized systems for the identification, registration and control of the prison population was reported by some countries. One of them stressed that automatic data processing reduced the risk of an inmate being detained longer than the term stipulated. Another country reported that the use of computers had permitted the compilation of a census of all its prisoners, and that it was planning to produce, on that basis, annual publications showing offences, sentences, previous records, and other individual data, without, however, identifying the prisoners concerned.

Report of the Secretary-General, Implementation of the United Nations Standard Minimum Rules for the Treatment of Prisoners, at 8, U.N. Doc. A/CONF.121/15 (1985).

21. S.M.R., R. 8.

22. *See* Covenant on Civil and Political Rights, *supra* note 15, art. 10, para. 2(a) which insists that: "Accused persons shall, save in exceptional circumstances, be segregated from convicted persons and shall be subject to separate treatment appropriate to their status as unconvicted persons." Reservations were made to this provision on ratifying the Covenant by Australia, Belgium and the Netherlands. *See Multilateral Treaties Deposited with the Secretary-General, Status as at 31 December 1991*, at 134, 135, 139, U.N. Doc. ST/LEG/SER.E/10 (1992).

criminal offenses.[23] Young prisoners must be kept separate from adults.[24]

Several Rules deal with standards for accommodation. Where sleeping accommodation is in individual cells or rooms, each prisoner must occupy at night a separate cell or room. Should special reasons, such as temporary overcrowding, make it necessary for the central prison administration to create an exception to this rule, it is not desirable to have two prisoners in a cell or room.[25] Dormitories must be occupied by prisoners carefully selected as being suitable to associate with one another in those conditions.[26] Accommodation, and particularly sleeping accommodation, shall meet all requirements of health, with due regard being paid to climatic conditions and particularly to cubic content of air, minimum floor space, lighting, heating, and ventilation.[27] (However, no particular standards are laid down for these items. Presumably, the object is for individual states to be be encouraged to have a policy in place.) Windows must be large enough to enable prisoners to read or work by natural light, and constructed so as to allow the entrance of fresh air whether or not there is artificial ventilation.[28]

23. *Cf.* Covenant on Civil and Political Rights, *supra* note 15, art. 11 stating that: "No one shall be imprisoned merely on the ground of inability to fulfil a contractual obligation."

24. *See id.*, art. 10, para. 2(b) (asserting that: "Accused juvenile persons shall be separated from adults and brought as speedily as possible for adjudication"). Article 10, para. 3 adds that the "penitentiary system shall comprise treatment of prisoners the essential aim of which shall be their reformation and social rehabilitation. Juvenile offenders shall be segregated from adults and be accorded treatment appropriate to their age and legal status." Australia, Austria, Belgium, Denmark, Finland, Iceland, Luxembourg, the Netherlands, New Zealand, Norway, Sweden, Trinidad and Tobago, and the United Kingdom made reservations to one or both of these provisions. *United Nations, Multilateral Treaties Deposited with the Secretary-General, Status as at 31 December 1991* 134–142, U.N. Doc. ST/LEG/SER.E/10 (1992). New Zealand's case is typical: "New Zealand reserves the right not to apply article 10(2) (b) or article 10(3) in circumstances where the shortage of suitable facilities makes the mixing of juveniles and adults unavoidable; and further reserves the right not to apply article 10(3) where the interests of other juveniles in an establishment require the removal of a particular juvenile or where mixing is considered to be of benefit to the persons concerned." *Id.* at 140. *See also* P.R. WILLIAMS, TREATMENT OF DETAINEES: EXAMINATION OF ISSUES RELEVANT TO DETENTION BY THE UNITED NATIONS HUMAN RIGHTS COMMITTEE 68 (1990) (describing the reservations in general); *infra* note 133; *Report of the Human Rights Committee*, U.N. GAOR, 44th Sess., Supp. No. 40, at 173, U.N. Doc. A/44/40 (1989) (reiterating obligation to separate and ignoring the widespread existence of reservations).

25. S.M.R., R. 9(1). *See* R. 19 (separate bed, clean and sufficient bedding).

26. *Id.* R. 9(2).

27. *Id.* R. 10.

28. The designers of the United Nations building in Vienna where the Crime Prevention and Criminal Justice Branch is located had apparently not read this exhortation—

Sufficient artificial light must be provided for prisoners to read or work without injury to their eyesight.[29] There must be adequate toilet[30] and bathing facilities,[31] and the institution must be kept "scrupulously clean."[32]

As far as clothing is concerned, prisoners who are not allowed to wear their own clothing shall be provided with an outfit of clothing suitable for the climate and adequate to keep them in good health. Such clothing may not be degrading or humiliating,[33] and must be kept clean and in proper condition.[34]

Food must be provided at the usual hours which is both of wholesome quality and well-prepared and served.[35] Drinking water is to be available whenever the prisoner needs it.[36] There are to be exercise and sport facilities.[37]

Six Rules (22 through 26) are devoted to medical services. The Rules insist that every institution maintain the services of at least one qualified medical officer with some knowledge of psychiatry. The medical services should be organized in close relationship with the general health administration of the community or nation.[38] Sick prisoners who require specialist treatment are to be transferred to specialized institutions or civil hospitals. The services of a qualified dentist must be available.[39] Women's institutions require pre-natal and post-natal care and treatment. Birth should occur, wherever practicable, outside the prison, and the fact that a child is born inside the prison may not be mentioned on the birth certificate. If nursing children remain in the prison with their mothers, a nursery must be provided, staffed by qualified personnel.[40]

---

the windows do not open and air conditioning must be used even when fresh air would do the trick.

29. S.M.R., R. 11.

30. *Id.* R. 12.

31. *Id.* R. 13 (bath or shower "at least once a week in a temperate climate"). *See* R. 15 (water and toilet articles to be supplied); R. 16 (care of hair and beard, in order that "prisoners may maintain a good appearance compatible with their self-respect").

32. *Id.* R. 14.

33. *Id.* R. 17(1).

34. *Id.* R. 17(2).

35. *Id.* R. 20(1).

36. *Id.* R. 20(2).

37. *Id.* R. 21.

38. Paragraph 9 of the 1990 Statement of Basic Principles seems to go a little further than this when it asserts: "Prisoners shall have access to the health services available in the country without discrimination on the grounds of their legal situation." *Supra* note 9.

39. S.M.R., R. 22.

40. *Id.* R. 23.

The medical officer is to see and examine all prisoners as soon as possible after admission, with the intent of discovering possible physical or mental illness, segregating prisoners suspected of infectious or contagious disease, identifying any physical or mental defects that might hamper rehabilitation, and determining of the physical capacity of every prisoner for work.[41] The medical officer should daily see all sick persons, all who complain of illness, and any to whom the officer's attention is particularly directed. The officer must report to the director whenever he considers that a prisoner's physical or mental health has been or will be injuriously affected by any condition of imprisonment.[42]

Two distinguished commentators have referred to the "cathartic effect of an authentic governmental grievance machinery which would provide an outlet for complaints and dissatisfaction."[43] It is in this spirit that a set of rules on discipline and punishment (Rules 27–32) contain fundamental standards of human rights of both a procedural and a substantive nature.

These Rules begin with the general proposition that discipline and order shall be maintained with firmness, but with no more restriction than is necessary for safe custody and well-ordered community life.[44] Another general principle requires that no prisoner shall be employed in the service of the institution in any disciplinary capacity. This does not, however, preclude the functioning of systems based on self-government under which social, educational, or sports activities or responsibilities are entrusted, under supervision, to prisoners who are formed into groups for the purposes of treatment.[45]

The principle of legality is then firmly spelled out. Conduct constituting a disciplinary offense, the types and duration of punishment that may be inflicted, and the authority competent to impose such punishment must always be determined by the (statutory) law or by the regulation of the competent administrative authority.[46] No one may be punished except in accordance with such a law or regulation and never twice for the same offense. The accused must be informed of the case

41. *Id.* R. 24.
42. *Id.* R. 25. The medical officer must also regularly inspect and advise on general conditions in the institution and the director must act on those recommendations. S.M.R., R. 26. These Rules on medical aspects foreshadow the 1982 Principles of Medical Ethics. *See* Chapter 4 *supra*, at notes 21 & 23.
43. Besharov & Mueller, *supra* note 5, at 844.
44. S.M.R., R. 27.
45. *Id.* R. 28.
46. *Id.* R. 29.

against him and given a proper opportunity to mount a defense. Where necessary and practicable, the prisoner shall be allowed to make a defense with the aid of an interpreter.[47]

Corporal punishment, punishment by placement in a dark cell, and all cruel, inhuman, or degrading punishments shall be completely prohibited as punishments for disciplinary offenses.[48] Punishment by close confinement or reduction of diet must not be inflicted unless the medical officer has examined the prisoner and certified in writing that the individual is fit to sustain it. Daily medical visits must be made to those undergoing such punishment.[49]

Instruments of restraint, such as handcuffs, chains, irons, and strait-jackets, shall never be applied as punishment. Furthermore, chains or irons shall not be used as restraints. Other instruments of restraint may be used only in limited circumstances, and then only for as long as

47. *Id.* R. 30.

48. *Id.* R. 31. Principle 6 of the 1988 *Body of Principles for the Protection of All Persons under Any Form of Detention or Imprisonment, supra* note 9, restates the idea more generally: "No person under any form of detention or imprisonment shall be subjected to torture or to cruel, inhuman or degrading treatment or punishment." A footnote adds that:

> The term "cruel, inhuman or degrading treatment or punishment" should be inter-preted so as to extend the widest possible protection against abuses, whether physical or mental, including the holding of a detained or imprisoned person in conditions which deprive him, temporarily or permanently, of the use of any of his natural senses, such as sight or hearing, or of his awareness of place and the passing of time.

49. *Id.* R. 32. Questions have been raised about whether these disciplinary measures go far enough. In 1972, a working group on the rules commented:

> 26. The Group concurred substantially with the observation of the Consultant that the Rules regarding the imposition of discipline and, especially, Rules 31 and 32 were largely insufficient. Attention was directed towards the importance of considering scientific findings regarding the effects of sensory deprivation in relation to the use of isolation as a form of punishment. While it was noted that conditions of isolation within a prison differed in significant respects from those in experimental laboratories, none the less the research findings of behavioural scientists should not be ignored.
>
> 27. There was also agreement that the tacit approval which the Rules gave to the practice of depriving a prisoner of food as a disciplinary measure should be ques-tioned. Clearly, no punishment imposed by prison authorities should impair the physical or mental health of the person found guilty of a disciplinary violation.

Report of the Secretary-General on the Meeting of the Working Group of Experts on the Standard Minimum Rules for the Treatment of Prisoners, held at United Nations Headquarters, from 25 to 29 September 1972, at 7, U.N. Doc. E/AC.57/8 (1973). Paragraph 7 of the 1990 Statement of Basic Principles, picks up this theme when it states that: "Efforts addressed to the abolition of solitary confinement as a punishment, or to the restriction of its use, should be undertaken and encouraged." *Supra* note 9.

strictly necessary: (a) as a precaution against escape during a transfer, provided that they shall be removed when the prisoner appears before a judicial or administrative authority; (b) on medical grounds by direction of the medical officer; or (c) by order of the director, if other methods of control fail, in order to prevent a prisoner from injuring himself or others, or from damaging property.[50]

Upon admission every prisoner must be provided with written information about the regulations governing the treatment of prisoners in that person's category, the disciplinary requirements of the institution, the authorized methods of seeking information and making complaints, and anything else necessary for the person to understand the rights and obligations of prisoners and to adapt to life in the institution.[51] A complaint procedure must be in place.[52]

Prisoners, "under necessary supervision," are entitled to be in contact with the outside world, including family and friends.[53] If the prisoners are foreign nationals, they are entitled to diplomatic contact with consular representatives.[54]

Every institution is to have an adequately stocked library and prisoners are to have access to it.[55]

Provision is also made for religious observances. Where there is a sufficient number of prisoners of the same religion, a qualified representative of that religion shall be appointed or approved. The representative shall be allowed to hold regular services and pay pastoral visits. Access to a qualified representative of any religion shall not be refused to any prisoner. However, if a prisoner objects to the visit of a religious representative, that objection must be respected.[56] To the

50. S.M.R., R. 33. To emphasize that the whole system must be sensitive to the issue, Rule 34 requires that the patterns and manner of use of instruments of restraint shall be decided by the central prison administration.

51. *Id.* R. 35. If the prisoner is illiterate the information must be conveyed orally.

52. *Id.* R. 36.

53. *Id.* R. 37.

54. *Id.* R. 38.

55. *Id.* R. 40. They are also to have access to newspapers, periodicals, "wireless transmissions" (television?) and lectures. *Id.* R. 39. *See* R. 90, *infra* note 93 (permitting untried prisoners also to obtain material such as newspapers outside the library system at their own expense). Rule 39 should probably be similarly broad. Besharov & Mueller, *supra* note 5, at 846.

56. S.M.R., R. 41. The Rule would be stronger if it protected the prisoner expressly from being required to attend religious services. In the presentation of its second report under the Covenant on Civil and Political Rights, the New Zealand Government noted that "As a consequence of comments made by the Human Rights Committee during examination of New Zealand's report in 1983, Regulation 97(4) of the Penal Institutions Regulations 1961 under which an inmate could be required to attend services of worship has been revoked." [NEW ZEALAND] MINISTRY OF EXTERNAL RELATIONS AND TRADE,

extent practicable, every prisoner should be allowed to satisfy the needs of religious life by attending services in the institution and having in his or her possession the books of religious observance and instruction of that person's denomination.

Rule 43 concerns with the retention of a prisoner's property. If property is taken from the prisoner upon admission, it must be placed in safe keeping, be made the subject of an inventory and kept carefully pending its ultimate return.[57]

Rule 44 concerns the basic decencies of maintaining contact between prisoner and family. Upon the death of, or serious injury to the prisoner, or his removal to an institution for the treatment of mental "affections" (illnesses), the director must at once inform a spouse, if any, or the nearest relative and must in any event inform any other person previously designated by the prisoner. A prisoner must be informed at once of the death or serious illness of any near relative and should be authorized to visit in the case of a critical illness, either under escort or alone. Every prisoner has the immediate right to inform his family of the imprisonment or of the transfer to another institution.[58]

When prisoners are being removed to or from an institution, they must be exposed as little to public view as possible. Proper safeguards must be adopted to protect the prisoners from insult, curiosity, and publicity in any form. They must not be transported in conveyances with inadequate ventilation or light or in any way which would subject them to unnecessary physical hardship.[59]

The matter of institutional personnel was one which received con-

---

HUMAN RIGHTS IN NEW ZEALAND: THE PRESENTATION OF NEW ZEALAND'S SECOND PERIODIC REPORT TO THE HUMAN RIGHTS COMMITTEE, Information Bulletin No. 30 (1990). *See Report of the Human Rights Committee*, U.N. GAOR, 39th Sess., Supp. No. 40, para. 170, at 35, U.N. Doc. A/39/40 (1984) (noting the relevant questioning). *See also* R. 6(2), *supra* note 19 (discussing religious freedom and observance and requiring "respect" for the "religious beliefs and moral precepts of the group to which the prisoner belongs."). Rules 6(2) and 41 are fairly consistent with the guarantee of freedom of religion in the Universal Declaration of Human Rights, and the more expansive formulations of the Declaration on the Elimination of All Forms of Intolerance and of Discrimination Based on Religion or Belief. *See supra* note 18, art. 18 (Universal Declaration); *Declaration on the Elimination of All Forms of Intolerance and of Discrimination Based on Religion or Belief*, G.A. Res. 36/55, U.N. GAOR, 36th Sess., Supp. No. 51, at 171, U.N. Doc. A/36/51 (1981). The latter, however, is somewhat more explicit on the right *not* to have a religion. Paragraph 3 of the 1990 Statement of Basic Principles, is quite weak and undercuts the comparable provision in the Standard Minimum Rules when it asserts that: "It is, however, desirable to respect the religious beliefs and cultural precepts of the group to which prisoners belong, *whenever local conditions so require*" (emphasis added.) *Supra* note 9.

57. S.M.R., R. 43.
58. *Id.* R. 44.
59. *Id.* R. 45.

siderable attention during the early years of the United Nations. No fewer than nine of the Standard Minimum Rules are devoted to it and these Rules were reiterated in more detail in a resolution adopted at the 1955 Congress entitled "Recommendations on the Selection and training of personnel for Penal and Correctional Institutions."[60] The general proposition stated is that the prison administration must provide for the careful selection of every grade of personnel "since it is on their integrity, humanity, professional capacity, and personal suitability for the work that the proper administration of the institutions depends."[61] Both the personnel and the public at large should be encouraged to appreciate that "this work is a social service of great importance."[62] Thus, personnel should be full-time professionals with civil service status and security of tenure, attractive salaries, benefits, and conditions of work.[63] They must be adequately trained upon entering duty and have continuing in-service training.[64] The personnel must so perform their duties as to influence the prisoners for good and command their respect.[65] So far as possible, the personnel must include a sufficient number of specialists such as psychiatrists, psychologists, social workers, teachers, and trade instructors.[66] The director, deputy director, and the majority of other personnel shall be able to speak the language of the greatest number of prisoners, or a language understood by the greatest number of them. Where necessary, the services of an interpreter shall be used.[67]

In an institution for both men and women, the part of the institution set aside for women must be under the control of a responsible woman officer who shall have custody of the keys for that part of the institution. No male member of the staff may enter the part of the institution set aside for women unless accompanied by a woman officer. Women prisoners may be attended and supervised only by women officers,

---

60. *First United Nations Congress on the Prevention of Crime and the Treatment of Offenders, Geneva, 22 Aug.–3 Sept. 1955, Report Prepared by the Secretariat,* at 73, U.N. Doc. A/CONF.6/1 (1956).

61. S.M.R., R. 46(1).

62. *Id.* R. 46(2).

63. *Id.* R. 46(3). *See* R. 50 (director to be full-time, properly qualified and reside in premises or immediate vicinity); R. 52 (if institution large enough for full-time medical services at least one practitioner should live in or near it).

64. *Id.* R. 47.

65. *Id.* R. 48.

66. *Id.* R. 49(1). Social workers, teachers and trade instructors should be full-time, but this is not to preclude additional part time or volunteer people. *Id.* R. 49(2). *See id.* R. 77 (education for all capable of profiting thereby, integrated with the educational system of the country so that after release prisoners may continue education without difficulty).

67. *Id.* R. 51.

though this does not preclude male members of the staff, particularly doctors and teachers, from carrying out their duties in institutions or parts of institutions set aside for women.[68]

Officers may not use force on a prisoner except in cases of self defense, attempted escape, or active or passive physical resistance to an order based on law or regulations. Officers using such force must use no more than is strictly necessary and must report the incident immediately to the director. They should be given special training in restraining aggressive prisoners and should not be armed except in special circumstances.[69]

A final rule of general application is systemic. There must be a regular inspection of penal institutions and services by qualified and competent inspectors. The inspectors' task is to ensure that the institution is administered in accordance with existing laws and regulations and with a view to bringing about the objectives of penal and correctional services.[70]

3. Rules Applicable to Special Categories

(a) Prisoners Under Sentence

The rules applicable to prisoners under sentence begin with a number of "guiding principles" which expand upon the Preliminary Observations. It is recognized that imprisonment and other measures which result in cutting off the offender from the outside world are afflictive by the very fact of taking from the person the right of self-determination by depriving that person of liberty. Hence, the prison system must not, except as incidental to justifiable segregation or the maintenance of discipline, aggravate the suffering inherent in such a situation.[71] This statement is followed by a fairly standard exposition of the rehabilita-

---

68. *Id.* R. 53.

69. *Id.* R. 54. Only persons specially trained in their use may be provided with arms. *Id.*

70. *Id.* R. 55. One standard such inspectors—or those who do ad hoc examinations of penal systems—should be encouraged to apply is the Standard Minimum Rules themselves. *See* COUNCIL OF EUROPE, EUROPEAN PRISON RULES 78 (1987).

71. S.M.R., R. 57. Significantly, para. 5 of the 1990 Statement of Basic Principles, states that: "Except for those limitations that are demonstrably necessitated by the fact of incarceration, all prisoners shall retain the human rights and fundamental freedoms set out in the Universal Declaration of Human Rights, and, where the State concerned is a party, the International Covenant on Economic, Social and Cultural Rights, the International Covenant on Civil and Political Rights and its Optional Protocol, and such other rights as are set out in other United Nations covenants." (Footnotes omitted.) *Supra* note 9.

tive approach to punishment. It is asserted that the purpose and justification of deprivation of liberty is ultimately to protect society against crime. The Rules maintain that this end can only be achieved if the period of imprisonment is used to ensure, so far as possible, that upon return to society the offender is not only willing but able to lead a law-abiding and self-supporting life.[72] The regime of the institution, moreover, should seek to minimize differences between prison life and life at liberty which tend to lessen the responsibility of the prisoners or the respect due their dignity as human beings.[73] Steps must be taken before the expiration of the sentence, such as a pre-release regime, to prepare the prisoner for the return to society.[74] And the "duty of society," as the Rules put it, does not end with release. There should be government or private agencies capable of providing efficient aftercare directed towards lessening prejudice against the prisoner and towards social rehabilitation.[75] Prisoners are to be classified into treatment groups for maximal individualization of care.[76] The number of prisoners in closed institutions should not be so large that the individualization of treatment is hindered,[77] nor so small that proper facilities cannot be provided.[78]

Systems of privileges appropriate for the different classes of prisoners should be established at every institution, in order to encourage

72. S.M.R., R. 58. *See id.* R. 59 (an institution should utilize all the remedial, educational, moral, spiritual and other forms of assistance which are appropriate and available, and should seek to apply them according to the individual treatment needs of the prisoners); *id.* R. 62 (detect and treat any physical or mental illnesses or defects which may hamper rehabilitation); *id.* R. 65 (will and ability to lead law-abiding and self-supporting lives); *id.* R. 66 (all appropriate means, including religious care where possible, education, vocational guidance and training, social casework, employment counselling, physical development and strengthening of moral character).

73. *Id.* R. 60(1). *See also* R. 61 (concluding that treatment should emphasize not the exclusion of offenders from the community, but their continuing part in it.) *But see* R.G. Singer, *Privacy, Autonomy, and Dignity in the Prison: A Preliminary Inquiry Concerning Constitutional Aspects of the Degradation Process in Our Prisons*, 21 BUFF. L. REV. 669 (1972)(criticizing the traditional way in which prisons set out to destroy the dignity of the individual).

74. S.M.R., R. 60(2).

75. *Id.* R. 64. Paragraph 10 of the 1990 Statement of Basic Principles asserts that "With the participation and help of the community and social institutions, and with due regard to the interests of victims, favourable conditions shall be created for the reintegration of the ex-prisoner into society under the best possible conditions." *Supra* note 9.

76. S.M.R., R. 63(1), 63(2). Open institutions are recommended for some groups. *Id. See also id.* R. 67, 68, 69 (these rules are the same as R.63 except more detailed).

77. *Id.* R. 63(3). In some countries, the paragraph asserts as a factual matter, it is considered that the populations in such institutions should not exceed five hundred. In open institutions it should be as small as possible.

78. *Id.* R. 63(4).

good conduct, develop a sense of responsibility and obtain the interest and co-operation of the prisoners in their treatment.[79]

Prison work was viewed by the drafters of the Rules both as salutary in itself and as preparation for life on the outside. All mentally and physically fit prisoners must be required to work, but prison labor must not be of an afflictive nature. So far as possible, work required of the prisoners must be such as will maintain or increase their ability to earn an honest living after release.[80] It is preferable that institutional industries and farms should be operated by the administration and not by private contractors, but if the work is not so controlled prisoners must be under supervision of the administration's personnel.[81] Health and safety standards must be maintained and there must be indemnification against industrial injury and disease.[82] There is to be a system of "equitable remuneration" for the work of prisoners. Prisoners are to be allowed to spend at least a part of their earnings on approved articles for their own use and to send a part of their earnings to their family. Another part should also be set aside by the administration as savings to be handed over on release.[83]

A final group of rules in the section concerned with prisoners under sentence deals with social relations and after-care. These rules require that an effort be made to maintain and improve the relations between a prisoner and the prisoner's family in the best interests of both.[84] From

---

79. S.M.R., R. 70. While the most recent *1990 Report of the Secretary-General on the Rules*, indicates a wide degree of acceptance of Rule 70, there are those who see it as an anachronism. *See* table *infra* p. 172. Thus the *1980 Report of the Secretary-General* states:

> In some countries (Italy, Federal Republic of Germany, France), the principles of this Rule are not implemented simply because they are not applicable, since by law the same privileges must apply to all inmates, although there may be differences in this regard among the different institutions. Moreover, in accordance with Rule 71 of the European version of the Standard Minimum Rules, adopted in 1973, the concept of obtaining the prisoner's co-operation by means of a system of privileges has been abandoned. Therefore all prisoners have the opportunity to participate in various forms of leisure activities and can make use of other programmes.

1980 Report of the Secretary General, supra note 2, at 10.

80. S.M.R., R. 71. *See id.* R. 72 (organized as far as possible like employment on the outside, but interests of prisoners not to be subordinated to profit motive). Paragraph 8 of the 1990 statement of Basic Principles, provides that "Conditions shall be created enabling prisoners to undertake meaningful remunerated employment which will facilitate their reintegration into the country's labour market and permit them to contribute to their families' financial support and to their own." *Supra* note 9.

81. S.M.R., R. 73.

82. *Id.* R. 74. *See id.* R. 75 (regulation of working hours).

83. *Id.* R. 76.

84. *Id.* R. 79.

the beginning of the sentence efforts should be made to foster relations with agencies and persons outside the prison who can promote the interests of the family and the prisoner's eventual social rehabilitation.[85]

(b) Insane and Mentally Abnormal Prisoners

While there are only two rules dealing with insane and mentally abnormal prisoners, they are quite emphatic. Those found to be insane may not be detained in prison; and arrangements must be made to remove them to mental institutions as soon as possible. In the meantime, they must be under special supervision of a medical officer. Prisoners who suffer from other mental diseases or abnormalities must be observed and treated in specialized institutions under medical management. The medical or psychiatric service of the penal institutions must provide for the psychiatric treatment of all other prisoners who are in need of such treatment.[86] Finally, steps should be taken to ensure, if necessary, continuation of psychiatric treatment after release and the provision of social-psychiatric after-care.[87]

(c) Prisoners Under Arrest or Waiting Trial

Section C refers to what are, for the most part, described as "untried prisoners"[88] and proclaims that this category of prisoners are to benefit by a special regime which is set out in the rules that follow in its essential requirements only.[89] Untried prisoners must be kept separate from the convicted. Young untried prisoners must be kept separate from adults and in principle detained in separate institutions.[90] Untried prisoners must sleep singly in separate rooms with the reservation of different local custom in respect of the climate.[91] Within limits, they may obtain their own food,[92] books, newspapers, and what are coyly

85. *Id.* R. 89. *See id.* R. 81 (encouraging the activities of services and agencies, governmental and otherwise that assist in the social rehabilitation of prisoners).

86. *Id.* R. 82.

87. *Id.* R. 83.

88. *See id.* R. 84(1)(defining "untried prisoners" as "Persons arrested or imprisoned by reason of a criminal charge against them who are detained either in police custody or in prison custody (jail) but have not yet been tried or sentenced."). Paragraph (2) of Rule 84 uses the term "unconvicted prisoners" (undefined) in asserting that such persons are presumed to be innocent and must be treated as such.

89. *Id.* R. 84(3).

90. *Id.* R. 85. *See also supra* note 24.

91. *Id.* R. 86.

92. *Id.* R. 87.

described as "other means of occupation,"[93] wear their own clothes,[94] and use their own doctors and dentists.[95] They must be allowed to inform their families immediately and have reasonable communication with and visits from them.[96] They must be allowed to apply for free legal aid and to receive visits from a legal adviser to plan a defense. For this purpose the prisoner must, if he so desires, be supplied with writing material. Interviews between the prisoner and his or her legal adviser may be within the sight but not within the hearing of a police or institution official.[97]

(d) Civil Prisoners

There is only one provision of the Rules that deals specifically with civil prisoners.[98] Rule 94 provides that in countries where the law permits imprisonment for debt, or by order of a court under any non-criminal process, those so imprisoned shall not be subjected to any greater restriction or severity than is necessary to ensure safe custody and good order. Their treatment shall be not less favorable than that of untried prisoners, with the reservation, however, that they may possibly be required to work.[99]

(e) Persons Arrested or Detained Without Charge

The final and controversial category of prisoners arrested or detained without charge was added in 1977.[100] The category was contro-

93. *Id.* R. 90.
94. *Id.* R. 88.
95. *Id.* R. 91.
96. *Id.* R. 92.
97. *Id.* R. 93.
98. *See supra* note 21.
99. S.M.R., R. 94. The phrase "may possibly" is about the most tentative language in the whole of the Rules which are generally drafted in a much more emphatic style. The whole Rule sits awkwardly with article 11 of the International Covenant on Civil and Political Rights, *supra* note 15, art. 11, which provides that "No one shall be imprisoned merely on the ground of inability to fulfil a contractual obligation." The precise reach of article 11 is, however, unclear. For example, Congo's reservation apparently permits imprisonment as a last resort and in cases of fraud. Belgium objected to that reservation as "unnecessary." *See United Nations, Multilateral Treaties Deposited with the Secretary-General, Status as at 31 December 1991*, at 135, 142, U.N. Doc. ST/LEG/SER.E/10 (1992). There is certainly something of a trend against such imprisonment. *See 1990 Report of the Secretary-General on the Rules, supra* note 2, at 27 (commenting that "Almost half of the countries reported that, in their countries, this Rule was not applicable as their national laws did not permit such imprisonment.").
100. S.M.R., R. 95. *See supra* note 10 (on the 1977 amendment). *See also* J. Graven, *Importance and Scope of Minimum Rules for the Protection of Non-delinquent Detainees*, 26 INT'L

versial since some would have preferred simply to prohibit the creation of such a group, rather than to regulate the incidents of such classification. Rule 95 provides that, without prejudice to Article 9 of the International Covenant on Civil and Political Rights,[101] persons arrested or imprisoned without charge shall be given the same protection as that accorded under Part I (Rules of General Application)[102] and Part II, Section C (Prisoners Under Arrest or Waiting Trial)[103]. Relevant provisions of Part II, Section A (Prisoners Under Sentence)[104] shall also be applicable when this is to the benefit of this special group of persons in custody, provided that no measures are taken implying that re-education or rehabilitation is in any way appropriate to persons not convicted of any criminal offense.

C. Surveys of Implementation of the Rules

As noted in an earlier chapter, the United Nations has now carried out five surveys on the implementation of the Rules reported in time for the congresses in 1970,[105] 1975,[106] 1980,[107] 1985[108] and 1990.[109] Neither the volume of responses to the surveys nor the picture that emerges from them gives any impression of vast enthusiasm among the Foreign Offices and Justice Departments of the world. Daniel Skoler in his perceptive piece on implementation of the Rules, published in 1975, comments that:

A major goal in formulating and approving the Standard Minimum Rules was to encourage their enactment (explicitly or in substance) in national penal codes. However, the record of actual incorporation of the Standard Minimum

---

REV. CRIM. POL'Y 56 (1968) (outlining the background to this category). *See also Body of Principles for the Protection of All Persons under Any Form of Detention or Imprisonment, supra* note 9 (defining "detained person" as "any person deprived of personal liberty except as a result of conviction for an offence").

101. *See supra* note 15. Article 9 deals with the right to liberty and security of persons and freedom from arbitrary arrest and detention. The article guarantees that anyone arrested has the right to be informed of the reasons therefor, to be promptly brought before a judge and to an enforceable right to compensation for unlawful arrest or detention. It is subject to some derogation under article 4 "in time of public emergency which threatens the life of the nation." The effect of the reference to article 9 in the text of R. 95 is probably to create a presumption against the legality of a "detention."

102. *See supra* notes 18–70.

103. *See supra* notes 88–97.

104. *See supra* notes 71–85.

105. U.N. Doc. A/CONF.43/3, Annex (1970).

106. U.N. Doc. A/CONF.56/6, Annex I (1975).

107. U.N. Doc. A/CONF.87/11, A/CONF.87/11 Add. (1980).

108. U.N. Doc. A/CONF.121/15, A/CONF.121/15 Add. 1 (1985).

109. U.N. Doc. A/CONF.144/11 (1990).

Rules in legislation and administrative regulation is hazy, not well documented, and largely disappointing. . . . U.N. data collection efforts appear to have yielded not much more than enthusiastic but vague declarations that the Standard Minimum Rules had "influenced" recent code enactments—and this from only a minority of states surveyed.[110]

His comment is just as valid when applied to the survey reported to the 1990 Havana Congress.[111] In this section of the chapter, I offer some comments on the 1990 report, bearing in mind that the main lines of what the questionnaire discovered are fairly similar to those of previous surveys,[112] although it is perhaps a little more upbeat than some.[113]

The 1990 report analyzes the responses of a grand total of 49 responding states—less than one third of the then United Nations membership. One might think this a little thin for what is, after all, the longest standing set of United Nations norms! The authors of the

110. *Skoler*, supra note 5, at 459–60. Given the paucity of other literature, the Secretary-General's surveys are still the main source for any indications of the impact of the Rules. Occasionally, one encounters anecdotal evidence that the Rules have some impact in concrete instances. The discussion of the UNICRI technical co-operation project entitled *Social Rehabilitation and Economic Development at El-Katta Prison Farm in Egypt*, is devoted to a model project being developed in the light of the relevant provisions of the Rules. UNITED NATIONS INTERREGIONAL CRIME AND JUSTICE RESEARCH INSTITUTE (UNICRI), ANNUAL REPORT (1989). *See* P. Mackowiak, *Formulation and application of United Nations standards and norms in criminal justice*, in HELSINKI INSTITUTE FOR CRIME PREVENTION AND CONTROL AFFILIATED WITH THE UNITED NATIONS, COURSE ON UNITED NATIONS CRIMINAL JUSTICE POLICY 183, 191 (1985)(discussing claims of substantial application and dissemination of the Rules in Poland).

111. *1990 Report of the Secretary-General, supra* note 2.

112. *See 1990 Report of the Secretary-General, supra* note 2, at 27–29 (making some thoughtful suggestions about future action, notably ways of ensuring more effective implementation of the Rules and recommendations for future surveys). The most important of these are noted in Chapter 9 *infra*, note 99.

113. *Cf. 1975 Report, supra* note 2, at 59:

Regarding the *de facto* implementation of specific Rules, it must be said that although more than 70 percent of the total number of replies are in the "implemented" category . . . some of the perhaps most important Rules are among those least effectively implemented. Thus, only half of the countries have been able to achieve the guidelines in Rules 9 and 14, dealing with accommodations and fundamentals for securing decent living conditions for prisoners. Furthermore, a great number of countries face tremendous difficulties in following the recommendations concerning institutional personnel (Rules 46–54), a fact that might be deemed more serious, since the application of the spirit of the Rules is to a very large extent dependent upon the availability of adequately trained staff with appropriate levels of education, intelligence and knowledge of institutional problems. In terms of protection of the fundamental rights of prisoners against arbitrary treatment, the Rules dealing with discipline and punishment (Rules 27–32) are of a basic nature, and it is therefore unsatisfactory that only about 60 per cent of the replying countries claim to observe these guidelines fully.

report, however, present the response rate as favorably as possible by noting that forty countries have taken part in at least three of the last four surveys, and that the countries participating for the first time in 1990—Ecuador, Jordan, Malawi, South Africa, and Uganda—bring to 100 the number of countries that have taken part in at least one survey.[114]

Early questions in the survey asked in a general way about the application, dissemination, and implementation of the Rules.

Governments were asked first about the extent to which the Rules had been embodied in national legislation or other regulations. Most respondents who replied to the question said that either the substance of the Rules was covered by existing legislation or that the Rules had been embodied in prison laws, regulations, or rules. Two claimed that most, but not all, of the substance was so incorporated; one said that some of the substance was covered and another said, candidly, that the substance of the Rules was not covered.[115]

Most countries reported that the Rules had been translated and published in the official language or languages of the country. And most reported that the Rules were available to law enforcement officials and correctional personnel. Of the six countries which reported that the material was not so available, two stated that regulations based on the Rules were available instead.[116]

Most claimed that the Rules were used in the training of staff.[117] Dissemination to prisoners did not fare as well. About 60 percent of the countries that answered the question about this matter agreed that "the Rules were made available at some time during the period of confinement, at least in the form of the legal codes in which they were embodied."[118] A further 30 percent indicated more vaguely that the Rules were routinely explained, or explained on request, or that at least some explanatory work was undertaken.[119] Moreover, in response to a ques-

---

114. *1990 Report of the Secretary-General, supra* note 2, at 12.

115. *Id.* at 12.

116. *Id.*

117. *Id.*

118. *Id.* at 13. Note the way one set of pro se U.S. litigants was laughed out of court:

The plaintiffs' claim for distribution of the United Nations Standard Minimum Rules for the Treatment of Prisoners is . . . without merit. The federal courts will not interfere in the administration of a prison when there is evidence of facilities sufficient to provide prisoners with meaningful access to the courts. [citation omitted.] In this case, the lengthy and detailed submissions by the plaintiffs are clear and sufficient evidence of their access to the courts.

Bottom v. Mondale, No. 79 Civ. 6228, Slip. Op. (S.D.N.Y. Sept. 30, 1980) (LEXIS, Genfed library, Dist file). Some non sequiturs here!

119. *Id.*

tion whether prisoners and persons under detention received copies of the Rules in their own language or in a language they understood, fewer than a quarter of the thirty-nine countries that answered this question indicated that such persons automatically received the Rules in such a form.[120]

So far as actual implementation is concerned, respondents were asked to state the extent of compliance with each Rule in a form suitable for tabulation and to give an explanation for any discrepancies between the Rules and their own law or practice. This survey resulted in the production of the accompanying tables,[121] which indicate some quite striking trends, as summarized here in Table 1. For the most part, the responses indicate that states claim to give effect to the Rules in a fairly routine fashion, although there was no single instance of a Rule fairly routine fashion, although there was no single Rule for which total compliance was claimed by all respondents. Whether this high degree of deference represents reality on the ground is another question, one the survey technique is ill equipped to answer.

To the extent that the particular numbers in the columns are meaningful (obviously the sample leaves a lot to be desired statistically), the two most accepted principles are Rules 6 and 7. Rule 6 contains the basic exhortation that the Rules are to be applied with no discrimination as to race, color, sex, language, religion, political or other opinion, national or social origin, property, birth, or other status but that it is necessary to respect the religious beliefs of the group to which the prisoner belongs.[122] Of the usable responses no one admitted that the rule was not implemented. While forty said it was implemented, three said it was implemented partially and one said it was recognized in principle. The requirement of a bound register in Rule 7[123] again found no state admitting non-application, with forty-one claiming full implementation and two partial. Rule 34, which requires that the patterns and manner of use of instruments of restraint shall be decided by the central prison administration and that such instruments shall not be applied for any longer time than is absolutely necessary,[124] also enjoyed widespread

120. *Id.*

121. *See* U.N. Doc. A/CONF. 144/11, at 14–18 (1990) (tables). Only 46 of the 49 responding states gave material which, by and large, could be tabulated Rule by Rule. Rules 1–5 are "Preliminary Observations" which do not lend themselves to survey analysis and, thus, the questions on the Rules begin with R. 6. *See* Table 1 *infra*, pp. 170–74.

122. *See supra* note 18.

123. *See supra* note 20. An answer suggesting non-application or partial application here may mask a computerized system that meets the spirit of the Rule.

124. *See supra* note 50.

support, although two states acknowledged that they did not implement it. Similarly, there was widespread acceptance of the provisions of Rule 36 on opportunities by prisoners to make complaints,[125] Rule 37 on contact by prisoners with the outside world,[126] and Rule 38 on contact by foreigners with diplomatic and consular representatives.[127] None of these should be especially threatening to well-intentioned governments, although one suspects that the material on contacts with the outside is often honored in the breach.

Solid, but by no means universal, support was also afforded Rule 31, which prohibits corporal punishment, punishment by placing in a dark cell, and all cruel, inhuman, or degrading punishments as punishments for disciplinary offenses.[128] Thirty-four states claimed to implement the rule in full, seven claimed partial implementation, and three said it was not implemented. Presumably no one claims the right to engage in cruel, inhuman, or degrading punishments, which are after all proscribed in various United Nations instruments,[129] so that the non- and partial implementers must be demanding the right to engage in corporal punishment or punishment in a dark cell,[130] although one might certainly argue that such actions are in themselves cruel, inhuman, or degrading. In the absence of more detail in the responses as reported in the Secretary-General's survey, it is difficult to draw any serious conclusions about where state practice is moving in respect of these issues of the basic dignity of prisoners. It is certainly an area where the United Nations should find some way to follow up and obtain more detailed and meaningful information.

The cases where there is substantial variation in the claimed degree

125. *See supra* note 52.
126. *See supra* note 53.
127. *See supra* note 54.
128. *See supra* note 48.
129. *See, e.g.*, Universal Declaration of Human Rights, *supra* note 18, art. 5; International Covenant on Civil and Political Rights, *supra* note 15, art. 7.
130. In fact the *1985 Report of the Secretary-General* recorded that: "Punishment in dark cells seemed still to be a prevailing practice in one region, thus at variance with Rule 31. Corporal punishment, also prohibited by Rule 31, was reported by one country, which used caning as a disciplinary measure." *Supra* note 2, at 10. *See also* THE HUMAN RIGHTS WATCH GLOBAL REPORT ON PRISONS, *supra* note 4 at xviii:

Though U.N. standards have been much criticized for vaguenes and imprecision, they are widely known and are accepted in principle. Yet many of these standards are clearly violated routinely and systematically throughout the world. For example, Rules 9–14 on decent accomodations; Rules 27–32 on discipline and the ban on corporal punishment; and Rules 35–36 on the availability of rules and fair disciplinary standards.

TABLE 1 Number and Type of Reply from Member States on the Implementation of the Standard Minimum Rules for the Treatment of Prisoners

Rule number	Subject	Implemented[1]	Implemented partially[2]	Recognized in principle[3]	Not implemented[4]	Not applicable[5]	No response[6]	Total[7]
6	Basic principle	40	3	1	-	-	2	46
7	Register	41	2	-	-	-	3	46
8	Separation of categories	25	16	1	2	-	2	46
9	Accommodation	22	12	6	3	-	3	46
10	Accommodation	32	7	4	1	-	2	46
11	Accomodation	35	6	2	1	-	2	46
12	Accomodation	36	6	1	1	-	2	46
13	Accomodation	34	6	2	2	-	2	46
14	Accomodation	37	5	1	1	-	2	46
15	Personal hygiene	37	5	2	-	-	2	46
16	Personal hygiene	38	4	1	1	-	2	46
17	Clothing and bedding	37	5	-	2	-	2	46
18	Clothing and bedding	38	4	1	1	-	2	46
19	Clothing and bedding	37	3	3	1	-	2	46
20	Food	36	8	-	-	-	2	46
21	Exercise and sport	31	13	-	-	-	2	46
22	Medical services	30	11	1	1	-	3	46
23	Medical services	29	11	2	1	-	3	46
24	Medical services	36	5	-	2	-	3	46
25	Medical services	33	8	-	2	-	3	46
26	Medical services	32	7	1	2	-	3	46
27	Discipline and punishment	41	3	-	-	1	2	46
28	Discipline and punishment	37	5	-	2	-	2	46

No.								
29	Discipline and punishment	39	3	-	2	-	2	46
30	Discipline and punishment	40	2	-	2	-	2	46
31	Discipline and punishment	34	7	-	3	-	2	46
32	Discipline and punishment	34	10	-	-	-	2	46
33	Instruments of restraint	40	4	-	,2	-	2	46
34	Instruments of restraint	42	1	-	2,	-	1	46
35	Information to and complaints by prisoners	34	9	1	,	-	2	46
36	Information to and complaints by prisoners	42	2	-	1	-	1	46
37	Contact with the outside world	44	1	-	-	-	1	46
38	Contact with the outside world	43	1	-	-	1	1	46
39	Contact with the outside world	42	3	-	-	-	1	46
40	Books	33	10	-	-	1	2	46
41	Religion	36	4	4	-	-	2	46
42	Religion	39	4	1	-	-	2	46
43	Retention of prisoners' property	42	1	-	1	-	2	46
44	Notification of death, etc.	39	4	1	-	-	2	46
45	Removal of prisoners	42	2	-	-	-	2	46
46	Institutional personnel	33	9	-	1	-	3	46
47	Institutional personnel	31	11	-	2	-	2	46
48	Institutional personnel	36	7	,1	1	-	2	46
49	Institutional personnel	31	11	2	,	-	2	46
50	Institutional personnel	34	8	1	1	-	2	46

TABLE 1 Continued

Rule number	Subject	Implemented[1]	Implemented partially[2]	Recognized in principle[3]	Not implemented[4]	Not applicable[5]	No response[6]	Total[7]
51	Institutional personnel	41	3	-	-	-	2	46
52	Institutional personnel	27	14	2	-	1	2	46
53	Institutional personnel	34	5	1	1	3	2	46
54	Institutional personnel	40	4	-	-	-	2	46
55	Inspection	38	3	1	2	-	2	46
(a) Prisoners under sentence								
56	Guiding principles	42	1	1	-	-	2	46
57	Guiding principles	40	3	1	-	-	2	46
58	Guiding principles	39	4	1	-	-	2	46
59	Guiding principles	39	4	1	-	-	2	46
60	Guiding principles	38	5	1	-	-	2	46
61	Guiding principles	40	4	-	-	-	2	46
62	Guiding principles	37	5	-	1	-	3	46
63	Guiding principles	29	12	2	1	-	2	46
64	Guiding principles	35	3	4	2	-	2	46
65	Treatment	39	4	-	-	-	3	46
66	Treatment	33	9	1	-	-	3	46
67	Classification and individualization	35	5	1	2	-	3	46
68	Classification and individualization	32	9	-	2	-	3	46
69	Classification and individualization	31	11	1	-	-	3	46
70	Privileges	37	4	-	3	-	2	46
71	Work	29	14	-	1	-	2	46

72	Work	37	6	-	1	-	2	46
73	Work	34	7	2	1	-	2	46
74	Work	34	5	3	2	-	2	46
75	Work	37	3	1	3	-	2	46
76	Work	30	12	1	1	-	2	46
77	Education and recreation	36	8	-	-	-	2	46
78	Education and recreation	39	5	-	-	-	2	46
79	Social relations and after-care	42	4	-	-	-	-	46
80	Social relations and after-care	41	4	1	-	-	-	46
81	Social relations and after-care	34	7	-	3	2	-	46

(b) Insane and mentally abnormal prisoners

82	Insane and mentally abnormal prisoners	35	7	2	1	1	-	46
83	Insane and mentally abnormal prisoners	31	4	5	1	1	4	46

(c) Prisoners under arrest or awaiting trial

84	Prisoners under arrest or awaiting trial	37	4	1	1	1	2	46
85	Prisonders under arrest or awaiting trial	25	12	2	4	1	2	46
86	Prisoners under arrest or awaiting trial	11	13	12	6	1	3	46
87	Prisoners under arrest or awaiting trial	33	8	-	2	1	2	46
88	Prisoners under arrest or awaiting trial	33	8	-	1	1	3	46
89	Prisoners under arrest or awaiting trial	31	10	-	1	1	3	46

TABLE 1 Continued

Rule number	Subject	Implemented[1]	Implemented partially[2]	Recognized in principle[3]	Not implemented[4]	Not applicable[5]	No response[6]	Total[7]
90	Prisoners under arrest or awaiting trial	39	3	-	-	1	3	46
91	Prisoners under arrest or awaiting trial	25	8	1	2	7	3	46
92	Prisoners under arrest or awaiting trial	37	5	-	-	1	3	46
93	Prisoners under arrest or awaiting trial	36	5	-	-	1	4	46
(d) Civil prisoners								
94	Civil prisoners	20	2	-	1	21	2	46
(e) Persons arrested or imprisoned without charge								
95	Persons arrested or imprisoned without charge	16	5	-	2	22	1	46

1. The term "implemented" means that the specific Rule is fully applied in law and in practice.
2. The term "implemented partially" means that the specific Rule is being applied only to a limited extent. Where a country gave different answers to different subsections of a Rule, that Rule has been classified as having been implemented partially by the country if at least one subsection of the Rule was implemented partially.
3. The term "recognized in principle" means that the specific Rule is not being implemented but would be if circumstances permitted; for example, if prisons are overcrowded, the accommodation of prisoners in single rooms may be impossible.
4. The term "not implemented" means that there is no intention at present of implementing the particular Rule.
5. The term "not applicable" means that the Rule does not apply in the prevailing circumstances (for example, when the law does not permit imprisonment for debt).
6. This category includes some responses that did not reveal the extent of the implementation of a particular Rule.
7. Three of the 49 countries taking part in the survey did not provide information for this tabular summary.

of implementation are, however, instructive. For example, Rule 8 requires separation of categories of prisoner.[131] Most countries reported "adherence" to the Rule but "Over 40 percent were unable to apply it fully, however, mainly for budgetary and economic reasons and because of overcrowding. Three countries said that their infrastructure was inadequate for the purpose. Several countries pointed out that while they were able to detain men and women in separate institutions and to keep young prisoners separately from adults, they could not always keep untried prisoners separately from convicted prisoners."[132] In fact, the separation of juveniles from adult prisoners is rather more controversial than would appear from this report of the Secretary-General's survey.[133]

Another case in point is Rule 9, which has a requirement of single-cell occupancy and careful selection of prisoners in dormitories. Approximately half the respondents reported that this Rule was not fully implemented, citing budgetary and economic reasons and overcrowding.[134]

Rules 22–26 deal with medical services. There were some problems with budgets and with the availability of medical personnel in general here. In particular, there appeared to be a shortage of the required persons skilled in psychiatry and in dentistry and even in pre- and post-

131. *See supra* note 21.

132. *1990 Report of the Secretary-General, supra* note 2, at 19.

133. *See supra* note 24 (providing some indications that keeping young prisoners separately from adults is not always the norm, nor universally accepted as the desirable rule). Indeed at the Eighth Congress in 1990, Latin American and Nordic delegates clashed strongly on the issue during the debate on para. 29 of the United Nations Rules for the Protection of Juveniles Deprived of Their Liberty. G.A. Res. 45/113, U.N. GAOR, 45th Sess., Supp. No. 49A, U.N. Doc. A/45/49 (1990). As finally adopted, the Rule reads: "In all detention facilities juveniles should be separated from adults, unless they are members of the same family. Under controlled conditions, juveniles may be brought together with carefully selected adults as part of a special programme that has been shown to be beneficial for the juveniles concerned." *Id.* This language gives some room for maneuver and the Nordic states would have liked something even softer. The Latin American states, on the other hand, would have preferred something stronger, like the language in the Committee on Crime Prevention and Control's draft before the congress which referred to mixing only in case of a special program "that has definitively been proven to be beneficial to the juveniles concerned." Letter from Matti Joutsen, Director, European Institute for Crime Prevention and Control to Roger S. Clark (Jan. 24, 1991). *See also the Convention on the Rights of the Child*, G.A. Res. 44/25, 44 U.N. GAOR, Supp. No. 49, at 166, art. 37(c), U.N. Doc. A/44/49 (1989) (adopting a softer formulation than the Minimum Rules). It provides that "every child deprived of liberty shall be separated from adults unless it is considered in the child's best interest not to do so." *Id.*

134. *Id.* at 19.

natal care for women.[135] The absence of adequate psychiatric personnel is indicated again in the case of those states that have trouble meeting the standards in Rules 82–83 for the care of insane and mentally abnormal prisoners.[136] Interestingly, no states deny the legitimacy of these Rules, they merely regret the lack of resources to give effect to them. One might perhaps have expected some assertions of skepticism about the value of psychiatry.

There were some difficulties also with Rules 71 to 76 concerning work for prisoners. Rule 71 begins by insisting that prison labor must not be of an afflictive nature. States seemed to have no trouble adhering to this principle although the survey does not indicate what kinds of mindless tasks pass for being non-afflictive. But Rule 71 also requires that mentally and physically fit prisoners must work, and that sufficient work of a useful nature shall be provided to keep prisoners actively employed over a normal working day. Only twenty-nine of the respondents claimed that these parts of the Rule were fully implemented, while fourteen stated that they were partially implemented. Various obstacles were mentioned by such states—budgetary, economic, and technical; one country mentioned a lack of tools.[137] Budgetary excuses were similarly given for the failure of about a third of the respondents to comply with Rule 76 concerning "equitable remuneration."[138]

Perhaps the most dramatic disparities between the Rules and even claimed implementation, however, occur with respect to the Rules on prisoners under arrest or awaiting trial. The responses concerning Rule 84 seem to suggest that the general notion of having a special regime for such persons is accepted in principle. But two of the corollaries of that have some difficulties. Rule 85, which requires that untried prisoners must be kept separate from the convicted, and that young untried prisoners must be kept separate from adults and in

135. *Id.* at 20. The survey responses to R. 49 (specialist institutional personnel) and R. 52 (resident medical personnel) show the same kinds of failings of the system.

136. *See id.* at 26.

137. *1990 Report of Secretary-General, supra* note 2, at 25. Worth recalling are other comments on the issue of work, recorded in the *1985 Report of the Secretary-General*:

> The role of labour unions in correctional work programmes was seen from different angles, due to different experiences. There were national as well as prison unions which protected the rights of prisoners and helped them to find jobs outside, and unions which protected the workers outside to avoid unfair competition with expensive products through "exploitation" of cheap labour.

1985 Report of the Secretary-General, supra note 2, at 16.

138. *Id.*

principle detained in separate institutions, is fully implemented only by about half of the responding countries. The familiar "budgetary, economic and technical difficulties and the lack of an infrastructure" were again relied upon as an explanation.[139] Furthermore, Rule 86 requires that untried prisoners must normally sleep singly in separate rooms. Only eleven of the usable responses claimed that this Rule was implemented fully. A further thirteen spoke of partial implementation; twelve claimed that it was recognized in principle; six conceded that it was not implemented; one claimed that it was "not applicable" and two gave no response. This is plainly the question that shows the most disparity in application.

D. Conclusion

The volume of responses to the Secretary-General's questionnaires is obviously not overwhelming and the value of the information received is debatable. The Rules have had substantial impact in some countries, but in others the impact has been marginal. The Rules are invoked from time to time in domestic litigation, either as an endeavor to incorporate international standards by way of the common law[140] or in order to give concrete content to abstract domestic constitutional or statutory material, state[141] or federal.[142] As a standard against which prisoners may make complaints domestically, however, the Rules have had only limited success. This is true even in some countries where there have been substantial endeavors to change the prison system in the past two decades or so. The United States, for example, has in recent years seen an outpouring of litigation over prisoners' rights. Yet, neither a Lexis search of the thousands of reported cases on prisoners' rights nor an examination of the enormous literature on that subject

---

139. *Id.* at 26.

140. *See* J. Hartman, *"Unusual" Punishment: The Domestic Effects of International Norms Restricting the Application of the Death Penalty*, 52 U. CIN. L. REV. 655 (1983) (using international standards as federal common law in the United States).

141. Sterling v. Cupp, 625 P.2d 123 (Or. 1981). *See* H. Linde, *Comments*, 18 INT'L LAWYER 61, 63 (1984) (Judge Linde was the author of Sterling v. Cupp.)

142. *See, e.g.*, Estelle v. Gamble, 429 U.S. 97 (1976); Detainees of the Brooklyn House of Detention for Men v. Malcolm, 520 F.2d 392 (2d Cir. 1975); Lareau v. Manson, 507 F. Supp. 1177, 1187 n.9 (1980), *aff'd. in part, mod. in part*, 651 F.2d 96 (2d Cir. 1981); Wolfish v. Levi, 439 F. Supp. 114, 154 (S.D.N.Y. 1977) (humiliating clothing, Dist. Ct. reversed on this point without any discussion of Standard Minimum Rules, 573 F.2d 118 (2d Cir. 1978) and point not discussed on final appeal in 441 U.S. 520 (1979)). *See also* G. Christenson, *The Uses of Human Rights Norms to Inform Constitutional Interpretation*, 4 HOUS. J. INT'L L. 39 (1981); Hartman, *supra* note 10, at 687–98; R. Lillich, *The United States Constitution and International Human Rights Law*, 3 HARV. HUM. RTS J. 53 (1990).

revealed more than a few references to the U.N. Rules.[143] Seminal articles and books on the topic fail to mention the Rules.[144] Knowledge of and training based on the Rules seems to be limited. Familiarity with the Rules is probably most widespread among international human rights groups who frequently invoke them in criticism of government behavior.[145]

Thus the challenge is one of implementation. I will come to the

143. *See supra* note 142 (citing the most significant cases). United States courts are not entirely alone in using such material, but the cases in other jurisdictions are also sparse. *See generally* Juvenile v. State, Judgment No. 64/89, Crim. App. No. 156/88 (Zimbabwe, 1989), *noted in* 84 Am. J. Int'l L. 768 (1990)(in which one of the majority relied upon the prohibition of corporal punishment of juveniles contained in the U.N. Standard Minimum Rules for the Administration of Juvenile Justice in interpreting the constitutional prohibition of "inhuman or degrading punishment."). *See also* G. Naldi, *Prisoners' Rights as Recently Interpreted by the Supreme Court of Zimbabwe: A Comparative Study with International Human Rights*, 4 Afr. J. Int'l & Comp. L. 715 (1992) (discussing use made of various international instruments including the Standard Minimum Rules). A Lexis search of British Commonwealth material turned up only two cases in which the Rules were relied upon. In McCann v. The Queen, 68 D.L.R.(3d) 661, 685 (Fed. Ct., Tr. Div.) (1976) a witness described the solitary confinement involved there as not meeting minimum U.N. standards, with the judge's apparent acquiescence. *Id.* at 692. In Ralston v. H.M. Advocate, 1989 Scot. L.T. 474 (H.C.J. Scot.), the Rules were referred to in the course of a losing argument about whether it was proper for the accused to be in chains and irons during his trial.

144. *See, e.g.*, E.B. Spaeth, *The Courts' Responsibility for Prison Reform*, 16 Vill. L. Rev. 1031 (1971); R.G. Singer, *Prisoners as Wards of the Court—A Nonconstitutional Path to Assure Correctional Reform By the Courts*, 41 U. Cin. L. Rev. 769 (1972); R.G. Singer, *Prisoners' Rights Litigation: A Look at the Past Decade, and a Look at the Coming Decade*, Fed. Probation, Dec. 1980, at 3; A.J. Bronstein, *Criminal Justice: Prison and Penology, in* Our Endangered Rights: The ACLU Report on Civil Liberties Today 221 (N. Dorsen ed. 1984); D. Rudovsky, et al., The Rights of Prisoners: The Basic ACLU Guide to Prisoners' Rights (4th ed. 1988). A very useful survey produced in 1974 for the Second Meeting of the United Nations Working Group of Experts on the Rules discusses techniques for the enforcement of prisoners' rights on a comparative basis—the Scandinavian Ombudsman, the Socialist Procuracy, the French Conseil d'Etat, the Japanese Civil Liberties Bureau, regional human rights Conventions, and judicial remedies in the U.S., Italy and France—but is quite thin on actual use of the Standard Minimum Rules, as is the literature in general. *See* Academy for Contemporary Problems, Remedies and Mechanisms for the Enforcement of the UN Standard Minimum Rules for the Treatment of Prisoners and Similar Guaranties and Principles of Offender Treatment: A Multinational Comparison and Analysis (1974).

145. *See, e.g.*, *Malawi: Authorities Chaining and Beating Prisoners, Amnesty Claims*, Inter Press Service, March 6, 1992, *available in* LEXIS, Nexis Library, INPRES File. (Amnesty International invokes S.M.R.); *Asia Watch Blasts Peking for Exploiting Prison Labor*, Central News Agency, September 19, 1991, *available in* LEXIS, Nexis Library, CENEWS File. (S.M.R. provisions on prison labor); Michael Conlon, *Group Compares Prison Conditions to Chile and South Africa*, Reuters, June 4, 1987, *available in* LEXIS, Nexis Library, ALLNWS File. (Amnesty International study of federal prison in Illinois).

theme of what more might be done in Chapters 9 and 10, which deal with that topic.

An optimist would probably add that the Rules have at least had some effect in encouraging the development of national or regional standards based on them, standards which are perhaps given greater attention than the inspiration for them. I have in mind such documents as the 1989 Standard Guidelines for Corrections in Australia,[146] or the European Prison Rules, most recently formulated by the Council of Europe in 1987.[147]

146. CONFERENCE OF CORRECTIONAL ADMINISTRATORS, STANDARD GUIDELINES FOR CORRECTIONS IN AUSTRALIA (1989). *See also Meeting of Commonwealth Law Ministers, Grand Baie, Mauritius, 15–19 November 1993, Communique,* 19 November 1993, paras 49–50 (referring to "illustrative draft of proposed guidelines for the treatment of prisoners within the Commonwealth" based on the Standard Minimum Rules).

147. *See* Recommendation No. R (87)3 of the Committee of Ministers to Member States, and Explanatory Memorandum, *in* COUNCIL OF EUROPE, EUROPEAN PRISON RULES (1987). A. Reynaud notes some "new ideas" in the European document, compared with the U.N. one:

"the distribution of prisoners", which replaces "separation of categories"; "reception arrangements for prisoners"; "moral assistance", which, alongside traditional spiritual assistance, is designed for prisoners who want non-religious spiritual help; and "control" (by a judicial or other authority) supplementing the concept of "inspection" provided for in 1955.

A. Reynaud, Expert Consultant to the Council of Europe, *in* COUNCIL OF EUROPE, HUMAN RIGHTS IN PRISONS 32 (1986). In addition, there are "extras" such as these: a walk or suitable exercise in the open air becomes a *right*; prisoners may not be submitted to medical or scientific experiments which may result in physical or moral injury; the medical officer must examine sick prisoners under conditions, and with a frequency, consistent with hospital standards; collective punishment is prohibited, as is the use of instruments of restraint as punishment; the scope for prisoners' relations with the outside world is increased; prisoners cannot be asked to do any especially dangerous or unhealthy work; safety, health precautions; and working hours for prisoners must be similar to those prevailing in the outside world.

Chapter 7
The Declaration of Basic Principles of Justice for Victims of Crime and Abuse of Power

A. The Drafting Process

The Victims Declaration[1] had a complicated gestation period which has been described in detail elsewhere.[2] It is necessary to recall here only so much as is crucial to an understanding of some of the puzzling aspects of the final product, in particular the somewhat unhappy ac-

---

1. *Declaration of Basic Principles of Justice for Victims of Crime and Abuse of Power*, G.A. Res. 40/34, U.N. GAOR, 40th Sess., Supp. No. 53, at 213, U.N. Doc. A/40/53 (1986) [hereinafter Victims Declaration]. *See also* E.S.C. Res. 1989/57, *Implementation of the Declaration of Basic Principles of Justice for Victims of Crime and Abuse of Power*, U.N. ESCOR, Supp. No. 1, at 43, U.N. Doc. E/1989/89 (1989); *Victims of crime and abuse of power*, E.S.C. Res. 1990/22, U.N. ESCOR, Supp. No. 1, at 25, U.N. Doc. E/1990/90 (1990); Other Resolution 27, *Protection of the human rights of victims of crime and abuse of power, Eighth United Nations Congress on the Prevention of Crime and the Treatment of Offenders, Havana, 27 August–7 September 1990, Report prepared by the Secretariat*, at 194, U.N. Doc. A/CONF.144/28/Rev.1 (1991) (detailing follow-up action). In preparation for the Tenth Session of the Committee on Crime Prevention and Control in 1988, the Secretariat produced a useful paper on what has been done, nationally and internationally, to promote the Victims Declaration. *Measures taken to implement the Declaration of Basic Principles of Justice for Victims of Crime and Abuse of Power, Report of the Secretary-General*, U.N. Doc. E/AC.57/1988/3 (1988). For the Eighth Congress it produced a *Report of the Secretary-General, Declaration of Basic Principles of Justice for Victims of Crime and Abuse of Power*. U.N. Doc. E/AC.57/1990/3 (1990).

2. *See generally*, in particular, M. Joutsen, The Role of the Victim of Crime in European Criminal Justice Systems: A Crossnational Study of the Role of the Victim 63–69 (HEUNI Publication Series No. 11, 1987); L.L. Lamborn, *The United Nations Declaration on Victims: Incorporating "Abuse of Power,"* 19 Rutgers L.J. 59 (1987); G.M. Kerrigan, *Historical Development of the United Nations Declaration, in* International Protection of Victims, 7 Nouvelles Etudes Pénales 91 (M.C. Bassiouni for Association Internationale de Droit Pénale, ed. 1988). There is much useful information on the Declaration in the AIDP volume.

commodation reached between the interests of victims of crime and those of victims of abuse of power.

The development of the Victims Declaration began at the Sixth United Nations Congress on the Prevention of Crime and the Treatment of Offenders held in Caracas in 1980 with the discussion of a very erudite working paper prepared by the Secretariat. Provocatively entitled "Crime and the Abuse of Power: Offences and Offenders Beyond the Reach of the Law?"[3] the paper represented a bold attempt to provide a conceptual framework for discussion of a broad package of ills that went far beyond concern with traditional street and juvenile crime—the areas with which previous congresses had been primarily concerned. This was the first congress held in a developing country. In responding to the stimulus provided by this event, the Secretariat paper raised some fundamental questions about the role of the criminal law in attempting to control various perceived evils at the national and transnational level. The paper also touched some raw nerves in the North-South debate, particularly on the protection of the environment and on the activities of transnational corporations.

The germ of the idea that led to the paper and to the ensuing debate in 1980 had in fact been floated at the Fifth United Nations Congress in Geneva in 1975 thus:

In addition to the dark number of offenders who escaped all official detection, there were numbers of "gilded" criminals—namely those who had political power and wielded it with impunity when injuring citizens and the community for the benefit of their oligarchy, or who possessed an economic power that was being developed to the detriment of the community as a whole. The offences of those criminals were comparable to those of certain criminal justice functionaries who violated the law by abuse of their power and remained unpunished because of that power. Such offences might range from bribery and corruption to torture of persons in custody.[4]

In arguing for a general category of offenses of abuse of power, the 1980 Secretariat working paper[5] described them as "beyond the reach of the law" in two senses, "first in the sense of acts that are not criminal or illegal according to existing laws, but are nevertheless harmful to society, and secondly, in the sense of acts that are already covered by legal prohibitions but are still beyond the reach of the law-enforcement

3. *Working paper prepared by the Secretariat, Crime and the Abuse of Power: Offences and Offenders Beyond the Reach of the Law*, U.N. Doc. A/CONF.87/6 (1980).

4. *Report prepared by the Secretariat, Fifth United Nations Congress on the Prevention of Crime and the Treatment of Offenders, Geneva, 1–12 Sept. 1975*, at 20–21, U.N. Doc. A/CONF.56/10 (1976).

5. *See supra* note 3, at 5.

process, owing to the selective and differential application of the law." Numerous examples of the category were discussed. One package of offenses involved economic abuse such as tax, credit and customs fraud, misappropriation and embezzlement, currency violations, environmental pollution and other damage, smuggling, and organized crime. Developing countries were said to be particularly concerned about over-pricing and transfer-pricing by powerful trading partners, monopolies, offenses against the patrimony, fraudulent sales, including those of unsafe products, adulterated food and obsolete or hazardous drugs, and various acts that constrain or distort development.[6] Other problems involved abuse of public power: torture, maltreatment, apartheid, persecution of political dissidents, elimination of political opponents by official or semi-official institutions, abuses of office, and infringements of the right of privacy, to name a few.[7]

In spite of the power of the Secretariat paper, there was no clear agreement about how—or even whether—all of these issues could be fitted together under a common rubric. Nor was there any agreement about the extent to which the criminal law should apply, or if this topic in general was a fit subject for a congress on *crime*! After some rambunctious debate and procedural maneuvering,[8] the 1980 Congress adopted a resolution which, *inter alia*, recommended that the public should be made aware of the harmful consequences of the abuse of economic and political power, including abuses committed or gener-

6. *Id.* at 8. While the Victims Declaration was in the drafting process, the General Assembly adopted a resolution which addressed some of these issues, under the title *Guidelines for Consumer Protection.* G.A. Res. 39/248, U.N. GAOR, 39th Sess., Supp. No. 51, at 179, U.N. Doc. A/39/51 (1985).

7. *Id.* at 9. As the working paper notes on page 10, some of these activities have been addressed in the International Law Commission's Draft Code of Crimes against the Peace and Security of Mankind; others have been suggested for inclusion in that instrument; others have not yet been suggested for criminalization there or elsewhere. *See Draft articles on the draft code of crimes against the peace and security of mankind provisionlly adopted by the International Law Commission on first reading*, Report of the International Law Commission on its forty-third session, 29 April-19 July 1991, U.N. GAOR, 46th Sess., Supp. No. 10, at 238, U.N. Doc. A/46/10 (1992); M. Berman & R. Clark, *State Terrorism: Disappearances*, 13 Rutgers L.J. 531 (1982).

8. The Abuse of Power resolution was one of only two to come to a vote in the Plenary of the Sixth Congress (the other was on extra-judicial executions). *Sixth United Nations Congress on the Prevention of Crime and the Treatment of Offenders, Caracas, Venezuela, 25 August-5 September 1980, Report prepared by the Secretariat*, at 78–79, U.N. Doc. A/CONF.87/14/Rev.1 (1981). While the Rules of the Congress required a two-thirds vote for the adoption of a resolution by a Plenary session of the congress, supporters of the resolution, aware that it was supported by only a bare majority in committee, moved to suspend the Rule in this instance and then voted the resolution through by a simple majority.

ated by the activities of transnational corporations.[9] It also recommended that the United Nations "should continue its present work on the development of guidelines and standards regarding abuse of economic and political power." This language would provide the mandate for the drafting of the Declaration on Victims, the main focus shifting from the etiology of victimization to the victims themselves—to those individuals and (to a lesser extent) groups on the losing end of the activities in question.[10]

The drafting was completed at the Seventh United Nations Congress, held in Milan in 1985, and the resulting Victims Declaration was approved by the General Assembly later that year. The drafting exercise would, however, carry with it the baggage of unresolved conceptual issues from the Sixth Congress. In fact, in some respects, the problem became even worse. An already large range of categories of victims collected a further one. As the effort to draft standards for the treatment of victims of abuse of power commenced, efforts were also afoot, primarily under the auspices of a non-governmental organization, the World Society of Victimology, to draft international standards concerning victims of crime.[11] A first draft was produced by Professor Irvin Waller of the University of Ottawa.[12]

There were many strands to the broad "victim movement" that gave rise to this latter initiative. The best nutshell description of it is by Matti Joutsen and Joanna Shapland:

The victim movement is commonly considered to have begun in the United States where, during the 1970's, it was essentially a feminist movement, with some associated developments for reform within the criminal justice system. The feminists drew attention to the particular problems faced by victims of sexual assault and (somewhat later) domestic violence. Some individual practitioners, working on a daily basis with victims . . . gradually grew to realize that the system was not meeting the needs of victims and, in many cases, was producing "secondary victimization". They argued that the concentration of

9. This issue of the transnationals, and in particular of a draft code of conduct for transnational corporations, was a divisive one between North and South. Efforts were continuing on the matter in other parts of the organization while the victims instrument was being developed. *See, e.g.*, F.I. Nixson, *Controlling the Transnationals? Political Economy and the United Nations Code of Conduct*, 11 INT'L J. SOC. L. 83 (1983).

10. The 1980 Congress agenda item on "Crime and the abuse of power: offences and offenders beyond the reach of the law" was not repeated in 1985. The Victims Declaration was ultimately discussed under topic 3 of the 1985 Congress, "Victims of crime." The agenda item, in itself, foreshadowed some narrowing of the place of abuse of power in the discussion.

11. *See* Joutsen, *supra* note 2, at 65; Lamborn, *supra* note 2, at 62–63.

12. I. Waller, *Declaration on the Protection of and Assistance to Crime Victims*, 3 WORLD SOC'Y OF VICTIMOLOGY NEWSL. 1, 9–12 (1983–84).

attention on crime prevention and on the punishment and rehabilitation of offenders meant that the victim was being ignored. Furthermore, due to specialization and bureaucratization, the social welfare and medical services remained unaware of, and thus unable to deal with, the special problems faced by victims.

When the victim movement took on a separate identity in the United States, it also became in many respects a conservative movement. One of the most vocal goals has been to increase the level of punishment for certain offences. However, the largest victim association—the National Organization for Victims Assistance (NOVA)—has sought to turn the orientation away from such "offender-bashing" towards helping victims and, in particular, promoting and ensuring victims rights. NOVA has sought to expand its activities beyond the victims of crime, and to include victims of "stark misfortune". Thus, NOVA has sent crisis teams into communities that have undergone mass murder or, for example, an aeroplane crash.[13]

The reference by Joutsen and Shapland to an aircraft crash drives home the hard intellectual question of just what traffic the "victim" label will bear. Are victims of crime at some level in the same category as victims of fire, plague, floods, pestilence, and war, that is to say, disasters whether made by humans or by natural causes? In the United Nations context, does it make sense to label some victims as having suffered human rights abuses (and thus under the jurisdiction of the Center for Human Rights), or as refugees (and under the jurisdiction of the High Commissioner for Refugees), or as having suffered a natural disaster (and thus under the aegis of the United Nations Department of Humanitarian Affairs). All of these people may need some compensation and assistance, just like victims of crime.[14] Indeed, the creation of the Department of Humanitarian Affairs of the United Nations Secretariat, which has some coordinating functions, in the course of the restructuring of the organization in the early 1990s represents, in part at least, an effort to reconfigure some of the categories.

13. M. Joutsen & J. Shapland, *Report of an ad hoc working group meeting, in* HELSINKI INSTITUTE FOR CRIME PREVENTION AND CONTROL AFFILIATED WITH THE UNITED NATIONS, PUBLICATION SERIES NO. 16, CHANGING VICTIM POLICY: THE UNITED NATIONS VICTIM DECLARATION AND RECENT DEVELOPMENTS IN EUROPE 1, 4 (1989). On United States developments in general, *see* J.H. STARK & H.H. GOLDSTEIN, THE RIGHTS OF CRIME VICTIMS (1985) (noting United States developments in general); L.N. Henderson, *The Wrongs of Victims Rights*, 37 STAN. L. REV. 937 (1985) (providing a much less sympathetic assessment of the movement).

14. *See, e.g.,* G.A. Res. 46/182, U.N. GAOR, 46th Sess., Supp. No. 49, U.N. Doc. A/46/49 (1992) (making the Assembly *"Deeply concerned* about the suffering of the victims of disasters and emergency situations, the loss in human lives, the flow of refugees, the mass displacement of people and the material destruction."). *See also infra* notes 53–56 (detailing categories of victims).

The two efforts at drafting an international statement coalesced, but not without some dissonance. With the encouragement of the United Nations Secretariat, Professor Leroy Lamborn, a prominent member of the World Society of Victimology, then drafted a "Declaration on Crime, Abuses of Power and the Rights of Victims."[15] A further draft, drawing on the work of a number of consultants, including the present author, was presented to the Committee on Crime Prevention and Control at its Eighth Session in March 1984 under the title "Draft Declaration on the Rights of Victims of Crime or Other Illegal Acts Involving Abuse of Power."[16]

This draft, along with the Waller and Lamborn drafts, was considered at the Interregional Preparatory Meeting for the Seventh Congress which was held in Ottawa in July of 1984.[17] That meeting produced a lengthy "Draft Declaration on Justice and Assistance for Victims"[18] with the understanding that the Secretariat would "effect all the necessary adjustments and customary editorial revisions"[19] to produce a final version for submission to the congress. In fact, the draft was discussed at a number of conferences in the ensuing months and the Secretariat "received comments about the Ottawa proposals from a variety of official, quasi-official and private sources."[20] As a result, the Seventh Congress was presented both with a tidied-up version of the Ottawa draft[21] and a considerably shortened version of it.[22]

The short version was the one on which the delegates to the Seventh Congress ultimately focused. As late as the closing stages of the Seventh Congress itself, that draft document tried to give equal weight to both aspects of the matter, victims of crime and victims of abuse of power. In commentaries on the two versions of the Victims Declaration

15. L. Lamborn, *Toward a United Nations Declaration on Crime, Abuses of Power and the Rights of Victims*, 3 WORLD SOC'Y OF VICTIMOLOGY NEWSL. 15, 16–20 (1983–84).

16. *Report of the Secretary-General, Guidelines for Measures on Behalf of Victims of Crime and Abuses of Power*, at 24–31, U.N. Doc. E/AC.57/1984/14 (1984).

17. *See Report of the Interregional Preparatory Meeting for the Seventh United Nations Congress on the Prevention of crime and the Treatment of Offenders on Topic III: "Victims of Crime,"* U.N. Doc. A/CONF.121/IPM/4 (1984).

18. *Id.* at 20 [hereinafter Ottawa Draft].

19. *Id.*

20. Lamborn, *supra* note 2, at 65–66.

21. *See Report of the Interregional Preparatory Meeting for the Seventh United Nations Congress on the Prevention of Crime and the Treatment of offenders on Topic III: "Victims of Crime": Addendum: Revised Draft Resolution Introducing the Draft Declaration on Justice and Assistance for Victims of Crimes or Other Acts Involving the Abuse of Power,* U.N. Doc. A/CONF.121/IPM/4/Add.1 (1985).

22. *Working Paper prepared by the Secretariat, Victims of Crime,* U.N. Doc. A/CONF.121/6 (1985).

prepared on behalf of the Secretariat for circulation at the congress,[23] I suggested that the drafting had proceeded on the basis that there are some shared similarities in the needs of various types of victims of crime including those under international law, victims of human rights violations, violations of certain standards of corporate conduct, and of other abuses of power, as that concept had been evolving in United Nations usage. (There was, of course, some overlap in the categories.) The victims of genocide, torture, disappearances, serious harm to the environment, dangerous consumer products, corruption, robbery, and rape all have certain common needs and certain common claims on the resources of society. This was the basic point—that the concept might be stated in such a way that it cried out the moral, and even legal, message that these unfortunates as a group had some special claims on society that others did not. The drafting represented an effort both to stake out the common ground and to refer to the specific needs of different classes of victims, where necessary. It proceeded on the assumption that the effort to find common ground was a worthwhile and intellectually challenging one.[24]

23. *See Commentary on Draft Declaration on Justice and Assistance for Victims of Crimes or Other Illegal Acts Involving the Abuse of Power, as contained in U.N. Doc. A/CONF.121/IPM.4/Add.1* (1985); *Commentary on Draft of Main Principles of Justice and Assistance for Victims of Crime or Illegal Abuses of Power* (1985) (unnumbered documents circulated as conference papers at the Milan Congress). The discussion in the text is based in part on those documents.

24. As a challenge to the drafter's art, the whole thing was a nightmare. The definition provision in Article II of the Ottawa Draft, *supra* note 18, which tried to hold everything together, read:

A "victim" is a person who has suffered physical or mental injury or harm, material loss or damage, or other social disadvantage as a result of conduct which:
(a) is a violation of national penal laws; or
(b) is a crime under international law; or
(c) constitutes a violation of internationally recognized human rights norms protecting life, liberty and personal security; or
(d) (i) otherwise amounts to an "abuse of power" by persons who, by reason of their political, economic or social position, whether they are public officials, agents or employees of the State or corporate entities, are "beyond the reach of the law"; or
(ii) although not presently proscribed by national or international law, causes physical, psychological or economic harm comparable to that caused by abuses of power constituting a crime under international law or a violation of internationally recognized human rights norms and creates needs in victims as serious as those caused by violations of such norms.

The term "victim" includes any person who has thus suffered loss, damage or injury whether as a individual or as a member of a group or collectivity.

When appropriate, the term "person" includes legal entities, organizations, associations, communities, the State or society as a whole.

supra note 18.

It became clear at the Seventh Congress, however, that there was much more enthusiasm among some delegations for the material on victims of crime—certainly a significant issue in its own right. It seemed for a while in Milan that all the abuse of power material would be stricken from the draft. This would be an ironical result since this was where the saga began five years earlier. In order to save the bare minimum, a decision was therefore made to split the Victims Declaration into two parts, one dealing in some detail with victims of crime and another treating the question of abuse of power in more skeletal form. At the same time, material aimed at the prevention of victimization was de-emphasized by being moved out of the Victims Declaration itself and buried in the adopting resolution.[25]

B. Contents of the Declaration

As adopted, then, the Victims Declaration is in two parts, Part A headed "Victims of Crime" and Part B headed "Victims of Abuse of Power." Some comments follow on each of these parts.[26]

1. Victims of Crime

"Victims" is defined in paragraph 1 of the Victims Declaration (apparently for the purposes of Part A only) to mean persons who, individually or collectively, have suffered harm, including physical or mental injury, emotional suffering, economic loss, or substantial impairment of their fundamental rights, through acts or omissions that are in violation of criminal laws operative within member states, including those laws proscribing criminal abuse of power.[27] A second para-

25. See Victims Declaration, *supra* note 1, para. 4 (calling upon states, inter alia, to implement social, health, including mental health, education, economic and specific crime prevention policies to reduce victimization and encourage assistance to victims in distress; and to prohibit practices and procedures conducive to abuse, such as secret places of detention and incommunicado detention). These two surviving prevention provisions are typical of the way in which the drafts emphasized both specific human rights concerns and a broader social approach. See also Chapter 4 *supra*, at notes 169–179 (detailing the continuation at the Eighth Congress and beyond of efforts to encourage broad social prevention initiatives).

26. See also Joutsen, *supra* note 2, at 298–324 (entitled *The Declaration of Basic Principles of Justice for Victims of Crime and Abuse of Power: Commentary*).

27. Victims Declaration, *supra* note 1, para. 1. "Criminal laws operative within Member States" is meant to be broad enough to include federal, state or local laws where a state's criminal law system is organized along such lines. The final reference to "criminal abuse of power" was a nod in the direction of the abuse of power concept, but it was limited to those abuses already criminalized.

graph[28] of the definition was designed primarily to deal with the problem of the perpetrator who is not criminally responsible and cases such as a "disappearance" where it is not clear who the perpetrator is. It provides that a person may be considered a victim, under the Victims Declaration, regardless of whether the perpetrator is identified, apprehended, prosecuted, or convicted and regardless of the familial relationship between the perpetrator and the victim. The definition adds[29] that the term "victim" also includes, where appropriate, the immediate family or dependents of the direct victim and persons who have suffered harm in intervening to assist victims in distress or to prevent victimization. The definition concludes[30] with a fairly standard non-discrimination clause asserting that the provisions of the Declaration shall be applicable to all, without distinction of any kind, such as race, color, sex, age, language, religion, nationality, political or other opinion, cultural beliefs or practices, property, birth or family status, ethnic or social origin, and disability. (Notable additions to the usual United Nations list are disability and age—concessions to the many people from the healing professions engaged in the exercise.)[31]

This definition sets the stage. Part A places on the stage four categories of claims possessed by victims of crime: access to justice and fair treatment, restitution, compensation, and assistance. I use the term "claim" to describe what victims may seek under the Victims Declaration because "rights" would be too strong. The Victims Declaration is of

---

28. *Id.* para. 2.

29. *Id.*

30. *Id.* para. 3.

31. The non-discrimination provision has perhaps to be balanced against paragraph 17 which suggests some classes of victims may have special needs and should receive some sort of affirmative action. It reads: "In providing services and assistance to victims, attention should be given to those who have special needs because of the nature of the harm inflicted or because of factors such as those mentioned in para. 3 above." (*See supra* text accompanying note 29 describing paragraph 3.) Joutsen comments:

> Research has indicated that there are a variety of factors (such as low education, low-income housing, unemployment, alcohol and drug abuse) that are strongly correlated with victimization, even multiple victimization. Certain other factors (such as age and sex) may also create special needs. Special mention should also be made here of victims of domestic abuse and sexual offences. The victims of such offences may have special problems in gaining access to justice or services, problems that might only be overcome by an "out-reach" service.

Supra note 2, at 320.

"Basic Principles" and throughout uses the precatory "should" rather than a mandatory "shall."[32]

(a) Access to Justice and Fair Treatment

So far as access to justice and fair treatment are concerned, the Victims Declaration asserts that victims should be treated with compassion and respect for their dignity. Victims are entitled to access to the mechanisms of justice and to prompt redress, as provided for by national legislation, for the harm they have suffered.[33] As Matti Joutsen puts it, "By treating such victims with compassion and respect they are assured that they have indeed suffered an injustice recognized by the community as such."[34] Joutsen continues:

Furthermore, some victims may be so shaken by the offence that they are not able to function as full members of the community. The showing of compassion and respect, something that can be done at minor cost, may well be enough in itself to help the victim to recovery. Compassion, however, should be balanced against respect; many victims may dislike an attitude that implies that, as victims, they are helpless persons in need of charity and assistance.[35]

Judicial and administrative mechanisms should, according to the Victims Declaration, be established and strengthened where necessary to enable victims to obtain redress through formal or informal procedures that are expeditious, fair, inexpensive, and accessible.[36] Victims should be informed of their rights in seeking redress through such mechanisms.[37] The responsiveness of the system should be enhanced.

32. *See* Chapter 5 *supra*, at note 64.
33. Victims Declaration, *supra* note 1, para. 4.
34. Joutsen, *supra* note 2, at 306.
35. *Id.*
36. Victims Declaration, *supra* note 1, para. 5. According to Joutsen:

The provision calls upon States not only to establish mechanisms where necessary but also to strengthen existing mechanisms. For example civil proceedings have been faulted in many connections for being complex and time-consuming. The provision in question would therefore suggest that the State should simplify and expedite the techniques of civil procedure, in particular with respect to the enforcement of claims. From the point of view of the victim, however, it may be more expeditious to have his civil claim appended to criminal proceedings, as is indeed possible in many European countries.

Supra note 2, at 307.
37. *Id.* para. 5. The "right to know one's rights" is receiving increasing emphasis in the human rights literature. *See* V. Pechota, The Right to Know One's Human Rights: A Road Toward Individual Freedom (1983).

Enhancement should be achieved, for example, by informing victims of their role and the scope, timing, and progress of the proceedings and the disposition of their cases, especially where serious crimes are involved and where they have requested such information. It should also be done by allowing the views and concerns of victims to be presented and considered at appropriate stages of the proceedings where their personal interests are affected, without prejudice to the accused and consistent with the relevant national criminal justice system. Victims should also receive proper assistance throughout the legal process. Measures should be taken to minimize inconvenience to victims, protect their privacy, and ensure their safety, as well as that of their families and witnesses on their behalf, from intimidation and retaliation. Unnecessary delay should be avoided in the disposition of cases and in the execution of orders or decrees granting awards to victims.[38] Bearing in mind that the criminal process is not necessarily simply a vehicle for punishment, the Victims Declaration suggests that informal mechanisms for the resolution of disputes, including mediation, arbitration, and customary justice or indigenous practices, should be utilized where appropriate to facilitate conciliation and redress for victims.[39] For some, the use of such techniques might obviate the need for prosecution. Nevertheless, the Victims Declaration leaves it "open to the criminal laws of the jurisdiction in question to proceed with the prosecution of the alleged offence regardless of possible dispute resolution and conciliation between the offender and the victim."[40]

Thus, the section of the Victims Declaration on access to justice and fair treatment builds upon two main underlying propositions. The first is that substantive rights are meaningful only in the context of fair procedures to give effect to those rights. The second is that victims ought to be involved more in the criminal justice process than is currently the case in many legal systems and that they should be treated fairly and with dignity by the other actors in the system.

(b) Restitution

In the restitution section, the Victims Declaration starts with the assertion that offenders or third parties responsible for their behavior should, where appropriate, make fair restitution to victims, their fam-

---

38. *Id.* para. 6. These rather mild provisions about the involvement of victims in the criminal process represented something of a concession to those governments (like that of the United Kingdom) which strongly opposed any extension of rights to victims over sentencing, case disposal or the course of trial. Joutsen, *supra* note 2, at 309.

39. *Id.* para. 7.

40. Joutsen, *supra* note 2, at 310.

ilies, or dependents. Such restitution should include the return of property or payment for the harm or loss suffered, reimbursement of expenses incurred as a result of the victimization, the provision of services, and the restoration of rights.[41] Governments are exhorted to review their practices, regulations, and laws in order to consider restitution as an available sentencing option in criminal cases, in addition to other options.[42] In the final version of the Victims Declaration, the types of loss for which restitution may be given are left at large. At an earlier stage of the drafting, effort had been made to determine if some general principles on the subject could be drawn from various legal systems.[43]

Some of the drafting of the Declaration took place soon after the chemical disaster in Bhopal and reflected an effort to respond to that event and to suggest directions in which the criminal law might expand

41. Victims Declaration, *supra* note 1, para. 8. "Restoration of rights" might have some impact in respect of common crime (such as disappearances as finally dealt with) but it was intended by the original drafters more to deal with cases of human rights violations and other abuses of power—with "state crime" in a broad sense. Examples of "restitution" in such cases might include a return from exile, restoration of civil rights, reinstatement of a license to practice law, or issue of a passport.

42. *Id.* para. 9. *See* B. Galaway, *Use of Restitution as a Penal Measure in the United States*, 22 HOWARD L.J. 8 (1983) (discussing the role of restitution as an "intermediate sanction" between probation and imprisonment). As envisaged by the drafters, the Victims Declaration was meant to permit restitution in particular cases, either in addition to or as an alternative to other sanctions. In some legal systems the term "restitution" is used in a narrow sense to refer only to the return of stolen property. The Victims Declaration uses it the broad way Galaway does, to refer to a sanction "by which an offender is required to restore victim losses through either money payment or services." *Id.* at 9.

43. Thus, the Ottawa Draft, *supra* note 18, Article IV, paragraph 2, provided:

2. Victims shall be entitled to obtain reparation for at least the following kinds of loss, damage or injury:
(a) loss of life;
(b) impairment of health;
(c) pain and suffering, both physical and mental;
(d) loss of liberty;
(e) loss of income, earning capacity or support;
(f) loss of or damage to property or deprivation of the use of property;
(g) special damages, i.e., the expenses reasonably incurred by the victim as a result of the victimization, for example medical, legal, transportation, funeral and burial expenses;
(h) intangible damage, such as loss of reputation.

Comparative law and international law have not yet developed a sophisticated approach to these problems. *See generally*, C. GRAY, JUDICIAL REMEDIES IN INTERNATIONAL LAW (1990). For a recent effort to address such issues in the context of claims against Iraq arising from its invasion of Kuwait, *see* J. Crook, *The United Nations Compensation Commission—A New Structure to Enforce State Responsibility*, 87 AM. J. INT'L L. 144 (1993).

in such cases. In language that managed to survive from the earlier abuse of power emphasis, there is in Part A of the Declaration a reference to restitution in environmental cases. In cases of substantial harm to the environment, it is written that where restitution is ordered, it should include, as far as possible, restoration of the environment, reconstruction of the infrastructure, replacement of community facilities and reimbursement of the expenses of relocation, whenever such harm results in the dislocation of a community.[44]

In a concluding paragraph, the restitution section of the Victims Declaration provides that where public officials or other agents acting in an official or quasi-official capacity have violated national criminal laws, the victims should receive restitution from the state whose officials or agents were responsible for the harm inflicted. In cases where the Government under whose authority the victimizing act or omission occurred is no longer in existence, the state or government successor should provide restitution to the victims.[45] This provision was aimed especially at the problem of the disappeared. In earlier drafts of the Victims Declaration, the disappeared were treated as a problem of a breach of international law creating a criminal offense and the documents gave the same rights to victims of crime under international law as to victims of crimes under national (domestic) law.[46] Ultimately, what one might call the "newly restored democracy lobby," notably Argentina and Uruguay, took the position that, since disappearances were illegal under their domestic laws at all relevant times, it was appropriate to treat problems of restitution in such cases along with restitution to victims of other common crimes. The category of victims of crime under international law was thus excised from the draft, an unfortunate development since it also included victims of war crimes, genocide, torture, and apartheid.

44. Victims Declaration, *supra* note 1, para. 10. The role of the criminal law in the protection of the environment is still a burning issue. In E.S.C. Res. 1992/22, pt. VI, para. 1, the Economic and Social Council set as a "priority theme" for the Commission on crime Prevention and Criminal Justice "(a) National and transnational crime, organized crime, economic crime, including money laundering, *and the role of criminal law in the protection of the environment.*" (Emphasis added.) E.S.C Res. 1992/22, U.N. ESCOR, Supp. No. 1, U.N. Doc. E/1992/92, at 22 (1992).

45. *Id.* para. 11. *See generally* Y. Danieli, *Preliminary Reflections from a Psychological Perspective*, in SEMINAR ON THE RIGHT TO COMPENSATION AND REHABILITATION FOR VICTIMS OF GROSS VIOLATIONS OF HUMAN RIGHTS AND FUNDAMENTAL FREEDOMS, MAASTRICHT, 11–15 MARCH 1992, 196 (T. Van Boven, C. Flinterman, F. Grunfeld & I. Westendorp eds., 1993) (discussing the role of restitution and compensation in such cases, especially as part of the healing process)

46. *See, e.g.*, Ottawa Draft, *supra* note 24.

(c) Compensation

The Victims Declaration next addresses the matter of compensation. "Compensation" was the term chosen as a drafting technique to refer to recompense made by the state, as opposed to recompense made by the offender, for which the term "restitution" had been called into service. When recompense is not fully available from the offender or other sources, states are exhorted to provide financial compensation to (a) victims who have sustained significant bodily injury or impairment of physical or mental health as a result of serious crimes, and (b) the family, in particular dependents of persons who have died or become mentally or physically handicapped as a result of such victimization.[47]

Moreover, the establishment, strengthening, and expansion of national funds for compensation to victims is to be encouraged. Where appropriate, other funds may also be established for this purpose, including those cases where the state of which the victim is a national is not in a position to compensate the victim for the harm.[48] "Not in a position" is perhaps a euphemism. The drafters were actually contemplating those situations where the state itself is involved in the victimization and will not acknowledge its obligation to correct its harm. In such situations, the Victims Declaration encourages the establishment, strengthening, or expansion of such international funds as the United Nations Voluntary Fund for the Victims of Torture[49] or the Trust Fund for South Africa which assists victims of apartheid.[50]

47. Victims Declaration, *supra* note 1, para. 12.

48. *Id.* para. 13.

49. G.A. Res. 36/151, U.N. GAOR, 36th Sess., Supp. No. 51, at 185, U.N. Doc. A/36/51 (1982). The Fund, according to para. 1 (a) of the resolution, receives voluntary contributions for distribution "as humanitarian, legal and financial aid to individuals whose human rights have been severely violated as a result of torture and relatives of such victims, priority being given to aid to victims of violations by States in which the human rights situation has been the subject of resolutions or decisions adopted by either the [General] Assembly, the Economic and Social Council or the Commission on Human Rights."

50. *See* G.A. Res. 2054 B (XX), U.N. GAOR, 20th Sess., Supp. No. 14, at 17, U.N. Doc. A/6014 (1966) (creating the Trust Fund for South Africa). *See also* Other resolution 27, *supra* note 1, para. 5 (requesting the Secretary-General "to make appropriate provisions to study the feasibility of establishing an international fund, within the framework of the United Nations crime prevention and criminal justice programme, for the compensation of, and assistance to, victims of transnational crimes and for the promotion of international research, data collection and dissemination and the establishment of policy guidelines in this respect."). Moves are still afoot to make this operational. *See also* E.S.C. Res. 1990/22, *supra* note 1, which requests the Secretary-General to "further develop international means of recourse and redress for victims where national channels may be insufficient."

It will be noted that the measure of recompense from the state is not necessarily as expansive as that which, at least theoretically, it may be possible to exact from the offender by way of restitution. The state may not necessarily be expected to pay substantial sums for pain and suffering or moral damage.[51] The analogy here is more likely to be with the kind of limited scheduled benefits payable in a workers' compensation scheme[52] than those payable by tortfeasors in a tort system. It may be reasonable, moreover, to expect people in developed countries at least to carry private insurance against property damage—which is not covered by this part of the Declaration—or even to absorb some losses, whether to person or property, themselves.

The provisions in the Declaration concerning payments to victims of crime were inspired in large part by the experience of countries which have created special schemes for the support of victims of such offenses, especially of the violent kind.[53] However, there is no reason why the standards of the Declaration in respect of such victims could not be met through comprehensive social security or social insurance schemes. In this respect, the New Zealand experience is telling.[54] In 1963, New Zealand adopted the world's first criminal injuries compensation scheme, a widely applauded initiative[55] that became a model elsewhere. In the following few years, however, considerable attention was given to methods of dealing with injuries incurred on the job, in automobile accidents, and indeed with unexpected personal injuries in general. The result was the adoption of the Accident Compensation Act 1972 which abolished the tort system as a means of compensating for personal injuries and established a state administered compensation scheme which subsumed the regime for the compensation of criminally caused injuries.[56] (It did not, however, deal with property

51. *See supra* note 43 (describing the types of damages that offenders may be required to pay).

52. *See generally*, G. PALMER, COMPENSATION FOR INCAPACITY: A STUDY OF LAW AND SOCIAL CHANGE IN NEW ZEALAND AND AUSTRALIA 219–29 (1979).

53. *See generally*, P. BURNS, CRIMINAL INJURIES COMPENSATION: SOCIAL REMEDY OR POLITICAL PALLIATIVE FOR VICTIMS OF CRIME? (1980).

54. *Id.* at 131.

55. *See e.g.*, L.L. Lamborn, *The Propriety of Governmental Compensation of Victims of Crime*, 41 GEO. WASH. L. REV. 446, 448 (1972).

56. The accident compensation scheme is discussed thoroughly in PALMER, *supra* note 52. BURNS devotes the whole of Chapter 2 to "The Rationales of Criminal Injuries Compensation Schemes" and examines various theories for why victims of (violent) crime have some special claim to societal resources, *supra* note 53. The drafting of the Victims Declaration proceeded with an intuited rather than articulated premise that the various classes of victims encompassed therein had a strong claim on the state. The ultimate New Zealand disposition suggests that some states may find the broad class even larger.

damages.) In retrospect, one can view the discussion of compensation for criminal injuries in that jurisdiction as a minor skirmish along the way to the creation of a much more comprehensive scheme. Yet, admitting this is not to deny the importance of the criminal injuries compensation issue!

(d) Assistance

The provisions of the Victims Declaration on assistance start from the rather obvious premise that some victims need more than money to make them whole. A support system must be in place. It need not be provided or run entirely by the state. Indeed, voluntary or indigenous modes may be most appropriate in some societies. But even in such cases, the state may need to contribute to the resources of the system by such means as financial assistance, logistical help, and expert advice. Medical, counseling, and legal assistance are among the resources that may be immediately necessary, to say nothing of emergency financial assistance. Some of these costs may be recoverable in due course from the perpetrator as part of "restitution", but it is unrealistic to expect that the recovery rate from that source will be high.

Thus, the Victims Declaration asserts that victims should receive the necessary material, medical, psychological, and social assistance through governmental, voluntary, community-based, and indigenous means.[57] Victims should be informed of the availability of health and social services and other relevant assistance and be readily afforded access to them.[58] Many plans to assist victims, including both compensation and assistance schemes, have had limited impact because of the lack of publicity for their operations. Hence victims should be told of their options at an early stage. Police, justice, health, social service, and other personnel concerned should receive training to sensitize these groups to the needs of victims, and guidelines to ensure proper and prompt aid.[59]

Part A, then, sets out in some detail a comprehensive group of rights—access to justice, restitution, compensation and assistance—to which victims of crime are entitled.

2. Victims of Abuse of Power

Part B of the Victims Declaration contains a rather brief and confusing set of standards, consisting of only four fairly cryptic paragraphs. It

57. Victims Declaration, *supra* note 1, para. 14.
58. *Id.* para. 15.
59. *Id.* para. 16.

begins with another definition, apparently for the purposes of this part, although the drafting is not altogether precise. The lack of precision may be attributable in part to the haste with which the final compromises were reached in Milan that allowed at least much of the Victims Declaration to survive. It may also be traceable to a tacit decision to obfuscate rather than give up all efforts at gaining consensus.[60] Be that as it may, the Part B definition paragraph provides that the meaning of victims is to include

persons who, individually or collectively, have suffered harm, including physical or mental injury, emotional suffering, economic loss or substantial impairment of their fundamental rights, through acts or omissions that do not yet constitute violations of national criminal laws, but are violations of internationally recognized norms relating to human rights.[61]

At the very least, the concept of "internationally recognized norms relating to human rights" includes those standards contained in the Universal Declaration of Human Rights[62] and the two Covenants on human rights,[63] but could encompass material contained in many other instruments. Arguably this language was designed as a definition of victims which would apply to each of the later provisions of Part B. However, the only subsequent provision which actually utilizes the concept is a paragraph suggesting that states should consider negotiating multilateral treaties relating to victims, as defined.[64]

---

60. The author attempted unsuccessfully to persuade some friendly delegations to try to clean up the drafting in the Third Committee of the General Assembly. *See* Memorandum from Roger Clark To Anyone Interested, Draft United Nations Declaration of Basic Principles of Justice A. Relating to Victims of Crime, and B. Relating to Victims of Abuse of Power (Sept. 23, 1985). (The title alone was simplified in the Assembly.)

61. Victims Declaration, *supra* note 1, art. 18. Earlier versions of the Declaration (such as the Ottawa Draft, *supra* note 18) used the concept of victims of crime under international law as a general category to describe some of the classes of persons who were to be brought under the aegis of the instrument, including the victims of genocide, war crimes, apartheid, disappearances and torture. That concept was criticized by several governments, in some cases as a general category and in others for its specifics, and its use was dropped in the final version. Joutsen, *supra* note 2, at 321. In the author's view, the attacks on the concept of crimes under international law were thoroughly misguided. *See* R. Clark, *Offenses of International Concern: Multilateral State Treaty Practice in the Forty Years Since Nuremberg*, 57 NORDIC. J. INT'L L. 49 (1988) (for a response).

62. G.A. Res. 217A (III), U.N. GAOR, 3th Sess, pt.1, Resolutions 71, U.N. Doc. A/810 (1949).

63. International Covenant on Economic, Social and Cultural Rights, G.A. Res. 2200 (XXI), U.N. GAOR, 21st Sess., Supp. No. 16, at 49, U.N. Doc. A/6316 (1967); International Covenant on Civil and Political Rights, *id.* at 52.

64. Victims Declaration, *supra* note 1, para. 20.

Instead of using the term "victims" according to the definition, the other two paragraphs of Part B take a slightly different tack which echoes the earlier emphasis on abuse of power. In doing so, these two paragraphs do not necessarily regard an abuse of power as synonymous with breaching internationally recognized norms relating to human rights. One of these paragraphs suggests that states should consider incorporating into national law "norms proscribing abuses of power" and providing remedies to victims of such abuses. In particular, the paragraph states that such remedies should include restitution and/or compensation, and necessary material, medical, psychological, and social assistance and support.[65] The other paragraph urges states to periodically review existing legislation and practices to ensure their responsiveness to changing circumstances. It encourages states to enact and enforce, if necessary, "legislation proscribing acts that constitute serious abuses of political or economic power," as well as promoting policies and mechanisms for the prevention of such acts, and to develop and make readily available appropriate rights and remedies for victims of such acts.[66] The plain meaning of the quoted language, "abuses of power," and "serious abuses of political or economic power," is not necessarily the same as violations of "internationally recognized norms relating to human rights."

A leading scholarly commentator on the Victims Declaration, Leroy Lamborn (also one of the drafters) has suggested a contextual way in which some sense can be made of the definitional provisions and subsequent structure of Part B. Lamborn suggests that:

An internally consistent and rational way of integrating the various terms used starts by noting that the title of the section is "B. Victims of abuse of power." In light of this title and the fact that section A for its separate purposes defines "victims" as persons harmed by conduct "in violation of criminal laws operative within Member States," the only reasonable interpretation of the definitional paragraph of Section B is that the subjects of the definition are not "victims" but rather "victims of abuse of power." Thus "victims of abuse of power" are "persons who . . . have suffered harm . . . through acts or omission that do not yet constitute violations of national criminal laws but of internationally recognized norms relating to human rights." That being the case, the proposal of paragraph 19 that States "consider incorporating into the national law norms proscribing abuses of power and providing remedies to victims of such abuses" is most reasonably construed to mean that States should consider incorporating into the national law norms proscribing abuses of power, *that is, internationally recognized norms relating to human rights.*[67]

65. *Id.* para. 19.
66. *Id.* para. 21.
67. Lamborn, *supra* note 2, at 84–85 (emphasis in original).

This is certainly a plausible way of interpreting the ultimate language and structure of the abuse of power part of the Declaration. It rather plainly entails a narrowing of the scope of Part B from anything beyond human rights law—a narrowing that some, but not all, of the states represented in Milan were pleased to achieve.

This narrowing rationalization still leaves some, perhaps small, sphere of action for Part B which, if the reader bears in mind what Part A has promised, makes some potential contribution to evolving international law on the treatment of victims beyond that already contained in mainstream human rights instruments. In particular it points in the direction of restitution and compensation.[68] Nevertheless, the whole episode suggests that, while states were prepared, at least at the level of exhortation,[69] to make a serious effort to improve the plight of victims of crime, an opportunity for a broader conceptualization was lost.

68. In 1989, the Sub-Commission on Prevention of Discrimination and Protection of Minorities entrusted a Special Rapporteur to undertake a study on the right to restitution, compensation and rehabilitation for victims of gross violations of human rights and fundamental freedoms, taking into account relevant existing international human rights norms on compensation and relevant decisions and views of international human rights organs, with a view to exploring the possibility of developing some basic principles and guidelines. See *Preliminary report submitted by Mr. Theo Van Boven, Special Rapporteur*, U.N. Doc. E/CN.4/Sub.2/1990/10 (1990); *Progress report submitted by Mr. Theo Van Boven, Special Rapporteur, Study concerning the right to restitution, compensation and rehabilitation for victims of human rights and fundamental freedoms*, U.N. Doc. E./CN.4/Sub.2/1991/7 (1991); *Second progress report submitted by Mr. Theo Van Boven, Special Rapporteur*, U.N. Doc. E/CN.4/Sub.2/1992/8 (1992). *See generally* SEMINAR, *supra* note 45. When the state is responsible for gross violations, whether it be by an existing regime or a previous one, the focus for the assessment of recompense is the "restitution" part of the Victims Declaration, with its emphasis on making the victim as nearly whole as it is possible to do with money and appropriate legal mandates, rather than the "compensation" part of the Victims Declaration, where the state is making a contribution to the victim because it is not possible to collect from the wrongdoer. *Supra* notes 41–45, 47–56. The state responsible for gross violations is the functional equivalent of the criminal for restitution purposes.

69. There have been several efforts to keep states honest by encouraging efforts at "implementing" the Victims Declaration. Note, in particular, *Measures for the Implementation of the Declaration of Basic Principles of Justice for Victims of Crime and Abuse of Power* submitted by a committee of experts that met at the International Institute of Higher Sciences, Syracuse Italy, in May 1986, and later endorsed by various non-governmental organizations. U.N. Doc. E/AC.57/1988/NGO/1 (1988); *Guide for Practitioners regarding the implementation of the Declaration of Basic Principles of Justice for Victims of Crime and Abuse of Power*, U.N. Doc. A/CONF.144/20 (1990); *Model Training Curricula prepared by the Society for Traumatic Stress Studies*, U.N. Doc. E/AC.57/1990/NGO/3 (1990); *Report of the International Workshop on Victim Protection and Conflict Resolution, Oñati, Spain, 12–16 May 1993*; *supra* notes 2, 12 (citing the AIDP and HEUNI publications).

Chapter 8
International Cooperation in the Criminal Process

A. Introduction

The focus here is on a package of model treaties on international criminal cooperation that were approved at the Seventh and Eighth United Nations Congresses on the Prevention of Crime and the Treatment of Offenders in 1985 and 1990. These models represent an attempt to capture the state of the art in international cooperative practice. The model treaties in question are a Model Agreement on the Transfer of Foreign Prisoners,[1] a Model Treaty on Extradition,[2] a Model Treaty on Mutual Assistance in Criminal Matters,[3] a Model Treaty on the Transfer of Proceedings in Criminal Matters,[4] a Model Treaty on the Transfer of Supervision of Offenders Conditionally Sentenced or Conditionally Released,[5] and a Model Treaty for the Prevention of Crimes that Infringe on the Cultural Heritage of Peoples in the Form of Movable Property.[6] I shall endeavor both to analyze the documents themselves and to place them in their legal and historical context.

---

1. *Seventh United Nations Congress on the Prevention of Crime and the Treatment of Offenders, Milan, 26 August-6 September 1985, Report prepared by the Secretariat*, at 53, U.N. Doc. A/CONF.121/22/Rev.1 (1986) [hereinafter Model Prisoner Transfer Agreement].

2. G.A. Res. 45/116, U.N. GAOR, 45th Sess., Supp. No. 49A, at 211, U.N. Doc. A/45/49 (1991) [hereinafter Model Extradition Treaty].

3. G.A. Res. 45/117, *id.* at 215 [hereinafter Model Mutual Assistance Treaty].

4. G.A. Res. 45/118, *id.* at 219 [hereinafter Model Transfer of Proceedings Treaty].

5. G.A. Res. 45/119, *id.* at 221 [hereinafter Model Transfer of Supervision Treaty].

6. *Eighth United Nations Congress on the Prevention of Crime and the Treatment of Offenders, Havana, Cuba, 27 August—7 September 1990, Report prepared by the Secretariat*, at 110, U.N. Doc. A/CONF.144/28 (1990) [hereinafter Model Cultural Heritage Treaty]. This model was not ultimately adopted as a G.A. resolution. *See infra* notes 144–146.

B. Background to the Models

In the simpler world of the nineteenth century, most of the impetus for encouraging transnational cooperation in criminal matters was generated by fleeing thieves and murderers. The basic response was the development of a network of bilateral extradition treaties which provided the means for the return of fugitives to justice.[7] Few countries were ever entirely systematic in their pattern of treaties and there were always relatively safe havens left in the cracks. Moreover, many former colonial territories including some developed countries like my own, New Zealand, failed to negotiate more than a handful of their own treaties after attaining independence. For the most part, these countries have relied on succession to the treaties of the former metropolitan power. If my unscientific examination of the literature is any guide, the most interesting issue in extradition for decades was the political offender exception, a dash of human rights in an otherwise law and order structure, normally written into at least those treaties between states with a Western European political tradition.[8]

Along with the invention of the multilateral treaty in the nineteenth century, however, came a gradual realization that there were some societal ills that were of international concern and should be dealt with in part by the criminal law on a transnational and multilateral basis.[9]

---

7. Within the British Empire, rendition of the likes of thieves and murderers between parts of that entity was facilitated by Imperial legislation. The modern Commonwealth has its successor to that in the "Scheme" initiated in 1966, and amended in 1983 and 1986. The approach of the Scheme (which is not a treaty) is the adoption by most members of the Commonwealth of what amounts to parallel legislation permitting return of fugitives under circumstances where extradition would be appropriate between two non-Commonwealth countries or between a Commonwealth country and a non-Commonwealth country. *See Commonwealth Scheme for the Rendition of Fugitive Offenders, in* COMMONWEALTH SECRETARIAT, COMMONWEALTH SCHEMES ON MUTUAL ASSISTANCE IN THE ADMINISTRATION OF JUSTICE 1 (n.d.). The actual workings of the Scheme are similar to a network of bilateral treaties. The Commonwealth has been active on efforts on cooperation in general. *See, e.g.,* COMMONWEALTH SECRETARIAT, ACTION AGAINST TRANSNATIONAL CRIMINALITY, PAPERS FROM THE 1991 OXFORD CONFERENCE ON INTERNATIONAL AND WHITE COLLAR CRIME (1992); W. C. Gilmore, *International Cooperation in the Administration of Justice: Developments and Prospects* in COMMONWEALTH SECRETARIAT, II ACTION AGAINST TRANSNATIONAL CRIMINALITY, PAPERS FROM THE 1992 OXFORD CONFERENCE ON INTERNATIONAL AND WHITE COLLAR CRIME 147 (1993) (providing a good overview of the field in general). *See also* D. McCLEAN, INTERNATIONAL JUDICIAL ASSISTANCE (1992) (discussing many aspects of international cooperation).

8. C. VAN DEN WIJNGAERT, THE POLITICAL OFFENCE EXCEPTION TO EXTRADITION 72 (1980).

9. *See* M.C. BASSIOUNI, A DRAFT INTERNATIONAL CRIMINAL CODE AND DRAFT STATUTE FOR AN INTERNATIONAL CRIMINAL TRIBUNAL 355–475 (1987) (providing a comprehensive list of multilateral treaties in the criminal law area).

Early examples were the slave trade,[10] the trade in women and children,[11] trade in obscene publications,[12] forgery of currency[13] and trade in illicit drugs.[14] These have continued to be of some moment, but were joined, as the twentieth century progressed and the United Nations came into existence, by perhaps more politically charged items such as genocide,[15] war crimes,[16] apartheid,[17] and various terrorist offenses (like aircraft hijacking,[18] attacks on diplomats,[19] the taking of hostages,[20] and torture[21]).

10. *See, e.g.*, Declaration Relative to the Universal Abolition of the Slave Trade [Congress of Vienna, Act XV], Feb. 8, 1815, 2 Martens Nouveau Récueil de Traités 432; Slavery Convention, signed at Geneva, Sept. 25, 1926, 60 L.N.T.S. 253; Supplementary Convention on the Abolition of Slavery, the Slave Trade, and Institutions and Practices Similar to Slavery, signed at Geneva, Sept. 7, 1956, 266 U.N.T.S. 3.

11. *See, e.g.*, International Agreement for the Suppression of the "White Slave Traffic," signed at Paris, Mar. 18, 1904, 1 L.N.T.S. 83; International Convention for the Suppression of the Traffic in Women and Children, signed at Geneva, Sept. 30, 1921, 9 L.N.T.S. 415; Convention for the Suppression of the Traffic in Persons and of the Exploitation of the Prostitution of Others, opened for signature at Lake Success, New York, May 4, 1949, 96 U.N.T.S. 271.

12. *See, e.g.*, Agreement for the Suppression of the Circulation of Obscene Publications, signed at Paris, May 4, 1910, 7 Martens Nouveau Récueil de Traités (ser. 3) 266; International Convention for the Suppression of the Circulation of and Traffic in Obscene Publications, *opened for signature* at Geneva, Sept. 12, 1923, 27 L.N.T.S. 169.

13. *See* International Convention for the Suppression of Counterfeiting Currency, signed at Geneva, Apr. 20, 1929, 112 L.N.T.S. 371.

14. *See, e.g.*, International Opium Convention, signed at the Hague, Jan. 23, 1912, 8 L.N.T.S. 187; Single Convention on Narcotic Drugs, signed at New York, Mar. 30, 1961, 520 U.N.T.S. 151; United Nations Convention Against Illicit Traffic in Narcotic Drugs and Psychotropic Substances, U.N. Doc. E/CONF.82/15 (1988).

15. Convention on the Prevention and Punishment of the Crime of Genocide, G.A. Res. 260 A (III), U.N. GAOR, 3d Sess., pt.1, Resolutions 174, U.N. Doc. A/810 (1948) [hereinafter Convention on Genocide].

16. Geneva Conventions of 12 August 1949, 75 U.N.T.S. 287.

17. International Convention on the Suppression and Punishment of the Crime of Apartheid, G.A. Res. 3068 (XXVIII), U.N. GAOR, 28th Sess., Supp. No. 30, at 75, U.N. Doc. A/9030 (1974) [hereinafter Convention on Apartheid].

18. Convention for the Suppression of Unlawful Seizure of Aircraft, signed at the Hague, Dec. 16, 1970, 10 I.L.M. 133 (1971) [hereinafter Convention on Aircraft]; Convention for the Suppression of Unlawful Acts Against the Safety of Civil Aviation, signed at Montreal, 23 September 1971, 10 I.L.M. 1151 (1971) [hereinafter Convention on Aviation].

19. CONVENTION ON THE PREVENTION AND PUNISHMENT OF CRIMES AGAINST INTERNATIONALLY PROTECTED PERSONS, INCLUDING DIPLOMATIC AGENTS, G.A. Res. 3166 (XXVIII) Dec. 14, 1973, U.N. GAOR, 28th Sess., Supp. No. 30, at 146, U.N. Doc. A/9030 (1974).

20. International Convention Against the Taking of Hostages, G.A. Res. 34/146, U.N. GAOR, 34th Sess., Supp. No. 46, at 245, U.N. Doc. A/34/46 (1980) [hereinafter Hostage Convention].

21. Convention Against Torture and other Cruel, Inhuman or Degrading Treatment

Each of such activities became the subject of international efforts at control, centered on one or more multilateral treaties which typically require parties to the treaty to criminalize the activity and make an effort to prosecute, or to extradite to someone else who will prosecute, those who engage in it. The current fuel to encouraging international cooperation is thus abhorrence of the egregious violator of basic rights, the terrorist, the drug cartel, and organized crime in general. These areas are not, however, in all respects different from traditional crime and there is, in fact, much cross-fertilization. More cooperation in dealing with traditional problems is worth some effort, too. In the long run, cooperation on traditional crime may be of more practical value than attempts to deal with obviously trendy topics.

At all events, the multilateral treaties commonly proceed with some fairly standard variations on the arsenal of international cooperation.[22] Some of them try to facilitate extradition by adding the offense in question to the list of extraditable offenses contained in existing bilateral treaties, or by providing that the multilateral treaty itself may be regarded as sufficient basis for extradition, even in the absence of another treaty. Making such an offense "extraditable" still left the political offender issue open. In some cases, such as the genocide[23] and apartheid[24] Conventions, the treaty simply denies that political offender status may ever attach to the person charged with a treaty offense. In other cases, such as the hijacking and offenses against aircraft conventions, a state may take the position that the accused is a political offender, but must nonetheless bring the case before its prosecutorial authorities with a view to bringing the accused to trial.[25] The regional European Convention for the Suppression of Terrorism[26] assimilates some of the broader multilateral terrorism treaties to the Genocide and Apartheid models as between the parties to the regional convention. It provides that, for the purposes of extradition between its contracting states, an offense within the scope of the Hague Convention for the Suppression of Unlawful Seizure of Aircraft[27] and the Montreal Convention for the Suppression of Unlawful Acts against the

---

or Punishment, G.A. Res. 39/46 of U.N. GAOR, 39th Sess., Supp. No. 51, at 197, U.N. Doc. A/39/51 (1985).

22. *See* R. S. Clark, *Offenses of International Concern: Multilateral State Treaty Practice in the Forty Years Since Nuremberg*, 57 Nordic J. Int'l L. 49 (1988) (expanding upon these notions).

23. Convention on Genocide, *supra* note 15, art. VII.

24. Convention on Apartheid, *supra* note 17, art. XI.

25. *See* Clark, *supra* note 22, at 66–67.

26. Convention for the Suppression of Terrorism, done at Strasbourg, Nov. 10, 1976, Europ. T.S. No. 90 [hereinafter Convention on Terrorism].

27. Convention on Aircraft, *supra* note 18.

Safety of Civil Aviation[28] shall not be regarded as a political offense or as an offense inspired by political motives.[29]

Such treaties respond to the absence of an international penal tribunal by treating nation states as the agents by necessity of the international system. They thus encourage the exercise of jurisdiction on theoretical bases which have always seemed esoteric to the common law mind, such as the nationality of the accused, the nationality of the victim (so-called "passive personality" jurisdiction), and universal jurisdiction.[30]

Rather plainly, though, the multilateral treaties have not addressed all of the relevant problems of international cooperation. What is more, the treaties rely for their efficacy on the network of bilateral relations already mentioned, since they in effect incorporate those relationships by reference. This has led to efforts both to modernize the bilaterals[31] (not only as to extradition but also as to areas of cooperation beyond that) and to encourage states that do not have a serious network of bilaterals to enter into negotiations with others. This is indeed the role of the models adopted in 1985 and 1990. It has been taken as a given that a massive global treaty tying together all the loose ends is simply not likely to occur. [32] Thus, painstaking work must be done by individual countries to put the pieces together mostly on a bilateral basis,[33] although some further regional developments might

28. Convention on Aviation, *supra* note 18.

29. Convention on Terrorism, *supra* note 26, art. 1 (which also denies political offense status to various acts constituting offenses against internationally protected persons, kidnapping and the taking of hostages and various acts involving a danger to the public).

30. Clark, *supra* note 22, at 85–86. *See* COUNCIL OF EUROPE, EUROPEAN COMMITTEE ON CRIME PROBLEMS, EXTRATERRITORIAL JURISDICTION (1990), *reprinted in* 3 CRIM. L.F. 441 (1992) (discussing theories of jurisdiction).

31. *See* E.A. Nadelmann, *The Role of the United States in the International Enforcement of Criminal Law*, 31 HARV. INT'L L.J. 37, 64 (1990) (detailing the strategy of United States modernization efforts). There is a wealth of suggestive material on international cooperation efforts from a United States viewpoint in Professor Nadelmann's important recent book, E.A. NADELMANN, COPS ACROSS BORDERS: THE INTERNATIONALIZATION OF U.S. CRIMINAL LAW ENFORCEMENT (1993).

32. At a fairly early stage of the negotiations that led to the restructuring of the U.N. program in 1991, Vasily Ignatov, expert from the then Soviet Union on the Committee on Crime Prevention and Control, drafted a "United Nations Convention on Crime Control" which was essentially an extradition/mutual assistance arrangement. (April 1991 draft on file with the author.) This idea was not proceeded with. The Soviet Union had a good deal of bilateral and regional experience in the cooperation area. *See* G. Ginsburgs, *The USSR and the Socialist Model of International Cooperation in Criminal Matters*, 17 REV. SOCIALIST L. 199 (1991); G. Ginsburgs, *The Soviet Union and International Cooperation in Penal Matters*, 41 INT'L & COMP. L.Q. 85 (1992). *See also* L. Hannikainen, *How to Interpret and What to Do to the Treaty on Aircraft Seizures with the Soviet Union*, 2 FINNISH Y.B. INT'L L. 538 (1991). *See also infra* notes 34, 40 (referring to Soviet practice).

33. *See* the trenchant comment by Nadelmann, "Multilateral arrangements suffer

be expected. Consequently, the U.N. models are all drafted primarily in language that assumes the treaty to be a bilateral one, but occasionally there are lapses where the language reads more like that of a multilateral arrangement. Little tidying up is required to utilize the models in either mode. Moreover, although there is some existing practice of a different nature,[34] each of the models deals with a single subject-matter (extradition, mutual legal assistance, etc.). The models can, of course, be arranged in various permutations and combinations by the ultimate consumers.

Foreign Offices and Justice Departments, especially those in developing countries and even small developed ones, simply do not have the resources to re-invent the wheel each time they enter into negotiations. Hence it was deemed helpful to have some widely-accepted models to which one could refer as a type of international formbook.

This enterprise represents something of a new departure for the United Nations. As we have seen in earlier chapters,[35] the organization has had a great deal of experience with the drafting of other kinds of "instruments." Included in these would be multilateral treaties such as the Covenants on Human Rights,[36] and resolutions of a softer legal nature which contribute to the development of international custom, such as the Universal Declaration of Human Rights[37] and the Standard

---

from their tendency to settle on the lowest common denominator of cooperation. Bilateral treaties, on the other hand, afford the opportunity to push the negotiating partner to include those provisions of greatest interest and advantage to the United States." Nadelmann, *supra* note 31, 31 HARV. INT'L L. J. at 65. It is, of course, not only the United States that may seek such advantages—mutual ones even! *See also* A. Eser, *Common Goals and Different Ways in International Criminal Law: Reflections from a European Perspective*, 31 HARV. INT'L L.J. 117 (1990) (discussing the practical and cultural problems encountered by negotiators in the area, especially those dealing across different legal systems); C. Blakesley & O. Lagodny, *Finding Harmony Amidst Disagreement over Extradition, the Role of Human Rights, and Issues of Extraterritoriality Under International Criminal Law*, 24 VAND. J. TRANSNAT'L L. 1 (1991) (discussing the challenge of reaching agreement between common law and civil law systems).

34. France, for example, has a number of comprehensive agreements with former French African colonies which deal in one instrument with extradition and mutual assistance in criminal and civil matters. The former socialist countries had a large number of treaties on "legal cooperation in civil, family and penal matters" which included extradition and other matters. *See* UNITED NATIONS DIVISION OF NARCOTIC DRUGS, EXTRADITION FOR DRUG-RELATED OFFENSES 15 (1985).

35. *See generally* Chapters 1 & 4 *supra*.

36. International Covenant on Economic, Social and Cultural Rights, G.A. Res. 2200 (XXI), U.N. GAOR, 21st Sess., Supp. No. 16, at 49, U.N. Doc. A/6316 (1967); International Covenant on Civil and Political Rights, *id.* at 52.

37. G.A. Res. 217A (III), U.N. GAOR, 3d Sess., pt.1, Resolutions 71, U.N. Doc. A/810 (1948).

Minimum Rules for the Treatment of Prisoners.[38] But these examples are instruments of a different juridical nature and represent a benchmark to follow while acknowledging that states will almost certainly introduce some variations as they tailor the contents to their own needs and legal structure.[39]

C. The Model Treaties

1. The Model Agreement on the Transfer of Foreign Prisoners

The first of the model treaties was the lone one adopted in 1985, the Model Agreement on the Transfer of Foreign Prisoners.[40] Its ration-

---

38. E.S.C. Res. 663 (XXIV) C, U.N. ESCOR, 24th Sess., Supp. No. 1, at 11, U.N. Doc. E/3048 (1957). *See* Chapter 6 *supra*.

39. *See also* L. Radzinowicz, *International Collaboration in Criminal Science*, *in* THE MODERN APPROACH TO CRIMINAL LAW 467, 478–79 n.2 (L. Radzinowicz & J.W.C. Turner eds. 1945) (detailing earlier efforts by the International Penal and Penitentiary Commission to develop a model extradition treaty); *Report of the Sixth Committee, United Nations Draft Rules for the Conciliation of Disputes between States*, U.N. Doc. A/45/742 (1990), *reprinted in* 30 I.L.M. 229 (1991) (describing an analogous effort at drafting a model bilateral agreement). The technique of devising model agreements to deal with developing areas of the law is not unknown in domestic legal practice. *See American Bar Association, Electronic Messaging Services Task Force, The Commercial Use of Electronic Data Interchange—A Report and Model Trading Partner Agreement*, 45 BUS. LAW. 1645 (1990) (for a recent example of this phenomenon). The United Nations Commission on International Trade Law is considering whether it might be possible to produce a model electronic data interchange agreement with global possibilities in the commercial community. *Report of the United Nations Commission on International Trade Law on the work of its twenty-third session, 25 June–6 July 1990*, U.N. GAOR, 45th Sess., Supp. No. 17, at 9, U.N. Doc. A/45/17 (1990). The work in the United States of the Uniform Law Commissioners is also analogous. *See generally* R.A. Leflar, *Minimizing State Conflicts of Law*, 4 DET. C.L. REV. 1325 (1983); HANDBOOK OF THE NATIONAL CONFERENCE OF COMMISSIONERS ON UNIFORM STATE LAWS (1979). This technique of drafting model laws has also appeared on the international scene. *See the UNCITRAL Model Law on International Commercial Arbitration, Report of the United Nations Commission on International Trade Law on the work of its eighteenth session*, Annex I, U.N. GAOR, 40th Sess., Supp. No. 17, U.N. Doc. A/40/17 (1985) (noted "with particular satisfaction" by the General Assembly in G.A. Res. 40/71, U.N. GAOR, 40th Sess., Supp. No. 53, at 307, U.N. Doc. A/40/53 (1986)); R. Lillich, *Model Law on the Oil Embargo Against South Africa*, U.N. CENTRE AGAINST APARTHEID, NOTES AND DOCUMENTS, No. 10/91 (1991); L.E. Teitz, *Taking Multiple Bites of the Apple: A Proposal to Resolve Conflicts of Jurisdiction and Multiple Proceedings*, 26 INT'L LAWYER 21 (1992). *See also infra* note 163.

40. Model Prisoner Transfer Agreement, *supra* note 1. The written legislative history of this and the other model treaties is rather thin. *See* Chapter 3 *supra*, at note 7 (the criminal justice part of the United Nations does not make either verbatim or summary records of its sessions). At best there are rapporteurial or secretariat accounts of the

ales are succinctly stated in two preambular paragraphs of the adopting resolution which has the congress "[r]ecognizing the difficulties of foreigners detained in prison establishments abroad owing to such factors as differences in language, culture, customs and religion," and "[c]onsidering that the aim of social resettlement of offenders could best be achieved by giving foreign prisoners the opportunity to serve their sentence within their country of nationality or residence."[41]

---

debates together with what can be gleaned by considering successive drafts and explanatory notes thereon. There is some useful material in the *Note by the Secretariat prepared for the Seventh Congress* under the title *Model agreement on the transfer of foreign prisoners and recommendations for the treatment of foreign prisoners*. U.N. Doc. A/CONF.121/10 (1985). Prisoner transfers have been developed most in European, North American and Soviet bloc practice. The first example was apparently Scandinavian uniform legislation in 1963. *See* H. Epp, *The European Convention*, in 2 INTERNATIONAL CRIMINAL LAW 253, 254 (M.C. Bassiouni ed. 1986). Then came the European Convention on the International Validity of Criminal Judgments, May 28, 1970, Europ. T. S. No. 70 (the Convention was broad enough in scope to encompass prisoner transfers but was complicated procedurally and not widely ratified). European practice (in which the U.S., Canada, and more recently the Bahamas, have also participated) was solidified in the Convention on the Transfer of Sentenced Persons, Mar. 21, 1983, Europ. T.S. No. 112. *See generally, Council of Europe, Information memorandum prepared by the Directorate of Legal Affairs, Convention on the Transfer of Sentenced Persons*, Doc. PC-OC (92) 5 (1992); B.A. RISTAU & M. ABBELL, INTERNATIONAL JUDICIAL ASSISTANCE, Chapter XIV (describing United States practice). The first U.S. treaties were those with Mexico and Canada in 1976 and 1977 respectively. *See* Note, *Criminal Law: Exchange of Prisoners*, 18 HARV. INT'L L.J. 703 (1977); A. Abramovsky & S.J. Eagle, *A Critical Evaluation of the Mexican-American Transfer of Penal Sanctions Treaty*, 64 IOWA L. REV. 275 (1979) (debating the advisability and constitutionality of the exercise in the American context); D. Vagts, *A Reply to "A Critical Evaluation of the Mexican-American Transfer of Penal Sanctions Treaty"*, *id.* at 325; I.P. Stotzky & A.C. Swan, *Due Process Methodology and Prisoner Exchange Treaties: Confronting an Uncertain Calculus*, 62 MINN. L. REV. 733 (1978). The Soviet bloc practice (instituted multilaterally by treaty in 1978) is discussed in Ginsburgs, *supra* note 32, 41 INT'L & COMP. L.Q. 85, G.E. Glos, *Convention on the Transfer of Prisoners Among the Communist Countries*, 9 INT'L J.L. LIB. 262 (1978) (which also reproduces the text of the agreement), and in P. Mackowiak, *Formulation and application of United Nations standards and norms in criminal justice*, in HELSINKI INSTITUTE FOR CRIME PREVENTION AND CONTROL AFFILIATED WITH THE UNITED NATIONS, COURSE ON UNITED NATIONS CRIMINAL JUSTICE POLICY 183, 192–93 (1985) (noting that by 1985 some 30 Polish prisoners had been transferred back to Poland). There is a British Commonwealth Scheme of 1986 which has not yet become effective. *See* K. Best, *The Problems of Prisoner Transfer*, 18 COMMONWEALTH L. BULL. 333 (1992) (detailing the Commonwealth Scheme and British experience).

41. Model Prisoner Transfer Agreement, *supra* note 1, paras. 2, 3 (preamble). This is the idealistic rationale for such treaties—and sometimes the real explanation. The following, written concerning the first two transfer treaties negotiated by the United States, argues that:

> The Canadian treaty appears genuinely intended to aid prisoner rehabilitation, parolee supervision, and law enforcement cooperation between the two countries.

The Model Prisoner Transfer Agreement itself begins with a set of general principles. The desirability of fostering "social resettlement" is again stressed.[42] A transfer should be effected on the basis of mutual respect for national sovereignty and jurisdiction.[43] There must be double criminality: a transfer should be effected in cases where the offense giving rise to conviction is punishable by deprivation of liberty by the judicial authority of both the "sending" (or "sentencing") state and the state to which the transfer is to be effected (the "administering state") according to their national laws.[44] A transfer may be requested either by the sentencing or the administering state. The prisoner, as well as close relatives, may express to either state an interest in the transfer. To that end, the states in question must inform the prisoner of their competent authorities.[45] A transfer shall be dependent on the agreement of both the sentencing and the administering state, and shall also be based on the consent of the prisoner.[46] The prisoner must be fully informed of the possibility and of the legal consequences of the

---

The Mexican treaty, however, is principally a response to both popular and congressional concern with allegations that Americans in Mexican jails were subject to intolerable living conditions, acts of brutality, and extortion by prison officials and fellow prisoners.

Stotzky & Swan, *supra* note 40, at 736. Another writer, Epp, adds a bureaucratic consideration: "Moreover, the prison authorities were confronted with increasing difficulties caused by foreign prisoners, in particular in countries where the proportion of foreigners within the prison population was high (twenty percent in Sweden and Belgium, twenty-five percent in Switzerland, and fourteen percent in the Netherlands)." Epp, *supra* note 40, at 253.

42. Model Prisoner Transfer Agreement, *supra* note 1, para. 1.

43. *Id.* para. 2.

44. *Id.* para. 3.

45. *Id.* para. 4.

46. *Id.* para. 5. As the Secretary-General explained it:

The requirement that prisoners must consent to the transfer ensures that transfers are not used as a method of expelling prisoners, or as a means of disguised extradition. Moreover, since prison conditions vary considerably from country to country, and the prisoner may have very personal reasons for not wishing to be transferred, it seems preferable to base the proposed model agreement on the consent requirement.

Secretary-General's Note, *supra* note 40, paras. 4–5. Practice under existing treaties is mixed. *See* Epp, *supra* note 40, at 264 (1983 European Convention requires consent but 1970 European Convention and 1978 Soviet bloc convention do not). The U.S. treaties require consent. Issue has been joined on whether "consent" in the face of intolerable prison conditions is "freely" given or refused. *See* Abramovsky & Eagle, *supra* note 40; Vagts, *supra* note 40; Stotzky & Swan, *supra* note 40; A. Abramovsky, *A Critical Evaluation of the American Transfer of Penal Sanctions Policy*, 1980 WISC. L. REV. 25.

transfer, in particular whether or not he or she might be prosecuted for other offenses committed before the transfer.[47] Moreover, the administering state should be given the opportunity to verify the free consent of the prisoner.[48] In cases where the prisoner is incapable of making a free determination, that person's legal representative is competent to consent to the transfer.[49]

As a general rule, at the time of the request for a transfer, the prisoner must be required to serve at least six months of the sentence. However, a transfer should also be granted in cases of indeterminate sentences.[50]

One provision is in the pious hope category: the decision whether to transfer a prisoner shall be taken without delay.[51]

The Model Prisoner Transfer Agreement also contains a double jeopardy provision. A person transferred may not be tried again in the administering state for the same act on which the sentence to be executed is based.[52]

Following these provisions are a number of what the model describes as "procedural regulations." A rather basic proposition requires that a transfer shall in no case aggravate the situation of the prisoner.[53] The extent to which the prisoner may be better off (aside from the benefit of returning to his or her own country) is complex. When the transfer occurs, the authorities of the administering state must (a) continue the enforcement of the sentence immediately or through a court or administrative order; or (b) convert the sentence, thereby substituting for the sanction imposed in the sentencing state a sanction prescribed by the law of the administering state for a corresponding offense.[54] In the case of continuing enforcement, the administering state is bound by the legal nature and duration of the sentence as determined by the sentencing state. If, however, this sentence is by its nature or duration incompatible with the law of the administering state, the state may adapt the sanction to the punishment or measure prescribed by its own

47. Model Prisoner Transfer Agreement, *supra* note 1, para. 6.

48. *Id.* para. 7.

49. *Id.* para. 9.

50. *Id.* para. 11.

51. *Id.* para. 12.

52. *Id.* para. 13. Principles of double jeopardy are quite undeveloped at the international level. This and other models represent tentative efforts to move in the direction of exploring the matter further. *See infra* notes 78, 129. *See also* D. Thiam, Special Rapporteur, International Law Commission, *Fifth Report on the Draft Code of Offenses Against the Peace and Security of Mankind*, at 5–6, 12, U.N. Doc. A/CN.4/404 (1987) (detailing some tentative efforts to raise the issue).

53. Model Prisoner Transfer Agreement, *supra* note 1, para. 19.

54. *Id.* para. 14.

law for a corresponding offense.[55] In the case of conversion of sentence, the administering state shall be entitled to adapt the sanction as to its nature or duration according to its national law, taking into due consideration the sentence passed in the sentencing state. A sanction involving the deprivation of liberty shall, however, not be converted to a pecuniary sanction.[56] The administering state is bound by the findings as to the facts in so far as they appear from the judgement imposed in the sentencing state. Thus, the sentencing state has the sole competence for a review of the sentence.[57] The period of deprivation of liberty already served by the sentenced person in either state shall be fully deducted from the final sentence.[58] A final "procedural regulation" deals with costs. Any costs incurred because of a transfer and related to transportation shall be borne by the administering state, unless otherwise decided by both the sentencing and administering states.[59]

Two brief paragraphs deal with what is described as "enforcement and pardon." One asserts that the enforcement of the sentence shall be governed by the law of the administering state.[60] The other confirms that both the sentencing and the administering state shall be competent to grant pardon and amnesty.[61]

As adopted by the Seventh Congress, the Model Prisoner Transfer Agreement was accompanied by a set of nine recommendations of an essentially human rights and humanitarian nature on the treatment of foreign prisoners.[62] These recommendations insist that foreign prisoners must be treated in a non-discriminatory fashion. They must also be informed without delay of their right to request contact with their consular authorities, as well as of any other relevant information regarding their status. Contact of foreign prisoners with families and community agencies should be facilitated, by providing the necessary opportunities for visits and correspondence, with the consent of the prisoner. Humanitarian international organizations, such as the Inter-

---

55. *Id.* para. 15.

56. *Id.* para. 16.

57. *Id.* para. 17. Few states are likely to agree to treaties that permit the administering state's courts to review the original decision on the merits. *See generally* Vagts, *supra* note 40; Rosado v. Civiletti, 621 F. 2d 1179 (2d Cir. 1980), *cert. denied.*, 449 U.S. 856 (1980) (considering Mexico-U.S. treaty).

58. *Id.* para. 18.

59. *Id.* para. 20. Presumably other costs—notably the cost of imprisonment in the administering state—lie where they fall.

60. *Id.* para. 21.

61. *Id.* para. 22. This could enable the executive in the administering State to rectify some miscarriages of justice where the courts would be powerless. *See supra* at note 57.

62. *Report of the Seventh United Nations Congress, supra* note 1, Annex II, at 57.

national Committee of the Red Cross, should be given the opportunity to assist foreign prisoners. The recommendations were formulated taking into account that among the foremost measures for alleviating the problems of foreign prisoners, including those whose transfer cannot be effected, is the provision of information and contacts, including information in their own languages.[63]

2. The Model Treaty on Extradition

The Model Treaty on Extradition[64] follows a fairly standard modern format, based to a substantial degree on recent Australian extradition treaties.[65] The parties would agree to extradite to each other, upon request and subject to the terms of the treaty, a person who is wanted in the requesting state for prosecution for an extraditable offense or for the imposition or enforcement of a sentence in respect of such an offense.[66] Extraditable offenses are defined, as is now usual, not by a list of specific offenses, but by severity of penalty:

[E]xtraditable offenses are offenses that are punishable under the laws of both Parties by imprisonment or other deprivation of liberty for a maximum period of at least [one/two] year(s), or by a more severe penalty. Where the request for extradition relates to a person who is wanted for the enforcement of a sentence of imprisonment or other deprivation of liberty imposed for such an offense, extradition shall be granted only if a period of at least [four/six] months of such sentence remains to be served.[67]

(The bracketed numbers reflect some disagreement about the appropriate parameters.)

The Model Extradition Treaty contains both mandatory and op-

---

63. *Note by the Secretariat, supra* note 40, at 8.

64. Model Extradition Treaty, *supra* note 2.

65. Australia has in recent years been unusually aggressive in tidying up its inventory of extradition treaties. It has brought new treaties or other arrangements into force with Argentina, Austria, Belgium, Denmark (arrangement), Ecuador, Germany, Fiji (arrangement), Finland, France, Greece, Iceland (arrangement), Ireland, Italy, Japan (arrangement), Luxembourg, Mexico, Monaco, Netherlands, Norway, Philippines, Portugal, South Africa (arrangement), South Korea and Spain. As of May 27, 1992, further treaties were awaiting ratification with Indonesia, Uruguay, U.S.A., and Venezuela. Further negotiations are nearing completion. Letter from Herman F. Woltring, Attorney-General's Department, Canberra, A.C.T., Australia, to Roger Clark (July 20, 1992). *See* H. Woltring, *Extradition Law*, 61 VICTORIAN L. INST. J. 919 (1987).

66. Model Extradition Treaty, *supra* note 2, art. 1.

67. *Id.* art. 2, para. 1. *See Contemporary Practice of the United States Relating to International Law, Modernization of Extradition Treaties*, 86 AM. J. INT'L L. 547 (1992) (testimony by Alan J. Kreczko, Deputy Legal Adviser, Department of State) (describing recent U.S. practice along these lines).

tional grounds for refusing extradition. Extradition *will* be refused if the offense for which extradition is requested is regarded by the requested state as an offense of a political nature.[68] A bracketed variation on this is, included, however. It provides that:

Reference to an offence of a political nature shall not include any offence in respect of which the Parties have assumed an obligation, pursuant to any multilateral convention, to take prosecutorial action where they do not extradite, nor any other offence agreed by the Parties not to be an offence of a political character for the purposes of extradition.[69]

The effect of the first part of this variant is functionally the same as the approach taken in the European Convention on the Suppression of Terrorism.[70] The parties would in effect agree that the *extradite-or-prosecute* obligation in treaties such as the Convention Against the Taking of Hostages[71] or the aircraft conventions[72] would be treated, between themselves, as an absolute obligation to *extradite*. The latter part of the bracketed material is probably redundant. In effect, it confirms the existing obligation of parties to the Genocide and Apartheid Conventions[73] not to treat the offenses contained therein as political.[74] Extradition will also be refused if the requested state has substantial grounds for believing that the request for extradition has been made for the purpose of prosecuting or punishing a person on account of that person's race, religion, nationality, ethnic origin, political opinions, sex, or status, or that the person's position may be prejudiced for any of those reasons.[75] Similarly, it will be refused if the person whose extradition is requested has been or could be subjected in the requesting state to torture, or cruel, inhuman, or degrading treatment or punishment or if that person has not received or would not receive the

68. *Id.* art. 3(a).

69. *Id.*

70. Convention on Terrorism, *supra* note 26.

71. Hostage Convention, *supra* note 20.

72. Aircraft and Aviation Conventions, *supra* note 18.

73. Genocide Convention, *supra* note 15; Apartheid Convention, *supra* note 17.

74. Modern practice in the international crime area seeks, as noted above, to deal with the "safe haven" problem in two over-lapping ways. Sometimes it encourages prosecution through extradition by denying political offender status to those engaging in activities such as some varieties of terrorism; sometimes it permits a denial of extradition on a ground such as political offender status, but nonetheless compels prosecution in the state denying extradition. The nod in the model treaty goes towards extradition rather than prosecution.

75. Model Extradition Treaty, *supra* note 2, art. 3(b). Language along these lines first appeared in the 1976 European Convention for the Suppression of Terrorism. *Supra* note 26. There is perhaps something of a trend in multilateral practice for such a provision to replace the political offender exception as the latter is whittled away.

minimum guarantees in criminal proceedings, as contained in the International Covenant on Civil and Political Rights.[76] It will be refused if the offense for which extradition is requested is an offense under military law, which is not also an offense under ordinary criminal law.[77] It will also be refused if there has been a final judgment rendered against the person in the requested state in respect of the offense for which extradition is requested[78] or the person whose extradition is sought has, under the law of either party, become immune from prosecution or punishment for any reason, including lapse of time or amnesty.[79] Finally it will be refused if the judgment of the requesting state has been rendered *in absentia*, if the convicted person has not had sufficient notice of the trial nor the opportunity to arrange his or her defense, and has not had or will not have the opportunity to have the case retried in his or her presence.[80]

A footnote on grounds for refusal adds almost casually what is probably the nub of the matter for some: "Some countries may wish to add . . . the following ground for refusal: 'If there is insufficient proof, according to the evidentiary standards of the Requested State, that the person whose extradition is requested is a party to the offence.'"[81] Common law countries have generally insisted in the past on some sort of prima facie case requirement, but there is something of a trend away from it in the more recent treaties.[82] There are two significant issues raised here: whether there should be any proof threshold at all and whether the requested state should defer to the evidentiary rules of the requesting state.[83] Both are controversial and raise awkward questions

76. Model Extradition Treaty, *supra* note 2, art. 3(f).

77. *Id.* art. 3(c).

78. *Id.* art. 3(d). "Final judgment" appears broad enough to include both conviction and acquittal. The principle of *ne bis in idem*, or the rule against double jeopardy, is not clearly established under international customary law, so it is important to spell it out by treaty. *See* EXTRADITION FOR DRUG-RELATED OFFENSES, *supra* note 34, at 53–55, C.L. BLAKESLEY, TERRORISM, DRUGS, INTERNATIONAL LAW AND THE PROTECTION OF HUMAN LIBERTY 262 (1992). *See also supra* note 52, and *infra* at note 129.

79. *Id.* art. 3(e).

80. *Id.* art. 3(g).

81. *Id.* at 213 n.98. Significantly, the Commonwealth debated deleting the prima facie case requirement from the Commonwealth Scheme. *See, e.g., Commonwealth Secretariat, Meeting of Commonwealth Law Ministers, Zimbabwe, 26 July—1 August 1986, Memorandum by the Commonwealth Secretariat and the Government of Australia,* Secretariat Doc. LMM (86) 5. *See also* Woltring, *supra* note 65, at 920; D.M. Kennedy, et al., *The Extradition of Mohammed Hamadei,* 31 HARV. INT'L L.J. 5, 17–18 (1990); W.C. Gilmore, *International Action Against Drug Trafficking: Trends in United Kingdom Law and Practice,* 24 INT'L LAWYER 365, 371–72 (1990).

82. *See supra* note 81.

83. *See* EXTRADITION FOR DRUG-RELATED OFFENSES, *supra* note 34, at 41–43, 56.

not only of a human rights nature but also about the extent to which one legal system should trust the quality of decision-making in the legal system of a treaty partner. One writer suggests that the argument for the requirement of a prima facie case "is based on the belief that it is unfair, under any system, to imprison the person sought in extradition and to send him to a distant place without providing some evidence of the validity of the charge against him."[84] This weighs rather heavily against the argument based on administrative simplicity on the other side.

Extradition *may* be refused if the person whose extradition is requested is a national of the requested state.[85] In the past it has been the case that, where extradition is refused on the basis of the accused's nationality, a prosecution may proceed in the country of nationality, pursuant to domestic legislation, but it was uncommon until the past few decades for treaties to make this obligatory. The present model, however, does just that. It provides that where extradition is refused on the ground of nationality, the requested state shall, if the requesting state so requests, submit the case to its competent authorities with a view to taking appropriate action against the person.[86]

84. Blakesley, *supra* note 78, at 219.
85. Model Extradition Treaty, *supra* note 2, art. 4(a). A recent commentator notes:

Most civil law countries, as well as some common law countries, regard the nonextradition of their citizens as an important principle deeply ingrained in their legal traditions. They justify the principle on various grounds, including the state's obligation to protect its citizens, lack of confidence in the fairness of foreign judicial proceedings, the many disadvantages a defendant confronts in trying to defend himself in a foreign state before a strange legal system, as well as the additional disadvantages posed by imprisonment in a foreign jail where family and friends may be distant and the chances of rehabilitation are significantly diminished.

Nadelmann, *supra* note 31, at 67.
86. Model Extradition Treaty, *supra* note 2, art. 4(a). Functionally, this provision in the model extradition treaty would work the same way as a request for the transfer of proceedings to the state of nationality. *See* Model Treaty on Transfer of Proceedings, *infra* note 120. There is no magic to a provision requiring this type of vicarious administration of justice in the face of lethargy by the other treaty party. Note, for example, the discussion by Nadelmann, of the relatively unsuccessful efforts by United States authorities to galvanize Mexican prosecutors into action (art. 9 of the Mexico-U.S. treaty has a mild prosecution requirement). Nadelmann, *supra* note 31, at 70. Where a national is not extradited "the requested Party shall submit the case to its competent authorities for the purpose of prosecution, provided that Party has jurisdiction over the offense." *See* EXTRADITION LAWS AND TREATIES, UNITED STATES, No. 590.19 (I. Kavass & A. Sprudzs comp. 1979). In a recent cause célèbre, U.S. v. Alvárez-Machain, 112 S. Ct. 2188 (1992), the defendant, a Mexican citizen, was accused of involvement in the torture/murder of a U.S. federal agent in Mexico. The U.S. did not even bother to ask formally for extradition, and instead arranged a kidnapping. The U.S. Supreme Court upheld U.S. jurisdic-

Extradition may be refused in a number of cases other than nationality, including those close cousins of *ne bis in idem* cases where the competent authorities of the requested state have decided not to institute or to terminate proceedings against the person for the offense in respect of which extradition is requested,[87] and where a prosecution in respect of the offense for which extradition is requested is pending in the requested state.[88] Again, it may be refused if the offense carries the death penalty under the law of the requesting state, unless that state gives such assurance as the requested state considers sufficient that the death penalty will not be imposed, or, if imposed, will not be carried out.[89]

The model contains standard machinery provisions[90] and re-asserts the "rule of specialty." Under this rule, a person surrendered under the treaty shall not be proceeded against, sentenced, detained, re-extradited to a third state, or subjected to any other restriction of liberty in the territory of the requesting state for any offense committed before surrender, other than an offense for which extradition was granted, or any other offense as to which the requested state consents.[91]

Finally, the model reiterates the current "non-solution" to the problem of how to deal with concurrent requests from different countries for the same person. It accomplishes this by providing that where there are concurrent requests, a party "shall, at its discretion, determine to which of those states the person is to be extradited."[92] The problem is potentially acute in the terrorism area where multiple bases for juris-

---

tion notwithstanding Mexico's protests and a further strong amicus curiae brief filed by Canada. Mexico's view that this constitutes a denial of the effect of article 9 of the treaty was forcefully expressed in Brief for the United Mexican States as Amicus Curiae in Support of Affirmance, at 13–17, United States v. Alvárez-Machain (1991) (No. 91-712). The earliest example I have found in *multilateral* state practice of a provision requiring the state of nationality to prosecute a non-extraditable citizen for offenses committed abroad is article 9 of the 1949 Convention for the Suppression of the Traffic in Persons and of the Prostitution of Others, G.A. Res. 317 (IV), U.N. GAOR, 4th Sess., Resolutions, at 33, U.N. Doc. A/1251 (1950).

87. *Id.* art. 4(b).

88. *Id.* art. 4(c).

89. *Id.* art. 4(d). A footnote adds that some countries may wish to apply the same restriction to the imposition of a life, or indeterminate sentence—an interesting commentary on evolving contemporary attitudes towards modes of punishment.

90. Notably, article 5 on channels of communication and required documents, article 7 on certification and authentication, article 9 on provisional arrest, article 11 on surrender of the person, and article 13 on surrender of property found in the requested state that has been acquired as a result of the offence or that may be required as evidence, is contained in the standard machinery provisions.

91. *Id.* art. 14.

92. *Id.* art. 16.

diction may be asserted in respect of the same incident but no clear priority is assigned. It may also arise in situations where the accused is wanted in more than one place for different offenses. General international law provides no guidance about priorities in such cases, merely forcing states to negotiate in each instance. The draft recognizes this approach with an acknowledgement that the state having possession of the accused is in the ultimate position of calling the shots if no agreement can be reached. The state can, however, be encouraged to take certain factors into account in good faith in making a decision.

Some attention was given to this problem at the Eighth United Nations Congress in the context of the struggle against terrorism, although the only recommendation that emerged was that "Jurisdictional priorities should be established giving territoriality the first priority."[93] The Commonwealth Scheme[94] provides help in some cases (it seems more help in cases of requests for different offenses arising out of distinct events rather than requests in respect of the same incident). Under the Commonwealth Scheme, the requested state must consider all the circumstances, including (a) the relative seriousness of the offenses, (b) the relative dates on which the requests were made, and (c) the citizenship or other national status of the fugitive and his ordinary residence. The recent Australian treaties echo this language.[95]

Simply granting priority to the territorial state does not catch the full range of considerations in respect of multiple extradition requests relating to the same incident, either in respect of international crimes or in respect of ordinary crimes. As a commentary on the transfer of criminal proceedings noted:

The assumption that it is normally most appropriate to prosecute an offence where it has been committed is not justified. Rehabilitation of the offender which is increasingly given weight in modern penal law requires that the sanction be imposed and enforced where the reformative aim can be most successfully pursued, that is normally in the State where the offender has family or social ties or will take up residence after the enforcement of the sanction. On the other hand, it is clear that difficulties in securing evidence will

---

93. Other Resolution 25, on *Terrorist criminal activities, Report of the Eighth United Nations Congress, supra* note 6, at 181, para. 7. The Model Extradition Treaty itself has a nod in the direction of territoriality in another situation: where there is a dispute between the requesting and the requested state over who should exercise its jurisdiction. Article 4 (f) gives as an optional ground of refusal that the offense "is regarded under the law of the requested State as having been committed in whole or in part within that State."

94. *See supra* note 7, para. 13.

95. *See, e.g.*, Austl. Stat. R. 1988, No. 293 (noting the provisions of Article 9 of the treaty with the Netherlands).

often be a consideration militating against the transmission of proceedings from the State where the offence has been committed to another State.[96]

Meanwhile, some evolving state treaty practice exists which adapters of the U.N. model may wish to examine. For example, it has been suggested that "The influence of the primary effects approach or most substantial connection test is seen in some of Canada's more recent treaties."[97]

3. The Model Treaty on Mutual Assistance in Criminal Matters

The Model Treaty on Mutual Assistance in Criminal Matters[98] has benefited, like the model extradition treaty, from a great amount of work done on it by the Australian Government which has been actively engaged in negotiating such treaties.[99] This Model Treaty also has

96. European Committee on Crime Problems, Council of Europe, Explanatory Report on the European Convention on the Transfer of Proceedings in Criminal Matters 15 (1970). Terrorism offenses may be different from other crimes because rehabilitation considerations may not weigh heavily with ideological offenders.

97. See S.A. Williams, *Human Rights Safeguards and International Cooperation in Extradition: Striking the Balance*, 3 Crim. L. F. 191, 207 (1992) (referring to treaties with India and the United States). "[T]he treaty with India provides that although a request may be refused by the requested state if the fugitive may be tried for the same offense in its own courts, in deciding whether or not to refuse the requested state shall consider whether the requesting state has felt or will feel more gravely or imminently the effects or consequences of the offense." *Id.* The treaty with the U.S. provides that the requested state is to consider all relevant factors, including but not limited to: the place where the act was committed or was intended to be committed or where the injury occurred or was intended to occur; the respective interests of the contracting parties; the nationality of the victim; and the availability and location of the evidence. *Id.*

98. Model Mutual Assistance Treaty, *supra* note 3.

99. By May 27, 1992 Australia had recent Mutual Assistance treaties in force with Austria, Canada, Hong Kong (limited to drug trafficking offenses), Japan, the Netherlands, Spain, Switzerland, and the U.K. (limited to drug trafficking offenses only). Treaties were awaiting ratification with Argentina, Finland, Italy, Luxembourg, Mexico, Philippines, Portugal and Switzerland. Other negotiations were at an advanced stage. Letter from Herman Woltring, *supra* note 65. *See* D. Stafford, *Mutual Legal Assistance in Criminal Matters: The Australian Experience*, in Commonwealth Secretariat, Action Against Transnational Criminality, *supra* note 7, at 26; A. Ellis & R.L. Pisani, *The United States Treaties on Mutual Assistance in Criminal Matters*, in 2 International Criminal Law (Procedure) 151 (M.C. Bassiouni ed., 1986) (detailing recent United States practice); B.A. Ristau & M. Abbell, International Judicial Assistance, Criminal, ch. XII; E.A. Nadelmann, *The Role of the United States in the International Enforcement of Criminal Law*, 31 Harv. Int'l L.J. 37, 58–64 (1990); G.R. Watson, *Offenders Abroad: The Case for Nationality-Based Criminal Jurisdiction*, 17 Yale J.Int'l L. 41 (1992); *Contemporary Practice of the United States Relating to International Law, Mutual Legal Assistance Treaties*, 86 Am. J. Int'l L. 549 (1992) (testimony of Alan J. Kreczko, Deputy Legal Adviser of the

some similarities to the Scheme Relating to Mutual Assistance in Criminal Matters within the Commonwealth, adopted in 1986.[100] The basic obligation of the model treaty is that the parties shall afford each other the widest possible measure of mutual assistance in investigations or court proceedings in respect of offenses the punishment of which, at the time of the request for assistance, falls within the jurisdiction of the judicial authorities of the requesting state.[101]

The types of assistance may include:

(a) Taking of evidence or statements from persons;
(b) Assisting in making available of detained persons or others to give evidence or assist in investigations;
(c) Effecting service of judicial documents;
(d) Executing searches and seizures;
(e) Examining objects and sites;
(f) Providing information and evidentiary items; and
(g) Providing originals or certified copies of relevant documents and records, including bank, financial, corporate or business records.[102]

Mutual assistance is a somewhat limited concept of great practical importance. The draft underscores the limitations by indicating areas to which "assistance" does not extend, although such areas *may* be covered by other treaty obligations. Notably, the treaty is not a mode of extradition. The treaty does not require the enforcement in the requested state of criminal judgments imposed in the requesting state[103] and it does not address the transfer of persons in custody to serve sentences; nor does it deal with the transfer of proceedings in criminal matters.[104] A mutual assistance treaty, in short, is useful in conjunction with other treaty relationships that deal with associated aspects of the general problem of cooperation.

Department of State)[hereinafter Kreczko testimony]; NADELMANN SUPRA note 31, Chapter 6 (U.S. practice). *See also* L. Gardocki, *The Socialist System, in* 2 INTERNATIONAL CRIMINAL LAW SUPRA at 133 (describing the socialist countries' experience in the area, often as part of a larger package of conventions "on legal co-operation in civil, family and criminal matters").

100. Commonwealth Secretariat, *supra* note 7, at 11. *See* D. McClean, *Mutual Assistance in Criminal Matters: The Commonwealth Initiative*, 37 INT'L & COMP. L.Q. 177 (1988).

101. Model Mutual Assistance Treaty, *supra* note 3, art. 1, para. 1.

102. *Id.* art 1, para. 2.

103. Except as permitted by the law of the requested state and the Optional Protocol to the draft. *See infra* note 110.

104. Model Mutual Assistance Treaty, *supra* note 3, art. 1, para. 3.

States are required to designate competent authorities to process requests[105] and the form for requests and modes of dealing with them are set out.[106]

Assistance may be refused where the requested state "is of the opinion that the request, if granted, would prejudice its sovereignty, security, public order (*ordre public*) or other essential public interests."[107] Assistance may also be refused on political offender and human rights grounds which largely track the grounds for refusal under the model extradition treaty.[108]

In one striking way, the model treaty differs from the Commonwealth Scheme.[109] The latter includes in its standard list of modes of assistance "tracing, and forfeiting the proceeds of criminal activities," but nothing to this effect appears in the United Nations model treaty itself. The matter is, however, singled out for an "Optional Protocol to the Model Treaty on Mutual Assistance in Criminal Matters Concerning the Proceeds of Crime."[110] Parties to the Optional Protocol would agree that a requested state will endeavor to trace assets, investigate financial dealings, and obtain other information or evidence that may help secure the recovery of proceeds of crime.[111] The requested state must, to the extent permitted by its law, give effect to or permit enforcement of a final order forfeiting or confiscating the proceeds of crime made by a court of the requesting state or take other appropriate action to secure the proceeds following a request.[112]

105. *Id.* art. 3. The designation of competent authorities will typically permit Ministry of Justice to Ministry of Justice communication. Common law countries communicating in the past with civil law countries have faced the problem that the civil law countries, given their different court and prosecutorial structure, have been comfortable only when dealing with judicial requests. As one commentator notes, "While this practice may be consistent with the investigative role of judges in these countries, it has seriously hampered the ability of the United States [and other common law countries] to obtain necessary assistance, since parallel responsibility in the United States is assigned to prosecutors rather than judges." Kreczko testimony, *supra* note 99.

106. *Id.* art. 5.

107. *Id.* art. 4, para. 1(a).

108. *Id.* art. 4, para. 1(b), (c). *See* Model Extradition Treaty, *supra* note 2.

109. Commonwealth Scheme Relating to Mutual Assistance, *supra* note 100.

110. Model Mutual Assistance Treaty, *supra* note 3, at 218 [hereinafter Optional Protocol]. "Proceeds of crime" is defined broadly as "any property suspected, or found by a court, to be property directly or indirectly derived or realized as a result of the commission of an offence or to represent the value of property and other benefits derived from the commission of an offence." Optional Protocol, art. 1. *See also Report of the Ad Hoc Expert Group Meeting on Strategies to Deal with Transnational Crime, Smolenice, 27–31 May 1991*, at 16, U.N. Doc. E/CN.15/1992/4/Add.1 (1992) (model decree for the confiscation of criminal proceeds).

111. Optional Protocol, *supra* note 110, para. 3.

112. *Id.* para. 5.

An explanatory note to the Optional Protocol suggests that it is included "on the ground that questions of forfeiture are conceptually different from, although closely related to, matters generally accepted as falling within the description of mutual assistance."[113] It continues that states may wish to include such provisions because of their significance in dealing with organized crime. Forfeiture seems to be in vogue both in domestic law[114] and in current bilateral[115] assistance practice, so it is not surprising that some effort is made to deal with it here.

4. The Model Treaty on the Transfer of Proceedings in Criminal Matters

The Model Treaty on the Transfer of Proceedings in Criminal Matters[116] proceeds on the basis that when a person is suspected of having

113. Optional Protocol, *supra* note 110, at 218 n.125.

114. *See, e.g.,* B. Fisse, *Confiscation of Proceeds of Crime: Funny Money, Serious Legislation,* 13 CRIM. L.J. 368 (1989); Gilmore, *supra* note 81, at 389–90; D. McClean, *Seizing the Proceeds of Crime: The State of the Art,* 38 INT'L & COMP. L.Q. 334 (1989). Closely related is the control of money laundering. *See, e.g.,* INTERNATIONAL EFFORTS TO COMBAT MONEY LAUNDERING, (W.C. Gilmore, ed. 1992); *Note by the Secretary-General, Money Laundering and associated issues: the need for international cooperation,* U.N. Doc. E/CN.15/1992/4/Add.5 (1992); M. BEARE & S. SCHNEIDER, TRACING OF ILLICIT FUNDS: MONEY LAUNDERING IN CANADA (Ministry of the Solicitor-General of Canada, Working Paper No. 1990–06, 1990); THE MONEY TRAIL: CONFISCATION OF PROCEEDS OF CRIME, MONEY LAUNDERING AND CASH TRANSACTION REPORTING (B. Fisse, D. Fraser & G. Coss eds. 1992). The United Nations has not produced a model on this. *But see,* H.G. Nilsson, *The Council of Europe Laundering Convention: A Recent Example of a Developing International Criminal Law,* 2 CRIM. L.F. 419 (1991).

115. Examples of forfeiture may be observed in some of the recent Australian treaties. *See, e.g.,* Treaty Between Australia and the Republic of the Philippines on Mutual Assistance in Criminal Matters, Apr. 28, 1988, art. 1, para. 3(e), art. 18 (on file with the author); Treaty between Australia and the Kingdom of the Netherlands on Mutual Assistance in Criminal Matters, Oct. 28, 1988, art. 1, para. 2(h), art. 18 (on file with the author). It also appears in dramatic detail in one recent multilateral treaty, the December 1988 United Nations Convention Against Illicit Traffic in Narcotic Drugs and Psychotropic Substances. U.N. Doc. E/CONF.82/15 (1988). Article 5 of that Convention has fairly strong provisions requiring legislative, judicial, and administrative action to effect confiscations. *See* Kreczko testimony, *supra* note 99, at 550 (describing developing U.S. practice in the area).

116. Model Transfer of Proceedings Treaty, *supra* note 4. According to the Report of the Experts who met in Baden in 1987 to work on the draft of this model:

The model agreement on transfer of proceedings . . . could contribute to a reduction of pre-trial detention and to the solution of problems of concurrent jurisdictions and plurality of proceedings which laid an additional burden on national criminal justice systems and caused unnecessary hardship for offenders. This model agreement might eventually lead to the reciprocal formal acknowledgement of the validity of foreign criminal judgements and, thus, may constitute significant progress towards the fur-

committed an offense under the law of a state which is party to the treaty, that state may, if the interests of the proper administration of justice so require, request another state which is a party to commence proceedings in respect of the offense.[117] For the purposes of the Model Transfer of Proceedings Treaty, a request provides the requested state with the necessary jurisdiction in respect of the offense if that state does not already maintain jurisdiction under its own law. Indeed, the Model Transfer of Proceedings Treaty obligates the parties to take the necessary legislative measures to ensure that a request of the requesting state to take proceedings shall allow the requested state to exercise the necessary jurisdiction.[118] This kind of jurisdiction is referred to, particularly in European usage, as "vicarious administration of justice."[119] One suspects that the most likely field of application for such a treaty is where an accused has returned to his or her state of nationality and an extradition request is futile since that state does not extradite nationals.[120] It is not, however, intended that the Model Transfer of Proceedings Treaty should be limited to such cases. It is meant to

---

ther establishment of international recognition of the principle of double jeopardy (*ne bis in idem*).

Report of the International Expert Meeting on United Nations and Law Enforcement, Baden near Vienna, 16 to 19 November 1987, at 63, [hereinafter *Baden Report*].

117. Model Transfer of Proceedings Treaty, *supra* note 4, art. 1, para. 1.

118. *Id.* art. 1, para. 2.

119. *See* J. Meyer, *The Vicarious Administration of Justice: An Overlooked Basis of Jurisdiction*, 31 HARV. INT'L L.J. 108 (1990) (providing a useful introduction to theory and practice in the area).

120. There is a good discussion of the situations in which transfer treaties are useful and on the genre in general in J. Schutte's chapter, *The European System*, in Bassiouni, *supra* note 40, at 319. As noted earlier in the discussion of extradition, there may be a case based on the rehabilitation of the offender for trial and subsequent punishment in his or her country of origin. *Supra* note 85. If the states in question have an extradition treaty with provision for the prosecution of non-extraditable nationals then the present treaty would be redundant in the particular cases suggested in the text but may be useful in other instances. *Supra* note 86. Moreover, transfer of custodial or non-custodial punishment to the state of origin after conviction may serve the same ultimate purpose as transfer of proceedings. Thus, the various forms of cooperation treaties discussed may often be alternative routes to the same end. It is suggested in a publication of the United Nations International Drug Control Program that:

> Transfer of proceedings is not only a significant tool, which may replace extradition, but sometimes it also makes extradition possible, because the transfer of proceedings can provide the basis for a civil law State to effect surrender without postponement, despite the fact that in its territory criminal proceedings are pending for an offence other than that covered by the request for extradition.

EXTRADITION FOR DRUG RELATED OFFENSES, *supra* note 34, at 50.

encompass as well situations where the requested state would not be in a position to effect the extradition of a national of a third state. While the idea is not altogether unprecedented,[121] selling this Model Transfer of Proceedings Treaty to common law countries is somewhat difficult since they do not usually exercise jurisdiction over what their nationals do abroad.

As in the other models, the parties are to designate channels of communication;[122] certain documents are required;[123] and various formalities are spelled out.[124] Dual criminality is required.[125] Various grounds of refusal are given[126] including cases where the suspected person is not a national of or ordinarily resident in the requested state; the act is an offense under military law which is not also an offense under ordinary criminal law; the offense is in connection with taxes, duties, customs, or exchange; or the offense is regarded by the requested state as being of a political nature.

The suspected person is entitled to express to either state his or her interest in the transfer of proceedings,[127] although the factors to be taken into account in deciding whether to give effect to those views are not articulated. Both states are required to ensure that the rights of the victim, in particular the victim's right to restitution or compensation, shall not be affected by the transfer.[128] The suspect's right not to be prosecuted twice is protected.[129] A framework for dealing with multiple prosecution possibilities[130] is also suggested by language asserting that where criminal proceedings are pending in two or more states

---

121. Note, for example, New Zealand's exercise of jurisdiction over diplomats who commit offenses abroad but who are immune from local jurisdiction at the place of commission. Crimes Act of 1961, § 8A, *substituted by* the External Relations Act of 1988 § 14(1) (N.Z.). A number of British Commonwealth countries (anomalously) exercise jurisdiction over bigamy committed abroad by nationals but not over more serious offenses such as murder. *See, e.g.*, The King v. Lander [1919] N.Z.L.R. 305 (C.A.) (the "constitutionality" of such legislation, if not its wisdom, was conceded by the 1930s). New Zealand, in fact, claims a kind of vicarious theory of jurisdiction in respect of offenses committed by anyone, anywhere on a ship if that ship then comes within New Zealand waters and the flag state of the ship consents. *See generally*, R.S. Clark, *Criminal Code Reform in New Zealand? A Martian's View of the Erewhon Crimes Act 1961 with Some Footnotes to the 1989 Bill*, 21 VICT. U. W. L. REV. 1, 14–18 (1991).

122. Model Transfer of Proceedings Treaty, *supra* note 4, art. 2.

123. *Id.* art. 3.

124. *Id.* arts. 3, 4 & 5.

125. *Id.* art. 6.

126. *Id.* art 7.

127. *Id.* art. 8.

128. *Id.* art. 9.

129. *Id.* art. 10.

130. *See supra* notes 92–97.

against the same suspect in respect of the same offense, the states concerned shall conduct consultations to decide which of them alone should continue the proceedings. An agreement reached thereupon shall have the consequences of a request for transfer of proceedings.[131]

5. The Model Treaty on the Transfer of Supervision of Offenders Conditionally Sentenced or Conditionally Released

The fourth of the 1990 models is the Model Treaty on the Transfer of Supervision of Offenders Conditionally Sentenced or Conditionally Released.[132] It is a follow-up to the 1985 model on persons sentenced to imprisonment and deals with sentencing options not addressed in 1985. This Model Transfer of Supervision Treaty applies to a person who has been found guilty and (a) placed on probation without sentence having been pronounced, (b) given a suspended sentence involving deprivation of liberty, or (c) given a sentence, the enforcement of which has been modified (parole) or conditionally suspended, in whole or in part, either at the time of the sentence or subsequently.[133] The sentencing state may request another party to the Model Transfer of Supervision Treaty ("the administering state") to take responsibility for applying the terms of the decision.[134] The rationale for the scheme is, as in other instances, found in the preamble to the draft. It argues that such transfers should further the ends of justice, encourage the use of alternatives to imprisonment, facilitate the social resettlement of sentenced persons, and further the interests of victims of crime.[135] The draft contains similar grounds for refusal to those contained in the Treaty on the Transfer of Proceedings.[136] The sentenced person is entitled to express his or her views on the transfer[137] and the rights of the victim, especially to restitution or compensation, must not be adversely affected as a result of the transfer.[138]

131. Model Transfer of Proceedings Treaty, *supra* note 4, art. 13.

132. According to the Experts who met in Baden in 1987 to work on the draft of this and other instruments, the model "could contribute to a reduction in the numbers of persons required to serve prison sentences and to the social resettlement of foreign offenders by avoiding imprisonment through the increased application of supervision alternatives." *Baden Report, supra* note 116, at 63.

133. Model Transfer of Supervision Treaty, *supra* note 5, art. 1, para. 1.

134. *Id.* art 1, para. 2.

135. *Id.* para. 5 (preamble). *See* Chapter 4 *supra*, at notes 120–123 (detailing efforts to encourage alternatives to imprisonment). The interests of victims referred to are presumably those in obtaining recompense from the offender.

136. *Id.* art. 7; *supra* note 126.

137. *Id.* art. 8.

138. *Id.* art. 9.

The acceptance by the administering state of the responsibility for applying the sentence extinguishes the competence of the sentencing state to enforce the sentence.[139] The supervision is to be carried out in accordance with the law of the administering state. That state alone has the right of revocation. The administering state may, to the extent necessary, adapt to its own law the conditions or measures prescribed, provided that such conditions or measures are, in terms of their nature or duration, not more severe than those pronounced in the sentencing state.[140] The sentencing state alone shall have the right to decide on any application to reopen the case.[141] Each party, however, may grant pardon, amnesty, or commutation of the sentence in accordance with the provisions of its Constitution or other laws.[142]

6. The Model Treaty for the Prevention of Crimes That Infringe on the Cultural Heritage of Peoples in the Form of Movable Property

The last of the 1990 models is the Model Treaty for the Prevention of Crimes that Infringe on the Cultural Heritage of Peoples in the Form of Movable Property.[143] This was the most controversial of the drafts considered at the Eighth Congress. As the Chief of the Crime Prevention and Criminal Justice Branch has noted, it was crafted in association with UNESCO, ILANUD, UNAFEI, UNICRI, the Australian Institute of Criminology, the Australian National Cultural Heritage Commission and experts from various regions.[144] However, it did not receive the careful consideration of members of the Committee on Crime Prevention and Control that the other drafts had received. It was revised by a drafting group of experts in Chicago in June of 1990 and the revised version did not become available until the Eighth Congress.[145] Consequently some delegates would have preferred to put more work into it, for reasons of professional pride and language refinement. The subject-matter is, moreover, of considerable political significance, especially between developed countries with large collec-

---

139. *Id.* art. 10.
140. *Id.* art. 11, para. 1.
141. *Id.* art. 12, para. 1.
142. *Id.* art. 12, para. 2.
143. Model Cultural Heritage Treaty, *supra* note 6.
144. E. Vetere, *The Role of the United Nations: Working for a More Effective International Co-operation, in* PRINCIPLES AND PROCEDURES FOR A NEW TRANSNATIONAL CRIMINAL LAW, PROCEEDINGS OF AN INTERNATIONAL WORKSHOP ORGANIZED BY THE SOCIETY FOR THE REFORM OF CRIMINAL LAW AND THE MAX PLANCK INSTITUTE FOR FOREIGN AND INTERNATIONAL CRIMINAL LAW, FREIBURG-IM-BREISGAU, GERMANY, 21–25 MAY 1991 at 19 (A. Eser & O. Lagodny eds. 1992).
145. U.N. Doc. A/CONF.144/L.2 (1990).

tions of precious objects from elsewhere and developing countries which would like them back. As a result, it was adopted as an "other instrument" by the Eighth Congress, rather than appearing as a separate General Assembly resolution, and was part of the group of recommendations "welcomed" in the Assembly's omnibus Eighth Congress resolution as a model not cast in stone.[146]

"Movable cultural property" is defined for the purposes of the treaty as referring to property which, on religious or secular grounds, is specifically designated by a state party as being subject to export control by reason of its importance for archaeology, prehistory, history, literature, art or science, and as belonging to one or more of a lengthy list of categories.[147] Each state party undertakes:

   (a) To take the necessary measures to prohibit the import of movable cultural property (i) which has been stolen in the other State Party or (ii) which has been illicitly exported from the other State Party;

   (b) To take the necessary measures to prohibit the acquisition of, and dealing within its territory with, movable cultural property which has been imported contrary to the prohibitions resulting from the implementation of subparagraph (a) above;

   (c) To legislate in order to prevent persons and institutions within its territory from entering into international conspiracies with respect to movable cultural property;

   (d) To provide information concerning its stolen movable cultural property to an international data base agreed upon between the States Parties;[148]

   (e) To take the measures necessary to ensure that the purchaser of stolen movable cultural property that is listed on the international data base is not considered to be a purchaser who has acquired such property in good faith;

146. G.A. Res. 45/121, U.N. GAOR, 45th Sess., Supp. No. 49A, at 223, U.N. Doc. A/45/49 (1991). *See* Chapter 5 *supra*, at notes 59–61 (discussing this Resolution). *See also* R. Paterson, *The United Nations Model Treaty on Crimes Against Cultural Property*, 4 CRIM. L.F. 213 (1993).

147. Model Cultural Heritage Treaty, *supra* note 6, art. 1, para. 1. The list includes rare collections and specimens of fauna, flora, minerals, and anatomy, and objects of paleontological interest; products of archaeological excavations or discoveries; pictures, paintings, and drawings; and rare manuscripts and incunabula.

148. A footnote to the draft text at this point suggests that there should be further development of the data base approach. *See* Government of Canada, Proposal for the International Exchange of Information to Combat Crimes Against Cultural Movable Property (1990) (giving a concrete suggestion along these lines).

(f) To introduce a system whereby the export of movable cultural property is authorized by the issue of an export certificate;

(g) To take the measures necessary to ensure that a purchaser of imported movable cultural property which is not accompanied by an export certificate issued by the other State Party and who did not acquire the movable cultural property prior to the entry into force of this treaty shall not be considered to be a person who has acquired the movable cultural property in good faith;

(h) To use all the means at its disposal, including the fostering of public awareness, to combat the illicit import and export, theft, illicit excavation, and illicit dealing in movable cultural property.[149]

Further, each party promises to take the necessary measures to recover and return, at the request of another State Party, any movable cultural property covered by the treaty.[150] To emphasize the criminal law nature of the treaty, Article 3, headed "Sanctions," requires each party to impose sanctions upon (a) persons or institutions responsible for the illicit import or export of movable cultural property; (b) persons or institutions that knowingly acquire or deal in stolen or illicitly imported movable cultural property; and (c) persons or institutions that enter into international conspiracies to obtain, export, or import movable cultural property by illicit means.[151]

Article 4 of the Model Cultural Heritage Treaty covers procedures to be followed. Requests for recovery and return are to be made through diplomatic channels, with supporting documentation.[152] Expenses incidental to the return of the property are to be borne by the requesting State Party and no person or institution shall be entitled to claim any form of compensation from the State Party returning the property claimed. Neither shall the requesting State Party be required to compensate in any way such persons or institutions as may have participated in illegally sending abroad the property in question, although it must pay fair compensation to any person or institution that in good

---

149. Model Cultural Heritage Treaty, *supra* note 6, art. 2, para. 1 (numerous footnotes omitted).

150. *Id.* art. 2, para. 2.

151. *Id.* art. 3. A footnote to article 3 makes the rather obvious point in the circumstances that "States Parties should consider adding certain types of offences against movable cultural property to the list of extraditable offenses covered by an extradition treaty." The present model is not an extradition treaty but is intended as part of a package of relationships and the other parts of the package need to be dovetailed.

152. *Id.* art. 4, para. 1.

faith acquired or was in legal possession of the property.[153] The States Parties agree to make available to each other such information as will assist in combating crimes against cultural movable property.[154] Each party is, moreover, to provide information concerning laws which protect its movable cultural property to an international data base agreed upon between the States Parties.[155]

D. Conclusion

This completes the discussion of model treaties. Given that many states need to do substantial work on their basic extradition law and treaties, it is unlikely that the more sophisticated models will command widespread acceptance in the near future. But the congresses and the follow-up to them that occurs within the United Nations represent important opportunities to spread among criminal justice professionals, the basic constituency of the United Nations congresses, further knowledge of the range of co-operative opportunities suggested by modern state practice.

It was appreciated that there was no great likelihood that such issues would be solved in a multilateral fashion (except perhaps among regional, or other like-minded groupings)[156] and that the emphasis should, accordingly, be on suggesting to states the framework within which their negotiators might proceed, but leaving them to tailor-make the final details. I suggest that this is a useful enterprise in which to be engaged.[157] One should not underestimate the paucity of resources in

153. *Id.* art. 4, para. 2. A footnote suggests that "State Parties may wish to consider whether the expenses and/or the expense of providing compensation should be shared between them." A further note suggests that "States Parties may wish to consider the position of a blameless possessor who has inherited or otherwise gratuitously acquired a cultural object which had been previously dealt with in bad faith."

154. *Id.* art. 4, para. 3

155. *Id.* art. 4, para. 4.

156. Thus, as was noted *supra* pp. 203–4, the documents are drafted primarily on the assumption that they will be used for bilaterals, but they are readily adaptable to wider—notably regional—use. The models, indeed, owe much to treaties developed in the European region. The less than overwhelming number of ratifications that have occurred there, however, suggest that these are areas where much education is required before states are actually going to do the nitty gritty work to bring the treaties into force. *See* E. Muller-Rappard, *The European System, in* 2 INTERNATIONAL CRIMINAL LAW (PROCEDURE) 96 (M.C. Bassiouni ed. 1986).

157. According to a report prepared by the Secretary-General for the Eighth Congress, 17 of 49 states that replied to a questionnaire item on the subject reported that they were using the Model Agreement on the Transfer of Foreign Prisoners for bilateral negotiations. *Report of the Secretary-General, Implementation of the Standard Minimum Rules for the Treatment of Prisoners,* at 7, U.N. Doc. A/CONF.144/11 (1990). There is one more draft currently in the pipeline, on the transfer of enforcement of penal sanctions. This is

many a Ministry of Foreign Affairs or Ministry of Justice when it comes to acting on the international plane and the documents are meant to be helpful in such cases.

Ultimately, however, there is no escaping the considerable work involved in the network of individual exercises in diplomacy that are necessary to put the edifice of cooperation in place. In this respect, it is to be hoped that the new United Nations emphasis on technical cooperation[158] will play some part. The experience to date has been somewhat mixed, as a 1992 Secretariat report[159] indicates. The Secretariat, on request of the Economic Community of West African States (ECOWAS), had assisted that organization at two working sessions in formulating the draft text of a regional convention on mutual assistance in criminal matters. ECOWAS then convened two meetings of legal experts in Lagos to examine the text and it was sent on for consideration by a meeting of ECOWAS Ministers of Justice. Because of lack of funds, however, the Secretariat was not able to attend the Lagos meetings or to provide further requested assistance, involving a review of the legal situation of ECOWAS member states, a drafting of legal documents, and relevant training initiatives. By the same token, the Secretariat was unable to pursue requests from other Member States and sub-regional organizations for assistance in adapting United Nations models on assistance in criminal matters as a basis for bilateral or multilateral arrangements, although the support of potential donor countries had been sought. Further funding was being sought in 1993

---

broader in scope than the transfer of convicted persons (incarcerated or otherwise). *See Conclusions and recommendations of the International Expert Group Meeting for the Elaboration of a Model Treaty on the Transfer of Enforcement of Penal Sanctions, Siracusa, 3–8 December 1991,* U.N. Doc. E/CN.15/1992/4/Add.3 (1992) ("penal sanctions" defined to include deprivation of liberty, fines, confiscations and disqualifications). *See also* the Convention Between the Governments of Denmark, Norway and Sweden Regarding the Recognition and Enforcement of Judgments in Criminal Matters, Mar. 8, 1948, 27 U.N.T.S. 128 (1949) (seemingly the first state practice in this area). Given that the Crime Prevention and Criminal Justice Branch is not currently devoting any resources to the drafting of new instruments, the draft on the transfer of enforcement of penal sanctions is not likely to emerge in the near future.

158. *See* Chapter 2 *supra,* at notes 73–74.

159. *Report of the Secretary-General, Progress report on United Nations activities in crime prevention and criminal justice, including detailed information on current programme budget and extrabudgetary activities of the Crime Prevention and Criminal Justice Branch of the Centre for Social Development and Humanitarian Affairs,* at 13–14, U.N. Doc. E/CN.15/1992/2 (1992). Another regional group has shown some interest in the U.N. models. The members of the South Pacific Forum agreed in July 1992 "that members should review their extradition legislation and, if required, take steps to introduce and bring into force legislation based on the United Nations Model Treaty on Extradition or on the current London Scheme for the Rendition of Fugitive Offenders within the Commonwealth." *Declaration by the South Pacific Forum on Law Enforcement Cooperation, Twenty Third South Pacific Forum: Forum Communique, Honiara, Solomon Islands 8–9 July 1992,* at 18, SPFS(92)18.

to assist ECOWAS with training on mutual legal asssistance and with the development of a regional extradition convention.[160]

As in other respects, the United Nations International Drug Control Program provides a model to envy. The Drug Control Program has three legal experts available full-time to assist in whatever way they are asked. What follows is a list of the various ways in which the legal experts may be utilized to give effect to the drug abuse conventions, notably the 1988 Convention Against Illicit Traffic in Narcotic Drugs and Psychotropic Substances[161]:

- Advice on the nature and extent of obligations under the conventions;
- Review and evaluation of drug abuse control legislation and infrastructures;
- Advice on any legislative or administrative measures to implement the conventions or enhance their effectiveness;
- Advice on implementation measures adopted by other countries with similar legal concepts and systems (including provision of relevant legislation);
- Provision of expert consultants to help prepare any necessary legislative drafting instructions or to draft the legislation itself;
- Advice and assistance in elaborating suitable arrangements to strengthen domestic, regional and inter-regional drug abuse control capacity (for example, on matters such as confiscation, extradition, mutual legal assistance, controlled delivery, etc);
- Advice on the resolution of particular implementation problems arising;
- Advice on ratification or accession procedures and documentation.[162]

It is to be hoped that the Crime Prevention and Criminal Justice Branch can move its own more broadly focused program in a similar direction,[163] or even find a way to tap into some of the resources of the Drug Control Program.

160. *Operational activities completed or proposed to the United Nations Crime Prevention and Criminal Justice Branch since the first session of the Commision on Crime Prevention and Criminal Justice in April 1992*, U.N. Doc. E/CN.15/CRP.9 (1993).

161. *See supra* note 32.

162. U.N. International Drug Control Program (June 1, 1991) (Flier).

163. For some efforts along these lines, *see* Ad Hoc Expert Group Meeting on "Model Legislation to Foster Reliance on Model Treaties," Vienna 18–21 October 1993, Background Paper for Participants (mimeo, on file with the author); *Conclusions and recommendations of the Meeting of Experts on Implementing Legislation to Foster Reliance on Model Treaties, Vienna, 18–21 October 1993*, U.N. Doc. E/CN.15/1994/4/Add.1 (1994).

Part IV
Implementation of Norms and Standards

Chapter 9
Efforts at Implementation During the Life of the Committee on Crime Prevention and Control

A. The General Assembly's Plea for "Realistic and Effective" Implementation Machinery

The burst of substantive law-making activity by the Committee on Crime Prevention and Control and the congresses in the past decade fits a little awkwardly with a significant 1986 policy statement by the General Assembly entitled "Setting international standards in the field of human rights."[1] That statement applies at least in spirit to the work in the area of crime prevention and criminal justice. In its preambular paragraphs, the statement recalls the "extensive network of international standards in the field of human rights" and reaffirms the primacy of the Universal Declaration of Human Rights and the two Covenants. It concedes that there are still areas where further development is needed but asserts that "the effective implementation of these standards is of fundamental importance." The first operative paragraph of the resolution insists that Member States and the United Nations itself should "accord priority" to the implementation of existing standards. Among the guidelines given in the resolution for the development of new instruments, when the urge to procreate becomes irresistible, is that they should "[p]rovide, where appropriate, realistic and effective implementation machinery, including reporting systems."

Over the last several years of its life, the Committee on Crime Prevention and Control diligently tried to follow this exhortation to implementation, even as it, the congresses and the bodies to which they

1. G.A. Res. 41/120, U.N. GAOR, 41st Sess., Supp. No. 53, at 178, U.N. Doc. A/41/53 (1987).

report—ECOSOC and the General Assembly—indulged themselves in the proliferation of instruments discussed in other chapters. How "realistic and effective" the effort to engage in implementation has been is open to debate. The expansion in activities aimed at implementation is, however, a fine example of the gradual accumulation of particular precedents followed by an ultimate, and ongoing, attempt to generalize and rationalize them. Yet much of it has been done with smoke and mirrors in a period of limited resources but widening expectations. The system finally ground to a halt through overload.

B. What is Meant by Implementation?

To the best of my knowledge, "implementation" has never been authoritatively defined in any international instrument. In United Nations usage, it usually consists of two elements. First, implementation connotes an effort to encourage states to apply international norms in their domestic laws and practices. Second, it suggests some kind of international machinery to supervise or follow-up on the exhortations to do so.

The machinery most commonly encompasses a requirement for self-reporting by states on progress made or claimed to have been made. This reporting may be accompanied by some critical review by a committee or other body. The whole exercise will normally be associated with an effort to disseminate information about the norms in question, and perhaps even about the extent to which particular states comply with them. Technical assistance may sometimes be provided on a bilateral or multilateral basis, either to help in compliance, or in the reporting process, or both.

Another kind of machinery, one to "supervise" the way states fulfill their obligations, is a complaint procedure which will respond to individual or class complaints of infringements. This is sometimes described as a "violations" approach.[2]

The Committee on Crime Prevention and Control's efforts prior to its demise relied heavily on reporting and merely skirmished with the idea of a violations approach, which had political implications and required a capacity for action that was simply not available. As we shall see, the kind of reporting entailed so far is different from that carried out under the auspices of the more familiar "treaty bodies" such as the Committee on Human Rights and the Committee on the Elimination

2. *See* HUMAN RIGHTS SOURCEBOOK 349–53 (A.P. Blaustein, R.S. Clark & J.A. Sigler eds. 1987) (giving a typology of United Nations procedures).

of all Forms of Racial Discrimination. We are in territory where there is both "soft law" and "soft procedure."[3] There were also many references to technical assistance during the life of the Committee on Crime Prevention and Control, in its resolutions, and in resolutions of ECOSOC, the congresses and the General Assembly, but the actual delivery was limited by a severe lack of resources. Under the new arrangements, technical assistance is advertised as carrying more of the burden.

C. Early History and the Scope of This Chapter

Early moves in the direction of implementation of the items in the Crime Prevention and Criminal Justice Program began with efforts in the late 1950s to collate and disseminate information on the extent to which various states were giving effect to the norms in question. Apparently, this rested on two theories. The first was that the exercise in collecting the information was cathartic for the state doing the gathering and the second was that information on other people's actions was interesting, and perhaps even useful, to other members of the international community who could assess their own efforts against the wider practice.[4] Early moves toward the collection and dissemination of information occurred, not surprisingly given the inherent significance of the topics within the organization, in the areas of the Standard Minimum Rules for the Treatment of Prisoners and of capital punishment.

I shall discuss in this chapter, in a more or less chronological order, these early reporting efforts followed by more recent efforts in the Committee on Crime Prevention and Control and ECOSOC both to enhance the reporting process and to expand it into broader attempts at implementation. The chronological treatment permits an exposition of the manner in which the Crime Prevention Committee's implementation functions developed by accretion. It will lead logically into the final chapter, Chapter 10, which examines some theoretical issues on implementation (or on "use and application" which seems to be the currently preferred terminology in some quarters) and makes some suggestions about the future.

---

3. *See* Chapter 5 *supra*, at note 73.

4. *See* Chapter 10 *infra*, at notes 19–35 (discussing further the rationale for reporting systems). The second of the reasons mentioned in the text is consistent with the organization's basic interest in networking in the criminal justice area. Chapter 1 *supra*, at notes 56–58.

D. Reporting on and Implementing the Standard Minimum Rules

1. First Steps, 1957–1984

In its resolution approving the Standard Minimum Rules (Rules) in 1957,[5] ECOSOC requested governments to inform the Secretary-General regularly of the progress made with regard to the implementation of the Rules.[6] Questionnaires on the application of the Rules were addressed to Governments by the Secretary-General in 1967, 1974, 1979, 1984, and 1989.[7] The responses were somewhat sparse,[8] although it is possible to glean some interesting material from their content.[9]

At the Fourth United Nations Congress held in Kyoto in 1970, there was a general discussion of "the Standard Minimum Rules for the Treatment of Prisoners in the Light of Recent Developments in the Correctional Field."[10] A sub-item in this discussion was the question of implementation. Suggestions made in the course of this debate are still very current two decades later. For example, the methods of implementation suggested were classified in the Report of the Fourth Congress as dissemination, training, information, and establishing machinery for these purposes.[11] All these ideas are still topical in discussions at the Commission on Crime Prevention and Criminal Justice.

---

5. E.S.C Res. 663C (XXIV), U.N. ESCOR, 24th Sess., Supp. No. 1, at 11, U.N. Doc. E/4048 (1957).

6. The resolution recommended that the Secretary-General be informed every five years of the progress made with regard to the application of the Rules and authorized the Secretary-General to make arrangements for the publication of the information received "and to ask for supplementary information if necessary." The power to request supplementary information has lain dormant. *See also infra* text accompanying note 107. The idea of reporting on the application of the Standard Minimum Rules in fact went back to the League of Nations period. Chapter 1 *supra*, at note 26.

7. *See* U.N. Docs. A/CONF.43/3, Annex (1970); A/CONF.56/6, Annex I (1975); A/CONF.87/11, A/CONF.87/11 Add. (1980); A/CONF.121/15, A/CONF.121/15 Add.1 (1985); A/CONF.144/11 (1990)(Reports of these surveys).

8. Forty-four governments replied to the survey sent out in 1967, 62 to that sent in 1974, only 38 to that sent in 1979, 62 again in respect of 1984's and 49 to that in 1989. *Id.*

9. *See* Chapter 6 *supra*, at notes 105–139.

10. *See Working Paper prepared by the Secretariat, The Standard Minimum Rules for the Treatment of Prisoners in Light of Recent Developments in the Correctional Field,* U.N. Doc. A/CONF.43/3 (1970) [hereinafter *Working Paper prepared by the Secretariat*].

11. *Fourth United Nations Congress on the Prevention of Crime and the Treatment of Offenders, Kyoto, Japan, 17–26 August 1970, Report Prepared by the Secretariat,* at 22, U.N. Doc. A/CONF.43/5 (1971). *See Working Paper prepared by the Secretariat, supra* note 10, at 36:

The discussion continued at a meeting of a Working Group of Experts on the Rules, called together by the Secretary-General in September 1972, a Working Group whose formation had been foreshadowed at the Fourth Congress. Much of the discussion concerned possible amendments to the Rules,[12] but the question of implementation was also addressed. The Group concluded that the United Nations "should make greater efforts to propagate the Rules, collect data and provide more facilities for information and education on the Rules."[13] Among the other suggestions strongly endorsed by the Group was the development of a commentary on the Rules which would furnish guidelines to Governments faced with the problem of deciding how the Rules might be given fuller effect.[14] The Group also argued that it was important to

---

> The possibility of incorporating [the Rules] into national and local law and practice depends . . . upon the extent to which they are publicized, propagated and understood by everyone likely to be concerned with or interested in their subject-matter. . . . This suggests the need for an international campaign designed to disseminate the provisions of the Rules, which has not yet been undertaken on any considerable scale.

Note also the analogy drawn with the way in which the Geneva Conventions are to be posted in all prisoner of war camps. *Id.* In fact, the Geneva Conventions go even further into the area of dissemination than merely posting copies in the camps. Common article 47, of the First Convention, article 48 of the Second Convention, article 127 of the Third and article 144 of the Fourth Convention state that:

> The High Contracting Parties undertake, in time of peace as in time of war, to disseminate the text of the present Convention as widely as possible in their respective countries, and, in particular, to include the study thereof in their programmes of military and, if possible, civil instruction, so that the principles thereof may become known to the entire population, in particular to the armed fighting forces, the medical personnel and the chaplains.

The International Red Cross and Red Crescent Movements publish a magazine on dissemination of the Conventions, aptly titled DISSEMINATION. Many of the educational and publicity ideas in it are readily adaptable to standards other than those of the Geneva Conventions. *See also* NATIONAL IMPLEMENTATION OF INTERNATIONAL HUMANITARIAN LAW (M. Bothe, et al., eds. 1990); *Roundtable, Implementing the Rules of War: Training, Command and Enforcement,* 1972 PROC. AM. SOC'Y INT'L L. 183 (describing the difficult work of incorporating the Geneva Conventions into national legal orders).

12. The discussion ultimately led to an amendment in 1977 extending the coverage of the Rules to those arrested or imprisoned without charge. *See* Chapter 6 *supra,* at note 101; *infra* note 23.

13. *Report of the Secretary-General on the Meeting of the Working Group of Experts on the Standard Minimum Rules for the Treatment of Prisoners, held at United Nations Headquarters, from 25–29 September 1972,* at 13, U.N. Doc. A/AC.57/8 (1973) [hereinafter *Working Group of Experts*].

14. *Id.* at 13–14. This idea had been floated in the 1970 *Working Paper prepared by the Secretariat, supra* note 10, at 49–50. To the best of my knowledge the commentary was

communicate to the various organs and agencies of the United Nations, especially those concerned with national development, the relevance of the Rules in planning for effective crime prevention and control in developing countries.[15] Early steps had to be taken, according to the Experts, to stimulate the translation of the Rules into the official languages of the substantial number of Member States in which they were not available.[16] Where feasible, the aid of United Nations information centers, other international organizations, United Nations associations, and other non-governmental actors should be asked to assist in publicity. The cooperation of the academic community and national correspondents in social defense was also thought to be helpful.[17]

Most of these ideas were incorporated in a set of draft procedures for the implementation of the Rules contained in the working paper prepared by the Secretariat for the Fifth Congress.[18] There was support at the Fifth Congress for more vigorous efforts to assure dissemination of the Rules. It was also argued that the United Nations should give

---

never completed, although a draft was considered at the second meeting of the Working Groups of Experts in 1974. *See Report of the Working Group of Experts on the Standard Minimum Rules for the Treatment of Prisoners on its Second Meeting*, 33 INT'L REV. CRIM. POL'Y 87 (1977). The basic idea, which is essentially an effort to appeal to the professionalism of the relevant workers in the field, has, however, been applied recently to the Declaration on the Rights of Victims. *See Measures for the Implementation of the Declaration of Basic principles of Justice for Victims of Crime and Abuse of Power*, U.N. Doc. E/AC.57/1988/NGO/1 (1988)(submitted by a committee of experts that met at the International Institute of Higher Sciences, Syracuse, Italy in May 1986, and later endorsed by various non-governmental organizations); *Guide for Practitioners on the Basic Principles of Justice for Victims of Crime and Abuse of Power*, U.N. Doc. E/AC.57/1990/CRP.1 (1990); *Model Training Curricula*, U.N. Doc. E/AC.57/1990/NGO/3 (1990)(prepared by the Society for Traumatic Stress Studies). A related endeavor is that of producing manuals for those in the field. *See, e.g., Practical measures against corruption: manual prepared by the Secretariat*, U.N. Doc. A/CONF.144/8 (1990). Manuals on Juvenile Justice and Domestic Violence are in the course of preparation for the Secretariat.

15. *Working Group of Experts, supra* note 13, at 3–4.

16. This is a very common problem with U.N. human rights standards in general—starting with the Universal Declaration of Human Rights. The Secretary-General's 1990 survey of the implementation of the Standard Minimum Rules, *supra* note 7, at 12, records that almost all the respondent countries reported that the Rules had been translated and published in the official language(s) of their country as a separate document. This perhaps indicates some progress, but leaves an enormous number of unofficial languages unaccounted for.

17. *Working Group of Experts, supra* note 13, at 4.

18. *Working Paper Prepared by the Secretariat, The Treatment of Offenders, in Custody or in the Community, with Special Reference to the Implementation of the Standard Minimum Rules for the Treatment of Offenders adopted by the United Nations*, at 73, U.N. Doc. A/CONF.56/6, Annex III (1975).

serious consideration to the need for appropriate implementation machinery. It was suggested that this might be done through the establishment of a sub-committee of the Committee on Crime Prevention and Control, through the extension of the service of the Working Group of Experts on the Standard Minimum Rules or the creation of a new committee on the treatment of prisoners.[19] However, nothing specific was recommended to ECOSOC or the General Assembly.

ECOSOC empowered the Crime Prevention Committee to follow up the matter early in 1976 as part of an omnibus resolution dealing with the "question of the human rights of all persons subjected to any form of detention or imprisonment."[20] At its Fourth Session in 1976, the Crime Prevention Committee adopted, for consideration by ECOSOC, a set of procedures for the implementation of the Rules based on the Secretariat draft for the 1975 Congress.[21] This effort was "welcomed" by the General Assembly that year[22] and the Assembly invited ECOSOC to consider the draft procedures "with due priority." The priority that was due, however, was apparently rather low.[23] Nothing

19. *Fifth United Nations Congress on the Prevention of Crime and the Treatment of Offenders, Geneva, 1–12 September 1975, Report Prepared by the Secretariat,* at 36, U.N. Doc. A/CONF.56/10 (1975).

20. E.S.C. Res. 1993 (LX), U.N. ESCOR, 60th Sess., Supp. No. 1, at 23, U.N. Doc. E/5850 (1976). The resolution, which refers also to questions of torture, the right to be free from arbitrary arrest, detention and exile, and to human rights of those subjected to any form of detention or imprisonment, is an interesting example of ECOSOC combining—perhaps even coordinating—work being done both under the auspices of the Committee on Crime Prevention and Control and under the auspices of the Commission on Human Rights. The relevant paragraph in the resolution was added in the Social Committee, on the initiative of the Representative of Greece, to an existing Western European/Latin American draft. *Report of the Economic and Social Council on the work of its organizational session for 1976 and of its sixtieth and sixty-first sessions,* at 56, U.N. GAOR, 31st Sess., Supp. No. 3, U.N. Doc. A/31/3 (1976). The Greek representative did little to explain the initiative other than to note that the congress had limited time to consider the matter. U.N. Doc. E/AC.7/SR 781, at 2 (1976).

21. *Report of the Committee on Crime Prevention and Control on its Fourth Session, 21 June— 2 July 1976, Draft Procedures for the Effective Implementation of the Standard Minimum Rules for the Treatment of Prisoners,* Annex VI, at 74, U.N. Doc. E/CN.5/536 (1976). Analogies were drawn in a footnote with the ECOSOC reporting system, with reports made concerning the Declaration on the Elimination of Discrimination Against Women, G.A. Res. 2263 (XXII), U.N. GAOR, 22d Sess., Supp. No. 16, at 35, U.N. Doc. A/6716 (1968), and with the reports required under the 1960 Single Convention on Narcotic Drugs, 520 U.N.T.S. 204.

22. G.A. Res. 31/85, U.N. GAOR, 31st Sess., Supp. No. 39, at 102, U.N. Doc. A/31/39 (1976).

23. ECOSOC did act the following year on a related move to extend the field of application of the Rules by adding a new Rule 95 dealing with persons arrested or imprisoned without charge ("detained"). E.S.C. Res. 2076 (LXII), U.N. ESCOR, 62d

emerged from ECOSOC on the subject in the next few years. A half-hearted discussion of the item "United Nations Norms and Guidelines in Criminal Justice: From Standard-Setting to Implementation, and Capital Punishment" at the Sixth United Nations Congress did not result in the adoption of any specific proposals.[24]

2. The 1984 Procedures

It was not until 1984 that the Economic and Social Council, acting on a new recommendation of the Committee on Crime Prevention and Control, was moved to try harder and ultimately approved the so-called Procedures for the Effective Implementation of the Standard Minimum Rules for the Treatment of Prisoners (Procedures).[25] The nine year delay presumably allowed a consensus to develop, but it did little to improve the drafting. The Procedures as finally adopted were substantially in the terms proposed by the Secretariat draft in 1975 and the Crime Prevention Committee version of 1976.

The Procedures are a blend of provisions encouraging states to institutionalize the Rules in their own system and a tentative effort at international accountability through the involvement of the Secretary-General and the Committee on Crime Prevention and Control.

States whose standards fall short of the Rules are exhorted to adopt them. In adopting the Rules, states are expected to adapt them to existing law and culture, without deviation from the spirit and purpose of the Rules. Moreover, states are requested to embody the Rules in national legislation and other regulations. The Rules are to be made available to all persons concerned, particularly to law enforcement officials and correctional personnel, for the purposes of enabling their application and execution in the criminal justice system. The Rules, as embodied in national law, are also to be made available, in an understandable form, to prisoners and all persons under detention, on their admission and during confinement.

Sess., Supp. No. 1, at 35, U.N. Doc. E/5988 (1977). This action perhaps symbolizes the way in which, as late as the 1970s, it was often easier to make progress on substance than on efforts at implementation—even limited ones.

24. See *Report prepared by the Secretariat, Sixth United Nations Congress on the Prevention of Crime and the Treatment of Offenders, Caracas, Venezuela, 25 August-5 September 1980*, at 46–50, U.N. Doc. A/CONF.87/14/Rev.1 (1981).

25. E.S.C. Res. 1984/47, U.N. ESCOR, Supp. No. 1, at 29, U.N. Doc. E/1984/84 (1984). The ECOSOC Resolution was later endorsed by the General Assembly. G.A. Res. 39/118, U.N. GAOR, 39th Sess., Supp. No. 51, at 211, U.N. Doc. A/39/51 (1984). *See generally*, M.C. Bassiouni, *The U.N. Procedures for the Effective Implementation of the Standard Minimum Rules for the Treatment of Prisoners*, in FESTSCHRIFT FÜR DIETRICH OEHLER 525 (R.D. Herzberg ed. 1985).

The Procedures established a somewhat more precise reporting requirement than that in the earlier 1957 resolution. States were required to inform the Secretary-General every five years of the extent of the implementation, the progress made with regard to the application of the Rules, and the factors and difficulties, if any, affecting their implementation.[26] This information would be conveyed mainly by responding to the Secretary-General's questionnaire. Taking into account these reports, as well as other relevant material available within the United Nations system, the Secretary-General was required to prepare independent periodic reports on progress made and to submit them to the Committee on Crime Prevention and Control. In preparing the independent reports, the Secretary-General was authorized to enlist the cooperation of the specialized agencies and of relevant intergovernmental organizations and non-governmental organizations in consultative status with ECOSOC.[27]

In order to increase awareness of these standards, the Secretary-General was required to disseminate the Rules, implementing procedures and reports on the subject to as wide an audience as possible. In a further effort to have knowledge of the Rules permeate national and international administrations, the Secretary-General was also required to ensure the widest possible reference to and use of the text of the Rules by the organization in all its relevant programs, including technical assistance activities.

As part of its technical cooperation and development programs, the United Nations was instructed to (a) aid governments, at their request, in setting up and strengthening comprehensive and humane correctional systems; (b) make available to Governments requesting them the services of experts and regional and interregional advisers on crime prevention and criminal justice;[28] (c) promote national and regional seminars and other meetings at the professional and non-professional levels to further the dissemination of the Rules and the Procedures; and (d) strengthen substantive support to regional research and training institutes in crime prevention and criminal justice that are associ-

---

26. Some variant of the language about "factors and difficulties" that "affect" implementation (presumably in a negative way) has become something of a boiler-plate formula in U.N. human rights instruments. It seems to have been first used in substantially the form it appears here in article 17 of the International Covenant on Economic, Social and Cultural Rights, G.A. Res. 2200 (XXI), U.N. GAOR, 21st Sess., Supp. No. 16, at 49, U.N. Doc. A/6316 (1967) and article 40 of the International Covenant on Civil and Political Rights, *id.*, at 52. Recording difficulties might generate offers of technical assistance. *See infra* note 53; Chapter 10 *infra*, at notes 30–31.

27. *See* Chapter 10 *infra*, at notes 50–58 (giving comments on the role of NGOs).

28. *See id.* at notes 79–84.

ated with the United Nations.[29] The research and training institutions, in cooperation with national institutions, were encouraged to develop curricula and training manuals on the Rules and Procedures, suitable for use in criminal justice education programs at all levels,[30] as well as in specialized courses on human rights and other related subjects.

For its part, the Committee on Crime Prevention and Control was instructed to keep the Rules under review with an aim of elaborating new rules, standards and procedures and following up the implementing procedures, including periodic reporting.[31] Moreover, the Crime Prevention Committee was instructed to assist the General Assembly, the Economic and Social Council and any other United Nations human rights bodies, as appropriate, in developing recommendations relating to reports of *ad hoc* inquiry commissions on matters pertaining to the application and implementation of the Standard Minimum Rules. This power remained dormant as nothing "appropriate" emerged.

A final provision in the Procedures asserted that nothing in their content should be construed as precluding resort to any other means or remedies available under international law or set forth by other United Nations bodies and agencies for the redress of violations of human rights. This was specifically said to include the procedure on consistent patterns of gross violations of human rights under Economic and Social Council resolution 1503 (XLVIII) of May 27, 1970,[32] the communication procedure under the Optional Protocol[33] to the International Covenant on Civil and Political Rights[34] and the communication procedure under the International Convention on the

---

29. *See* Chapter 3 *supra*, at notes 112–142 (describing these bodies).

30. I have located some decent materials designed for use in United Nations training courses on human rights in the administration of justice but none specifically on the Standard Minimum Rules. *See, e.g., United Nations Training Course in Human Rights in the Administration of Justice, organized by the United Nations Division of Human Rights in cooperation with the Government of the Arab Republic of Egypt, 18 June—7 July 1973* (1973). I have not been able to locate any materials on the Rules that were prepared for national programs.

31. The Commentary adopted as part of the Procedures suggested: "The Committee should therefore clearly define existing shortcomings in or the reasons for the lack of implementation of the Rules, *inter alia*, through contacts with the judiciary and ministries of justice of the countries concerned, with a view to suggesting appropriate remedies." There was some promise of action by the Committee here, although left vague was the extent to which it was a promise to become involved in specific situations rather than in merely propagating generalities.

32. U.N. ESCOR, 48th Sess., Supp. No. 1A, at 8, U.N. Doc. E/4832/Add.1 (1970).

33. G.A. Res. 2200A (XXI), U.N. GAOR, 21st Sess., Supp. No. 16, at 59, U.N. Doc. A/6316 (1967).

34. *See supra* note 26.

Elimination of All Forms of Racial Discrimination.[35] This was the only hint of a "violations" approach to implementation[36] and it was, it will be noted, a reference to procedures other than those of the Committee on Crime Prevention and Control itself.

"Communications" is of course, United Nations jargon for complaints or petitions. The "1503" procedure has hardly been an effective response to the gross violations of human rights with which it is concerned,[37] but it does at least represent a commitment by the organization to take *some* action in concrete cases. The Human Rights Committee's now well established experience under the Optional Protocol,[38] and the Committee on Racial Discrimination's thinner and more recent experience,[39] suggest that some questions of violations of human rights are amenable to an international complaints procedure.

The present saving provision in the Procedures thus opens up several possibilities for future work by the Commission on Crime Prevention and Criminal Justice. First, the existing human rights procedures may provide analogies for a new complaints procedure that the Commission or a sub-group of it might engage in.[40] Second, since the norms and standards with which the Standard Minimum Rules are concerned overlap those in other United Nations instruments, the Procedures invite greater efforts by the Crime Prevention and Criminal Justice Program in general to have its norms taken into account by other United Nations organs.[41] And third, they raise the possibility that there might develop parallel procedures which would need to be coordinated.[42]

One thing at least was clear with the adoption of the Procedures in 1984: a vision of "implementation" had become a part of the currency of the Program. The issue now became how to make it work and how

35. G.A. Res. 2106 A (XX), U.N. GAOR, 20th Sess., Supp. No. 14, at 47, U.N. Doc. A/6014 (1966).

36. *See supra* note 2.

37. *See generally* H. TOLLEY, THE U.N. COMMISSION ON HUMAN RIGHTS 70–82 (1987). *See also, In-depth Evaluation of the Human Rights Programme, Report of the Secretary-General,* U.N. Doc. A/AC.51/1989/2 (1989)(for some devastating criticism of the procedure).

38. The numerous "views" of the Committee under the Protocol are reproduced in its annual reports and *Human Rights Committee, Selected Decisions Under the Optional Protocol,* U.N. Doc. CCPR/C/OP/1 (1985).

39. *Report of the Committee on the Elimination of Racial Discrimination,* U.N. GAOR, 46th Sess., Supp. No. 18, at 93–94, U.N. Doc. A/46/18 (1992) (only two opinions had been adopted by 1992 with respect to complaints against the 14 states accepting the jurisdiction of the Committee).

40. *See* Chapter 10 *infra* (conclusion).

41. *See id.,* at notes 59–78.

42. *See id.,* conclusion.

far to expand beyond the area of the Standard Minimum Rules. The impetus to so expand was strengthened by comparable, if not quite so far reaching, efforts that had been occurring in respect of capital punishment. It is to these that I now turn.

E. Reports on Capital Punishment

The United Nations began systematically gathering material with respect to laws and practice concerning the death penalty in the 1960s.[43] In 1973, ECOSOC moved to place this effort on a regular cycle by asking for the Secretary-General to present updated analytical reports at five-yearly intervals.[44] In 1956,[45] on the urging of the United States, the Council had introduced a voluntary procedure for states to report periodically on the condition of human rights in their countries on a cycle dealing with different topics. States were now invited in the 1973 capital punishment resolution to include in such periodic reports any further changes of their situation concerning capital punishment. They were also invited to inform the Secretary-General of any new research carried out by qualified national institutions and of any governmental action undertaken to promote research in this field.

In 1956, and even in 1973, none of the human rights treaty reporting regimes had come into being and the voluntary system could have represented both a valuable exercise in its own right and a useful dry run for the treaty bodies. In fact, not much was made of it in practice and the treaty bodies had eventually to invent the wheel for themselves. The voluntary reporting system seldom garnered a high per-

43. *See* E.S.C. Res. 747 (XXIX), U.N. ESCOR, 29th Sess., Supp. No. 1, at 4, U.N. Doc. E/3373 (1960) (requesting a factual review), Capital Punishment (1962) (written primarily by Marc Ancel) (prepared in response) Capital Punishment Developments, 1961 to 1965 (1967) (written primarily by Norval Morris) (prepared in response). Both documents prepared in response were published jointly as U.N. Sales Pub. No. E.67.IV.15 (1968). *See also* R. Hood, *The Question of the Death Penalty and the New Contributions of the Criminal Sciences to the Matter: A Report to the United Nations Committee on Crime Prevention and Control*, U.N. Doc. E/AC. 57/1988/CRP.7 (1988) (English text also published in book form by Oxford University Press (1989)).

44. E.S.C. Res. 1745, U.N. ESCOR, 54th Sess., Supp. No. 1, at 4, U.N. Doc. E/5367 (1973). On the inadequacies of voluntary reporting, *see generally*, R.S. Clark, A United Nations High Commissioner for Human Rights 35–38 (1972).

45. E.S.C. Res. 624 B (XXII), U.N. ESCOR, 22d Sess., Supp. No. 1, at 11, U.N. Doc. E/2929 (1956), *amended by* E.S.C. Res. 1074 C (XXXIX), U.N. ESCOR, 39th Sess., Supp. No. 1, at 24, U.N. Doc. E/4117 (1965). By 1956 it was clear that the United States would not proceed with the ratification of the human rights Covenants in the near future and the voluntary reporting system was an effort at an alternative strategy. The power of the organization to create a voluntary reporting system was not disputed during the debates on this item. U.N. Docs. E./CN.4/SR. 514–546 (1956).

centage of compliance, or much useful information, and efforts to breathe life into the examination of reports foundered. In December 1980 the General Assembly decided to terminate certain activities the Secretary-General had identified as obsolete, ineffective, or of marginal usefulness. This included the system of periodic reports, which, because of the disappointing way it had developed, warranted all three of these descriptions.[46] This experience does not augur well for the Crime Program's efforts.

Be that as it may, the capital punishment resolutions thus emphasized reporting, and the five-yearly reporting on capital punishment survived the 1980 demise of the more general voluntary periodic reporting system. There was, however, little mandate through the 1960s and 1970s for much more than this, although the organization was on record as favoring a move toward abolition of capital punishment and had lauded developments in this direction.[47] But the 1960 and 1973 resolutions did help to solidify a movement toward requesting reporting that was to lead to the imposition of several more reporting provisions, and broader efforts at a whole developing package of implementation measures, in the late 1980s. Moreover, the 1984 Capital Punishment Safeguards resolution, discussed in an earlier chapter,[48] endeavored to impose some limitations on state behavior in the area of capital punishment; those requirements in turn generated a call for their implementation.

F. Expansion of the Field of Reporting and Implementation

Strong impetus for expansion of the field also came from the General Assembly's omnibus resolution expressing its pleasure with the fruits of the 1985 Milan Congress. That resolution, among other items, invited the Committee on Crime Prevention and Control:

at its ninth session, to review the Milan Plan of Action, the resolutions and recommendations unanimously adopted by the Seventh United Nations

---

46. G.A. Res. 35/209, U.N. GAOR, 35th Sess., Supp. No. 48, at 235, U.N. Doc. A/35/48 (1981).

47. *See* Chapter 4 *supra*, at note 29. There is some mild sanction of "shame" on states that continue to be listed as "retentionist" in the Secretary-General's summaries of the periodic reports. States that moved in an abolitionist direction could, on the other hand, expect some positive reinforcement in the next Secretary-General's Report.

48. E.S.C. Res. 1984/50, U.N. ESCOR, Supp. No. 1, at 33, U.N. Doc. E/1984/84 (1984), discussed in Chapter 4 *supra*, at notes 28–42. The Safeguards resolution was adopted in the same ECOSOC Session as the Procedures on the Standard Minimum Rules. *Supra* this Chapter, at notes 25–42.

Congress . . . and their implications for the programmes of the United Nations system and to make specific recommendations on the implementation thereof in its report to the Economic and Social Council at its first regular session of 1986.[49]

In fact it took the Crime Prevention Committee both its Ninth and Tenth Sessions to deal, albeit not tidily, with this task. It did so in a series of resolutions and parts of resolutions forwarded for ECOSOC approval.

ECOSOC Resolution 1986/10, adopted on the recommendation of the Crime Prevention Committee at its Ninth Session, was a hodge-podge collection of items under the general heading "Implementation of the conclusions of the Seventh United Nations Congress on the Prevention of Crime and the Treatment of Offenders."[50] Particularly germane to the present matter were two parts of the resolution which imposed regular periodic reporting requirements. Part II of the resolution dealt with the Standard Minimum Rules for the Administration of Juvenile Justice ("Beijing Rules").[51] States were invited to inform the Secretary-General every five years, beginning in 1987, of the "progress achieved in the application" of the Rules. The Secretary-General was asked to "report regularly thereon" to the Committee on Crime Prevention and Control.[52]

Under Part V of the resolution, states were invited to inform the Secretary-General every five years, beginning in 1988, "of the progress achieved in the implementation of the Basic Principles of the Independence of the Judiciary, including their dissemination, their incorporation into national legislation, *the problems faced in their implementation at the national level and assistance that might be needed from the Secretary-General*."[53] The Secretary-General was asked to report on the matter to the Eighth Congress.[54]

---

49. G.A. Res. 40/32, U.N. GAOR, 40th Sess., Supp. No. 53, at 204, U.N. Doc. A/40/53 (1985).

50. *Implementation of the Conclusions of the Seventh United Nations Congress on the Prevention of Crime and the Treatment of Offenders*, E.S.C. Res. 1986/10, U.N. ESCOR, Supp. No. 1, at 12, U.S. Doc. E/1986/86 (1986).

51. *See* Chapter 4 *supra*, at notes 57–66.

52. An initial report was made to the Committee on Crime Prevention and Control in 1988 and an updated version of it was before the Eighth Congress as *Implementation of United Nations Standard Minimum Rules for the Administration of Juvenile Justice, Report of the Secretary-General*, U.N. Doc. A/CONF.144/4 (1990).

53. Emphasis added. *See supra* note 26 (on the connection between problems and assistance). The part of the resolution dealing with the Juvenile Rules speaks merely of "progress achieved in the application" of the Rules and does not have the detail of the part on the Judiciary about problems encountered and potential assistance by the Secretary-General. Plainly, there was no set formula agreed upon in the Committee on

Another part of ECOSOC Resolution 1986/10,[55] Part IX, dealt with the Code of Conduct for Law Enforcement Officials. Obliquely, it assumed a requirement to report to the Secretary-General by speaking to the content of such reports. States were asked

to pay particular attention, in informing the Secretary-General of the extent of the implementation and the progress made with regard to the application of the Code, to the use of force and firearms by law enforcement officials, and to provide the Secretary-General with copies of [sic. or?][56] abstracts of laws, regulations and administrative measures concerning the application of the Code, as well as information on possible difficulties in its application.

No time-frame was stated aside from the Secretary-General's obligation to make five-yearly reports to the Crime Prevention Committee, beginning in 1987.[57] Presumably states were supposed to report when asked by the Secretary-General.

Finally, Part III of the 1986 resolution[58] recommended that "continued attention should be given to implementation of the Basic Principles of Justice for Victims of Crime and Abuse of Power . . . ." This attention would occur at the Crime Prevention Committee's next Session.

While the details varied, and no one appeared to be thinking through the whole picture, the movement to expand the field was gathering steam.

There was still no consideration of the general issues involved at the Committee on Crime Prevention and Control's Tenth Session in 1988. Nevertheless, the Crime Prevention Committee produced a series of separate draft resolutions for ECOSOC that heralded an effort to move in much more detail in the direction taken at the previous Session. Included were resolutions entitled Implementation of the Declaration

---

Crime Prevention and Control or the Crime Prevention and Criminal Justice Branch for drafting the reporting requirement, even though the material was incorporated in a single conglomerate resolution.

54. *See Implementation of the Basic Principles on the Independence of the Judiciary, Report of the Secretary-General*, U.N. Doc. A/CONF.144/19 (1990) (Report on the Judiciary for 1990 Congress). *Compare* the request made to the Secretary-General to report "regularly" to the *Committee* on the Beijing Rules, *supra* note 52. Ultimately, in that instance, the Secretary-General reported to the Congress as well as to the Committee on Crime Prevention and Control. *Id.*

55. *Supra* note 50.

56. The model is the resolution implementing the Standard Minimum Rules, *supra* note 25, and it uses "or."

57. *See Progress made with respect to the implementation of the Code of Conduct for Law Enforcement Officials, Report of the Secretary-General*, U.N. Doc. E/AC.57/1988/8 and Adds 1–2 (1988) (containing the first effort).

58. *Supra* note 50.

of Basic Principles of Justice for Victims of Crime and Abuse of Power,[59] Procedures for the effective implementation of the Basic Principles on the Independence of the Judiciary,[60] Guidelines for the effective implementation of the Code of Conduct for Law Enforcement Officials,[61] Concerted international action against the forms of crime identified in the Milan Plan of Action,[62] Implementation of United Nations standards and norms in crime prevention and criminal justice,[63] Implementation of the safeguards guaranteeing protection of the rights of those facing the death penalty,[64] Effective prevention and investigation of extra-legal, arbitrary, and summary executions,[65] United Nations Standard Minimum Rules for the Administration of Juvenile Justice (Beijing Rules),[66] and Domestic Violence.[67]

No two of the resolutions were exactly alike but they proceeded along substantially similar lines, with a blend of activities to be carried out by states, the Secretariat and the Committee on Crime Prevention and Control. A differently-stated reporting obligation was laid down in the resolution on the Independence of the Judiciary and the reporting obligation apparently imposed in 1986 was clarified in the resolution on the Code of Conduct for Law Enforcement Officials.[68] The general

59. E.S.C. Res. 1989/57, U.N. ESCOR, Supp. No. 1, at 43, U.N. Doc. E/1989/89 (1989).

60. E.S.C. Res. 1989/60, *id.* at 46. This resolution largely tracks the 1984 resolution on implementation of the Standard Minimum Rules. Presumably, the Resolution superseded the 1986 resolution on implementing the Basic Principles. *Supra* note 53.

61. E.S.C. Res. 1989/61, *id.* at 47.

62. E.S.C. Res. 1989/62, *id.* at 48.

63. E.S.C. Res. 1989/63, *id.* at 49.

64. E.S.C. Res. 1989/64, *id.* at 51. *See* Chapter 4 *supra*, at notes 43–47.

65. E.S.C. Res. 1989/65, *id.* at 52. *See* Chapter 4 *supra*, at notes 95–111.

66. E.S.C. Res. 1989/66, *id.* at 54.

67. E.S.C. Res. 1989/67, *id.* at 54.

68. The upshot was that there were now reporting obligations on at least the following:

Standard Minimum Rules for the Treatment of Prisoners, and Procedures for Their Effective Implementation;

Capital Punishment, and Safeguards Guaranteeing Protection of the Rights of Those Facing the Death Penalty;

Code of Conduct for Law Enforcement Officials, and Guidelines for Its Effective Implementation;

United Nations Standard Minimum Rules for the Administration of Juvenile Justice;

Basic Principles on the Independence of the Judiciary, and Procedures for their Implementation;

resolution on implementation of United Nations norms and standards[69] introduced two new elements into the mix.

First, the Secretary-General was requested to prepare a compilation of all existing United Nations standards and norms in crime prevention and criminal justice and publish them in a form similar to that of HUMAN RIGHTS: A COMPILATION OF INTERNATIONAL INSTRUMENTS, the organization's very useful collection of normative texts.[70]

Second, the general resolution called for strengthening the role of the Committee on Crime Prevention and Control, including reviewing the application of existing standards; assisting other United Nations organs with reports and recommendations relating to their work; and fostering more active involvement of its members, *inter alia*, through the designation of resource persons from members on priority topics. In conjunction with this, the Secretary-General was asked to take appropriate action to establish pre-sessional working groups of the Crime Prevention Committee which would prepare items for discussion, oversee the elaboration of questionnaires to be used for reporting, examine replies from governments and other sources of information,

---

Declaration of Basic Principles of Justice for Victims of Crime and Abuse of Power;

Alternatives to Imprisonment and Reduction of the Prison Population;

Implementation of the Recommendations of the Seventh Congress; and

Survey of Crime Trends, Operations of Criminal Justice Systems and Crime Prevention Strategies.

See Provisional agenda of the pre-sessional Working Group on the Implementation of United Nations Standards and Norms in Crime Prevention and Criminal Justice, U.N. Doc. E/AC.57/1990/WG/1 (1990), (containing a list prepared by the Secretariat for the Committee on Crime Prevention and Control). The document also refers to an obligation to report "regularly" concerning the Model Agreement on the Transfer of Foreign Prisoners, but I have been unable to confirm the mandate for this. The document also notes that the Committee on Crime Prevention and Control was mandated to keep the Principles on the effective prevention and investigation of extra-legal, arbitrary and summary execution under constant review. This perhaps implies a reporting obligation.

69. E.S.C. Res. 1989/63, *supra* note 63.

70. Just which were the relevant standards and norms was not defined. By default these standards were left to the Secretariat, in consultation with members of the Committee on Crime Prevention and Control, to make the choices. A preliminary text appeared in time for the Eighth Congress. *Compendium of United Nations Standards and Norms in Crime Prevention and Criminal Justice*, U.N. Doc. A/CONF.144/INF.2 (1990). Revised to include the 1990 instruments, the text was published in 1992. U.N. Doc. ST/CSDHA 16, U.N. Sales Pub. No. E.92.IV.1 (1992). At the time of writing, the Compendium was still available only in English but the Secretariat was negotiating with governments for its production in other languages.

and "identify general problems that may impinge on the effective implementation of standards and norms and recommend viable solutions with action-oriented proposals based on the principles of international co-operation and solidarity." [71]

The model of the 1984 ECOSOC Resolution on implementation of the Standard Minimum Rules is apparent, as is the new part of the venture which proffers a wish by the Crime Prevention Committee and ECOSOC that more use be made of the expertise of the members of the Crime Prevention Committee, both during and between sessions.

Such then, is the package of implementation efforts that had been put together as the countries of the world approached the Eighth Congress in 1990. During that year, both the Committee on Crime Prevention and Control and the Eighth Congress took steps aimed at consolidating and synthesizing the moves just discussed. I turn to these efforts.

G. Efforts at Consolidation (1990)

With the approval by ECOSOC of the implementation resolutions proposed by the Crime Prevention Committee at its Ninth and Tenth sessions in 1986 and 1988, the time was now ripe for reflection on where this was leading. A plethora of reporting requirements now existed, drafted at various times and in varying degrees of detail.[72] Could they be consolidated? Were there some general principles on implementation that might now be formulated?

Along with approving the Crime Prevention Committee's 1988 efforts, ECOSOC at its 1989 Session[73] had also agreed to the establishment by the Secretary-General of pre-sessional working groups of the Crime Prevention Committee with broad terms of reference. Relying on this authority, a group met for two days before the Crime Prevention Committee's February 1990 meeting to consider, under the title "Implementation of United Nations Standards and Norms in Crime Prevention and Criminal Justice," how to begin to synthesize and rationalize a hodge-podge into a system.

The Working Group[74] had before it a number of reports of the

71. E.S.C. Res. 1989/63, *supra* note 63. The pre-sessional working groups were designed on the model of the groups formed by the Commission on Human Rights and its Sub-Commission on Prevention of Discrimination and Protection of Minorities.

72. *Supra* note 68.

73. E.S.C. Res. 1989/63, *supra* note 63.

74. *See Implementation of the Conclusions and Recommendations of the Seventh United Nations Congress on the Prevention of Crime and the Treatment of Offenders, Report of the Pre-Sessional*

Secretary-General made in response to many of the implementation resolutions, and notes verbales and questionnaires used in their preparation. It also examined some other reports on the United Nations human rights program, especially the *Note by the Secretary-General*, on *The effective implementation of international instruments on human rights, including reporting obligations under international instruments of human rights* (the *Alston Report*).[75]

In the course of the discussion,[76] it was suggested that in order to make the best use of resources it might be desirable to cluster or merge certain surveys (including the periodic crime surveys) according to the objectives of the standards concerned. What was described as a tripartite classification of a thematic nature, but which really contained four categories, was suggested: (a) those standards which were basically issues of human rights,[77] such as the Standard Minimum Rules, the Death Penalty Safeguards, and the Principles on the Effective Prevention and Investigation of Extra-Legal, Arbitrary and Summary Executions; (b) those standards which were concerned with promoting or protecting the integrity of criminal justice administration, such as the Code of Conduct for Law Enforcement Officials, the Basic Principles on the Independence of the Judiciary, the Standard Minimum Rules for the Administration of Juvenile Justice, the Basic Principles on the Role of Lawyers, the Basic Principles on the Role of Prosecutors, and the Standard Minimum Rules for Non-Custodial Measures; and c) those standards which were essentially matters of administration, such as model treaties on extradition, mutual assistance and transfer of proceedings in criminal matters, and transfer of supervision of foreign offenders who have been conditionally sentenced or conditionally released. In addition, reports were also required on what were referred

---

Working Group, U.N. Doc. E/AC.57/1990/WG.2 (1990) [hereinafter *Report of the Pre-Sessional Working Group*].

75. U.N. Doc. A/44/668 (1989) [hereinafter *Alston Report*].

76. *Report of the Pre-Sessional Working Group*, *supra* note 74, at 9.

77. A narrower concept of human rights is being used here than I have adopted for my general purposes in this book. It seems to equate human rights with civil and political rights (or even more narrowly with only some civil and political rights). Perhaps the category would be better called "individual human rights in the administration of justice." So long, however, as it is realized that the descriptions of the categories are for purposes of the present analysis, there is no need to get into the potential semantic argument. *See United Nations Norms and Guidelines in Crime Prevention and Criminal Justice, Working Paper prepared by the Secretariat*, at 24, U.N. Doc. A/CONF.144/18 (1990) [hereinafter *1990 Congress Working Paper*] (in which the Secretariat describes the category as "basically issues of penal policy or the administration of justice and human rights." This is still vague but is clearer than the Crime Prevention Committee's formulation.)

to as "more general subjects," such as crime trends, the Milan Plan of Action, the Guiding Principles for Crime Prevention and Criminal Justice in the Context of Development and a New International Economic Order, and the Declaration on Basic Principles of Justice for Victims of Crime and Abuse of Power.[78]

The categories are hardly water-tight or mutually exclusive. One might wonder whether the instruments have all been located in the correct categories. (For example, the instrument on Victims probably belongs in the "human rights" category.) However, the basic priorities suggested in the Working Group make relative sense and suggest that the highest priority would be given to the issues of "human rights,"[79] followed by those concerned with the "integrity of the system," especially as regards matters for which there were particular grounds of concern, for example the Code of Conduct for Law Enforcement Officials. Matters of administration would take the next lowest position and it seems that "general" matters would be at the bottom of the resource pile.[80]

Devising some rough and ready categories also suggested different ways in which any implementation body might operate in different contexts, ways other than simply reporting and sharing information.[81] Thus, it was noted that human rights issues (as defined) are by their nature an area where fact-finding is difficult. There might be a case in this context for an "implementation body" formed either by members of the Crime Prevention Committee or by other experts who would be entitled to visit countries, to make enquiries at first hand, and to report their findings. Resources would need to be allocated, and there would be some difficult issues such as whether the body could demand access to institutions, or receive representations from organizations and individuals, and about its relationship with other human rights bodies. "While these issues were not addressed in detail," the Report asserts, "it was considered doubtful whether the implementation of the relevant instruments could be effectively monitored without a body of this kind."[82]

78. *See Report of the Pre-Sessional Working Group, supra* note 74, at 9.

79. It does not appear that either the Working Group or the full Committee on Crime Prevention and Control was trying to develop a hierarchical ranking of the organization's norms in order of importance. At most, they were concerned with a kind of triage approach to the allocation of scarce resources in which violations affecting identifiable people and situations would have the first claim.

80. *See Report of the Pre-Sessional Working Group, supra* note 74, at 9.

81. *Id.* at 10.

82. *Id.* The *Report of the Pre-Sessional Working Group,* at 11, notes a way in which the Secretariat is already involving itself in the area and of which more might be made. "It was further noted that the Director-General of the United Nations Office at Vienna had

Issues concerning the integrity of the criminal justice system, it was suggested, did not lend themselves so readily to this kind of inspection. "They involved training for those who worked in criminal justice services, public information and accountability, and political and managerial commitment at ministerial and top management levels."[83]

Some discussion also occurred in the working group on the relationship between the work in the area of crime prevention and criminal justice and other parts of the United Nations human rights system. The value of the existing standards, not only for the criminal justice program itself but also for the work of the Human Rights Committee, was stressed "as demonstrated by the Committee's recent reports."[84] Coordination could be enhanced by inviting representatives of other bodies to participate in sessions of the Crime Prevention Committee and vice versa.[85]

---

contributed, through her good offices, to the commutation of the death sentences imposed on juveniles under 18 years of age at the time of the crime, and the amendment, by the country concerned, of its Juvenile Offenders Act, in 1989, raising the minimum age for the imposition of a death sentence to 18 years." This kind of action is also relevant to the notion of "contacts" mentioned in note 31 *supra. See infra* note 89. *See also* B. Ramcharan, Humanitarian Good Offices in International Law (1983) (discussion the whole question of "good offices" by the Secretariat). The involvement of the Vienna Office in this is known only to the initiated. A possible model for a committee authorized to make inspections is the committee set up under the European Convention for the Protection of Detainees from Torture and from Cruel, Inhuman or Degrading Treatment or Punishment, drafted in 1987. *See* A. Cassese, *A New Approach to Human Rights: The European Convention for the Prevention of Torture*, 83 Am. J. Int'l L. 128 (1989).

83. *Id.*

84. *Id.* at 11. The reference is presumably to questioning of states representatives using benchmarks such as the Standard Minimum Rules for the Treatment of Prisoners as indicative of what the obligations are under the criminal justice provisions of the Covenant on Civil and Political Rights, *supra* note 26. *See* Chapter 10 *infra* at notes 59–60 (citing some examples).

85. It was further recommended, *id.*, that the Chair of the Crime Prevention Committee or a representative should be invited to attend the periodic coordination meetings of the chairs of the human rights treaty bodies. This coordination meeting, which occurred in 1984, 1988, 1990 and 1992 is taking on a significant life as a serious part of the United Nations supervisory system. The meeting is attended by the Chairs or other representatives of the Human Rights Committee, the Committee on Economic, Social and Cultural Rights, the Committee on the Elimination of Racial Discrimination, the Committee on the Elimination of Discrimination Against Women, the Committee Against Torture and the Group of Three established under the International Convention on the Suppression and Punishment of the Crime of Apartheid. *See generally, Report of the fourth meeting of persons chairing the human rights treaty bodies*, in *Note by the Secretary-General, Effective implementation of international instruments on human rights, including reporting obligations under international instruments on human rights*, U.N. Doc. A/47/628 (1992). The participation of the Chair of the expert Committee on Crime Prevention and Control may just have been appropriate, although this would mean redefining the category as "expert" committees rather than "treaty-based" committees. The creation of the new Commission

The resolution ultimately proposed by the Working Group, and approved by the full Crime Prevention Committee and later by ECOSOC,[86] reiterated the now familiar lines of approach that can be traced back to the 1984 ECOSOC Resolution on the Standard Minimum Rules. States were exhorted to institutionalize the norms and standards[87] in their laws and practices and to encourage teaching and publicity of them. The states were requested to report to the Secretary-General on their efforts at implementation. In turn, the Secretary-General was asked to ensure the widest possible dissemination of the standards[88] and of the periodic reports on their implementation. Technical assistance would be encouraged. The regional and inter-regional

---

probably renders the idea moot since the Chairs of other relevant functional ECOSOC Commissions, notably the Commission on Human Rights, the Commission on Social Development, and the Commission on the Status of Women, do not attend. The idea could arise again should the Commission create a sub-group of independent experts.

86. E.S.C. Res. 1990/21, U.N. ESCOR, Supp. No. 1, at 23, U.N. Doc. E/1990/90 (1990).

87. As in the case of ECOSOC's general resolution in 1989, E.S.C. Res. 1989/63, *supra* note 63, this 1990 resolution, E.S.C. Res. 1990/21, *supra* note 86, leaves the precise scope of "norms and standards" at large. In three preambular paragraphs, however, ECOSOC "bear[s] in mind" the Milan Plan of Action and the Guiding Principles for Crime Prevention and Criminal Justice in the Context of Development and a New International Economic Order, the Declaration of Basic Principles of Justice for Victims of Crime and Abuse of Power, the Safeguards Guaranteeing Protection of the Rights of Those Facing the Death Penalty, the Code of Conduct for Law Enforcement Officials, the Basic Principles on the Independence of the Judiciary, the Standard Minimum Rules for the Treatment of Prisoners, the United Nations Standard Minimum Rules for the Administration of Juvenile Justice, the Principles on the Effective Prevention and Investigation of Extra-Legal, Arbitrary and Summary Executions, the Model Agreement on the Transfer of Foreign Prisoners, the Procedures for the Effective Implementation of the Standard Minimum Rules for the Treatment of Prisoners, the Procedures for the Effective Implementation of the Basic Principles on the Independence of the Judiciary, and the Guidelines for the Effective Implementation of the Code of Conduct for Law Enforcement Officials. *See also supra* note 70 (on possible content for the term "norms and standards").

88. One premise of this book is that there is widespread ignorance of the whole U.N. Crime Prevention and Criminal Justice Program apart from a few insiders. The Geneva-based human rights program and the New York-based Department of Public Information have been engaged in a vigorous publicity campaign the past few years to raise the visibility of the Geneva program, although that campaign is seen by some as flawed. *See* INTERNATIONAL LEAGUE FOR HUMAN RIGHTS, HUMAN RIGHTS AT THE UNITED NATIONS: A WORLD CAMPAIGN FOR HUMAN RIGHTS (In Brief No. 22) (1989). The Vienna Office and the Department of Public Information in New York went to considerable pains to disseminate material, both of a technical and a popular nature, about the Eighth United Nations Congress on the Prevention of Crime and the Treatment of Offenders. *See 1990 Congress Working Paper, supra* note 77, at 17. It seems likely that this effort at raising visibility in general will continue. The better-heeled Drug Control Program is in a superior position when it comes to producing glossies extolling its work.

United Nations institutes on crime prevention and criminal justice would be involved. The Committee on Crime Prevention and Control was, for its part, to keep the standards under review and follow up their implementation, "including [making] recommendations on the determination of their future application and identification of existing obstacles to, or shortcomings in, their implementation, *inter alia*, through contacts with the Governments of the countries concerned, with a view to suggesting appropriate remedies." The Chair of the Crime Prevention Committee was authorized to designate members of that committee, with due regard to appropriate regional representation, to assist the Crime Prevention Committee in the periods between its sessions in the implementation of specific standards, so long as this was "without financial implications for the United Nations." The practice of convening a pre-sessional working group would continue. Finally, the Eighth Congress was invited to consider the means by which to accord adequate priority to the implementation of existing standards and the possibility of consolidating reporting arrangements.

The content of the resolution suggests that the Committee on Crime Prevention and Control was not yet ready to reach into individual countries to try in an accusatorial way to throw the spotlight of public exposure on violations of criminal justice standards. For the most part, it was still very much in the "promotional" mode which has always characterized much United Nations human rights action. Yet the references in the 1990 resolution to Crime Prevention Committee "contacts" with Governments, and to allotting specific tasks to members, contained some possibilities for development. The term "contacts" was no doubt carefully chosen, perhaps even for its ambiguity. Did it refer to an effort to deal with specific situations? Or was it meant simply to refer to generalized networking? The potential for dealing with particular situations was certainly there.[89]

---

89. *See also* the reference in the Procedures for Implementing the Standard Minimum Rules to "contacts with the judiciary and ministries of justice of the countries concerned." *Supra* note 31. The main model for these interventions seems to be the International Labor Organization's "direct contacts" procedure. It has existed since 1967 in conjunction with the supervisory regime of the Organization's Committee on the Application of Conventions and Recommendations. "Direct contacts" require the consent of the state concerned and entail a meeting between a representative of the Organization and "persons thoroughly acquainted with all aspects of the case, including government representatives with sufficient responsibility and experience to speak with authority about the position in their country and about their own government's attitudes and intentions in the matter." *See Principles Governing the Procedure of Direct Contacts in* HUMAN RIGHTS SOURCEBOOK 513 (A.P. Blaustein, R.S. Clark & J.A. Sigler eds. 1987). In addition to this report-based contact system, the I.L.O. later began using direct contacts as part of its complaint-based system. *See* G. von Potobsky, *The Experience of the ILO, in* INTERNA-

This resolution was certainly the high water mark of the Committee on Crime Prevention and Control's work on implementation before its abolition. Indeed, it was a peak for the program as a whole. In retrospect, the most interesting question, so far unanswered, is whether it represented a model for the future or merely an instructive failure.

Under the 1990 ECOSOC resolution,[90] the Crime Prevention Committee was expected to pursue the matter of its procedures further at its Twelfth Session, which was never held, taking into account a number of "issues":

(a) Measures to increase the level of support to programs of technical co-operation and advisory services in crime prevention and criminal justice to permit more effective implementation, including special projects designed and carried out at the country level and more active involvement of potential funding agencies;

(b) The role of the United Nations, in particular the Committee on Crime Prevention and Control, in promoting the implementation of existing standards, including modalities for strengthening existing review procedures, more active inter-sessional involvement of Crime Prevention Committee members and other experts;

(c) The relationship between the effectiveness of implementation and the work-load of the Crime Prevention Committee and the Secretariat;

(d) The growing burden imposed on many states by the expansion of reporting obligations, and the need for technical assistance;[91]

(e) The problem of inadequate reporting or excessive delays;

(f) The question of additional or alternative sources of information;

(g) The inability of the Crime Prevention and Criminal Justice Branch of the Centre for Social Development and Humanitarian Affairs, for reasons of inadequate staffing and other financial constraints, to provide the Crime Prevention Committee with the administrative and technical support it would require.

This list of issues demonstrates both the resolve to forge ahead and a realistic tallying of the obstacles to further movement.

TIONAL LAW AND FACT-FINDING IN THE FIELD OF HUMAN RIGHTS 160, 164 (B. Ramcharan ed. 1982). The Committee on Crime Prevention and Control's tentative hints seem to be in the direction of report-based efforts rather than starting a complaint system, but there is always the possibility of evolution.

90. *Supra* note 86, para. 6.

91. *See Alston Report, supra* note 75, at 21–22; *Report of the fourth meeting of persons chairing the human rights treaty bodies, supra* note 85, at 11–12.

H. The Eighth Congress (1990)

The Eighth Congress added significantly to the reporting work-load. Reports were required by the resolutions adopting the Standard Minimum Rules for Non-Custodial Measures (the Tokyo Rules),[92] the Guidelines for the Prevention of Juvenile Delinquency (the Riyadh Guidelines),[93] the Standard Minimum Rules for the Protection of Juveniles Deprived of Their Liberty,[94] the Basic Principles on the Use of Force and Firearms by Law Enforcement Officials,[95] the Basic Principles on the Role of Lawyers,[96] and the Guidelines on the Role of Prosecutors.[97]

Along with adding to the implementation work-load, the Eighth Congress adopted a strong resolution recommending that "the role of the Committee on Crime Prevention and Control should be supported so as to enable it to function more effectively as the monitoring body for United Nations norms and guidelines in the field of criminal justice and to assist the Economic and Social Council with recommendations."[98] The resolution requested that the Secretary-General, subject to the provision of extra-budgetary funds, convene an *ad hoc* group of experts which would submit concrete proposals to the Crime Prevention Committee at its Twelfth Session for (a) promoting the implementation of existing standards; (b) consolidating and rationalizing arrangements for the effective evaluation and monitoring of the standards; and (c) improving the techniques to aid in such evaluations.[99]

92. G.A. Res. 45/110, U.N. GAOR, 45th Sess., Supp. No. 49A, at 195, U.N. Doc. A/45/49 (1991) (quinquennial reporting).

93. G.A. Res. 45/112, *id.* at 200 (reporting "regularly").

94. G.A. Res. 45/113, *id.* at 204 (reporting "regularly").

95. Other instrument 2, *Eighth United Nations Congress on the Prevention of Crime and the Treatment of Offenders, Havana, 27 August-7 September 1990, Report Prepared by the Secretariat,* at 110, U.N. Doc. A/CONF.144/28/Rev.1 (1991) (quinquennial reporting).

96. Other instrument 3, *id.* at 117 (quinquennial reporting).

97. Other resolution 26, *id.* at 188 (quinquennial reporting).

98. Other resolution 29, *Development of future procedures for evaluating the extent to which Member States implement United Nations norms and guidelines in criminal justice and crime prevention, Report of the Eighth Congress, supra* note 95, at 197.

99. *Id.* para. 1. Some suggestions were made in the resolution about possible techniques for improving the process such as statistical studies and pilot surveys. *Id.* para. 2. In connection with pilot studies, reference is made to a suggestion said to be in contained paragraph 110 of the 1990 *Report of the Secretary-General on the implementation of the Standard Minimum Rules for the Treatment of Prisoners,* U.N. Doc. A/CONF.144/11 discussed in Chapter 6 at notes 111–139. Paragraph 110 does not in fact contain this particular (sensible) idea, but it does have several others, including the suggestions that "Arrangements should be made to enable countries to be referred to for the purposes of clarifying any replies where there could be uncertainty in interpretation," and "It would

I. The 1991 Meeting of Experts

The expectation of the Eighth Congress was thus that a group of experts would make some further suggestions to the Committee on Crime Prevention and Control in time for its 1992 meeting. By the time that the Experts met, however, it was apparent that the Crime Prevention Committee would most likely be abolished. Accordingly, the Meeting of Experts reported in a general way and its report became part of the documentation for the first meeting of the Commission on Crime Prevention and Criminal Justice.[100]

Particular attention was given at the Meeting of Experts to matters of technical assistance and to what the group described as "monitoring."

The development of technical cooperation projects was encouraged.[101] Such projects should take into account, and be coordinated with, those of various United Nations agencies and programs, and those of other agencies.[102] Additional interregional and regional advisers[103] should, in the view of the Meeting of Experts, be appointed on either a permanent or an ad hoc basis. Their mandate should include the promotion and implementation of United Nations standards, and the provision of technical assistance for the monitoring process.[104]

According to the participants in the meeting, monitoring should be recognized as an essential component of the implementation process. The principal purpose of monitoring is to know as accurately as possible what has already been achieved in order to implement standards. Such knowledge will enable measures to be taken to tackle difficulties in implementing the standards.[105] Moreover, since effective monitoring requires considerable resources, which are beyond the current capabilities of the United Nations, the Meeting of Experts proposed

---

also help invaluably if independent observers were invited to assist in the interpretation of the replies when they have been received." *Id.* at 28–29, para. 110.

100. *See Note by the Secretary-General, Conclusions and recommendations of the Meeting of Experts for the Evaluation of Implementation of United Nations Norms and Guidelines in Crime Prevention and Criminal Justice, Vienna, 14–16 October 1991*, U.N. Doc. E/CN.15/1992/4/Add.4 (1992) [hereinafter *Meeting of Experts*]. Most of the necessary extrabudgetary funds were provided by the Government of the United Kingdom, with contributions from Canada and from the European Institute for Crime Prevention and Control affiliated with the United Nations. There was little discussion of the report of the *Meeting of Experts* at the first two meetings of the Commission on Crime Prevention and Criminal Justice. *See* Chapter 10 *infra*, at notes 1–4 (describing the action taken).

101. *Id.* at 7. *See* Chapter 3 *supra*, at notes 39–43, Chapter 8 *supra*, at notes 158–151, & Chapter 10 *infra*, at notes 79–95 (describing, in general, technical assistance).

102. *Meeting of Experts*, *supra* note 100, at 7.

103. *See* Chapter 3 *supra*, at notes 42 & 43 (detailing the role of the "regional advisers").

104. *Id.*

105. *Id.* at 8. *See supra* note 26 (analysing the concept of "difficulties").

that new structures should be established to provide effective monitoring. These structures should involve the creation by the Commission on Crime Prevention and Criminal Justice of a subgroup to advise on overall monitoring policy and practice, and of working groups to take responsibility for monitoring work on one or more standards.[106] The experts also recommended that there should be an established procedure for referring back to individual countries for clarification of particular responses. Member States should be invited to name a contact person for this purpose.[107] Further, information should be sought on both the *de jure* and the *de facto* situations, with care taken to avoid ambiguity as to which situation a particular question, or piece of information supplied, refers.[108]

The Meeting of Experts also gave some tentative thought to the matter of "thematic" priorities.[109] It was acknowledged that, given limited resources, it was obviously impossible to give equal attention to all of the organization's standards and guidelines. Referring to the work of the 1990 pre-sessional working group of the Committee on Crime Prevention and Control,[110] the Meeting of Experts suggested that a further effort might be made to develop categories of different norms and standards. Concluding on this point, the Meeting of Experts suggested that "Priority might be assigned on the basis of the further development of such categories, and the categorizations might also suggest different strategies for implementing different categorizations of standards."[111]

J. Conclusion

A variety of ideas on implementation had been floated during the life of the Committee on Crime Prevention and Control, but the system was suffering from near-terminal overload. Thus some crucial questions of rationale and strategy remained for the new Commission on Crime Prevention and Criminal Justice. In the next chapter, I turn to some of these questions and try to put the tentative moves made so far in the Crime Prevention Commission into perspective.

106. *Id.* The participants obviously had in mind what became paragraphs 27 and 28 of the Annex to G.A. Res. 46/152. U.N. GAOR, 46th Sess., Supp. No. 49, at 217, U.N. Doc. A/46/49 (1992) (on Creation of an Effective United Nations Crime Prevention and Criminal Justice Programme). *See* Chapter 2 *supra*, at notes 80–97 (discussing these provisions). *See also* Chapter 10 *infra*, note 3.

107. *Id.* at 10. *See supra* note 6; Chapter 10 *infra*, at notes 49–58 (idea of supplementing information goes back at least to 1957 but has lain dormant).

108. *Id.*

109. *See supra*, text accompanying notes 76–83.

110. *Id.*

111. *Meeting of Experts*, *supra* note 100, at 3.

Chapter 10
Implementation: What the Future Might Hold

A. Introduction

In the crush of business at the inaugural meeting of the Commission on Crime Prevention and Criminal Justice in 1992, the question of the implementation of norms and standards did not play a prominent role. Nevertheless, it was the subject of a draft resolution introduced by France on behalf also of Austria, Canada, the Netherlands, and the United Kingdom. The two most important preambular paragraphs and the operative paragraph of the draft are sufficiently interesting to reproduce in full:

Recalling . . . Commission on Human Rights resolution 1992/31 of 28 February 1992, entitled "Human rights in the administration of justice", in which that Commission invited the Commission on Crime Prevention and Criminal Justice to explore ways and means of cooperating with the human rights programme in the field of the administration of justice, with special emphasis on the effective implementation of standards and norms, . . .

Noting the large number of United Nations standards and the consequent need for new structures in order to provide for the effective implementation and monitoring of those standards,

Decides to establish, at its second session, a sessional working group on implementation entrusted with the task of advising the Commission on Crime Prevention and Criminal Justice and preparing its work on the implementation, including the monitoring, of United Nations standards and norms in the field of crime prevention and criminal justice, especially with a view to selecting priorities and ascertaining how the practical work involved should best be carried out.[1]

Reaction to the draft was mixed. While some representatives were enthusiastic, others thought that it was far too early to commit the

---

1. U.N. Doc. E/CN.15/1992/L.12 (1992), reprinted in *Report of the Commission on Crime Prevention and Criminal Justice on its First Session, Vienna, 21 to 30 April 1992*, at 76, U.N. ESCOR, Supp. No. 10, U.N. Doc. E/1992/30 (1992).

limited resources of the Crime Prevention Commission to the setting up of even a sessional working group on this part of its work. The upshot was that the draft was withdrawn when an appropriate paragraph was included in what ultimately became the Economic and Social Council's omnibus resolution on the work of the Crime Prevention Commission. This paragraph made the consideration of standards and norms a standing item on the agenda of the Crime Prevention Commission[2] and the item was duly discussed in the 1993 session. It can reasonably be expected that the effort to create some expert structure[3] to enhance the monitoring process will be repeated in later sessions of the Commission on Crime Prevention and Criminal Justice. At its session in 1993, the Commission on Crime Prevention and Criminal Justice discussed the norms and standards item in a working group of the whole. In practice this meant that whoever from among the representatives of members of the Crime Prevention Commission and observer states turned up participated. Something on a smaller and more expert scale might be expected for the future.

At the 1993 session of the Commission on Crime Prevention and Criminal Justice, it became apparent that the reporting system had ground to a halt and that a decision had been made within the Secretariat simply to devote no resources to it. Accordingly, a decision was made to begin again in a modest way "a process of information-gathering to be undertaken by means of surveys."[4] Since it was not believed to be possible to tackle everything at once, initial efforts would be made in respect of the Standard Minimum Rules for the Treatment of Pris-

---

2. E.S.C. Res. 1992/22, U.N. ESCOR, Supp. No. 1, at 22, U.N. Doc. E/1992/92 (1992). Pt. VII, para. 3 of the resolution provided that "the Commission should include in its agenda, beginning at its second session, a standing item on the existing United Nations standards and norms in the field of crime prevention and criminal justice, which serve as recommendations to Member States, and on, *inter alia*, their use and application." "Use and application" was the best language that could be obtained in the face of opposition from states that were unenthusiastic about "implementation" or "monitoring." The Secretariat reported to the Commission in *Existing United Nations standards and norms, which serve as recommendations to Member States, in the field of crime prevention and criminal justice in the light of and including their use and application, Report of the Secretary-General,* U.N. Doc. E/CN.15/1993/6 (1993).

3. The 1992 proposal for a sessional working group evidently entailed choosing the members of the group from among those representing their governments at the Commission meeting. *See,* however, *Creation of an Effective United Nations Crime Prevention and Criminal Justice Programme,* G.A. Res. 46/152, U.N. GAOR, 46th Sess., Supp. No. 49, Annex, para. 28, U.N. Doc. A/46/49 (1992) (contemplating the possibility of creating an expert body, not necessarily confined to meeting during sessions of the Commission for such purposes as these). *See also* Chapter 2 *supra,* at notes 80–97; Chapter 9 *supra,* at notes 81–82, 105–106.

4. E.S.C. Res. 1993/34, pt. III. para. 7 (1993).

oners, the Code of Conduct for Law Enforcement Officials (together with the Basic Principles on the Use of Force and Firearms by Law Enforcement Officials), the Declaration of Basic Principles of Justice for Victims of Crime and Abuse of Power, and the Basic Principles on the Independence of the Judiciary. Underlying all of the discussion on the process was an appreciation that, in a world of limited resources, not everything can be done at once by any international implementation system.[5] Thus, in a rough and ready way, the United Nations has opted in the human rights area to give most emphasis to the Universal Declaration of Human Rights, the two Covenants and the Convention on the Elimination of All Forms of Racial Discrimination. The International Labor Organization has emphasised giving effect to its conventions on freedom of association as being crucial to the survival of a healthy trade union movement,[6] although it has concentrated on other material as well. The Commission on Crime Prevention and Criminal Justice will face a continuing need to marshal the resources of the program.

Above and beyond the question of priorities, the 1992 draft resolution and the discussion in 1992 and 1993 suggests that future efforts at implementation might be considered broadly under four categories: efforts involving reporting and monitoring; efforts at encouraging the use by the human rights organs of the United Nations system of the norms and standards created in the crime and criminal justice part; advisory services and other kinds of technical assistance; and the creation of other implementation mechanisms. Some comments will be made in the following sections about each of these categories.

B. Reporting: Its Rationale and Associated Problems

"Reporting mechanisms lie at the very heart of the United Nations system for the promotion of standards in the administration of justice and human rights."[7] So said the Secretariat in a report to the 1990 Congress. Needless to say, the Committee on Crime Prevention and Control, in taking the initiatives discussed in Chapter 9, did not invent

5. *See also* discussion of priorities in Chapter 9 *supra*, at notes 76–89.

6. *See* R. KIRGIS, INTERNATIONAL ORGANIZATIONS IN THEIR LEGAL SETTING 294, 413–25 (2d ed. 1993). And note Res. 1/1 of the Commission on Crime Prevention and Criminal Justice, entitled *Strategic management by the Commission on Crime Prevention and Criminal Justice of the United Nations crime prevention and criminal justice programme*, Report of the Commission on Crime Prevention and Criminal Justice on its First Session, *supra* note 1, at 38.

7. *United Nations Norms and Guidelines in Crime Prevention and Criminal Justice, Working Paper prepared by the Secretariat*, at 12, U.N. Doc. A/CONF.144/18 (1990) [hereinafter *1990 Congress Working Paper*].

the idea of reporting. There now exists a substantial history within the international system of efforts to create effective supervisory regimes based on reporting. Indeed, the Crime Prevention Committee merely acted against that backdrop, taking for granted that a reporting system is useful. Some examination of this premise and of its practical application is in order. It is also worth noting at the outset that it is not only in international law that self-reporting is relied upon as a supervisory device. Consider, for example, the regulation of insurance companies, banks, and casinos by such means. Similarly, the accreditation bodies of universities also rely heavily on the universities' "self-studies."

The history of reporting as an international human rights mechanism begins with the work of the International Labor Organization in the 1920s which sought to give effect both to ratified conventions and to recommendations,[8] and with the efforts of the League of Nations in dealing with minorities and with mandated territories.[9] Experience with reporting continued into the United Nations era, initially primarily in relation to obligations assumed in the Charter in respect of non-self-governing territories.[10] Reporting requirements, with some organ to read and comment on the reports, were written into the major human rights treaty regimes, notably the International Convention on the Elimination of All Forms of Racial Discrimination,[11] the Interna-

8. *See* E. LANDY, THE EFFECTIVENESS OF INTERNATIONAL SUPERVISION: THIRTY YEARS OF I.L.O. EXPERIENCE (1966). The I.L.O. is widely held up as a model of a successful monitoring regime. Article 19 of the I.L.O. Constitution requires reports both in respect of ratified conventions and in respect of recommendations, thus blurring the distinction between "legal" and other obligations. That the obligation to report is of constitutional dimensions obviously strengthens the position of the I.L.O. machinery.

9. *See generally* R.S. CLARK, A UNITED NATIONS HIGH COMMISSIONER FOR HUMAN RIGHTS 6–7 (1972).

10. U.N. CHARTER, art. 73 (non-self-governing territories in general), art. 88 (trust territories). In supporting the creation of the voluntary human rights reporting procedures discussed in Chapter 9 *supra*, at notes 43–46, and mechanisms to examine the reports, Mrs. Lord of the United States noted that "a similar procedure adopted with respect to information from non-self-governing territories had proved satisfactory." U.N. Doc. E/CN.4/SR.515, at 5–6 (1956). Reporting on trust and other non-self-governing territories was specifically required by the Charter. In the case of trust territories, the Charter also set up an organ, the Trusteeship Council, one of the functions of which was to to examine reports. Various committees were created over the years to examine reports from other non-self-governing territories. The challenge in the crime prevention and criminal justice area is whether something could be made of a system where neither the reports, nor the mechanism, are specifically mandated in treaty obligations.

11. G.A. Res. 2106A (XX), U.N. GAOR, 20th Sess., Supp. No. 14, at 47, U.N. Doc. A/6014 (1966). *See* K. Das, *Measures of Implementation of the International Convention on the Elimination of All Forms of Racial Discrimination with Special Reference to the Provisions Concerning Reports from States Parties to the Convention*, 4 HUM. RTS. J. 213 (1971).

tional Covenant on Economic, Social and Cultural Rights,[12] the International Covenant on Civil and Political Rights,[13] the Convention on the Elimination of Discrimination Against Women,[14] the Convention Against Torture and Other Cruel, Inhuman or Degrading Treatment or Punishment[15] and the Convention on the Rights of the Child.[16] There are two key aspects to such regimes. The first aspect is how seriously states take their reporting obligations and the second is how effective the relevant committee is able to be in overseeing this activity.

A "general comment"[17] issued in 1989 by the Committee on Economic, Social and Cultural Rights[18] endeavors to summarize the main objects of reporting. While some of the arguments are especially relevant to the particular treaty regime there involved, all of them are apposite to reporting in general and are worth recalling in the present context.

The comment begins with a broad statement of the objectives of the reporting requirements. This statement is interesting in its emphasis on what the reporting process can achieve *within the state concerned*. Its

12. G.A. Res. 2200 (XXI), U.N. GAOR, 21st Sess., Supp. No. 16, at 49, U.N. Doc. A/6316 (1967).

13. *Id.* at 52.

14. G.A. Res. 34/180, U.N. GAOR, 34th Sess., Supp. No. 46, at 193, U.N. Doc.A/34/46 (1980).

15. G.A. Res. 39/46, U.N. GAOR, 39th Sess., Supp. No. 51, at 197, U.N. Doc.A/39/51 (1985).

16. G.A. Res. 44/25, U.N. GAOR, 44th Sess., Supp. No. 49, at 166, U.N. Doc.A/44/49 (1990). The Committee on the Rights of the Child is the most recent to be created. *See United Nations Centre for Human Rights, Workshop on international human rights instruments and reporting obligations; preparation of reports to United Nations human rights treaty bodies, Moscow, 26–30 August 1991,* U.N. Doc. HR/PUB/91/5 (1992) (giving some useful comments on reporting to the treaty bodies).

17. Like other treaty committees, the Economic, Social and Cultural Committee is empowered to issue general comments. It has explained their purpose thus:

The Committee endeavors, through its general comments, to make the experience gained so far through the examination of these reports available for the benefit of all States parties in order to assist and promote their further implementation of the Covenant; to draw the attention of the States parties to insufficiencies disclosed by a large number of reports; to suggest improvements in the reporting procedures and to stimulate the activities of the States parties, the international organizations and the specialized agencies concerned in achieving progressively and effectively the full realization of the rights recognized in the Covenant.

Committee on Economic, Social and Cultural Rights, Report on the Third Session, 6–24 February 1989, U.N. ESCOR, Supp. No. 4, at 87, U.N. Doc. E/1989/22 (1989).

18. *Id.* [hereinafter *CESCR General Comment No. 1.*]

emphasis is similar to the basic thrust of the Crime Prevention and Criminal Justice Program's own not so clearly articulated efforts:

> The reporting obligations . . . are designed *principally* to assist each State party in fulfilling its obligations under the Covenant and, *in addition*, to provide a basis on which the [Economic and Social] Council, assisted by the Committee, can discharge its responsibilities for monitoring States parties' compliance with their obligations.[19]

The Economic and Social Committee insisted that the obligation to report is more than a formal, procedural responsibility. In the Economic and Social Committee's view, the processes of preparation and submission of the reports can and should serve a variety of more detailed objectives. Seven of these "objectives" are noted in the comment.

The first objective, particularly relevant to a country's first report, "is to ensure that a comprehensive review is undertaken with respect to national legislation, administrative rules and procedures, and practices in an effort to ensure the fullest possible conformity with the Covenant."[20] Such a review would presumably involve many different governmental agencies and other authorities, such as domestic Human Rights Commissions, concerned with various aspects of the norms in question.[21]

A second objective "is to ensure that the State party monitors the

19. *Id.* (emphasis added) The Committee's Rapporteur had previously suggested a similar emphasis in the course of a discussion of the role of reporting somewhat along the lines of the general comment. "It is often assumed that the ultimate test of a reporting system lies in what happens at the international level. By contrast, the range of functions identified above places the international monitoring component of the process in a secondary or supportive role. This emphasis has important implications for the Committee's approach to supervision since it makes clear that the principal burden of devising appropriate methods for implementation falls upon individual governments rather than on the Committee, the United Nations, or the specialized agencies." P. Alston, *Out of the Abyss: The Challenges Confronting the New U.N. Committee on Economic, Social and Cultural Rights*, 9 Hum. Rts. Q. 332, 356 (1987).

20. *CESCR General Comment No. 1, supra* note 18, at 88. Rosalyn Higgins, an experienced member of the Human Rights Committee has suggested that: "The very knowledge that legislation and other public acts will be scrutinized and measured against the requirements of the Covenant is an incentive to check proposed legislation or administrative decrees against the requirements of the Covenant. It is an encouragement to *a priori* compliance. The preparation of the reports is also a salutary exercise." R. Higgins, *Some thoughts on the implementation of human rights*, 89/1 Bulletin of Human Rights 60, 62–63 (1989).

21. I have explored this type of comprehensive review exercise more fully in another context in R. Clark, *Preventing and Combating Intolerance of Religion or Belief*, 20 World Ord. 19, 22–24 (1985–86).

actual situation with respect to each of the rights on a regular basis and is thus aware of the extent to which the various rights are, or are not, being enjoyed by all individuals within its territory or under its jurisdiction."[22] This is a time-consuming and costly process, as the Economic and Social Committee notes, and international assistance of a technical nature may be necessary to enable some states to fulfill their duties.

The main value of such an overview is to provide the basis for the elaboration of careful policies to give effect to international obligations. Hence, a third objective of reporting "is to enable the government to demonstrate that such principled policy-making has in fact been undertaken."[23]

A fourth objective "is to facilitate public scrutiny of government policies . . . and to encourage the involvement of the various economic, social and cultural sectors of society in the formulation, implementation and review of the relevant policies." [24] Thus, "the preparation of the report, and its consideration at the national level, can come to be of at least as much value as the constructive dialogue conducted at the international level between the Committee and representatives of the reporting State."[25] Properly done, with adequate publicity and involve-

---

22. *ESCR General Comment No. 1, supra* note 18, at 88. Democratic administrations are likely to carry out such reviews from time to time, even in the absence of a need to provide particular reports to international bodies; and international yardsticks have a part to play on such occasions. A 1988 review of the prisons system led the New Zealand Department of Justice to consider its own performance alongside the United Nations Standard Minimum Rules for the Treatment of Prisoners. *See* PRISONS IN CHANGE: THE SUBMISSION OF THE DEPARTMENT OF JUSTICE TO THE MINISTERIAL COMMITTEE OF INQUIRY INTO THE PRISONS SYSTEM, 83–93 (1988) (appendices). The Department's submission was noted in Chapter 5 *supra*, at note 70. The Ministerial Committee commented that:

> It is true . . . that in some respects conditions in New Zealand are in advance of the Rules, and their spirit has been embodied in some legislation bearing on prison administration.
>
> In other areas it is clear from our inspection of prisons and the submissions we received that neither the Rules nor their spirit are being complied with. . . . Clear examples of non-compliance with the Rules were to be found in accommodation in some institutions, with the use of toilet pots in poorly ventilated cells where inmates also had their meals; clothing in poor condition or short supply; inadequate complaints procedures; inadequate staff training; deficiencies in medical and dental care; and unacceptable shortcomings in the hearing of disciplinary charges.

The Committee also expressed its concern that the Rules were not specifically covered in the training course for prison administrators. MINISTERIAL COMMITTEE OF INQUIRY INTO THE PRISONS SYSTEM, PRISON REVIEW. TE ARA HOU: THE NEW WAY 190–191 (1989).

23. *ESCR General Comment No. 1, supra* note 18, at 88.

24. *Id.*

25. *Id.* at 89.

ment of a wide range of governmental and non-governmental actors, the review could constitute a substantial national self-examination and debate.[26]

A fifth objective is designed to provide

a basis on which the State party itself, as well as the Committee, can effectively evaluate the extent to which progress has been made towards the realization of the obligations contained in the Covenant. For this purpose, it may be useful for States to identify specific bench-marks or goals against which their performance in a given area can be assessed.[27]

To a degree, this objective is most applicable to international instruments that, like the Economic, Social and Cultural Covenant, require by their own terms "progressive realization" of the obligations contained therein, that is to say that they will be made operative in successive stages.[28] Some of the instruments which come under the aegis of the Crime Prevention and Criminal Justice Program, such as those on prevention of juvenile delinquency and of crime in general, on domestic violence, and even some aspects of the Standard Minimum Rules for the Treatment of Prisoners, proceed on a basis of progressive realization. Thus, the idea of creating benchmarks makes enormous sense for them. Other crime prevention and criminal justice standards are more akin to the obligations under the Covenant on Civil and Political Rights

---

26. The possibilities of such activity are suggested by the commentary—notably on capital and corporal punishment, prison conditions and freedom of speech—that the Human Rights Association of St. Vincent and the Grenadines did on its government's initial report for the Human Rights Committee. U.N. Doc. HR/CT/47 (1990). Undoubtedly, the Government's representative was deeply embarrassed in New York. *See Report of the Human Rights Committee*, vol.I, at 56–62, U.N. GAOR, 45th Sess., Supp. No. 40, U.N. Doc. A/45/40 (1990) (providing a sanitized account of his grilling). The report under the Covenant had evidently been prepared without any consultation. An earlier involvement of the populace could have been most productive. *See infra* note 53; P. Alston, *Implementing economic, social and cultural rights: the functions of reporting obligations*, 89/1 BULLETIN OF HUMAN RIGHTS 5, 11 (1989) (concluding "In the final analysis, if the reporting process succeeds in stimulating a genuine national dialogue about those rights, it will have achieved an enormous amount.").

27. *CESCR General Comment No. 1*, *supra* note 18, at 89.

28. Article 2, paragraph 1 of the Covenant on Economic, Social and Cultural Rights, *supra* note 12, for example, provides that:

Each State Party to the present Covenant undertakes to take steps, individually and through international assistance and co-operation, especially economic and technical, to the maximum of its available resources, with a view to achieving progressively the full realization of the rights recognized in the present Covenant by all appropriate means, including particularly the adoption of legislative measures.

which are expected to be given immediate application upon ratification.[29] The Anti-Torture Declaration and the Assembly's resolutions on extra-judicial killings are obvious examples of the latter. For them, something more than a benchmark is required.

A sixth objective was expressed by the Economic and Social Committee as that of enabling the state concerned "to develop a better understanding of the problems and shortcomings encountered in efforts to realize progressively the full range of . . . rights."[30] Hence, it is essential that states report in detail on the "factors and difficulties" inhibiting such realization. "This process of identification and recognition of the relevant difficulties then provides the framework within which more appropriate policies can be devised."[31]

The final objective asserted by the Economic and Social Committee is

to enable the Committee, and the States parties as a whole, to facilitate the exchange of information among States and to develop a better understanding of the common problems faced by States and a fuller appreciation of the type of measures which might be taken to promote effective realization of each of the rights contained in the Covenant.[32]

In addition to the obvious networking and exchange of ideas which this entails, a part of the process so familiar in the criminal justice area, this exchange enables the Economic and Social Committee to identify ways in which the international community might assist states in realizing the objectives of the Covenant. Articles 22 and 23 of the Covenant on Economic, Social and Cultural Rights provide a specific treaty basis for the expectation that one of the beneficial effects of the reporting process will be to channel bilateral and multilateral technical assistance

---

29. The Covenant on Civil and Political Rights, provides, for example, that "Where not already provided for by existing legislative or other measures, each State Party to the present Covenant undertakes to take the necessary steps, in accordance with its constitutional processes and with the provisions of the present Covenant, to adopt such legislative or other measures as may be necessary to give effect to the rights recognized in the present Covenant." *Supra* note 13, art. 2, para. 2. This reads like an obligation to give immediate effect to the Covenant obligations. *But see* F. Jhabvala, *The Practice of the Covenant's Human Rights Committee, 1976–82: Review of State Party Reports*, 6 HUM. RTS. Q. 81 (1984) (suggesting that the Human Rights Committee has largely settled for progressive implementation).

30. *CESCR General Comment No. 1, supra* note 18, at 89.

31. *Id.* Note the reference to difficulties in the resolutions dealing with the Committee on Crime Prevention and Control's implementation efforts. Chapter 9 *supra*, at note 26.

32. *Id.*

to further the objectives of the Covenant.[33] Not all of the treaty-based bodies have such provisions in their empowering conventions. Nevertheless, the General Assembly has invited all the treaty bodies to give priority attention to identifying the possibilities for technical assistance projects in the regular course of their work reviewing the periodic reports of state parties.[34] There is no reason why similar objectives should not be enshrined in the resolution-based approach in the criminal justice area.

The Economic and Social Committee's general comment thus summarizes some useful goals of reporting systems, goals which are substantially applicable to, and implicit in, the efforts that had been going on under the auspices of the Committee on Crime Prevention and Control, looking toward a broadened reporting system. In particular, the Crime Prevention Committee's reporting efforts discussed in

---

33. Article 22 of the Covenant on Economic, Social and Cultural Rights, *supra* note 12, provides that:

> The Economic and Social Council may bring to the attention of other organs of the United Nations, their subsidiary organs and specialized agencies concerned with furnishing technical assistance any matters arising out of the reports referred to in this part of the present Covenant which may assist such bodies in deciding, each within its field of competence, on the advisability of international measures likely to contribute to the effective progressive implementation of the present Convenant.

Article 23 provides:

> The States Parties to the present Covenant agree that international action for the achievement of the rights recognized in the present Covenant includes such methods as the conclusion of conventions, the adoption of recommendations, the furnishing of technical assistance and the holding of regional meetings and technical meetings for the purpose of consultation and study organized in conjunction with the Governments concerned.

See General comment No. 2, *Committee on Economic, Social and Cultural Rights, Report on the Fourth Session, 15 January-2 February 1990*, U.N. ESCOR, Supp. No. 3, at 86, U.N. Doc. E/1990/23 (1990). The comment stresses the need to consider the human rights dimension in development planning and draws attention to "the important opportunity provided to States parties, in accordance with article 22 of the Covenant, to identify in their reports any particular needs they might have for technical assistance or development cooperation." The opportunity seems broad enough to include a wish-list in some aspects of the criminal justice area.

34. G.A. Res. 44/135, U.N. GAOR, 44th Sess., Supp. No. 49, para. 6, at 212, U.N. Doc A/44/49 (1989). For followup, *see Report of the fourth meeting of persons chairing the human rights treaty bodies, Effective implementation of international instruments on human rights, including reporting obligations under international instruments on human rights, Note by the Secretary-General*, at 11–12, 20, U.N. Doc. A/47/628 (1992).

Chapter 9 may be viewed as aimed at the following of the Economic and Social Committee's objectives: first, a comprehensive review by the state; second, state monitoring of the actual situation; third, elaboration of policy; fourth, public scrutiny of government policies; and even the sixth, enabling the state to have a better understanding of its shortcomings.[35]

Yet one has to acknowledge that there are some serious obstacles to making the criminal justice reporting system successful. For a start, there is no clear legal obligation upon states to provide the necessary reports, as is the case in the treaty regimes.[36] The experience with "voluntary" reporting systems, including those in the criminal justice area, has been dismal.[37] Indeed, even treaty-based regimes find it difficult to persuade all states to report in a timely and comprehensive fashion.[38] Voluntary schemes fare even worse. If a state feels little

35. Given the "soft law" nature of the instruments in the criminal justice area, there is a further possible objective in some instances—gathering data that would permit an informed discussion on whether the instruments require further refining.

36. One could make the argument in the case of the criminal justice reports that complying with requests for information is required by the obligation of articles 55 and 56 of the Charter to take joint and separate action in co-operation with the organization to promote conditions of economic and social progress and development as well as universal respect for and observance of human rights. Obligations under these provisions have been evolving over the years. Yet the very existence of the treaty regimes undercuts the argument some since, when states are serious about requiring reports, they enter into explicit obligations to that effect.

37. *See* Professor Philip Alston, *Effective Implementation of International Instruments on Human Rights, Including Reporting Under International Instruments on Human Rights*, at 19, U.N. Doc. A/44/668 (1989) [hereinafter *Alston Report*]. *See* Chapter 9 *supra*, at notes 45–46. Of the reports presented by the Secretariat at the Eighth Congress, the number of states providing material (out of a U.N. membership of 159) ranged from a low of twenty-nine to a high of seventy-nine. *See Implementation of the Resolutions and recommendations of the Seventh United Nations Congress on the Prevention of Crime and the Treatment of Offenders, Report by the Secretary-General*, at 3, U.N. Doc. A/45/324 (1990); *1990 Congress Working Paper, supra* note 7, at 7–8 (summarizing the reports).

38. "It must suffice to note that the principal manifestations of the problems are inadequate or unsatisfactory reports and the non-submission of reports. While the former problem has been the subject of frequent comments in the various committees, its magnitude cannot be readily be measured. The latter problem, however, can be quantified. Thus, as at 1 June 1988, when 146 States were parties to one or more of the 6 treaties covered by the present study, the number of overdue reports totalled 626 (leaving aside the Convention against Torture, under which reports were not yet due at that date). This compared to a total of 460 overdue reports 2 years earlier (when only 3 less states were involved)." *Alston Report, supra* note 37, at 20. Improvement is not in sight. The report of the 1992 meeting of the chairs of the treaty bodies, *supra* note 34, at 19, records the participants' view that "The problem of excessively overdue reports and of the failure to submit initial reports continues to give rise to concern." The group suggested that countries failing to report should not be "immune" from discussion—

obligation to produce the reports, the self examination exercise will simply not occur. Given the past track record, this may be the case for perhaps a majority of states.

There is, moreover, no guarantee that the necessary resources will be found within the Secretariat to process the paper.[39] Even the treaty-based regimes have had difficulties in this respect, both those financed entirely out of the regular United Nations budget and those financed in whole or in part by the states parties.[40] There is a serious danger that the present effort will fare as badly.

Finally, there is the question of the fifth objective of reporting, that of "provid[ing] a basis on which the State party itself, as well as the Committee, can effectively evaluate the extent to which progress has been made." The interplay between the state and the evaluative body, demonstrated in the evaluative body's consideration of the report, would strike most commentators as an essential element of the whole enterprise—even if great emphasis is placed on the salutary effects of the state's own review in the course of report-writing. In the case of the United Nations treaty committees, the interchange between the members of the Committee in question and representatives of the state whose report is being considered may be found in the relevant summary records of the oral proceedings of that Committee. This will not necessarily result in any formal finding that a particular state is or is not in compliance with the treaty under review, as interpreted by the reviewing Committee. It is, of course, hoped that the dialogue will have some impact on state practice and there are indications that this is in fact the case.[41]

---

their situation should be scheduled for discussion on the basis of otherwise available material. *Id.*

39. A document prepared for the 1992 session of the General Assembly even contemplated a reduction of activities relating to monitoring. *See Revised estimates under section 21D, Crime prevention and criminal justice, Report of the Secretary-General,* at 3, U.N. Doc. A/C.5/47/40 (1992). The proposed program for 1994–1995 presented to the Commission in April 1993 included an item for "promoting and assisting in the use or application of 16 existing instruments" but it was unclear how far this meant support of the surveys. *See, Note by the Secretary-General, Proposed programme of work in crime prevention and criminal justice for the biennium 1994–1995,* at 20, U.N. Doc. E/CN.15/1993/CRP.5 (1993). As amended after the decision of the Commission to concentrate intially on selected instruments, *supra* at notes 4–5, the estimates then referred to work on the five instruments discussed there. *See Proposed Programme Budget for the Biennium 1994–1995, pt.IV, International Cooperation for Development, Sec. 13, Crime Control,* at 10, U.N. Doc. A/48/6 Sec. 13 (1993)(issued 30 August 1993).

40. R. Clark & F. Gaer, *The Committee on the Rights of the Child: Who Pays?,* 7 N.Y.L. Sch. J. Hum. Rts. 123 (1989).

41. For example, one government remarks: "As a consequence of comments made by the Human Rights Committee during examination of New Zealand's report in 1983,

In the case of the International Labor Organization's procedures dealing with the application of conventions and recommendations,[42] there may be communications of various kinds between members of the Committee of Experts on the Application of Conventions and Recommendations and governments, including so-called "direct contacts" with governments.[43] Ultimately the General Conference of the I.L.O. may list countries guilty of a "continued failure to implement" particular conventions.[44] Such procedures, with their sophisticated mix of expert and political supervision, are a far cry from anything yet attempted in the crime prevention area. Here, what is carried out is a survey rather than an examination of the efforts of individual countries. A member of the Secretariat (or a consultant either hired for the purpose or lent by a member state) is the only one who views the particular reports and then endeavors to make a summary of them for the "Secretary General"'s report. No attempt at being critical, or even an effort to clarify or otherwise ask informational questions, is presently built in a practical way into the system. In this respect, a suggestion made by the authors of the 1990 Report of the Secretary-General on the Implementation of the Standard Minimum Rules for the Treatment of Prisoners is worth noting:

Arrangements should be made to enable countries to be referred to for the purposes of clarifying any replies where there could be uncertainty in interpretation. National correspondents may be the appropriate points of reference, but contacts will often be needed with the person directly responsible for

---

Regulation 97(4) of the Penal Institutions regulations 1961 under which an inmate could be required to attend services of worship has been revoked." SECOND PERIODIC REPORT TO THE HUMAN RIGHTS COMMITTEE, [NEW ZEALAND] MINISTRY OF EXTERNAL RELATIONS AND TRADE, INFORMATION BULLETIN No. 30 (March 1990).

42. *See supra* note 8.

43. *See* HUMAN RIGHTS SOURCEBOOK 403–419 (A.P. Blaustein, R.S. Clark & J.A. Sigler eds. 1987) (outlining the procedures prepared by I.L.O.) Note also the work of the European Committee for Co-operation in Prison Affairs, formed by the Council of Europe to encourage observance of the European Rules:

[The Committee] carried out the second quinquennial review in 1983 and followed this up with enquiries addressed to the prison administrations of a number of member states in order to clarify the position with regard to the implementation of certain rules or to encourage progress in particular areas in the light of the results of the review. Those specific enquiries, although modest in themselves, were the first ever made internationally in regard to the application of the rules. They received a co-operative and helpful response.

COUNCIL OF EUROPE, EUROPEAN PRISON RULES 75 (1987).

44. *See* F. KIRGIS, INTERNATIONAL ORGANIZATIONS IN THEIR LEGAL SETTING 534 (2d ed. 1993).

the reply and with the prison authorities, through ministries, in accordance with the procedures for the Effective Implementation of the Rules.[45]

Mild language empowering the Secretary-General to ask for supplementary information appeared as early as the 1957 ECOSOC resolution approving the Standard Minimum Rules,[46] but the political will to actually do so has not been there.

Indeed, there is an even broader issue here which involves the kind of material that may be used to supplement, and even contradict, the survey "information" supplied by states themselves. The former Committee on Crime Prevention and Control barely scratched the surface of this matter in paragraph 6 (f) of the last resolution on implementation that ECOSOC adopted on the advice of the Committee.[47] That paragraph included among the further issues on implementation that had to be addressed "the question of additional or alternative sources of information."[48] United Nations usage tends to give undue deference to government reports, especially those accorded the ultimate imprimatur of appearing as a United Nations document. Most of the material gathered under the Crime Prevention Committee's auspices came from the Governments concerned and was seldom notable for its candor.

What might be done to flesh out such material? For a start, if the Crime Prevention Commission or a sub-group were to begin looking seriously at individual government reports, those involved in the process could presumably be expected to bring some of their own expertise and knowledge to bear. The Secretariat might also be expected to share its information developed in the Secretariat unit that began as the Office for Research and the Collection of Information which was created in New York in 1987. The basic role of this unit (whose func-

---

45. *Report of the Secretary-General, Implementation of the Standard Minimum Rules for the Treatment of Prisoners*, at 28, U.N. Doc. A/CONF.144/11 (1990). The 1984 Procedures for the Effective Implementation of the Standard Minimum Rules for the Treatment of Prisoners, Chapter 9 *supra*, at note 31, contemplated that such "contacts" would take place through the Committee on Crime Prevention and Control. The proposal discussed in the text is a modest one by comparison with I.L.O. and treaty-based committee practice. At least one state made a much more radical proposal in its response to the survey: "It was suggested that an international body to inspect prisons and to offer advice should be created." *Id.* at 27. *See also* 1991 Meeting of Experts, Chapter 9 *supra*, at note 107 (suggesting followup questions to participants in surveys).

46. *See* E.S.C. Res. 663C (XXIV), U.N. ESCOR, 24th Sess., Supp. No. 1, at 11, U.N. Doc. E/4048 (1957); Chapter 9 *supra*, at notes 5–6.

47. E.S.C. Res. 1990/21, U.N. ESCOR, Supp. No. 1, at 23, U.N. Doc. E/1990/90 (1990); Chapter 9 *supra*, at notes 86–92.

48. *Id.*

tions have now been incorporated into the Department of Political Affairs) is to identify potential crisis areas and provide early warning to the Secretary-General of developing situations involving international peace and security.[49] From time to time, however, it must generate material specific to areas involving criminal justice. This should be shared with the Crime Prevention and Criminal Justice Program. Moreover, while the relevant treaties are all silent on the matter, all of the treaty-based committees have found ways to receive information on a formal[50] or informal basis[51] from human rights organizations, either of an international nature such as the International League for Human Rights[52] and Amnesty International, or local to the country concerned.[53] The legitimacy of this is widely accepted.[54] There is not likely to be any meaningful examination of reports under the auspices of the Commission on Crime Prevention and Criminal Justice unless

49. *See* B. RAMCHARAN, THE INTERNATIONAL LAW AND PRACTICE OF EARLY WARNING AND PREVENTIVE DIPLOMACY: THE EMERGING GLOBAL WATCH (1991); MONITORING HUMAN RIGHTS VIOLATIONS 120 (A. Schmid & A. Jongman ed. 1992) (Publication No. 43, Center for the Study of Social Conflicts, Faculty of Social Sciences, Leiden University); B. Ramcharan, *Early Warning at the United Nations: The First Experiment*, 1 INT'L J. REFUGEE L. 379 (1989).

50. *See Rules of the Committee Against Torture*, R. 62(1), U.N. Doc. A/43/46 (1988) (encouraging "non-governmental organizations in consultative status with the Economic and Social Council to submit to it information, documentation and written statements, as appropriate, relevant to the Committee's activities under the Convention").

51. *See generally* INTERNATIONAL LEAGUE FOR HUMAN RIGHTS, SOURCES OF INFORMATION USED BY TREATY COMMITTEES, A MEMORANDUM PREPARED FOR MEMBERS OF THE COMMITTEE ON THE ELIMINATION OF RACIAL DISCRIMINATION (Aug. 1990).

52. The International League for Human Rights, that pioneered this area, regularly submits commentaries on state reports to the Human Rights Committee, the Committee on the Elimination of Racial Discrimination, the Committee on the Elimination of Discrimination Against Women, and the Committee Against Torture.

53. For example, the remarks made by Mr. Wennergren, Expert from Sweden, during the discussion of the Report of St. Vincent and the Grenadines in the Human Rights Committee referred to a commentary on the Government's report made by the local Human Rights Association. U.N. PRESS RELEASE HR/CT/47 (March 20, 1990).

54. *See, e.g.*, INTERNATIONAL LEAGUE FOR HUMAN RIGHTS, *supra* note 51. (The memorandum was prepared in response to belated attacks on the procedure at the Committee on the Elimination of Racial Discrimination.) In a legal opinion on the work of the Committee on the Elimination of Racial Discrimination the U.N. Office of Legal Affairs concluded that the Committee on the Elimination of Racial Discrimination was not "precluded from using extraneous information for ancillary purposes, i.e. in evaluating the completeness of the reports submitted to it and in formulating requests for supplementary data, and the early practice of the Committee indicates that it does indeed rely on such information." 1972 U.N. Jurid. Y.B. 163, U.N. Doc. ST/LEG/SER.C/10. The opinion was rendered in the context of sharing material generated by the I.L.O. and UNESCO supervisory procedures, but the reasoning is applicable beyond information collected by the Specialized Agencies.

developments like these to utilize NGO material occur. Some forty-seven NGOs attended the Crime Prevention Committee's last meeting in 1990, twenty-seven attended the first meeting of the Crime Prevention Commission in 1992, and forty were present at the second meeting in 1993. NGOs have greatly contributed to the drafting of many of the norms and standards,[55] in disseminating those standards and commentaries on them, and in initiating and implementing development projects.[56] However, no NGOs have contributed significantly to the reporting process specifically in the criminal justice area.[57] An examination of typical survey reports of the Secretary-General suggests that either NGOs were not asked to contribute or they had not been persuaded that this was a good thing to do. If the effort at reporting and monitoring in the crime prevention and criminal justice area is to be successful, some of the cadre of NGOs that contribute to the human rights treaty reporting process must be encouraged to contribute here also.[58]

C. Use of Norms and Standards in the Human Rights Part of the United Nations System

The Geneva-based human rights part of the United Nations system is hardly hermetically sealed from what happens in other parts of the system, and the reverse is also true. There is considerable cross-fertilization, though it could be further enhanced. For example, the Human Rights Committee, in examining reports of states parties under the Covenant on Civil and Political Rights, fairly routinely inquires about the extent to which the Standard Minimum Rules on the Treatment of Prisoners are complied with.[59] Other human rights bodies also refer to

---

55. *See United Nations Rules for the Protection of Juveniles Deprived of Their Liberty*, G.A. Res 45/113, U.N. GAOR, 45th Sess., Supp. No. 49A, at 204, para. 3, U.N. Doc. A/45/49 (1991) (the document is unusual in its specificity when it thanks Amnesty International, Defence for Children International and Rädda Barnen, Swedish Save the Children, for their assistance in developing the rules).

56. *1990 Congress Working Paper*, *supra* note 7, at 18.

57. Compare, however, NGO contributions elsewhere in the human rights area. *Supra* notes 50–52.

58. For some suggestions about what NGOs might do, *see* the material produced under the auspices of the Dutch-based PIOOM (the Interdisciplinary Research Program on the Root Causes of Human Rights Violations). Schmid & Jongman, *supra* note 49.

59. *See, e.g., Report of the Human Rights Committee*, U.N. GAOR, 43d Sess., Supp. No. 40, at 17, 38, 76, 125 & 144. U.N. Doc. A/43/40 (1988) (questioning of representatives of Trinidad and Tobago, Denmark, Ecuador, Colombia, and Japan). *See also* P. WILLIAMS, TREATMENT OF DETAINEES: EVALUATION OF ISSUES RELEVANT TO DETENTION BY THE UNITED NATIONS HUMAN RIGHTS COMMITTEE 40–42 (1990).

the Standard Minimum Rules[60] and to other crime prevention and criminal justice material[61] in their work. The Sub-Commission on Prevention of Discrimination and Protection of Minorities has made considerable use of the Basic Principles on the Independence of the Judiciary,[62] the Basic Principles on the Role of Lawyers[63] and the Guidelines on the Role of Prosecutors[64] in its work in these areas.[65] Two other organs, staffed until recently by the Center for Social Development and Humanitarian Affairs in Vienna, the Committee on the Elimination of Discrimination Against Women and the Commission on the Status of Women, have taken the issue of domestic violence beyond the level reached in the Crime Prevention and Criminal Justice Program.[66]

60. *See, e.g., Ad Hoc Working Group of Experts on South Africa*, para. 73, U.N. Doc. E/CN.4/984/Add.8 (1969); *Ad Hoc Working Group on Chile*, para. 3, U.N. Doc. E/CN.4/1134 (1974); *Committee Against Torture, Report of the Committee Against Torture*, U.N. GAOR, 46th Sess., Supp. No. 46, at 21, U.N. Doc. A/46/46 (1991) (questioning of representative of Turkey); *id.* at 41 (remarks by representative of Panama). *See also Report of the Human Rights Committee*, U.N. GAOR, 44th Sess., Supp. No. 40, at 125, U.N. Doc. A/44/40 (1989) (questioning of Italian representative about compliance with the Code of Conduct for Law Enforcement Officials). Williams, *supra* note 59, at 42, gives examples of questioning about several non-treaty instruments by the Human Rights Committee. Much of the Williams discussion of rules relating to detention tracks material in the Civil and Political Covenant which is equally raised by the Standard Minimum Rules.

61. *See, e.g., Succinct information on developments in the human rights programme and on the activities of the United Nations programme on crime prevention and control as they relate to the question of human rights of persons subjected to any form of detention or imprisonment, Report of the Secretary-General*, U.N. Doc. E/CN.4/Sub.2/1991/22 (1991) (information provided to the Sub-Commission on Prevention of Discrimination and Protection of Minorities). The Sub-Commisssion has been engaged in a study on "the application of international standards concerning human rights of detained juveniles, in particular the separation of juvenile and adult offenders in penal institutions, detention pending trial, least possible use of institutionalization and the objectives of institutional treatment" which draws heavily on the Vienna material. *See, e.g., Application of international standards concerning the human rights of detained juveniles, Report prepared by the Special Rapporteur, Mrs. Mary Concepcion Bautista*, U.N. Doc. E/CN.4/Sub.2/1991/24 (1991); *Application of international standards concerning the human rights of detained juveniles, Note by the Special Rapporteur*, U.N. Doc. E/CN.4/Sub.2/1991/50 (1991).

62. *Seventh United Nations Congress on the Prevention of Crime and the Treatment of Offenders, Milan, 26 August-6 September 1985, Report prepared by the Secretariat*, at 58, U.N. Doc. A/CONF.121/22/Rev.1 (1986); Chapter 4 *supra*, at notes 87–94.

63. *Eighth United Nations Congress on the Prevention of Crime and the Treatment of Offenders, Havana, 27 August-7 September 1990*, at 117, U.N. Doc. A/CONF.144/28/Rev.1 (1991); Chapter 4 *supra*, at notes 138–149.

64. *Eighth United Nations Congress on the Prevention of Crime and the Treatment of Offenders, supra* note 63; Chapter 4 *supra*, at notes 150–161.

65. *See, Report on the independence of the judiciary and the protection of practising lawyers, prepared by Mr. Louis Joinet pursuant to resolution 1990/23 of the Sub-Commission on Prevention of Discrimination and Protection of Minorities*, U.N. Doc. E/CN.4/Sub.2/1991/30 (1991) [hereinafter *Joinet Report*].

66. *See* Chapter 4 *supra*, at notes 78–79.

A 1990 démarche by the Special Rapporteur on Extra-Legal, Arbitrary and Summary Executions, relying upon some other Vienna-created norms, is especially suggestive. The Committee on Crime Prevention and Control's efforts at the implementation of resolutions concerning extra-legal, summary, and arbitrary executions have been discussed in another chapter.[67] They relied primarily on the institutionalization of procedures at the domestic level under the guidelines of the 1989 Principles on the Effective Prevention and Investigation of Extra-Legal, Arbitrary and Summary Executions.[68] Meanwhile, in 1982, ECOSOC authorized the Chair of the Human Rights Commission to appoint a Special Rapporteur on Summary or Arbitrary Executions. Mr. Amos Wako was duly appointed to the position.[69] His mandate is to "examine the questions related to summary or arbitrary executions."[70] In doing so, he "may seek and receive information from Governments as well as specialized agencies, intergovernmental organizations and non-governmental organizations in consultative status with the Economic and Social Council."[71] This was a very broad mandate, wide open to cautious evolution. And, as one human rights group has put it:

Since 1982, Mr. Wako has continually expanded the scope of his concern, from a scholarly focus on *actual* deaths to an activist effort to do something about *imminent* deaths, to cases with the death penalty that lack legal safeguards, and to other suspicious deaths at the hands of governments or their agents.[72]

In his 1990 report to the Commission on Human Rights,[73] Mr. Wako describes the 1989 Principles devised under the auspices of the Committee on Crime Prevention and Control[74] as "a milestone for his mandate." He encourages Governments to bring their laws into com-

67. *Id.*, at notes 95–111.

68. E.S.C. Res. 1989/65, U.N. ESCOR, Supp. No. 1, at 52, U.N. Doc. E/1989/89 (1989).

69. E.S.C. Res. 1982/35, U.N. ESCOR, Supp. No. 1, at 27, U.N. Doc. E/1982/82 (1982). The appointment was initially for one year but has been extended. Mr. Wako was succeeded as Rapporteur in 1993 by Mr. Bacre Waly Ndiaye of Senegal.

70. *Id.* para.2.

71. *Id.* para. 4. He is to "submit a comprehensive report to the Commission on Human Rights . . . on the occurrence and extent of the practice of such executions together with his conclusions and recommendations." *Id.* para. 5.

72. International League for Human Rights, In Brief, No. 28, Human Rights at the United Nations: Halting Summary and Arbitrary Executions 1 (1990).

73. *Summary or arbitrary executions, Report by the Special Rapporteur, Mr. S. Amos Wako, pursuant to Economic and Social Council resolution 1988/38*, at 105, U.N. Doc. E/CN.4/1990/22 (1990).

74. *Supra* note 68.

pliance with the Principles and suggests that the consensus on standards will make his job easier, as he plans to use them as a yardstick:

Any Government's practice that fails to reach the standards set out in the principles may be regarded as an indication of the Government's responsibility, even if no government officials are found to be directly involved in the acts of summary or arbitrary execution.[75]

There are two very important points here for implementation of norms and standards developed in the Crime Prevention and Criminal Justice Program. First, like the Committee on Human Rights in its discussion of the Covenant on Civil and Political Rights in light of the Standard Minimum Rules for the Treatment of Prisoners,[76] the Special Rapporteur has treated the Principles as details to give concrete content to his own broadly-worded mandate. Second, here is a case where the Principles, arguably merely "soft law",[77] have been transformed by the Rapporteur, at least for the purposes of his mandate, into *rules* affecting the situation of real people.

Efforts such as those of the Committee on Human Rights and the Special Rapporteur on Summary or Arbitrary Executions are very satisfying from the point of view of the crime prevention and criminal justice part of the United Nations system. These efforts indicate that the Geneva-based part of the system takes the crime prevention and criminal justice work seriously. They also raise the question whether, in some respects, the Vienna-based program should simply defer to the other organs so far as implementation is concerned. The Geneva organs, it might be argued, have some kind of comparative advantage because of greater experience and existing resources. Certainly duplication is to be discouraged and one of the tasks facing the Commission on Crime Prevention and Criminal Justice is to find a principled way to spend the bulk of the resources available to it for implementation in a manner that can have most effect while avoiding unnecessary[78] duplication.

75. *Supra* note 73. Mr. Wako continued:

This resolution is a highly positive outcome of long and careful preparation and close co-operation among non-governmental organizations, Governments and United Nations organs. The Special rapporteur wishes to commend the serious work done in this regard by the Committee on Crime Prevention and Control and the vital contribution made by non-governmental organizations, and in particular by the Minnesota Lawyers International Human Rights Committee.

76. *See supra* note 59.
77. *See generally*, Chapter 5 *supra*, at notes 62–73.
78. Some "duplication" is useful on the principle that what is involved is simply reinforcement by another actor.

D. Advisory Services or Technical Cooperation

What is variously referred to somewhat indiscriminately as advisory services, technical cooperation, or technical assistance is regarded in various parts of the United Nations system as having substantial potential as an aid to implementation.[79] "Advisory services" (used in a narrow sense) in the crime prevention and criminal justice area currently consists primarily of the award of human rights fellowships for study to some thirty or so officials a year. There is also some limited technical assistance to states with human rights (including criminal justice) problems,[80] and some occasional seminars.[81] The Crime Prevention and Criminal Justice Branch itself does some of the facilitating in this area as does the Center for Human Rights,[82] the U.N. Development Program (UNDP) and the Department of Technical Co-operation of the United Nations Secretariat.[83] The regional and interregional institutes associated with the United Nations are also able to contribute through training courses and some specific projects.[84] The advisory services

---

79. *See, e.g.*, T. BUERGENTHAL, LAW-MAKING IN THE INTERNATIONAL CIVIL AVIATION ORGANIZATION 107–08 (1969) (detailing its use in the civil aviation area); *Turin points the way to a new relevance: International Training Centre offers a chance to re-tool creaky system*, SECRETARIAT NEWS, Oct., 1991, at 10 (describing use by International Labor Organization). *See also* Chapter 2 *supra*, at notes 73–76; Chapter 3 *supra*, at notes 39–44.

80. *See Report of the Secretary-General, Progress Report on United Nations Activities in Crime Prevention and Control*, at 8–10, U.N. Doc. E/AC.57/1990/2 (1989) (giving some examples). UNSDRI (as it then was) has made an assessment of potential needs in this area. U. ZVEKIC & A. MATTEI, RESEARCH AND INTERNATIONAL CO-OPERATION IN CRIMINAL JUSTICE: SURVEY ON NEEDS AND PRIORITIES OF DEVELOPING COUNTRIES, UNSDRI PUBLICATION No. 29 (1987). At the first meeting of the Commission on Crime Prevention and Criminal Justice, the Deputy Prime Minister in the newly-established democratic government of Albania made an impassioned plea for assistance. *See Report of the Commission on Crime Prevention and Criminal Justice on its First Session*, *supra* note 1, at 72. A training course for law enforcement officials, police, military, and prison personnel was organized in November 1992 by the United Nations Centre for Human Rights and the Crime Prevention and Criminal Justice Branch. Other efforts are being made to help in what is a daunting task. *See Operational activities contemplated by or proposed to the United Nations Crime Prevention and Criminal Justice Branch since the First session of the Commission on Crime Prevention and Criminal Justice in April 1992*, U.N. Doc. E/CN.15/1993/CRP.9 (1993) (table including efforts for Albania and many others).

81. *See, e.g.*, the *International Seminar on the Prevention and Treatment of Juvenile Delinquency and Community Participation, Beijing*, (Oct. 1988).

82. *See* CENTRE FOR HUMAN RIGHTS, FACT SHEET NO. 3, ADVISORY SERVICES AND TECHNICAL ASSISTANCE IN THE FIELD OF HUMAN RIGHTS (1988); *Joinet Report*, *supra* note 65, at 7–28, 58–63.

83. *See Interregional Advisory Services in the Field of Crime Prevention and the Treatment of Offenders*, 8 CRIME PREVENTION & CRIM. JUST. NEWSL. 6 (1983).

84. *See generally* Chapter 3 *supra*, at notes 112–142 (discussing the work of the institutes). The institutes have enaged in an impressive array of seminars and cooperative projects. Writing in November 1991, the Director of HEUNI commented: "Right

program in general has come under increasing scrutiny from human rights watchdogs, some of whom fear that it can be used as a fig-leaf to avoid holding governments accountable for their failings, while achieving little of substance.[85]

In fact, advisory services and other technical cooperation in the criminal justice area, funded from the regular United Nations budget, suffered a long period of decline in spite of numerous expressions of support for the concept by United Nations organs.[86] A former Chief of the Social Defence Section of the Secretariat, the predecessor to the present Crime Prevention and Criminal Justice Branch, has noted that "under the system of advisory services, instituted in 1946, direct technical assistance to Member States in the advancement of policy and practice in what was then known as social defence antedated the much larger and better-known programmes of technical assistance in economic development."[87] In the early stages, the industrialized countries availed themselves of the system but gradually the emphasis was placed on assisting developing countries.[88] There followed a reduction in requests for assistance and a dearth of funds specifically allocated to assistance in criminal justice. In spite of the emphasis in recent congresses on the complex relationship between crime and development, the 1990 Report of the Committee on Crime Prevention and Control suggested that

there appeared to be a widespread taboo against using development funds for crime prevention and criminal justice projects. That attitude was probably due

---

now, for example, HEUNI is funding a seven-week combined research/advisory mission by Professor David Fogel (University of Illinois at Chicago) to Albania, Bulgaria, the Czech and Slovak Republic, Hungary, Poland and the Soviet Union, on policing. We are also funding a series of 'needs assessment missions' on computerization in Poland." Letter from Matti Joutsen, to Roger S. Clark, Nov. 12, 1991).

85. *See, e.g.*, INTERNATIONAL LEAGUE FOR HUMAN RIGHTS, IN BRIEF, No. 7, HUMAN RIGHTS AT THE UNITED NATIONS: USING ADVISORY SERVICES (Oct. 1988); RÄDDA BARNEN (SWEDISH SAVE THE CHILDREN), UN ASSISTANCE FOR HUMAN RIGHTS (1988); LAWYERS COMMITTEE FOR HUMAN RIGHTS, ABANDONING THE VICTIMS: THE UN ADVISORY SERVICES PROGRAM IN GUATEMALA (1990); P. ALSTON & M. RODRIGUEZ-BUSTELO, TAKING STOCK OF UNITED NATIONS HUMAN RIGHTS PROCEDURES, REPORT OF A JANUARY 1988 WORKSHOP AT LAKE MOHONK, N.Y. 38–43 (1988).

86. *See, e.g.*, *Guiding Principles for Crime Prevention and Criminal Justice in the Context of Development and a New International Economic Order, Seventh United Nations Congress on the Prevention of Crime and the Treatment of Offenders, supra* note 62, at 5, paras. 41, 46 (1986); G.A. Res. 45/107, U.N. GAOR, 45th Sess., Supp. No. 49A, at 190, U.N. Doc A/45/49 (1991) (entitled *International co-operation for crime prevention and criminal justice in the context of development*).

87. E. Galway, *United Nations Technical Assistance in Crime Prevention and Control*, 34 INT'L REV. CRIM. POL'Y 22, 22 (1978).

88. *Id.* at 22–23.

to the failure to recognize how deleterious crime could be for the development efforts of a country. . . . Unless that taboo were discarded, very little of significance was likely to be achieved.[89]

The taboo was never absolute, but much more could be done with technical assistance on both a multilateral and a bilateral basis.[90]

Some items in the portion of the General Assembly's 1991 restructuring resolution[91] dealing with the Secretariat indicate a desire to make much more use of what is increasingly being described as "technical cooperation" under the new dispensation. The Secretariat is exhorted, *inter alia*, to "provide technical assistance and practical information for Member States, particularly through the global information network on crime prevention and criminal justice;"[92] "ensure that the potential donors of criminal justice assistance are put in touch with countries needing the help in question;"[93] and "make the case for assistance in the field of criminal justice to the appropriate funding agencies."[94] At the time of writing, efforts are being made to operationalize these tasks.[95] This may well become the area of implementation over the next few years on which the greatest emphasis is placed.

---

89. *Report of the Committee on Crime Prevention and Control on its Eleventh Session, Vienna, 5–16 February 1990*, at 183, U.N. ESCOR, Supp. No. 10, at 178–179, U.N. Doc. E/1990/31 (1990).

90. *See* "Other Resolution" 4, *International co-operation and mutual assistance through training programmes and exchange of expertise, Report of the Eighth Congress, supra* note 63, at 132. This resolution encourages states, especially developed ones, to make a range of programs—courses, tours, meetings, seminars, demonstration and pilot projects and actual "hands-on" experience with equipment or techniques—available to other states seeking such training, and recommends that the U.N. function as a coordinator of such activities. One modest area of technical assistance—relevant to the reporting area discussed in the text—is that of training officials from developing countries in the art of report-writing. UNITAR, with Ford Foundation funding, has been working on this in the human rights area, and has prepared a useful manual to assist officials in the drafting of the reports which they must submit. *United Nations Centre for Human Rights & United Nations Institute for Training and Research, Manual on Human Rights Reporting*, U.N. Doc. HR/PUB/91/1 (1991).

91. *Creation of an Effective United Nations Crime Prevention and Criminal Justice Programme*, G.A. Res. 46/152, U.N. GAOR, 46th Sess., Supp. No. 49, at 217, U.N. Doc. A/46/49 (1992).

92. *Id.*, Annex, para. 31(b).

93. *Id.*, Annex, para. 31(d).

94. *Id.*, Annex, para. 31(e).

95. *See* E.S.C. Res. 1992/22, U.N. ESCOR, Supp. No. 1, at 22, U.N. Doc. E/1992/92 (1992). The relevant parts of the resolution are discussed in Chapter 2 *supra*, at notes 72–76. One of the hopes for the creation of the International Scientific and Professional Advisory Council (ISPAC) is that it will be able to mobilize NGO efforts at technical assistance. *See* Chapter 2 *supra* at note 160. *See also* references *supra* note 80.

E. Other Mechanisms

Over the past decade a dramatic expansion has occurred in the creation of implementation mechanisms in the human rights area, mechanisms that are not based on treaty regimes.[96] In 1980, the Commission
on Human Rights created the first of a series of "thematic mechanisms," the Working Group on Enforced or Involuntary Disappearances.[97] The very broad mandate of the Working Group on Disappearances,[98] whose existence has been periodically extended one or
two years at a time, is to "examine questions relevant to enforced or
involuntary disappearances of persons."[99] Other than the general human rights obligations of the United Nations Charter, there is no
specific treaty obligation on disappearances. Instead, the effort here is
to give teeth to the General Assembly's resolutions on the subject. The
Working Group on Disappearances has been followed by other theme
mechanisms, the Special Rapporteur on Summary or Arbitrary Executions, to which reference has already been made;[100] the Special Rapporteur on Torture;[101] the Special Rapporteur on Intolerance Based
on Religion or Belief;[102] the Special Rapporteur on the Sale of Children;[103] and the Working Group on Arbitrary Detention.[104] Each of

96. *See* F. GAER, THE INTERNATIONAL LEAGUE FOR HUMAN RIGHTS, U.N. "SPECIAL
PROCEDURES" IN HUMAN RIGHTS: A GUIDE (1991).

97. C.H.R. Res. 20 (XXXVI), *Commission on Human Rights, Report on the Thirty-sixth
Session, 4 February–14 March 1980*, U.N. ESCOR, Supp. No. 4, at 180, U.N. Doc.
E/1980/13 (1980). *See* M. Berman & R. Clark, *State Terrorism: Disappearances*, 13 RUTGERS
L.J. 531 (1982); *Declaration on the Protection of All Persons from Enforced Disappearance*, G.A.
Res. 47/133.

98. The Group consists of five members of the Commission on Human Rights, serving
as experts in their individual capacities, *id.* para. 1.

99. *Id.*

100. *Supra* note 69.

101. *See* C.H.R. Res. 1985/33, *Commission on Human Rights, Report on the Forty-first
Session, 4 February–15 March 1985*, U.N. ESCOR, Supp. No. 2, at 71, U.N. Doc. E/1985/22
(1985) (appointing Special Rapporteur "to examine questions relevant to torture").

102. *See* C.H.R. Res. 1986/20, *Commission on Human Rights, Report on the Forty-second
Session, 3 February–14 March 1986*, U.N. ESCOR, Supp. No. 2, at 66, U.N. Doc. E/1986/
22 (1986) (appointing Special Rapporteur to "examine incidents and governmental
actions in all parts of the world which are inconsistent with the provisions of the
Declaration on the Elimination of All Forms of Intolerance and of Discrimination Based
on Religion or Belief [G.A. Res. 36/55, U.N. GAOR, 36th Sess., Supp. No. 51, at 171,
U.N. Doc. A/36/51 (1982)] and to recommend remedial measures as appropriate").

103. *See* C.H.R. Res. 1990/68, *Commission on Human Rights, Report on the Forty-sixth
Session, 29 January–9 March 1990*, U.N. ESCOR, Supp. No. 2, at 145, U.N. Doc.
E/1990/22 (1990) (appointing Special Rapporteur to "consider matters relating to the
sale of children, child prostitution and child pornography, including the problem of the
adoption of children for commercial purposes").

104. This working group, "composed of five independent experts," has the "task of

these mechanisms is meant to give effect to the relevant resolutions rather than to specific treaty obligations. They represent very clear precedents for the power of the organization to move in such a direction.[105] As a recent NGO study of the mechanisms concludes:

The Theme Rapporteurs are a series of innovative mechanisms established by the Commission on Human Rights to expand the UN's human rights fact-finding, reporting, and implementation of standards. In carrying out their mandates, the thematic Special Rapporteurs and Working Groups have, by and large, pressed substantially at the margins of what was acceptable and permissible human rights activity in the intergovernmental setting of the UN Commission on Human Rights.[106]

As precedents, moreover, the creation of the thematic mechanisms is of direct relevance to the work of the Commission on Crime Prevention and Criminal Justice. Apart from encouraging these mechanisms to make use of the Crime Program's instruments, the Crime Prevention Commission must ponder the possibilities of whether to move in such a direction itself. Should the Commission have a Working Group on the Standard Minimum Rules for the Treatment of Prisoners or a Rapporteur on Juvenile Justice or on Victims? While the power is there,[107] is the political will?

---

investigating cases of detention imposed arbitrarily or otherwise inconsistently with the relevant international standards set forth in the Universal Declaration of Human Rights [G.A. Res. 217A (III), U.N. GAOR, 3d Sess., 1st Pt., Resolutions, at 71, U.N. Doc. A/810 (1948)] or in the relevant international legal instruments accepted by the States concerned." *See* C.H.R.Res. 1991/42, *Commission on Human Rights, Report on the Forty-seventh Session, 28 January–8 March 1991*, U.N. ESCOR, Supp. No. 2, at 105, U.N. Doc. E/1991/22 (1991). *See generally* R. Brody, *The United Nations Creates a Working Group on Arbitrary Detention*, 85 Am. J. Int'l L. 709 (1991).

105. As a matter of Charter interpretation, the development presumably represents an effort to give content to the cooperative obligations in articles 55 and 56 of the Charter, discussed in Chapter 1 *supra*, at notes 18–20. One might also view the development as an application of the notions of implied powers and functional necessity derived from the Advisory Opinion, Reparation for Injuries Suffered in the Service of the United Nations, 1949 I.C.J. 174. There are also a number of "Country Special Rapporteurs and Similar Procedures" which represent further United Nations practice. *See* Gaer, *supra* note 96, at 9–27. Note also the action of the Human Rights Committee in appointing a Special Rapporteur for the Follow-up of Views, whose task is to monitor the effect given to the Committee's decisions under the Optional Protocol to the International Covenant on Civil and Political Rights, *supra* note 12, at 59. There is no specific treaty authority for this move. *See* A. de Zayas, *The Follow-up Procedure of the UN Human Rights Committee*, 47 Rev. Int'l Comm. Jur. 28 (1991).

106. Gaer, *supra* note 96, (summary n.p.).

107. Aside from the practice just discussed, there is the language of para. 28 of the Annex to G.A. Res. 46/152, *supra* note 3, which permits the Commission on Crime Prevention and Criminal Justice to "use the services of a limited number of qualified and

F. Conclusion

An unusually candid Working Paper prepared by the Secretariat for the Eighth Congress, noted stark reality: "It has even been suggested that priority be given to the implementation of existing standards over the initiation of new activities."[108] But even before the Eighth Congress approved several new instruments with reporting obligations,[109] the attempted implementation of which would surely strain resources even further, it was seen as too late:

> However, in view of the adoption of an increasing number of standards during the last five years, the implementation of which should be assured, bringing standard-setting to a temporary halt would not help to avert an impending deadlock, which could affect both the mechanisms and the procedures for overseeing compliance with United Nations instruments.[110]

That deadlock had come to pass by 1992–1993 and the reporting work had ground to a halt.

It is hard to be very sanguine about the prospects for an ambitious "implementation" program under the auspices of the Commission on Crime Prevention and Criminal Justice. It has limited Secretariat resources available to it and there is serious apathy even among vocal supporters of the criminal justice program when it comes to delivering reports or agreeing to the provision of budgetary funds. Despite this, there is some disposition to press on.

In the final years of the Committee on Crime Prevention and Control, the Crime Prevention and Criminal Justice Program was staking its claim to a serious place in the United Nations implementation system by endeavoring to make its reporting system work. By 1993, reporting had simply ceased, although it is now under way again in a limited way in response to a request from ECOSOC.[111] The program is now looking more seriously at the role of technical cooperation. Increasingly, however, with its organs such as the Working Group on Enforced or Involuntary Disappearances and its Special Rapporteurs on particular countries and its "theme" Rapporteurs such as those on Torture and on Summary or Arbitrary Executions, the Geneva-based human rights system has been showing a much greater disposition to go beyond reporting regimes and to deal with the individual problems

---

experienced experts, either as individual consultants or in working groups, in order to assist in the preparations for and follow-up work of the commission."

108. *1990 Congress Working Paper, supra* note 7, at 4.

109. *See* Chapter 9 *supra*, at notes 92–97.

110. *1990 Congress Working Paper, supra* note 7, at 4–5.

111. E.S.C. Res. 1993/34, pt. III, paras 7 and 8 (1993).

of individual people. As it moves further on "implementation," the Commission on Crime Prevention and Criminal Justice cannot be unmoved by such developments and no doubt will make sympathetic responses to them, both in its own functions and in working with other parts of the system. In doing so, it will need to be sensitive to questions of turf and comparative advantage. For instance, when should the Crime Prevention Commission encourage the appointment of theme Rapporteurs from its ranks, or of independent individuals or groups reporting to it? When should it acquiesce in having such mechanisms under the auspices of the Commission on Human Rights? When should it defer to the efforts of the Commission on Human Rights or the treaty-based committees? Should it, indeed, go any further down the present route, or should it instead leave the field substantially to the Geneva-based organs, thus avoiding duplication?

In so far as they have been acting as "human rights agencies," the Committee on Crime Prevention and Control, the congresses and the United Nations Crime Prevention and Criminal Justice Program in general have had the advantage over others of the human rights organs in emphasizing "technical" and "professional" aspects of the area. They have thus succeeded in avoiding some of the politicization of the others. If its first two meetings are any indication, the Commission on Crime Prevention and Criminal Justice could easily be mistaken for just another political body where nation states peddle their wares. The challenge to the Crime Prevention Commission and its working groups as they move to consider such implementation strategies as much more vigorous examination of governmental reports, involvement in concrete situations, the appointment of Special Rapporteurs, the creation of an early warning system for victims, or more serious involvement in technical cooperation activities, is to maintain the relatively non-politicized approach of the earlier organs.

Appendix

General Assembly Resolution 46/152 (1991)

The General Assembly,

Alarmed by the scope of criminality and by the dangers posed to the welfare of all nations by the rising incidence of crime generally and by the many forms of criminal activity that have international dimensions,

Also alarmed by the high cost of crime in both human and material terms, especially in its new and transnational forms, and aware of the effects of crime both on States and on individual victims,

Recalling that, in its resolution 45/108 of 14 December 1990, it decided to establish an intergovernmental working group to "produce a report elaborating proposals for an effective crime prevention and criminal justice programme and suggesting how that programme could most appropriately be implemented,"

Acknowledging with appreciation the work of the Intergovernmental Working Group on the Creation of an Effective International Crime and Justice Programme,[1] which met at Vienna from 5 to 9 August 1991,

Acknowledging also with appreciation the work of the Ministerial Meeting on the Creation of an Effective United Nations Crime Prevention and Criminal Justice Programme, held in Paris from 21 to 23 November 1991,

Recognizing that criminality is a major concern of all nations and that it calls for a concerted response from the international community aimed at preventing crime and recidivism, improving the functioning of criminal justice and law enforcement, and increasing respect for individual rights,

Acknowledging that a United Nations programme devoted to crime

1. *See* A/CONF.156/2.

prevention and criminal justice can only be effective with the direct involvement of Member States,

Convinced that the principal purpose of such a programme should be to provide practical assistance to States in combating both national and transnational crime,

Noting the principles contained in the Milan Plan of Action[2] and the Guiding Principles for Crime Prevention and Criminal Justice in the Context of Development and a New International Economic Order,[3] as well as other pertinent instruments formulated by United Nations congresses on the prevention of crime and the treatment of offenders and approved by the General Assembly,

Recalling the relevant resolutions in which it has stressed the importance of the Commission on Human Rights and the Centre for Human Rights at Geneva with regard to respect for human rights in the administration of justice,

Recognizing also the urgent need to promote and intensify international cooperation in crime prevention and criminal justice, and the fact that this cooperation can be effective only if it is executed with the direct participation of the receiving States, with due respect for their needs and priorities,

1. *Takes note with appreciation* of the report of the Ministerial Meeting on the Creation of an Effective United Nations Crime Prevention and Criminal Justice Programme;[4]

2. *Approves* the statement of principles and programme of action, annexed to the present resolution, recommending the establishment of a United Nations crime prevention and criminal justice programme;

3. *Supports* a clearer definition of its mandate with regard to crime prevention and criminal justice, under the aegis and guidance of the United Nations, whose aim will be to respond to the most pressing priorities and needs of the international community in the face of both national and transnational criminality;

4. *Requests* the Secretary-General to give a high level of priority within the United Nations framework, and within the overall existing United

2. *Seventh United Nations Congress on the Prevention of Crime and the Treatment of Offenders (Milan, 26 August–6 September 1985):* report prepared by the Secretariat (United Nations publication, Sales No. E.86.IV.1), chap. I, sect. A.

3. *Ibid.*, sect. B.

4. A/46/703.

Nations resources, to the activities of the United Nations crime prevention and criminal justice programme;

5. *Decides* that the United Nations crime prevention and criminal justice programme shall be devoted to providing States with practical assistance, such as data collection, information and experience sharing, and training, in order to achieve the goals of preventing crime within and among States and of improving the response to crime;

6. *Invites* Member States to give their political and financial support and to take measures that will ensure the implementation of the provisions of the statement of principles and programme of action as they relate to the strengthening of the United Nations crime prevention and criminal justice programme in terms of its structure, content and priorities;

7. *Requests* the Secretary-General to take the necessary action within the overall existing United Nations resources in accordance with the financial rules and regulations of the United Nations and to provide appropriate resources for the effective functioning of the United Nations crime prevention and criminal justice programme in accordance with the principles outlined in the statement of principles and programme of action;

8. *Urges* all entities of the United Nations system, including the regional commissions, the United Nations congresses on the prevention of crime and the treatment of offenders, the United Nations institutes for the prevention of crime and the treatment of offenders, the specialized agencies and the relevant intergovernmental and non-governmental organizations, to assist the United Nations crime prevention and criminal justice programme in fulfilling its tasks;

9. *Encourages* all developed countries to review their aid programmes in order to ensure that there is a full and proper contribution in the field of criminal justice within the overall context of development priorities;

10. *Decides* to recommend that a commission on crime prevention and criminal justice be established as a functional commission of the Economic and Social Council, which would hold its inaugural meeting during 1992, and recommends that the meeting of the Committee on Crime Prevention and Control scheduled for February 1992 be cancelled and to make available the funds necessary for the work of the new commission within the budget for the biennium 1992–1993;

11. *Requests* the Economic and Social Council at its organizational session of 1992:

(*a*) To dissolve the Committee on Crime Prevention and Control;

(*b*) To establish the commission on crime prevention and criminal justice as a new functional commission of the Economic and Social Council, in accordance with the recommendations contained in the statement of principles and programme of action;

(*c*) To endorse the role and functions of the United Nations congresses on the prevention of crime and the treatment of offenders, in accordance with the recommendations contained in the statement of principles and programme of action;

12. *Decides* that the present members of the Committee on Crime Prevention and Control should be invited to participate during the first two days of the inaugural session of the new commission, at the expense of their respective Governments, except in the case of Committee members from least developed countries, in order to facilitate an orderly transition;

13. *Also decides* to retain for the United Nations crime prevention and criminal justice programme, without prejudice to additional funds that may be made available by the Secretary-General, all funds currently allocated to the programme, as well as any savings realized by restructuring;

14. *Requests* the Secretary-General to report to the General Assembly at its forty-seventh session on measures taken to implement the statement of principles and programme of action.

ANNEX

Statement of Principles and Programme of Action of the United Nations Crime Prevention and Criminal Justice Programme
We, Member States of the United Nations,

Assembled in Paris to consider ways and means of promoting international cooperation in crime prevention and criminal justice and of strengthening the United Nations crime prevention and criminal justice programme in order to make it fully effective and responsive to the needs and priorities of Member States,

Considering that one of the purposes of the United Nations, as stated in the Charter of the United Nations, is to achieve international cooperation in solving international problems of an economic, social, cultural or humanitarian character, and in promoting and encouraging respect for human rights and for fundamental freedoms for all without distinction as to race, sex, language, or religion,

Convinced of the urgent need for more efficient international mechanisms to assist States and to facilitate joint strategies in the field of crime prevention and criminal justice, thus consolidating the role of the United Nations as the focal point in that field,

Noting the importance of the principles contained in the Milan Plan of Action[5] and the Guiding Principles for Crime Prevention and Criminal Justice in the Context of Development and a New International Economic Order,[6] as well as other pertinent instruments formulated by United Nations congresses on the prevention of crime and the treatment of offenders and approved by the General Assembly,

Reaffirming the responsibility assumed by the United Nations in crime prevention and criminal justice,

Bearing in mind the goals of the United Nations in the field of crime prevention and criminal justice, specifically the reduction of criminality, more efficient and effective law enforcement and administration of justice, the observance of human rights and the promotion of the highest standards of fairness, humanity and professional conduct,

Recognizing that it is essential to elicit active support for, and to provide the means of assistance for the development of, an effective United Nations crime prevention and criminal justice programme and to devise appropriate implementation mechanisms,

Deeply concerned about the extent and growth of crime, with its financial, economic and social consequences,

Alarmed at the high cost of crime in both human and material terms, as well as in its new national and transnational forms, and aware of the effects of crime both on States and on individual victims,

Recognizing that the primary responsibility for crime prevention and criminal justice rests with Member States,

Emphasizing the need for strengthened regional and international cooperation to combat crime and recidivism, to effect the improved

---

5. *Seventh United Nations Congress on the Prevention of Crime and the Treatment of Offenders (Milan, 26 August–6 September 1985):* report prepared by the Secretariat (United Nations publication, Sales No. E.86.IV.1), chap. I, sect. A.

6. *Ibid.*, sect. B.

functioning of criminal justice systems, to promote respect for individual rights and to safeguard the rights of victims of crime and the general security of the public,

Aware that there is unanimity about the need to create a new, vigorous United Nations crime prevention and criminal justice programme, as well as agreement on the need to establish an intergovernmental body for policy-making and priority-setting, to strengthen the effectiveness of the Secretariat unit within the Centre for Social Development and Humanitarian Affairs of the United Nations Office at Vienna, and to increase technical cooperation to help countries, particularly developing countries, translate United Nations policy-guidelines into practice, including training,

Determined to translate our political will into concrete action:

(*a*) By creating the essential mechanisms for practical collaboration against common problems;

(*b*) By providing a framework for inter-State cooperation and coordination to respond to the serious new forms and transnational aspects and dimensions of crime;

(*c*) By establishing information exchanges concerning the implementation and effectiveness of the United Nations norms and standards in crime prevention and criminal justice;

(*d*) By providing means of assistance, particularly to developing countries, for more effective crime prevention and more humane justice;

(*e*) By establishing an adequate resource base for a truly effective United Nations crime prevention and criminal justice programme,

Proclaim our strong commitment to the above-mentioned goals and agree on the following:

I. STATEMENT OF PRINCIPLES

1. We recognize that the world is experiencing very important changes resulting in a political climate conducive to democracy, to international cooperation, to more widespread enjoyment of basic human rights and fundamental freedoms, and to the realization of the aspirations of all nations to economic development and social welfare. Notwithstanding these developments, the world today is still beset by violence and other forms of serious crime. These phenomena, wherever they occur, constitute a threat to the maintenance of the rule of law.

2. We believe that justice based on the rule of law is the pillar on which civilized society rests. We seek to improve its quality. A humane and

efficient criminal justice system can be an instrument of equity, constructive social change and social justice, protecting basic values and peoples' inalienable rights. Every right of the individual should enjoy the protection of the law against violation, a process in which the criminal justice system plays an essential role.

3. We have in mind the fact that the lowering of the world crime rate is related to, among other factors, the improvement of the social conditions of the population. The developed countries and the developing countries are experiencing difficult situations in this respect. Nevertheless, the specific problems encountered by the developing countries justify priority being given to dealing with the situation confronting these countries.

4. We believe that rising crime is impairing the process of development and the general well-being of humanity and is causing general disquiet within our societies. If this situation continues, progress and development will be the ultimate victims of crime.

5. We also believe that the growing internationalization of crime must generate new and commensurate responses. Organized crime is exploiting the relaxation of border controls designed to foster legitimate trade and, hence, development. The incidence and scope of such crimes may increase further in the coming years unless sound preventive measures are taken. It is thus particularly important to anticipate events and to assist Member States in mounting suitable preventive and control strategies.

6. We recognize that many criminal offences have international dimensions. In this context, there is an urgent need for States to address, while respecting the sovereignty of States, problems arising in collecting evidence, extraditing offenders and promoting mutual legal assistance, for example, when such offences are committed across frontiers or when frontiers are used to escape detection or prosecution. Despite differences in legal systems, experience has shown that mutual assistance and cooperation can be effective countermeasures and can help to prevent conflicts of jurisdiction.

7. We also recognize that democracy and a better quality of life can flourish only in a context of peace and security for all. Crime poses a threat to stability and to a safe environment. Crime prevention and criminal justice, with due regard to the observance of human rights, is thus a direct contribution to the maintenance of peace and security.

8. We must ensure that any increases in the capacity and capabilities of perpetrators of crime are matched by similar increases in the capacity

and capabilities of law enforcement and criminal justice authorities. By pooling our knowledge and developing suitable countermeasures, success in the prevention of crime and the reduction of victimization can be maximized. We recognize in particular the need to improve and strengthen the means of the crime prevention and control authorities in the developing countries, whose critical economic and social situation is further increasing the difficulties in this area.

9. We call on the international community to increase its support of technical cooperation and assistance activities for the benefit of all countries, including developing and smaller countries, and for the purpose of expanding and strengthening the infrastructure needed for effective crime prevention and viable, fair and humane criminal justice systems.

10. We acknowledge the contributions of the United Nations crime prevention and criminal justice programme to the international community. We note that it is a long-recognized fact that inadequate resources have been devoted to the implementation of the programme, which has in the past been inhibited from achieving its potential. We also note that a strengthening of the resources devoted to the implementation of the programme was called for by the Sixth United Nations Congress for the Prevention of Crime and the Treatment of Offenders,[7] the Seventh United Nations Congress for the Prevention of Crime and the Treatment of Offenders[8] and the Eighth United Nations Congress for the Prevention of Crime and the Treatment of Offenders.[9] We further note that the Committee on Crime Prevention and Control, at its eleventh session, gave priority attention to the conclusions and recommendations of a subcommittee established to provide an overview of the problem of crime and to assess the most efficient means of stimulating practical international action in support of Member States, in pursuance of General Assembly resolution 44/72 of 8 December 1989. The Committee, in its resolution 11/3, unanimously approved a report of the subcommittee on the need for the creation of an effective international crime and justice programme.[10]

7. *Sixth United Nations Congress on the Prevention of Crime and the Treatment of Offenders (Caracas, 25 August–5 September 1980):* report prepared by the Secretariat (United Nations publication, Sales No. E.81.IV.4), chap. I, sect. A.

8. *Seventh United Nations Congress on the Prevention of Crime and the Treatment of Offenders (Milan, 26 August–6 September 1985):* report prepared by the Secretariat (United Nations publication, Sales No. E.86.IV.1), chap. I, sect. A.

9. *Eighth United Nations Congress on the Prevention of Crime and the Treatment of Offenders (Havana, 27 August–7 September 1990):* report prepared by the Secretariat (United Nations publication, Sales No. E.91.IV.2), chap. I, sect. A.

10. E/1990/31/Add.1.

That report, which was endorsed by the Eighth Congress,[11] was used as an important tool for the establishment of the United Nations crime prevention and criminal justice programme, in line with the provisions of General Assembly resolution 45/108.

11. We accordingly recommend intensified international cooperation in crime prevention and criminal justice, including the creation of an effective United Nations crime prevention and criminal justice programme.

12. We are convinced that there is a need for Governments to define more clearly the role and functions of the United Nations crime prevention and criminal justice programme and the Secretariat and to determine priorities within that programme.

13. We strongly believe that the review of the programme should aim at strengthening its effectiveness, improving its efficiency and establishing an adequate Secretariat support structure.

II. PROGRAMME OF ACTION

A. DEFINITION

14. The United Nations crime prevention and criminal justice programme shall bring together the work of the commission on crime prevention and criminal justice, the interregional and regional institutes for the prevention of crime and the treatment of offenders, the network of government-appointed national correspondents in the field of crime prevention and criminal justice, the Global Crime and Criminal Justice Information Network and the United Nations congresses on the prevention of crime and the treatment of offenders in providing assistance to Members States in their efforts to reduce the incidence and costs of crime and in developing the proper functioning of the criminal justice system. The establishment of this programme will be effected in accordance with the procedures defined below and within the framework of the total available resources of the United Nations.

B. Goals

15. The programme shall be designed to assist the international community in meeting its pressing needs in the field of crime prevention and criminal justice and to provide countries with timely and practical assistance in dealing with problems of both national and transnational crime.

11. *Eighth United Nations Congress, op. cit.*, chap. IV.

16. The general goals of the programme shall be to contribute to the following:

(*a*) The prevention of crime within and among States;

(*b*) The control of crime both nationally and internationally;

(*c*) The strengthening of regional and international cooperation in crime prevention, criminal justice and the combating of transnational crime;

(*d*) The integration and consolidation of the efforts of Member States in preventing and combating transnational crime;

(*e*) More efficient and effective administration of justice, with due respect for the human rights of all those affected by crime and all those involved in the criminal justice system;

(*f*) The promotion of the highest standards of fairness, humanity, justice and professional conduct.

C. SCOPE OF THE UNITED NATIONS CRIME PREVENTION AND CRIMINAL JUSTICE PROGRAMME

17. The programme shall include appropriate forms of cooperation for the purpose of assisting States in dealing with problems of both national and transnational crime. In particular, it may include:

(*a*) Research and studies at the national, regional and global levels on specific prevention issues and criminal justice measures;

(*b*) Regular international surveys to assess trends in crime and developments in the operation of criminal justice systems and in crime prevention strategies;

(*c*) Exchange and dissemination of information among States on crime prevention and criminal justice, particularly with regard to innovative measures and the results achieved in their application;

(*d*) Training and upgrading of the skills of personnel working in the various areas of crime prevention and criminal justice;

(*e*) Technical assistance, including advisory services, particularly in respect of the planning, implementation and evaluation of crime prevention and criminal justice programmes, training and the use of modern communication and information techniques; such assistance may be implemented by means of, for example, fellowships, study tours, consultancies, secondments, courses, seminars and demonstration and pilot projects.

18. Within the framework of the programme, the United Nations should directly carry out the above-mentioned forms of cooperation or should act as a coordinating or facilitating agent. Special attention should be paid to the creation of mechanisms to provide flexible and appropriate assistance and to respond to the needs of Member States at their request, without duplicating the activities of other existing mechanisms.

19. For the purpose of those forms of cooperation, Member States should establish and maintain reliable and effective channels of communication among themselves and with the United Nations.

20. The programme may also include, as appropriate, while respecting the sovereignty of States, a review of the effectiveness and application of and, where necessary, further development and promotion of international instruments on crime prevention and criminal justice.

D. PROGRAMME PRIORITIES

21. In developing the programme, areas of priority shall be determined in response to the needs and concerns of Member States, giving particular consideration to the following:

(*a*) Empirical evidence, including research findings and other information on the nature and extent of crime and on trends in crime;

(*b*) The social, financial and other costs of various forms of crimes and/or crime control to the individual, the local, national and international community, and to the development process;

(*c*) The need of developing or developed countries, which are confronting specific difficulties related to national or international circumstances, to have recourse to experts and other resources necessary for establishing and developing programmes for crime prevention and criminal justice that are appropriate at the national and local levels;

(*d*) The need for a balance within the programme of work between programme development and practical action;

(*e*) The protection of human rights in the administration of justice and the prevention and control of crime;

(*f*) The assessment of areas in which concerted action at the international level and within the framework of the programme would be most effective;

(*g*) Avoidance of overlapping with the activities of other entities of the United Nations system or of other organizations.

22. The commission on crime prevention and criminal justice shall not be bound by mandates conferred prior to its formation, but shall assess them on their merits by applying the above-mentioned principles.

E. STRUCTURE AND MANAGEMENT

1. Commission on crime prevention and criminal justice
23. A commission on crime prevention and criminal justice shall be established as a functional commission of the Economic and Social Council. The commission shall have the power to create ad hoc working groups and to appoint special rapporteurs, as it deems necessary.

Membership
24. The commission shall consist of forty Member States of the United Nations, elected by the Economic and Social Council on the basis of the principle of equitable geographical distribution. Its members shall serve for a term of three years, except that the terms of one half of the first elected members, whose names shall be chosen by lot, shall expire after two years.

Each Member State shall make every effort to ensure that its delegation includes experts and senior officials with special training and practical experience in crime prevention and criminal justice, preferably with policy responsibility in the field. Provisions should be made in the regular budget of the United Nations to defray the travel costs of the representatives of the least developed countries that are members of the Commission.[12]

Sessions
25. The commission shall hold annual sessions of not more than ten working days.

Functions
26. The commission shall have the following functions:

(*a*) To provide policy guidance to the United Nations in the field of crime prevention and criminal justice;

(*b*) To develop, monitor and review the implementation of the pro-

12. It is recommended that in order to commence the work of the commission as soon as possible, the geographical distribution should be as follows: African States (12), Asian States (9), Latin American and Caribbean States (8), Western European and other States (7), Eastern European States (4). The size and geographical distribution of the commission may be reviewed two years after the first session of the commission.

gramme on the basis of a system of medium-term planning in accordance with the priority principles provided in paragraph 21 above;

(c) To facilitate and help to coordinate the activities of the interregional and regional institutes;

(d) To mobilize the support of Member States for the United Nations crime prevention and criminal justice programme;

(e) To prepare the congresses and to consider suggestions regarding possible subjects for the programme of work as submitted by the congresses.

2. Committee on crime prevention and control

27. The Committee on Crime Prevention and Control should be dissolved by the Economic and Social Council upon the establishment by the Council of the commission on crime prevention and criminal justice. There will be a basic need for involving independent experts in the area of crime prevention and control.

28. The commission shall, when necessary, use the services of a limited number of qualified and experienced experts, either as individual consultants or in working groups, in order to assist in the preparations for and follow-up work of the commission. Their advice shall be transmitted to the commission for consideration. The commission shall be encouraged to seek such advice whenever such expertise is needed. One of the major tasks of the experts shall be to assist in the preparations for the congresses.[13]

3. United Nations congresses on the prevention of crime and the treatment of offenders

29. The United Nations congresses on the prevention of crime and the treatment of offenders, as a consultative body of the programme, shall provide a forum for:

(a) The exchange of views between States, intergovernmental organi-

---

13. The Secretariat shall keep a list of such experts. The experts shall be selected by the commission in collaboration with the Secretariat, the United Nations institutes for the prevention of crime and the treatment of offenders and non-governmental organizations. The commission, in consultation with Member States, shall develop a mechanism for that purpose. Such experts, who may be either governmental officials or other individuals, shall be chosen on the basis of equitable geographical distribution. They should be available to the programme in their individual independent capacity for at least three years. Expert group meetings shall take place subject to the conditions set out in paragraph 14.

zations, non-governmental organizations and individual experts representing various professions and disciplines;

(*b*) The exchange of experiences in research, law and policy development;

(*c*) The identification of emerging trends and issues in crime prevention and criminal justice;

(*d*) The provision of advice and comments to the commission on crime prevention and criminal justice on selected matters submitted to it by the commission;

(*e*) The submission of suggestions, for the consideration of the commission, regarding possible subjects for the programme of work.

30. In order to enhance the effectiveness of the programme and to achieve optimal results, the following arrangements should be implemented:

(*a*) The congresses should be held every five years, for a period of between five and ten working days;

(*b*) The commission shall select precisely defined topics for the congresses in order to ensure a focused and productive discussion;

(*c*) Quinquennial regional meetings should be held under the guidance of the commission on issues related to the agenda of the commission or of the congresses, or on any other matters, except when a region does not consider it necessary to hold such a meeting. The interregional and regional institutes should be fully involved, as appropriate, in the organization of those meetings. The commission shall give due consideration to the need to finance such meetings, in particular in developing regions, through the regular budget of the United Nations;

(*d*) Action-oriented research workshops on topics selected by the commission, as part of a congress programme, and ancillary meetings associated with the congresses should be encouraged.

4. Organizational structure of the secretariat and of the programme
31. The Secretariat shall be the permanent body responsible for facilitating the implementation of the programme, the priorities of which shall be established by the commission, and for assisting the commission in conducting evaluations of the progress made and analyses of the difficulties encountered. For that purpose, the Secretariat shall:

(*a*) Mobilize existing resources, including institutes, intergovernmental organizations, non-governmental organizations and other competent authorities for the implementation of the programme;

(*b*) Coordinate research, training and the collection of data on crime and justice, and provide technical assistance and practical information for Member States, particularly through the global information network on crime and criminal justice;

(*c*) Assist the commission in the organization of its work and in the preparation, in accordance with the directions of the commission, of the congresses and any other events relating to the programme;

(*d*) Ensure that the potential donors of criminal justice assistance are put in touch with countries needing the help in question;

(*e*) Make the case for assistance in the field of criminal justice to the appropriate funding agencies.

32. It is recommended to the Secretary-General that, in recognition of the high priority that should be accorded to the programme, an upgrading of the Crime Prevention and Criminal Justice Branch into a division should be effected as soon as possible, under the conditions set out in paragraph 14, bearing in mind the structure of the United Nations Office at Vienna.

33. The Professional staff of the Secretariat of the programme shall be called "Crime Prevention and Criminal Justice Officers."

34. The Secretariat of the programme shall be directed by a senior official responsible for the overall day-to-day management and supervision of the programme, communicating with the relevant government officials, the specialized agencies and intergovernmental organizations whose activities are relevant to the programme.

F. PROGRAMME SUPPORT

1. Interregional and regional institutes for the prevention of crime and the treatment of offenders

35. The activities of the United Nations institutes for the prevention of crime and the treatment of offenders[14] should be supported by Mem-

---

14. The United Nations institutes for the prevention of crime and the treatment of offenders consist of the following:

(*a*) The United Nations Asia and Far East Institute for the Prevention of Crime and the Treatment of Offenders, established in 1961 at Fuchu, Japan;

ber States and the United Nations, giving particular attention to the needs of such institutes located in developing countries. Given the important role of such institutes, their contributions to policy development and implementation, and their resource requirements, should be fully integrated into the overall programme, especially those of the African Regional Institute for the Prevention of Crime and the Treatment of Offenders.

2. Coordination among the interregional and regional institutes
36. The interregional and regional institutes should keep one another and the commission informed on a regular basis about their programme of work and its implementation.

37. The commission may request the interregional and regional institutes, subject to the availability of resources, to implement select elements of the programme. The commission may also suggest areas for inter-institute activities.

38. The commission shall seek to mobilize extrabudgetary support for the activities of the interregional and regional institutes.

3. Network of government-appointed national correspondents in the field of crime prevention and criminal justice
39. Member States should designate one or more national correspondents in the field of crime prevention and criminal justice as focal points for the purpose of maintaining direct communication with the Secretariat and other elements of the programme.

40. The national correspondents shall facilitate contact with the Secretariat on matters of legal, scientific and technical cooperation, training,

---

(*b*) The United Nations Interregional Crime and Justice Research Institute, established in 1968 at Rome;
(*c*) The United Nations Latin American Institute for the Prevention of Crime and [the] Treatment of Offenders, established in 1975 at San José, Costa Rica;
(*d*) The Helsinki Institute for Crime Prevention and Control, affiliated with the United Nations, established in 1981 at Helsinki;
(*e*) The African Regional Institute for the Prevention of Crime and the Treatment of Offenders, established in 1989 at Kampala.

In addition, three other institutes are currently cooperating closely with the United Nations in the field of crime prevention and criminal justice:

(*a*) The Arab Security Studies and Training Centre, at Riyadh;
(*b*) The Australian Institute of Criminology, at Canberra;
(*c*) The International Centre for Criminal Law Reform and Criminal Justice Policy, at Vancouver.

information on national laws and regulations, legal policy, the organization of the criminal justice system, crime prevention measures and penitentiary matters.

4. Global information network on crime and criminal justice
41. Member States shall support the United Nations in the development and maintenance of the global information network on crime and criminal justice in order to facilitate the collection, analysis, exchange and dissemination, as appropriate, of information and the centralization of inputs from non-governmental organizations and scientific institutions in the field of crime prevention and criminal justice.

42. Member States shall undertake to provide the Secretary-General on a regular basis and upon request with data on the dynamics, structure and extent of crime and on the operation of crime prevention and criminal justice strategies in their respective countries.

5. Intergovernmental and non-governmental organizations
43. Intergovernmental and non-governmental organizations and the scientific community are a valuable source of professional expertise, advocacy and assistance. Their contributions should be fully utilized in programme development and implementation.

G. FUNDING OF THE PROGRAMME
44. The programme shall be funded from the regular budget of the United Nations. Funds allocated for technical assistance may be supplemented by direct voluntary contributions from Member States and interested funding agencies. Member States are encouraged to make contributions to the United Nations Trust Fund for Social Defence, to be renamed the United Nations crime prevention and criminal justice fund. They are also encouraged to contribute in kind for the operational activities of the programme, particularly by seconding staff, organizing training courses and seminars, and providing the requisite equipment and services.

Alternative Visions

DRAFT INTERNATIONAL CONVENTION ON COOPERATION IN CRIME PREVENTION AND CRIMINAL JUSTICE (COSTA RICA, 1991)

(Circulated by Costa Rica to the Ministerial Meeting in Paris 21–23 November 1991 as U.N. Doc. A/CONF.156/CRP.1)

PREAMBLE

The States Parties to the present Convention,

Convinced of the need for international cooperation and concerted action to combat crime, particularly in its new and dangerous forms with transnational dimensions,

Aware of the key role of the United Nations as a world-wide coordinating centre for international cooperation in crime prevention and criminal justice,

Guided by the provisions of the Charter of the United Nations and the principles enshrined in the Caracas Declaration (General Assembly resolution 35/171, annex), and the Milan Plan of Action (see E.86.IV.1, chap. I, sect. A),

Considering that the strengthening of cooperation in crime prevention must become a priority task of the international combined,

Have agreed on the following:

PART I

Article 1

1. States Parties shall undertake, pursuant to the present Convention and the Protocols annexed thereto, to develop further the content, structure and practical application of the United Nations crime prevention and criminal justice programme and to strengthen interna-

tional cooperation in those areas, bearing in mind the fundamental principles of their legal systems.

2. States Parties shall undertake to collaborate among themselves and with the United Nations in a manner compatible with the principles of sovereign equality and territorial integrity.

Article 2
1. States Parties shall cooperate with each other and through the United Nations with a view to:

(a) Preventing and reducing transnational crime;

(b) Enhancing crime prevention and criminal justice policies;

(c) Establishing and maintaining appropriate channels of communication between the competent authorities and institutions;

(d) Facilitating and ensuring a rapid exchange of information by disseminating the appropriate data and mutual access to investigation systems and study centres;

(e) Improving the training of staff and other experts;

(f) Providing developing countries with technical assistance, including the relevant financial arrangements, as required.

2. States Parties shall adopt such measures as may be required to increase their cooperation with United Nations and other relevant entities, such as:

(a) Regional and interregional institutes for the prevention of crime and the treatment of offenders;

(b) Regional and interregional institutes for the prevention of crime and the treatment of offenders;

(c) National and international agencies and bodies involved in matters relating to crime prevention and criminal justice.

Article 3
1. To support the United Nations crime prevention and criminal justice programme, States Parties shall adopt such legislation as may be required and shall assist with the drafting, consolidation, revision and application of international instruments containing regulations and standards relating to crime prevention and criminal justice.

2. Such instruments may be annexed to the present Convention in the form of Protocols, with the agreement of the States Parties.

PART II

Article 4

1. There shall be established a Committee for Cooperation in Crime Prevention and Criminal Justice (hereinafter referred to as the Committee) which shall discharge the functions provided below. The experts shall be elected by the States Parties and shall serve in their individual capacity, consideration being given to equitable geographical distribution and to the representation of different forms of cultural development, as well as the principal legal systems.

2. The members of the Committee shall be elected by secret ballot from a list of persons nominated by States Parties. Each State Party may nominate one person from among its nationals.

3. The initial election shall be held no later than six months after the entry into force of the present Convention. At least three months before the date of each election, the Secretary-General of the United Nations shall send a letter to the States Parties inviting them to submit their nominations within two months. The Secretary-General shall prepare a list in alphabetical order of all the persons thus nominated, indicating the States Parties which have nominated them, and shall submit it to the States Parties.

4. The election of the Committee members shall be held at a meeting of the States Parties convened by the Secretary-General at United Nations Headquarters. At that meeting, two thirds of the States Parties shall constitute a quorum and the persons elected to the Committee shall be the nominees who obtain the greatest number of votes and an absolute majority of the votes of the representatives of States Parties present and voting.

5. The members of the Committee shall be elected for four years. The mandate of nine of the members elected at the first election, however, shall expire at the end of two years; immediately after the first election, the names of those nine members shall be chosen by lot by the Chairman of the Committee.

6. For the filling of unforeseen vacancies, the State Party whose expert has terminated his functions as a member of the Committee shall appoint another expert from among its nationals, subject to the approval of the Committee.

7. The members of the Committee shall, with the approval of the General Assembly receive emoluments from United Nations resources

on such terms and conditions as the Assembly may decide, having regard to the importance of the Committee's functions.

8. The Secretary-General of the United Nations shall provide the necessary staff and services for the effective performance of the functions of the Committee under the present Convention.

Article 5
1. States Parties shall submit to the Committee, through the Secretary-General of the United Nations, reports on measures taken pursuant to their commitments under the present Convention, within one year following the entry into force of the Convention, for the States Parties concerned; subsequently, States parties shall submit such reports every four years, as well as any other information requested by the Committee.

2. The reports may include factors and difficulties involved in complying with obligations under the present Convention.

Article 6
1. The Committee shall adopt its own regulations and procedures.

2. The Committee shall elect its officers for a term of two years.

Article 7
The Committee shall periodically inform the Economic and Social Council and the General Assembly of the United Nations of its activities and may make suggestions and general recommendations based on the reports received from States Parties. All suggestions and general recommendations shall be included in the report of the Committee together with comments, if any, from States Parties.

Article 8
1. The Committee shall normally meet for a period of not more than three weeks each year in order to consider the reports submitted pursuant to article 5 of the present Convention.

2. The meetings of the Committee shall normally be held at United Nations Headquarters or at any other place that the Committee deems appropriate.

Article 9
1. The specialized agencies shall be entitled to be represented at the consideration of the implementation of such provisions of the present

Convention as fall within the scope of their activities. The Committee may invite the specialized agencies to submit reports on the implementation of the Convention in areas falling within the scope of their activities.

2. Other entities of the United Nations shall be entitled to be represented, in addition to international, governmental and non-governmental organizations in accordance with the provisions of article 2.

PART III

Article 10
1. The present Convention shall be open for signature by all States.

2. The Secretary-General of the United Nations shall be designated as the depositary of the present Convention and any Protocols annexed thereto.

3. The present Convention shall be subject to ratification. Instruments of ratification shall be deposited with the Secretary-General of the United Nations.

4. Expressions of agreement to be bound by each of the Protocols annexed to the present Convention shall be optional for each State, provided that at the time of deposition of its instrument of ratification, acceptance or approval of the Convention, or of accession to it, that State gives notification of its agreement to be bound by each of its Protocols.

5. A State depositing its instrument of ratification, acceptance or approval of the present Convention, or of accession to it, may, at any time, notify the depositary of its agreement to be bound by each annexed Protocol, to which it is not yet bound.

6. Any Protocol to which a state Party is bound shall be, for that State Party, an integral part of the present Convention.

7. The present Convention shall be open to accession by all States. Accession shall be effected by depositing an instrument of accession with the Secretary-General of the United Nations.

Article 11
1. A request for the revision of the present Convention or of any Protocol annexed thereto may be made at any time by any State Party by means of a written notification addressed to the Secretary-General of the United Nations.

2. The General Assembly of the United Nations shall decide on the steps to be taken in response to such a request.

Article 12
1. The present Convention shall enter into force on the thirteenth day following the date on which the twentieth instrument of ratification or accession is deposited with the Secretary-General of the United Nations.

2. For each State ratifying or acceding to the present Convention after the twentieth instrument of ratification or accession has been deposited, the Convention shall enter into force on the thirtieth day following the date on which that State deposits its instrument of ratification or accession.

3. Each Protocol annexed to the present Convention shall enter into force on the thirtieth day following the date on which twenty States have notified their agreement to be bound by that Protocol.

4. For each State notifying its agreement to be bound by a Protocol annexed to the present Convention after the date on which twenty States have notified their agreement to be bound by that Protocol, the latter shall enter into force on the thirtieth day following the date on which that State notifies its agreement to be so bound.

Article 13
1. The Secretary-General of the United Nations shall receive and circulate to all States the text of reservations entered by States at the time of ratification or accession.

2. A reservation incompatible with the object and purpose of the present Convention shall not be permitted.

3. Reservations may be withdrawn at any time by notification to that effect addressed to the Secretary-General of the United Nations, who shall inform all States accordingly. Such notification shall take effect on the date on which it is received.

Article 14
1. Any dispute between two or more States Parties concerning the interpretation or application of the present Convention which is not settled through negotiation shall, at the request of one of them, be submitted for arbitration. If within six months from the date of the request for arbitration the States Parties do not succeed in reaching agreement on the arbitration arrangements, any one of them may

refer the dispute to the International Court of Justice by means of an application in line with the Statute of the court.

2. Each State Party may, at the time of signature or ratification of the present Convention, or accession thereto, declare that it does not consider itself bound by paragraph 1 of the present article. The other States Parties shall not be bound by that paragraph with respect to any State Party that has entered such a reservation.

3. Any State Party that has entered a reservation in accordance with paragraph 2 of the present article may at any time withdraw the reservation by notification to the Secretary-General of the United Nations.

4. When one of the States Parties to a dispute is not bound by one of the annexed Protocols, the other States Parties bound by the present Convention and the Protocols annexed thereto shall remain bound by these in their mutual relations.

Article 15
The present Convention, of which the Arabic, Chinese, English, French, Russian and Spanish texts are equally authentic, shall be deposited with the Secretary-General of the United Nations.

IN WITNESS WHEREOF the undersigned, duly authorized, have signed the present Convention.

INTERNATIONAL WORKSHOP ON PRINCIPLES AND PROCEDURES FOR A NEW TRANSNATIONAL CRIMINAL LAW

The Society for the Reform of Criminal Law and Max Planck Institute for Foreign and International Criminal Law

(May 21–24, 1991
at Freiburg im Breisgau, Federal Republic of Germany)

This International Workshop on "Principles and Procedures for a new Transnational Criminal Law" held at the Max Planck Institute for Foreign and International Criminal Law from May 21–24, 1991 notes that the General Assembly of the United Nations has established an intergovernmental working group to produce a report elaborating proposals for an effective crime prevention and criminal justice program for the United Nations and, in addition, to suggest how that program could most appropriately be implemented.

The General Assembly has also requested that a ministerial meeting be convened to consider the report of the intergovernmental working group to decide what the future crime prevention and criminal justice program of the United Nations should be.

Participants at this Workshop examined many aspects of growing phenomena of transnational crime and the response by governments and others to it, including the extra-territorial aspects of national laws and the need to harmonize these in many cases. The Workshop examined how international co-operation has increased dramatically in order to combat transnational crime by way of bi-lateral agreements and arrangements and multi-lateral convention. The Workshop also examined the possibility of establishing a supranational jurisdiction for a very limited number of crimes and what new mechanisms and institutions might be appropriate for enforcing them. In this examination, the Workshop recognized the importance of observing human rights in any system of criminal justice, including extradition, mutual assistance procedures, and the transfer of prisoners.

The Workshop was disturbed by the alarming threat and acknowledged gravity of the offences committed by organized crime, such as terrorism, drug trafficking, and trafficking in arms and persons, corruption and abuse of power, money laundering and economic criminality, all with their impact on local crime rates, and offences against eco-systems and cultural property, as well as offences against the peace and security of mankind.

The workshop concluded that although enormous strides have been made to date by governments and multi-governmental organizations in coordinating a response to the ever growing phenomena of transnational crime more can and must be done.

The recent discussion at the Eighth United Nations Congress 1990 in Havana and subsequently at the General Assembly in New York underscored the prevailing mood regarding the United Nations crime prevention and criminal justice program. This program is in urgent need of reform if it is to meet the needs of Member States. Although the United Nations program has assisted Member States in the development of their criminal policy and has been instrumental in the adoption of important standards and norms, in the provision of technical assistance, and in the production and exchange of useful information, at present it is unable to respond effectively to the numerous requests from Member States for assistance.

The Workshop would respectfully request the meeting of the intergovernmental working group and the subsequent meeting of ministers to seriously consider, among other options, the *creation of a new Specialized Agency*, independent of, yet linked to the United Nations (patterned after, for instance, the WHO, the ILO, the ICAO, or the IMO). This Agency would be an inter-governmental organization which would function on the basis of a special statute or constitution. The Agency could co-ordinate a new and strengthened international program of crime prevention and criminal justice in collaboration with national governments, specialized agencies, inter-governmental organizations, non-governmental organizations active in crime prevention on criminal justice, and all members of the international community concerned about these issues.

Should the meeting of ministers decide to proceed with the measures necessary to establish such a new Specialized Agency, its mandate could be to develop new *mechanisms, procedures, conventions, and institutions* necessary to combat transnational crime and to assist national governments to reduce crime domestically.

On the *national level*, this could particularly involve assistance with regard to

• information-gathering and analysis on the incidence of crime and the efficacy of the response to crime;

• preventing crime and helping the victims of crime;

• enhancing the criminal justice process by improving methods for the investigation of crime, developing pretrial and trial procedures as well as appellate review;

• developing the administration of sentences and the re-integration of offenders into society and the control of recidivism.

On the *international level*, the mandate of this New Agency could include

• the drafting of international conventions, declarations and recommendations pertaining to the definition of international offences.

• enhancing existing and developing new co-operative mechanisms, including such mechanisms as mutual assistance and extradition.

• the organization of trainee programs for developing countries,

• the drafting of model penal provisions dealing with selected offences.

On the *supranational* level, the mandate of this New Agency could include the development and encouragement of coordinated subregional, regional and international activities from the investigative through to the adjudicative stages, including the ascertainment of the practicality of establishing subregional and regional penal tribunals with transferred jurisdiction, in order to meet more effectively the problems of particularly severe national crime and of crime transcending national frontiers.

The Agency should have the capacity to provide a program of technical and other assistance in response to government request in order to ensure that the most recent developments in modern technology and expertise are placed at the disposal of all Member States.

Participants in the Workshop would be pleased as individuals and as a group to assist the intergovernmental working group and the meeting of ministers in any way they might deem useful to strengthen international co-operation to prevent crime and particularly its further growth.

Bibliography

ARTICLES AND NOTES

A. ARTICLES WITH NAMED AUTHORS

Abramovsky, A. *A Critical Evaluation of the American Transfer of Penal Sanctions Policy*, 1980 WISC. L. REV. 25

Abramovsky, A. & Eagle, S.J. *A Critical Evaluation of the Mexican-American Transfer of Penal Sanctions Treaty*, 64 IOWA L. REV. 275 (1979)

Alston, P. *Implementing economic, social and cultural rights: the functions of reporting obligations*, 89/1 BULLETIN OF HUMAN RIGHTS 5 (1989)

Alston, P. *Out of the Abyss: The Challenges Confronting the New U.N. Committee on Economic, Social and Cultural Rights*, 9 HUM. RTS. Q. 332 (1987)

American Bar Association, Electronic Messaging Services Task Force, *The Commercial Use of Electronic Data Interchange—A Report and Model Trading Partner Agreement*, 45 BUS. LAW. 1645 (1990)

Aust, A. *The Theory and Practice of Informal International Instruments*, 35 INT'L & COMP. L.Q. 787 (1986)

Barents, J. *Vanity Fair? International Congresses Reconsidered*, 53 AM. POL. SCI. REV. 1090 (1959)

Baxter, R.R. *Law in "Her Infinite Variety"*, 29 INT'L & COMP. L.Q. 549 (1980)

Berman, M. & Clark, R. *State Terrorism: Disappearances*, 13 RUTGERS L.J. 531 (1982)

Besharov, D. J. & Mueller, G.O.W. *The Demands of the Inmates of Attica State Prison and the United Nations Standard Minimum Rules for the Treatment of Prisoners: A Comparison*, 21 BUFF. L. REV. 839 (1972)

Best, K. *The Problems of Prisoner Transfer*, 18 COMMONWEALTH L. BULL. 333 (1992)

Blakesley, C. & Lagodny, O. *Finding Harmony Amidst Disagreement over Extradition, the Role of Human Rights, and Issues of Territoriality Under International Criminal Law*, 24 Vand. J. Transnat'l L. 1 (1991)

Bonnie, R. *Coercive Psychiatry and Human Rights: An Assessment of Recent Changes in the Soviet Union*, 1 CRIM. L. F. 319 (1990)

Bonnie, R. *Dilemmas in Administering the Death Penalty: Conscientious Abstention, Professional Ethics, and the Needs of the Legal System*, 14 L. & HUM. BEHAV. 67 (1990)

Bothe, M. *Legal and Non-Legal Norms—A Meaningful Distinction in International Relations?* 11 NETH. Y.B. INT'L L. 65 (1980)

Brody, R. *Introduction, The Independence of Judges and Lawyers: A Compilation of International Standards* 25–26 C.I.J.L. BULL. 3 (1990)

Brody, R. *The United Nations Creates a Working Group on Arbitrary Detention*, 85 AM. J. INT'L L. 709 (1991)

Cassese, A. *A New Approach to Human Rights: The European Convention for the Prevention of Torture*, 83 AM. J. INT'L L. 128 (1989)

Cerna, C. M. *The Normative Status of the Universal Declaration of Human Rights— The View from the United States*, in PROCEEDINGS AND COMMITTEE REPORTS OF THE AMERICAN BRANCH OF THE INTERNATIONAL LAW ASSOCIATION 1991– 1992 (1992)

Chinkin, C.M. *The Challenge of Soft Law: Development and Change in International Law*, 38 INT'L & COMP. L.Q. 850 (1989)

Christenson, G. *The Use of Human Rights Norms to Inform Constitutional Interpretation*, 4 HOUS. J. INT'L L. 39 (1981)

Clark, R. *Criminal Code Reform in New Zealand? A Martian's View of the Erewhon Crimes Act 1961 with Some Footnotes to the 1989 Bill*, 21 VICT. U. WELL. L. REV. 1 (1991)

Clark, R. *Human Rights and the U.N. Committee on Crime Prevention and Control*, 506 ANNALS 68 (1989)

Clark, R. *Offenses of International Concern: Multilateral State Treaty Practice in the Forty Years Since Nuremberg*, 57 NORDIC J. INT'L L. 49 (1988)

Clark, R. *Preventing and Combating Intolerance of Religion or Belief*, 20 WORLD ORD. 19 (1985–86)

Clark, R. *The Eighth United Nations Congress on the Prevention of Crime and the Treatment of Offenders*, 1 CRIM. L. F. 513 (1990)

Clark, R. & Gaer, F. *The Committee on the Rights of the Child: Who Pays?*, 7 N.Y.L. SCH. J. HUM. RTS. 123 (1989)

Clifford, W. *The Committee on Crime Prevention and Control*, 34 INT'L REV. CRIM. POL'Y 11 (1978)

Clifford, W. *The Standard Minimum Rules for the Treatment of Prisoners*, 66 PROC. AM. SOC. INT'L L. 232 (1972)

Conlon, M. *Group Compares Prison Conditions to Chile and South Africa*, Reuters, June 4, 1987, available in LEXIS, Nexis Library

Cornil, P. *International Standards for the Treatment of Prisoners*, 26 INT'L REV. CRIM. POL'Y 3 (1968)

Crook, J. *The United Nations Compensation Commission—A New Structure to Enforce State Responsibility*, 87 AM. J. INT'L L. 144 (1993)

Das, K. *Measures of Implementation of the International Convention on the Elimination of All Forms of Racial Discrimination with Special Reference to the Provisions Concerning Reports from States Parties to the Convention*, 4 HUM. RTS. J. 213 (1971)

de Zayas, A. *The Follow-up Procedure of the UN Human Rights Committee*, 47 REV. INT'L COMM. JUR. 28 (1991)

Eser, A. *Common Goals and Different Ways in International Criminal Law: Reflections from a European Perspective*, 31 HARV. INT'L L.J. 117 (1990)

Ferracuti, F. *The Role of Social Defence in the United Nations*, 32 REV. JUR. U. P.R. 683 (1963)

Finckenauer, J. & McArdle, T. *Institutional Treatment Possibilities for Young Offenders*, 39 & 40 INT'L REV. CRIM. POL'Y 119 (1990)

Fisse, B. *Confiscation of Proceeds of Crime: Funny Money, Serious Legislation*, 13 CRIM. L.J. 368 (1989)

Galaway, B. *Use of Restitution as a Penal Measure in the United States*, 22 Howard L.J. 8 (1983)

Galway, E. *United Nations Technical Assistance in Crime Prevention and Control*, 34 Int'l Rev. Crim. Pol'y 22 (1978)

Gilmore, W.C. *International Action Against Drug Trafficking: Trends in United Kingdom Law and Practice*, 24 Int'l Lawyer 365 (1990)

Ginsburgs, G. *The Soviet Union and International Co-operation in Penal Matters*, 41 Int'l & Comp. L.Q. 85 (1992)

Ginsburgs, G. *The USSR and the Socialist Model of International Cooperation in Criminal Matters*, 17 Rev. Socialist L. 199 (1991)

Glos, G.E. *Convention on the Transfer of Prisoners Among the Communist Countries*, 9 Int'l J.L. Lib. 262 (1978)

Graven, J. *Importance and Scope of the Minimum Rules for the Protection of Non-delinquent Detainees*, 26 Int'l Rev. Crim. Pol'y 56 (1968)

Hall Williams, J.E. *Two International Congresses*, 1 Brit. J. Criminology 254 (1961)

Hannikainen, L. *How to Interpret and What to Do to the Treaty on Aircraft Seizures with the Soviet Union*, 2 Finnish Y.B. Int'l L. 538 (1991)

Hartman, J. *"Unusual" Punishment: The Domestic Effects of International Norms Restricting the Application of the Death Penalty*, 52 U. Cin. L. Rev. 655 (1983)

Henderson, L.N. *The Wrongs of Victims Rights*, 37 Stan. L. Rev. 937 (1985)

Higgins, R. *Some thoughts on the implementation of human rights*, 89/1 Bulletin of Human Rights 60 (1989)

Jhabvala, F. *The Practice of the Covenant's Human Rights Committee, 1976–82: Review of State Party Reports*, 6 Hum. Rts. Q. 81 (1984)

Kennedy, D.M. et al. *The Extradition of Mohammed Hamadei*, 31 Harv. Int'l L.J. 5, 17–18 (1990)

Kerrigan, G.M. *Historical Development of the United Nations Declaration*, in International Protection of Victims, 7 Nouvelles Études Pénales 91 (M.C. Bassiouni ed. for Association Internationale de Droit Penale 1988)

Lamborn, L.L. *The Propriety of Governmental Compensation of Victims of Crime*, 41 Geo. Wash. L. Rev. 446 (1972)

Lamborn, L.L. *The United Nations Declaration on Victims: Incorporating "Abuse of Power"*, 19 Rutgers L.J. 59 (1987)

Lamborn, L.L. *Toward a United Nations Declaration on Crime, Abuses of Power and the Rights of Victims*, 3 World Soc'y of Victimology Newsl. 15 (1983–84)

Leflar, R.A. *Minimizing State Conflicts of Law*, 4 Det. C.L. Rev. 1325 (1983)

Lillich, R. *The United States Constitution and International Human Rights Law*, 3 Harv. Hum. Rts J. 53 (1990)

Linde, H. *Comments*, 18 Int'l Lawyer 61 (1984)

López-Rey, M. *Aspects and Problems of the Role of United Nations Assistance to Developing Countries in the Field of Social Defence*, 39 Revue Internationale de Droit Penale 21 (1968)

López-Rey, M. *The Co-operation of Non-Governmental Organizations with the United Nations in the Field of the Prevention of Crime and the Treatment of Offenders*, Associations Internationales, No. 1, 21 (1957)

López-Rey, M. *The First U.N. Congress on the Prevention of Crime and the Treatment of Offenders*, 47 J. Crim. L. Criminol. & Police Sci. 526 (1957)

López-Rey, M. *The Role of the United Nations Congresses on the Prevention of Crime and the Treatment of Offenders*, Fed. Probation, Sept. 1973, 24

López-Rey, M. *United Nations Activities in the Prevention of Crime and the Treatment of Offenders*, AM. J. CORRECTION, May—June 1960, 4

McClean, D. *Mutual Assistance in Criminal Matters: The Commonwealth Initiative*, 37 INT'L & COMP. L.Q. 177 (1988)

McClean, D. *Seizing the Proceeds of Crime: The State of the Art*, 38 INT'L & COMP. L.Q. 334 (1989)

Meyer, J. *The Vicarious Administration of Justice: An Overlooked Basis of Jurisdiction*, 31 HARV. INT'L L.J. 108 (1990)

Molina, L.F. *Comments on the "Universality" of the Code of Conduct for Law Enforcement Officials*, THIRD WORLD LEGAL STUD. 59 (1993)

Morris, T.P. *Second United Nations Congress on Prevention of Crime and the Treatment Officials*, 1990 THIRD WORLD LEGAL STUD. 59 (1993)

Morris, T.P. *Second United Nations Congress on Prevention of Crime and the Treatment of Offenders*, 1 BRIT. J. CRIMINOLOGY 261 (1961)

Nadelmann, E.A. *The Role of the United States in the International Enforcement of Offenders, London, August, 1960*, 1 EXCERPTA CRIMINOLOGICA 161 (1961)

Naldi, G. *Prisoners' Rights as Recently Intepreted by the Supreme Court of Zimbabwe: A Comparative Study with International Human Rights*, 4 AFR. J. INT'L & COMP. L. 715 (1992)

Neudek, K. *United Nations Crime Prevention and Criminal Justice Programme*, 1 EUROP. J. CRIM. POL'Y & RES. 185 (1993)

Nilsson, H.G. *The Council of Europe Laundering Convention: A Recent Example of a Developing International Criminal Law*, 2 CRIM. L.F. 419 (1991)

Nixson, F.I. *Controlling the Transnationals? Political Economy and the United Nations Code of Conduct*, 11 INT'L J. SOC. L. 83 (1983)

Palmer, G. *New Ways to Make International Environmental Law*, 86 AM. J. INT'L L. 259 (1992)

Panel, *A Hard Look at Soft Law*, 82 PROC. AM. SOC'Y INT'L L. 371 (1988)

Paterson, R. *The United Nations Model Treaty on Crimes Against Cultural Property*, 4 CRIM. L.F. 213 (1993)

Ramcharan, B. *Early Warning at the United Nations: The First Experiment*, 1 INT'L J. REFUGEE L. 379 (1989)

Riphagen, W. *From Soft Law to Jus Cogens and Back*, 17 VICT. U. WELL. L. REV. 81 (1987)

Robson, J.L. *Criminology in Evolution—The Impact of International Congresses*, 3 OTAGO L. REV. 5 (1973)

Rosen, S. *Draft Principles on the Effective Prevention and Investigation of Extra-Legal, Arbitrary and Summary Executions*, 5 NEWSLETTER AMNESTY INT'L LEGAL SUPPORT NETWORK 6 (1988)

Roundtable, *Implementing the Rules of War: Training, Command and Enforcement*, 1972 PROC. AM. SOC'Y INT'L L. 183

Salguero, R. G. *Medical Ethics and Competency to be Executed*, 96 YALE L.J. 167 (1986)

Schabas, W.A. *International Norms Concerning Capital Punishment of the Insane*, 4 CRIM. L.F. 95 (1993)

Schachter, O. *The Invisible College of International Lawyers*, 72 NW. U. L. REV. 217 (1977)

Schachter, O. *The Twilight Existence of Nonbinding International Agreements*, 71 AM. J. INT'L L. 296 (1977)

Seidl-Hohenveldern, I. *International Economic "Soft Law"* , 1979 II RECUEIL DES COURS 165

Silfverberg, K. *Suppression of the Traffic in Persons and the Exploitation of the Prostitution of Others*, 2 FINNISH Y.B. INT'L L. 66 (1991)

Singer, R.G. *Prisoners as Wards of the Court—A Nonconstitutional Path to Assure Correctional Reform By the Courts*, 41 U. CIN. L. REV. 769 (1972)

Singer, R.G. *Prisoners' Rights Litigation: A Look at the Past Decade, and a Look at the Coming Decade*, FED. PROBATION, Dec. 1980, 3

Singer, R.G. *Privacy, Autonomy, and Dignity in the Prison: A Preliminary Inquiry Concerning Constitutional Aspects of the Degradation Process in Our Prisons*, 21 BUFF. L. REV. 669 (1972)

Skoler, D.L. *World Implementation of the United Nations Standard Minimum Rules for the Treatment of Prisoners*, 10 J. INT'L L. & ECON. 453 (1975)

Spaeth, E.B. *The Courts' Responsibility for Prison Reform*, 16 VILL. L. REV. 1031 (1971)

Stotzky, I.P. & Swan, A.C. *Due Process Methodology and Prisoner Exchange Treaties: Confronting an Uncertain Calculus*, 62 MINN. L. REV. 733 (1978)

Sundberg, J. *The Wisdom of Treaty Making: A Glance at the Machinery Behind the Production of Law-Making Treaties and a Case Study of the Hague Hijacking Conference of 1970*, 16 SCANDINAVIAN STUD. IN L. 285 (1972)

Teitz, L.E. *Taking Multiple Bites of the Apple: A Proposal to Resolve Conflicts of Jurisdiction and Multiple Proceedings*, 26 INT'L LAWYER 21 (1992)

Thomas, D. & Beasley, M. *Domestic Violence as a Human Rights Issue*, 15 HUM. RTS Q. 36 (1993)

Treves, T. *The UN Body of Principles for the Protection of Detained or Imprisoned Persons*, 84 AM. J. INT'L L. 578 (1990)

Tulsky, F.N. *What Price Justice? Poor Defendants Pay the Cost as Courts Save on Murder Trials*, PHILADELPHIA INQUIRER, Sept. 3, 1992

Vagts, D. *A Reply to "A Critical Evaluation of the Mexican-American Transfer of Penal Sanctions Treaty"*, 64 IOWA L. REV. 325 (1979)

Viccica, A. *World Crime Trends*, 24 INT'L J. OFFENDER THERAPY & COMP. CRIMINOLOGY 270 (1980)

Waller, I. *Declaration on the Protection of and Assistance to Crime Victims*, 3 WORLD SOC'Y OF VICTIMOLOGY NEWSL. 1 (1983–84)

Watson, G.R. *Offenders Abroad: The Case for Nationality-Based Criminal Jurisdiction*, 17 YALE J.INT'L L. 41 (1992)

Wellens, K.C. & Borchardt, G.M., *Soft Law in European Community Law*, 14 EUROP. L. REV. 267 (1989)

Williams, S.A. *Human Rights Safeguards and International Cooperation in Extradition: Striking the Balance*, 3 CRIM. L. F. 191 (1992)

Woltring, H. *Extradition Law*, 61 VICTORIAN L. INST. J. 919 (1987)

Young, W. *Community Care as a Penal Sanction*, 1 CRIM. L.F. 297 (1990)

B. OTHER ARTICLES AND NOTES

Ad hoc Meeting of Experts on Social Defence Policies in relation to development planning, 27 INT'L REV. CRIM. POL'Y 57 (1969)

Asia and Far East Institute for the Prevention of Crime and the Treatment of Offenders, 20 INT'L REV. CRIM. POL'Y 76 (1962)

ASIA WATCH BLASTS PEKING FOR EXPLOITING PRISON LABOR, Central News Agency, September 19, 1991, available in LEXIS, Nexis Library

Contemporary Practice of the United States Relating to International Law, Modernization of Extradition Treaties, 86 AM. J. INT'L L. 547 (1992)

Contemporary Practice of the United States Relating to International Law, Mutual Legal Assistance Treaties, 86 Am. J. Int'l L. 549 (1992)

Criminal Law: Exchange of Prisoners, 18 Harv. Int'l L.J. 703 (1977)

Delinquent Detainees, 26 Int'l Rev. Crim. Pol'y 56 (1968)

Eighth UN Crime Congress, 16 Commonwealth L. Bull. 1381 (1990)

Establishment of the United Nations Latin American Institute for the Prevention of Crime and the Treatment of Offenders, 33 Int'l Rev. Crim. Pol'y 65 (1977)

General Assembly Resolution on the Creation of an Effective United Nations Crime Prevention and Criminal Justice Program, 3 Crim. L.F. 105 (1991)

Implementation of the Standard Minimum Rules for the Treatment of Prisoners, 26 Int'l Rev. Crim. Pol'y 69 (1968)

Interregional Advisory Services in the Field of Crime Prevention and the Treatment of Offenders, 8 Crime Prevention & Crim. Just. Newsl. 6 (1983)

Malawi: Authorities Chaining and Beating Prisoners, Amnesty Claims, Inter Press Service, March 6, 1992, available in LEXIS, Nexis Library

Progress report of the Secretary-General, Activities of the United Nations Interregional Crime and Justice Research Institute and the regional institutes for crime prevention and criminal justice 3 Crim. L. F. 481 (1992)

Report of the Working Group of Experts on the Standard Minimum Rules for the Treatment of Prisoners on its Second Meeting, 33 Int'l Rev. Crim. Pol'y 87 (1977)

Standard Minimum Rules for the Treatment of Prisoners, 2 N.Y.U. J. Int'l L. & Pol. 314 (1969)

Summary of the work programme of the Crime Prevention and Criminal Justice Branch of the United Nations Secretariat, 34 Int'l Rev. Crim. Pol'y 19 (1978)

The Work of the United Nations in the Field of the Prevention of Crime and the Treatment of Offenders, 1 Int'l Rev. Crim. Pol'y 3 (1951)

World-Wide Crime and the Responsibility of the International Community: A Declaration of the End of Complacency, 1 Crim. L.F. 571 (1990)

Books, Booklets, and Book Chapters

Academy for Contemporary Problems, Remedies and Mechanisms for the Enforcement of the UN Standard Minimum Rules for the Treatment of Prisoners and Similar Guaranties and Principles of Offender Treatment: A Multinational Comparison and Analysis (1974)

Alper, B.S. & Boren, J.F. Crime: International Agenda (1972)

Alston, P. & Rodríguez-Bustelo, M. Taking Stock of United Nations Human Rights Procedures, Report of a January 1988 Workshop at Lake Mohonk, N.Y. (1988)

American Law Institute, Restatement (Third) of the Foreign Relations Law of the United States (1987)

Amnesty International, Amnesty International Report 1991 (1991)

Amnesty International, United States of America: The Death Penalty and Juvenile Offenders (1991)

Australian Institute of Criminology, United Nations Criminal Justice Information Network (1990)

Bassiouni, M.C. A Draft International Criminal Code and Draft Statute for an International Criminal Tribunal (1987)

Bassiouni, M.C. *The U.N. Procedures for the Effective Implementation of the Standard Minimum Rules for the Treatment of Prisoners*, in Festschrift fur Dietrich Oehler (R.D. Herzberg ed. 1985)

Beare, M. & Schneider, S. TRACING OF ILLICIT FUNDS: MONEY LAUNDERING IN CANADA (Ministry of the Solicitor-General of Canada, Working Paper No. 1990-06, 1990)

Blakesley, C.L. TERRORISM, DRUGS, INTERNATIONAL LAW AND THE PROTECTION OF HUMAN LIBERTY (1992)

Blaustein, A.P., Clark, R.S. & Sigler, J.A. eds. HUMAN RIGHTS SOURCEBOOK (1987)

Bothe, M. et al. eds. NATIONAL IMPLEMENTATION OF INTERNATIONAL HUMANITARIAN LAW (1990)

Bronstein, A.J. *Criminal Justice: Prison and Penology*, in OUR ENDANGERED RIGHTS: THE ACLU REPORT ON CIVIL LIBERTIES TODAY (N. Dorsen ed. 1984)

Buergenthal, T. LAW-MAKING IN THE INTERNATIONAL CIVIL AVIATION ORGANIZATION (1969)

Burgers, J. & Danelius, H. THE UNITED NATIONS CONVENTION AGAINST TORTURE (1988)

Burgers, J. *An Arduous Delivery: The United Nations Convention Against Torture (1984)*, in EFFECTIVE NEGOTIATION: CASE STUDIES IN CONFERENCE DIPLOMACY (J. Kaufmann ed. 1989)

Burns, P. CRIMINAL INJURIES COMPENSATION: SOCIAL REMEDY OR POLITICAL PALLIATIVE FOR VICTIMS OF CRIME? (1980)

Butler, W. et al. PALAU: A CHALLENGE TO THE RULE OF LAW IN MICRONESIA; REPORT OF A MISSION ON BEHALF OF THE INTERNATIONAL COMMISSION OF JURISTS (1988)

Centre for the Independence of Judges and Lawyers, CIJL BULLETIN, SPECIAL ISSUE NO 25–26, THE INDEPENDENCE OF JUDGES AND LAWYERS: A COMPILATION OF INTERNATIONAL STANDARDS (Apr.–Oct. 1990)

Clark, R.S. A UNITED NATIONS HIGH COMMISSIONER FOR HUMAN RIGHTS (1972)

Commonwealth Secretariat, COMMONWEALTH SCHEMES ON MUTUAL ASSISTANCE IN THE ADMINISTRATION OF JUSTICE (n.d.)

Commonwealth Secretariat, ACTION AGAINST TRANSNATIONAL CRIMINALITY, PAPERS FROM THE 1991 OXFORD CONFERENCE ON INTERNATIONAL AND WHITE COLLAR CRIME (1992)

Commonwealth Secretariat, II ACTION AGAINST TRANSNATIONAL CRIMINALITY, PAPERS FROM THE 1992 OXFORD CONFERENCE ON INTERNATIONAL AND WHITE COLLAR CRIME (1993)

Conference of Correctional Administrators, STANDARD GUIDELINES FOR CORRECTIONS IN AUSTRALIA (1989)

Cornil, P. *John Howard, European Social Reformer*, in CHANGING CONCEPTS OF CRIME AND ITS TREATMENT (H.J. Klare ed. 1966)

Council of Europe, European Committee on Crime Problems, EXPLANATORY REPORT ON THE EUROPEAN CONVENTION ON THE TRANSFER OF PROCEEDINGS IN CRIMINAL MATTERS (1970)

Council of Europe, European Committee on Crime Problems, EXTRATERRITORIAL JURISDICTION (1990), reprinted in 3 CRIM. L.F. 441 (1992)

Council of Europe, EUROPEAN PRISON RULES (1987)

Council of Europe, HUMAN RIGHTS AND PRISONERS (1986)

Danieli, Y. *Preliminary Reflections from a Psychological Perspective*, in SEMINAR ON THE RIGHT TO COMPENSATION AND REHABILITATION FOR VICTIMS OF GROSS VIOLATIONS OF HUMAN RIGHTS AND FUNDAMENTAL FREEDOMS, MAASTRICHT, 11–15 MARCH 1992 (T. Van Boven, C. Flinterman, F. Grunfeld & I. Westendorp eds. 1993)

Ellis, A. & Pisani, R.L. *The United States Treaties on Mutual Assistance in Criminal*

Matters, in II INTERNATIONAL CRIMINAL LAW (PROCEDURE) (M.C. Bassiouni ed. 1986)

Epp, H. *The European Convention,* in II INTERNATIONAL CRIMINAL LAW (PRO-CEDURE) (M.C. Bassiouni ed. 1986)

Eser, A. & Lagodny, O. eds. PRINCIPLES AND PROCEDURES FOR A NEW TRANSNA-TIONAL CRIMINAL LAW, PROCEEDINGS OF A WORKSHOP ORGANIZED BY THE SOCIETY FOR THE REFORM OF CRIMINAL LAW AND THE MAX PLANCK IN-STITUTE FOR FOREIGN AND INTERNATIONAL CRIMINAL LAW, FREIBURG-IM-BREISGAU, GERMANY, 21–25 May 1991 (1992)

Fisse, B. Fraser, D. & Coss, G. eds. THE MONEY TRAIL: CONFISCATION OF PROCEEDS OF CRIME, MONEY LAUNDERING AND CASH TRANSACTION REPORT-ING (1992)

Gaer, F. for the International League for Human Rights, U.N. "SPECIAL PRO-CEDURES" IN HUMAN RIGHTS: A GUIDE (1991)

Garcia Barcelo, J. *Obstacles to the Implementation of the Standard Minimum Rules in Latin America,* 26 INT'L REV. CRIM. POL'Y 17 (1968).

Gilmore, W. C. *International Cooperation in the Administration of Justice: Develop-ments and Prospects* in Commonwealth Secretariat, II ACTION AGAINST TRANSNATIONAL CRIMINALITY, PAPERS FROM THE 1992 OXFORD CONFERENCE ON INTERNATIONAL AND WHITE COLLAR CRIME 147 (1993)

Gilmore, W.C. ed. INTERNATIONAL EFFORTS TO COMBAT MONEY LAUNDERING (1992)

Gobert, J.J. & Cohen, N.P. RIGHTS OF PRISONERS (1981)

Government of Canada, PROPOSAL FOR THE INTERNATIONAL EXCHANGE OF INFORMATION TO COMBAT CRIMES AGAINST CULTURAL MOVABLE PROPERTY (1990)

Gray, C. JUDICIAL REMEDIES IN INTERNATIONAL LAW (1990)

Heijder, A. *Codes of Professional Ethics Against Torture,* in Amnesty International, CODES OF PROFESSIONAL ETHICS (2d ed. 1984).

Helsinki Institute for Crime Prevention and Control, Affiliated with the United Nations (HEUNI), COURSE ON UNITED NATIONS CRIMINAL JUSTICE POLICY (1985)

Hood, R. THE DEATH PENALTY: A WORLDWIDE PERSPECTIVE (1989)

Human Rights Watch, THE GLOBAL REPORT ON PRISONS (1993)

International League for Human Rights, COMBATTING VIOLENCE AGAINST WOMEN (1993)

International League for Human Rights, HUMAN RIGHTS AT THE UNITED NATIONS: HALTING SUMMARY AND ARBITRARY EXECUTIONS (In Brief No. 28) (1990)

International League for Human Rights, HUMAN RIGHTS ·AT THE UNITED NATIONS: A WORLD CAMPAIGN FOR HUMAN RIGHTS (In Brief No. 22) (1989)

International League for Human Rights, HUMAN RIGHTS AT THE UNITED NATIONS: USING ADVISORY SERVICES (In Brief No. 7) (1988)

International League for Human Rights, SOURCES OF INFORMATION USED BY TREATY COMMITTEES, A MEMORANDUM PREPARED FOR MEMBERS OF THE COMMITTEE ON THE ELIMINATION OF RACIAL DISCRIMINATION (Aug. 1990)

International Penal and Penitentiary Foundation, STANDARD MINIMUM RULES FOR THE IMPLEMENTATION OF NON-CUSTODIAL SANCTIONS AND MEASURES INVOLVING RESTRICTIONS OF LIBERTY (1989)

Ivanov, S.A. *The International Labour Organisation: Control Over Application of the*

Conventions and Recommendations on Labour, in CONTROL OVER COMPLIANCE WITH INTERNATIONAL LAW (W.E. Butler ed. 1991)

Joutsen, M. & Shapland, J. *Report of an ad hoc working group meeting*, in HELSINKI INSTITUTE FOR CRIME PREVENTION AND CONTROL AFFILIATED WITH THE UNITED NATIONS, PUBLICATION SERIES NO. 16, CHANGING VICTIM POLICY: THE UNITED NATIONS VICTIM DECLARATION AND RECENT DEVELOPMENTS IN EUROPE (1989)

Joutsen, M. THE ROLE OF THE VICTIM OF CRIME IN EUROPEAN CRIMINAL JUSTICE SYSTEMS: A CROSSNATIONAL STUDY OF THE ROLE OF THE VICTIM (HEUNI Publication Series No. 11, 1987)

Kaufmann, J. CONFERENCE DIPLOMACY: AN INTRODUCTORY ANALYSIS (2d rev. ed. 1988)

Kavass, I. & Sprudzs, A. comp. EXTRADITION LAWS AND TREATIES, UNITED STATES (1979—)

Kirgis, F. INTERNATIONAL ORGANIZATIONS IN THEIR LEGAL SETTING (2d ed. 1993)

Krantz, S. CASES AND MATERIALS ON THE LAW OF CORRECTIONS AND PRISONERS' RIGHTS (3d ed. 1986)

Landy, E. THE EFFECTIVENESS OF INTERNATIONAL SUPERVISION: THIRTY YEARS OF I.L.O. EXPERIENCE (1966)

Lawyers Committee for Human Rights, ABANDONING THE VICTIMS: THE UN ADVISORY SERVICES PROGRAM IN GUATEMALA (1990)

Leive, D. M. INTERNATIONAL REGULATORY REGIMES: CASE STUDIES IN HEALTH, METEOROLOGY AND FOOD (1976)

Lillich, R. B. INTERNATIONAL HUMAN RIGHTS: PROBLEMS OF LAW, POLICY AND PRACTICE (2d ed. 1991)

Lillich, R. *Model Law on the Oil Embargo Against South Africa*, U.N. CENTRE AGAINST APARTHEID, NOTES AND DOCUMENTS, NO. 10/91 (1991)

Linke, R. *The Cooperation between Non-Governmental Organizations and the United Nations in the Field of Crime Policy*, in Helsinki Institute for Crime Prevention and Control affiliated with the United Nations, COURSE ON UNITED NATIONS CRIMINAL JUSTICE POLICY (1985)

López-Rey, M. A GUIDE TO UNITED NATIONS CRIMINAL POLICY (1985)

Mackowiak, P. *Formulation and application of United Nations standards and norms in criminal justice*, in Helsinki Institute for Crime Prevention and Control, Affiliated with the United Nations (HEUNI), COURSE ON UNITED NATIONS CRIMINAL JUSTICE POLICY (1985)

Mathiesen, T. *The U.N. Congress as a Culture* (paper delivered at the 18th Annual Conference of the European Group for the Study of Deviance and Social Control, in cooperation with the Coornhert-League for Penal Reform, Amsterdam) (Sept. 1990)

McClean, D. INTERNATIONAL JUDICIAL ASSISTANCE (1992)

Meron, T. HUMAN RIGHTS LAW-MAKING IN THE UNITED NATIONS (1986).

Ministerial Committee of Inquiry into the Prisons System [New Zealand], PRISON REVIEW. TE ARA HOU: THE NEW WAY (1989)

Ministry of External Relations and Trade, HUMAN RIGHTS IN NEW ZEALAND: THE PRESENTATION OF NEW ZEALAND'S SECOND PERIODIC REPORT TO THE HUMAN RIGHTS COMMITTEE, (Information Bulletin No. 30) (1990)

Morgenstern, F. LEGAL PROBLEMS OF INTERNATIONAL ORGANIZATIONS (1986)

Muller-Rappard, E. *The European System*, in II INTERNATIONAL CRIMINAL LAW (PROCEDURE) 96 (M.C. Bassiouni ed. 1986)

Nadelmann, E.A. COPS ACROSS BORDERS: THE INTERNATIONALIZATION OF U.S. CRIMINAL LAW ENFORCEMENT (1993)

Nagel, W.H. *International Collaboration in the Field of Criminology*, in LE DROIT PÉNAL: RECUEIL D'ÉTUDES EN HOMMAGE A JACOB MAARTEN VAN BEMMELEM (1965)

O'Donovan, D. *The Economic and Social Council*, in THE UNITED NATIONS AND HUMAN RIGHTS: A CRITICAL APPRAISAL (P. Alston ed. 1992)

Pechota, V. THE RIGHT TO KNOW ONE'S HUMAN RIGHTS: A ROAD TOWARD INDIVIDUAL FREEDOM (1983)

Palmer, G. COMPENSATION FOR INCAPACITY: A STUDY OF LAW AND SOCIAL CHANGE IN NEW ZEALAND AND AUSTRALIA (1979)

Quinn, P. *The General Assembly into the 1990s*, in THE UNITED NATIONS AND HUMAN RIGHTS: A CRITICAL APPRAISAL (P. Alston ed. 1992)

Rädda Barnen (Swedish Save the Children), UN ASSISTANCE FOR HUMAN RIGHTS (1988)

Radzinowicz, L. *International Collaboration in Criminal Science*, in THE MODERN APPROACH TO CRIMINAL LAW (L. Radzinowicz & J.W.C. Turner eds. 1945)

Radzinowicz, L. & Wolfgang, M.E. eds. CRIME AND JUSTICE: THE CRIMINAL IN CONFINEMENT (1971)

Ramcharan, B. HUMANITARIAN GOOD OFFICES IN INTERNATIONAL LAW (1983)

Ramcharan, B. THE INTERNATIONAL LAW AND PRACTICE OF EARLY WARNING AND PREVENTIVE DIPLOMACY: THE EMERGING GLOBAL WATCH (1991)

Ristau, B.A. & Abbell, M. INTERNATIONAL JUDICIAL ASSISTANCE, CRIMINAL

Robson, J.L. SACRED COWS AND ROGUE ELEPHANTS (1987)

Rodley, N.S. THE TREATMENT OF PRISONERS UNDER INTERNATIONAL LAW (1987)

Rubin, S. THE LAW OF CRIMINAL CORRECTION (1963)

Rudovsky, D. et al. THE RIGHTS OF PRISONERS: THE BASIC ACLU GUIDE TO PRISONERS' RIGHTS (4th ed. 1988)

Samson, K.T. *Human Rights Co-ordination within the UN System*, in THE UNITED NATIONS AND HUMAN RIGHTS: A CRITICAL APPRAISAL (P. Alston ed. 1992)

Schabas, W.A. THE ABOLITION OF THE DEATH PENALTY IN INTERNATIONAL LAW (1993)

Schmid, A. & Jongman, A. eds. MONITORING HUMAN RIGHTS VIOLATIONS (1992) (Publication No. 43, Center for the Study of Social Conflicts, Faculty of Social Sciences, Leiden University)

Schutte, J. *The European System*, in II INTERNATIONAL CRIMINAL LAW (PROCEDURE) (M.C. Bassiouni ed. 1986)

Sellin, T. *Lionel Fox and the International Penal and Penitentiary Commission*, STUDIES IN PENOLOGY DEDICATED TO THE MEMORY OF SIR LIONEL FOX, C.B., M.C. (M. López-Rey & C. Germain eds. 1964)

Singer, R.G. & Statsky, W.P. RIGHTS OF THE IMPRISONED: CASES, MATERIALS AND DIRECTIONS (1974)

Sloan, B. UNITED NATIONS GENERAL ASSEMBLY RESOLUTIONS IN OUR CHANGING WORLD (1991)

Stafford, D. *Mutual Legal Assistance in Criminal Matters: The Australian Experience* in Commonwealth Secretariat, ACTION AGAINST TRANSNATIONAL CRIMINALITY, PAPERS FROM THE 1991 OXFORD CONFERENCE ON INTERNATIONAL AND WHITE COLLAR CRIME (1992)

Stanley Foundation, REPORT OF THE TWENTY-SECOND UNITED NATIONS ISSUES

CONFERENCE, THE UNITED NATIONS: STRUCTURE AND LEADERSHIP FOR A NEW ERA (1991)

Stark, J.H. & Goldstein, H.H. THE RIGHTS OF CRIME VICTIMS (1985)

Tammes, A.J.P. *Soft Law*, in T.M.C. Asser Instituut, ESSAYS ON INTERNATIONAL AND COMPARATIVE LAW IN HONOUR OF JUDGE ERADES (1983)

Teeters, N.K. DELIBERATIONS OF THE INTERNATIONAL PENAL AND PENITENTIARY CONGRESSES: QUESTIONS AND ANSWERS 1872–1935 (1949)

Tolley, H. THE U.N. COMMISSION ON HUMAN RIGHTS (1987)

Toman, J. *Quasi-Legal Standards and Guidelines for Protecting Human Rights*, in GUIDE TO INTERNATIONAL HUMAN RIGHTS PRACTICE (H. Hannum ed. 2d ed. 1984)

United Nations, COMPENDIUM OF UNITED NATIONS STANDARDS AND NORMS IN CRIME PREVENTION AND CRIMINAL JUSTICE (1992)

United Nations, HUMAN RIGHTS: A COMPILATION OF INTERNATIONAL INSTRUMENTS (1988)

United Nations, MANUAL ON EFFECTIVE PREVENTION AND INVESTIGATION OF EXTRALEGAL, ARBITRARY AND SUMMARY EXECUTIONS (1991)

United Nations, THE UNITED NATIONS AND CRIME PREVENTION (1991)

United Nations Centre for Human Rights, FACT SHEET NO. 3, ADVISORY SERVICES AND TECHNICAL ASSISTANCE IN THE FIELD OF HUMAN RIGHTS (1988)

United Nations Centre for Human Rights, HUMAN RIGHTS FACT SHEET, NO. 1 ON HUMAN RIGHTS MACHINERY (1987)

United Nations Division of Narcotic Drugs, EXTRADITION FOR DRUG OFFENCES (1985)

United Nations Office at Vienna, Centre for Social Development and Humanitarian Affairs, VIOLENCE AGAINST WOMEN (1989)

Van den Wijngaert, C. THE POLITICAL OFFENCE EXCEPTION TO EXTRADITION (1980)

Vetere, E. *Las Reglas Minimas de las Naciones Unidas Para el Tratamiento de los Reclusos: Su Adopcion Y Application en Relacion a la Proteccion de los Derechos Humanos*, in P. David ed. CRIME AND SOCIAL POLICY: PAPERS IN HONOUR OF MANUEL LÓPEZ-REY Y ARROJO (1985)

Vetere, E. *The Role of the United Nations: Working for a More Effective International Co-operation*, in PRINCIPLES AND PROCEDURES FOR A NEW TRANSNATIONAL CRIMINAL LAW, PROCEEDINGS OF AN INTERNATIONAL WORKSHOP ORGANIZED BY THE SOCIETY FOR THE REFORM OF CRIMINAL LAW AND THE MAX PLANCK INSTITUTE FOR FOREIGN AND INTERNATIONAL CRIMINAL LAW, FREIBURG-IM-BREISGAU, GERMANY, 21–25 May 1991 (A. Eser & O. Lagodny eds. 1992)

von Potobsky, G. *The Experience of the ILO*, in INTERNATIONAL LAW AND FACT-FINDING IN THE FIELD OF HUMAN RIGHTS (B. Ramcharan ed. 1982)

Williams, P.R. TREATMENT OF DETAINEES: EXAMINATION OF ISSUES RELEVANT TO DETENTION BY THE UNITED NATIONS HUMAN RIGHTS COMMITTEE (1990)

Zvekic, U. & Mattei, A. RESEARCH AND INTERNATIONAL CO-OPERATION IN CRIMINAL JUSTICE: SURVEY ON NEEDS AND PRIORITIES OF DEVELOPING COUNTRIES (UNSDRI Publication No. 29) (1987)

Index

Procedural Aspects of International Law Series

Burns H. Weston, Series Editor (1994–   )
Robert Kogod Goldman, Editor (1977–1994)
Richard B. Lillich, Editor (1964–1977)

(Asterisks denote volumes published by the University of Pennsylvania Press. Ordering information for Volumes 1–18 may be obtained directly from the Procedural Aspects of International Law Institute.)

1. Richard B. Lillich. *International Claims: Their Adjudication by National Commissions.* 1962
2. Richard B. Lillich and Gordon A. Christenson. *International Claims: Their Preparation and Presentation.* 1962
3. Richard A. Falk. *The Role of Domestic Courts in the International Legal Order.* 1964
4. Gillian M. White. *The Use of Experts by International Tribunals.* 1965
5. Richard B. Lillich. *The Protection of Foreign Investment: Six Procedural Studies.* 1965
6. Richard B. Lillich. *International Claims: Postwar British Practice.* 1967
7. Thomas Buergenthal. *Law-Making in the International Civil Aviation Organization.* 1969
8. John Carey. *UN Protection of Civil and Political Rights.* 1970
9. Burns H. Weston. *International Claims: Postwar French Practice.* 1971
10. Frank Griffith Dawson and Ivan L. Head. *International Law, National Tribunals, and the Rights of Aliens.* 1971
11. Ignaz Seidl-Hohenveldern. *The Austrian-German Arbitral Tribunal.* 1972
12. Richard B. Lillich and Burns H. Weston. *International Claims: Their Settlement by Lump Sum Agreements.* 1975
13. Durward V. Sandifer. *Evidence Before International Tribunals* (Revised Edition). 1975
14. Roger Fisher. *Improving Compliance with International Law.* 1981
15. Richard B. Lillich and Burns H. Weston, eds. *International Claims: Contemporary European Practice.* 1982

16. Frederic L. Kirgis, Jr. *Prior Consultation in International Law: A Study of State Practice.* 1983
17. David Harris. *The European Social Charter.* 1984
18. Richard A. Falk. *Reviving the World Court.* 1986
*19. Joan Fitzpatrick. *Human Rights in Crisis: The International System for Protecting Rights During States of Emergency.* 1993
*20. Roger S. Clark. *The United Nations Crime Prevention and Criminal Justice Program: Formulation of Standards and Efforts at Their Implementation.* 1994

This book was set in Baskerville and Eras typefaces. Baskerville was designed by John Baskerville at his private press in Birmingham, England, in the eighteenth century. The first typeface to depart from oldstyle typeface design, Baskerville has more variation between thick and thin strokes. In an effort to insure that the thick and thin strokes of his typeface reproduced well on paper, John Baskerville developed the first wove paper, the surface of which was much smoother than the laid paper of the time. The development of wove paper was partly responsible for the introduction of typefaces classified as modern, which have even more contrast between thick and thin strokes.

Eras was designed in 1969 by Studio Hollenstein in Paris for the Wagner Typefoundry. A contemporary script-like version of a sans-serif typeface, the letters of Eras have a monotone stroke and are slightly inclined.

Printed on acid-free paper.